FOCUS ON
FESTIVALS

CONTEMPORARY EUROPEAN CASE STUDIES AND PERSPECTIVES

Edited by

Chris Newbold, Christopher Maughan, Jennie Jordan and Franco Bianchini

(G) Goodfellow Publishers Ltd

Published by Goodfellow Publishers Limited,
26 Home Close, Wolvercote, Oxford OX2 8PS
http://www.goodfellowpublishers.com

British Library Cataloguing in Publication Data: a catalogue record for
this title is available from the British Library.

Library of Congress Catalog Card Number: on file.

ISBN: 978-1-910158-15-9

 Design and typesetting by P.K. McBride, www.macbride.org.uk

Cover design by Cylinder

Printed by Marston Book Services, www.marston.co.uk

Contents

Notes on Contributors

Preface
  Christopher Maughan

Introduction: focusing on festivals
  Chris Newbold, Jennie Jordan, Franco Bianchini and Christopher Maughan

SECTION 1: PERSPECTIVES AND DEBATES — 1

Introduction — 2
  Christopher Maughan and Jennie Jordan

1 Festivals: Why, What, When? A case study of Berlin — 10
  Nele Hertling

2 Festivalisation: Patterns and Limits — 18
  Emmanuel Négrier

3 Festivals, Urbanity and the Public Sphere: reflections on European festivals — 28
  Monica Sassatelli

4 Festivals, Conformity and Socialisation — 40
  János Zoltán Szabó

5 Festivals as Communities of Practice: Learning by doing and knowledge networks
     amongst artists — 53
  Roberta Comunian

6 Festivals of Transition: *Greenlight Festival* Leicester — 66
  Richard Fletcher

SECTION 2: LEADERSHIP AND MANAGEMENT — 79

Introduction — 80
  Jennie Jordan

7 How to *Flow* — 88
  Satu Silvanto

8 *Romaeuropa Festival*: A Case Study — 98
  Lucio Argano

9 Festival Leadership in Turbulent Times — 107
  Jennie Jordan

10 *Mladi levi* Festival – Reflections and Memories — 118
  Nevenska Koprivšek

11 The *Diggers' Festival*: Organising a community festival with political connotations — 127
  Jacqui Norton

12 Volunteering for Festivals: Why and How?   138
    Anne-Marie Autissier

13 Festival City – Rotterdam   147
    David Dooghe

SECTION 3: IMPACTS, COMMUNITIES AND PLACES   **159**

    Introduction   160
    Chris Newbold

14 The Enchanted City: *Holstebro Festive Week* – an experiential and social cultural space   168
    Kathrine Winkelhorn

15 *Operaestate Festival Veneto*: A socio-cultural and economic analysis   180
    Luisella Carnelli

16 Street Performance: The unintended consequences of festivals   191
    Floriane Gaber

17 Diaspora Community Festivals and Tourism   201
    Yi Fu, Philip Long and Rhodri Thomas

18 Mela in the UK: A 'travelled and habituated' festival   214
    Rakesh Kaushal and Chris Newbold

19 A View from Australia   227
    Robyn Archer

SECTION 4: THE FUTURE OF FESTIVALS   **239**

    Introduction   240
    Franco Bianchini and Christopher Maughan

20 Festivals in the Network Society   245
    Greg Richards

21 The Public Festival: Inspiration and interconnectivity at the heart of festivals   255
    Kathrin Deventer

22 Belonging and Unbelonging: The cultural purpose of festivals   265
    Tessa Gordziejko

23 Transnational Festivals, a European alternativ*e: Les Boréales* and *Reims Scènes d'Europe* 276
    Anne-Marie Autissier

24 The Future of European Festivals   285
    Bernard Faivre d'Arcier

25 Some Reflections on the Future of Festival Practice in Europe   290
    Steve Austen

    Author Index   299

    Subject Index

List of figures

2.1	*Eurockéennes* Festival France	18
2.2	Changing trends in society's relationship to culture	20
4.1	Conceptual clarification of the festival phenomenon	44
4.2	Conformity indicators of festivals	47
4.3	Festivals and their relationships with different stakeholders	48
5.1	Knowledge and awareness connections between participating artists before *Fuse Medway Festival* 2011	61
5.2	Knowledge and awareness connections between participating artists after *Fuse Medway Festival* in 2011	61
8.1	Sasha Waltz and guest	103
13.1	Artist's impression of the daily use of a multifunctional urban location in Afrikaanderwijk	151
13.2	Artist's impression of the *Summer Carnival* taking place in a multifunctional urban location in Afrikaanderwijk	152
13.3	Artist's impression of the Coolsingel as a sight for a parade in Rotterdam	153
13.4	Artist's impression of the Coolsingel as the central meeting space of Rotterdam in winter	154
13.5	Artist's impression of the Coolsingel as the central meeting space of Rotterdam in summer	154
14.1	Key figures, Odin Teatret in 2011	169
14.2	Housewives dancing at *Holstebro*	176
15.1	*Operaestate* research table	182
18.1	*Leicester Belgrave Mela*	221
19.1	The Secret River	235

Notes on Contributors

Robyn Archer is a singer, writer, artistic director and public advocate for the arts. She is Artistic Director of *The Light in Winter* (which she created for Federation Square, Melbourne), Deputy Chair of *The Australia Council* (the Australian Government's arts funding and advisory body) and Strategic Advisor to Gold Coast Arts and Culture. She is a member of the *European House of Culture* and a mentor in the European Festivals Association's *Atelier* programme. Robyn is an *Officer of the Order of Australia* and has been awarded the *Chevalier de l'Ordre des Arts et des Lettres* (France) and Belgium's *Order of the Crown*. She was formerly Artistic Director of The National Festival of Australian Theatre, The Adelaide and Melbourne Festivals and Ten Days on the Island (which she created for Tasmania). She is the patron/ambassador for numerous organisations and recipient of many arts awards, most recently the *Helpmann Award* for Best Cabaret Performer 2013.

Lucio Argano is Professor of Cultural Management at the Roma Tre University and the Cattolica University of Milan. Currently he is the project manager of Perugia 2019, candidate for European Capital of Culture. Previously he has managed the *Rome Film Festival*, the Festival *Romaeuropa*, *Teatro Popolare di Roma* and *Auditorium of Rome*.

Steve Austen has been active in the European public domain since 1966, concentrating on performing arts, cultural policy, international cooperation and civil society issues. His CV includes: co-author of *Amsterdam Cultural Capital of Europe 1987*; setting up the informal working body *Gulliver*, with Günter Grass; Fellow of the Felix Meritis Foundation; founder of the Amsterdam Summer University; and board member of *A Soul for Europe*.

Anne-Marie Autissier is Director of the Institute of European Studies at Paris 8 University. Her main research interests include: a comparative study of cultural policies in Europe; the role of arts festivals in transnational cooperation; and cultural radio channels in France and Europe.

Franco Bianchini is Professor of Cultural Policy and Planning at Leeds Beckett University. From 1992 to 2007 he was Reader and Course Leader for the MA in European Cultural Planning at De Montfort University Leicester. Franco has been a member of the Editorial Board of *International Journal of Cultural Policy* since 1997 and of the Advisory Board of *ENCATC Journal of Cultural Management and Policy* since 2012. He was appointed in June 2001 to the selection panel responsible for the designation of Cork as *European Capital of Culture*. Franco acted as adviser to Liverpool Culture Company on the preparation of their successful bid for *European Capital of Culture* (2003) and on the implementation of *Cities on the Edge,* a project of cultural co-operation between Liverpool, Bremen, Gdansk, Istanbul, Marseilles and Naples (2004-2009). The project formed part of the programme of Liverpool European Capital of Culture 2008. From 2010 to 2014 he was a member of the team preparing the successful bid by the city of Matera, in Southern Italy, for the title of European Capital of Culture for 2019. Franco's books include *Urban Mindscapes of Europe* (co-editor, with Godela Weiss-Sussex, Rodopi, 2006), *Planning for the Intercultural City* (with Jude Bloomfield, Comedia, 2004), *Culture and Neighbourhoods: A Comparative Report* (with L. Ghilardi Santacatterina, Council of Europe, 1997), *The Creative City* (with Charles Landry, Demos, 1995) and *Cultural Policy and Urban Regeneration: the West European Experience* (co-editor, with Michael Parkinson, Manchester University Press, 1993).

Luisella Carnelli is a project manager, researcher and consultant for the Fitzcarraldo Foundation, in the field of Performing Arts. She has led or contributed to more than 50 research projects and consulting assignments, many of which have focused on the economic and socio-economic impact of cultural activities e.g. *Operaestate Festival 2012, MITO Settembre Musica 2012 Festival* and the *International Book Fair of Torino, 2013*. Additional research has included audience research at cultural events; audience development; and organization and strategy development.

Roberta Comunian is Lecturer in Creative and Cultural Industries at the Department of Culture, Media and Creative Industries at King's College London. Her work focuses on the relationship between arts, cultural regeneration projects and the cultural and creative industries. She is currently leading an AHRC research network exploring the connections between Higher Education and the Creative Economy and has published extensively on the career opportunities and patterns of creative graduates in UK.

Bernard Faivre d'Arcier served as director of the *Avignon Festival* from 1980 to 1984. He was appointed as cultural advisor to the Prime Minister and in 1986 launched the television channel La Sept, the French arm of the Franco-German channel Arte. From 1993 to 2003, Bernard was appointed for the second time as the director of *Avignon Festival*. He is presently consultant for many cultural institutions and chairs *La Biennale de Lyon*.

Kathrin Deventer is the Secretary General of the *European Festivals Association*. She believes in Europe and is convinced that arts and culture in general, and festivals in particular, play an important role in involving citizens more strongly in Europe. Kathrin is one of the founding members of the *European House for Culture* in Brussels and a member of *A Soul for Europe*'s strategy group.

David Dooghe has a life-long fascination with the relationship between humans and their surroundings, and this led him to study architecture at the LUCA School of Arts, Gent and urban design at the Rotterdam Academy of Architecture and Urban Design. As well as teaching at both institutes, he currently works as a researcher, strategist and designer on urban development.

Richard Fletcher is a part-time lecturer and researcher at De Montfort University. He has contributed to a range of interdisciplinary research and public engagement projects often within the theme of sustainable development. Richard has been involved in Transition Leicester since 2010 and has been part of the *Greenlight Festival* organising team since then.

Yi Fu is Lecturer in Cultural Heritage and Museum Studies at Zhejiang University, China. Her research interests include: festivals and society, intangible cultural heritage and society; museums and society; diaspora festivals and community relationships; diaspora communities, intangible cultural heritage and social relations; intangible cultural heritage, museums and tourism.

Floriane Gaber is a writer, researcher, journalist, teacher and cultural consultant. She is also a lecturer at the University of Paris III where she coordinated the ARAR (Association of Research on Street Arts). She has also taught at other universities: Paris XI, Evry and Cergy in press, expression and communication techniques, street arts, poetry reading and literature. She is a well-travelled European commentator and critic of street theatre, mime, circus and spoken/written word performance. She has been published widely and is a regular contributor to cultural and arts journals and magazines.

Tessa Gordziejko is a Creative Programmer with *iMove* (since September 2007) with which she worked on the creative programme for the *UK Cultural Olympiad* in 2012. Previously a writer, director, producer, production manager, stage manager, arts development consultant and trainer, she was Director of Arts & Business Yorkshire for six years. She has worked primarily in the performing arts, but also in media and visual arts and with museums and heritage organisations.

Nele Hertling is currently Vice-President of the Academy of Arts in Berlin and a co-founder and member of the strategy group of *A Soul for Europe*. One of Germany's most influential figures from German alternative culture, her career began with a degree in German Philology and Theatre from Humboldt University of Berlin. From 1963 to 1988 she worked as a Research Associate at the Academy of Arts in Berlin (West). In 1987 she took over the management of the Berlin workshop to develop the programme for *Berlin - European City of Culture* 1988 for which she was appointed its Artistic Director. From 1989-2003 she was Director of the Hebbel Theatre in Berlin, Artistic

Director of the *Theater der Welt* festival (1999). From summer 2003 to 2007 she was Director of the *Artists in Berlin Programme of the DAAD*. She has been a member and collaborator on numerous committees and networks, including the IETM (Informal European Theatre Meeting), *Theorem*, the advisory board of the Performing Arts of the Goethe Institute and the Board of Trustees of the Federal Cultural Foundation.

Jennie Jordan is Senior Lecturer in Arts and Festivals Management, De Montfort University Leicester, where she focuses on cultural leadership, cultural policy and audience engagement. Prior to her move into academia, Jennie had a varied background in the cultural and voluntary sectors. She was Head of Marketing at Phoenix Arts from 1995 to 1999, before joining regional audience development agency, Midlands Arts Marketing, and going on to work with the third sector development body, Engage East Midlands. Jennie has a significant track record as a consultant, having worked for the Department of Cultural Media and Sport, the Department of Food and Rural Affairs and national bodies such as Youth Music, Capacity Builders and Arts Council England. She is currently undertaking a PhD researching festivals and has written an Arts Council funded research paper as part of the *Discussion Papers in Arts and Festivals Management series*, which she co-edits with Chris Newbold, and she sits on the board of New Perspectives Theatre Company.

Rakesh Kaushal is a freelance writer and academic in media, culture and journalism, with twenty years' teaching and researching experience in universities that include Leicester, Cardiff and the University of the West of England.

Nevenka Koprivšek is a Director of *BUNKER Productions* and founder of the *Mladi levi Festival*, and also a member of IETM and DBM *Danse Bassin Méditerranée* (Ljubljana, Slovenia). She first trained and worked as actress, before moving into theatre direction and becoming artistic director for the Glej Theatre, 1989-97. In 1997 she founded *BUNKER* and since then has acted as the company's director.

Philip Long is Head of the Tourism Academic Group at Bournemouth University. His research interests include: festivals, cultural events and their tourism dimensions; connections between international film, television and tourism; diaspora communities, social exclusion and tourism. Philip is a Board member of the International Festivals and Events Association (Europe).

Christopher Maughan worked as an academic and researcher at De Montfort University for over 25 years. In 2002-3 he co-authored a major report on the economic and social impact of ten cultural festivals in the East Midlands of England. Since then he has contributed to the development of two festivals' tool-kits and published related work on festivals' life cycles, festivals and public authorities, and continues to undertake primary research on the economic impact of festivals. His work on festivals led to De Montfort University being a founder member of the European Festival Research Project and to him editing *Festivals in Focus* and undertaking a leading role in the editing of this companion collection.

Emmanuel Négrier is a CNRS senior research fellow in political science at CEPEL, University of Montpellier I (France). He dedicates a notable part of his investigations to festivals and public policies. He is the author or co-author of the following books: *Les Musiques du monde et leurs publics*, Le Mot et le Reste, 2014; *Music Festivals : a Changing World*, Michel de Maule ed. 2013; *Un territoire de rock*, L'Harmattan 2012; *Les publics des festivals*, Michel de Maule 2010.

Chris Newbold is Senior Lecturer in Arts and Cultural Industries Management and Programme Leader for the MSc. Cultural Events Management, De Montfort University Leicester. Chris has been working in media education for twenty five years, he has published on culture, media and research methods, and has produced two major text books in *Approaches to Media* (1995) and *The Media Book* (2002). He has just completed with Rakesh Kaushal an Arts Council England funded research project into mela festivals in the UK, and is joint series editor with Jennie Jordan of the *Discussion Papers in Arts and Festivals Management* series.

Jacqui Norton is Senior Lecturer in Arts and Festivals Management, De Montfort University Leicester. She has extensive experience of the music industry having worked for Chrysalis Music as Copyright Manager, and Zomba Production Music as Production Manager. She now runs her own music consultancy company and was a Director of a Community Interest Company, which aimed to promote social inclusion through song-writing. Jacqui is founder and director of the *Diggers Festival* in Northamptonshire.

Greg Richards is Professor of Leisure Studies at Tilburg University and Professor of Events at NHTV Breda University of Applied Sciences in the Netherlands. He has researched and published extensively on festivals and events, particularly the European Capital of Culture. Recent publications include *Eventful Cities* and *Exploring the Social Impact of Events* (both published by Routledge).

Monica Sassatelli is a cultural sociologist with a particular interest in cultural events and institutions, and has a focus on Europe. She is a Lecturer in the Sociology Department at Goldsmiths, University of London, where she is also co-director of the Centre for Urban and Community research. She co-edited the volume *Festivals and the Cultural Public Sphere* (with L. Giorgi and G. Delanty, Routledge 2011).

Satu Silvanto is a sociologist and cultural policy expert. Since 2003, she has been engaged in urban cultural policies as a researcher, project manager, adviser and, most recently, planning officer of the City of Helsinki Cultural Office. Satu is the editor of two books *Festivaalien Helsinki* (Helsinki – a festival city) and *Kaupunkilaisten kulttuurikeskus* (Cultural Centres for Urban Citizens). She has contributed to European publications, such as *The Europe of festivals: From Zagreb to Edinburgh, intersecting viewpoints* (edited by Anne-Marie Autissier), and participated in several European projects, such as *Eurocult21* (led by Eurocities), *Access of Young People to Culture* (Interarts), *Festival Policies of Public Authorities in Europe* (CIRCLE/EFRP). Today, her main interests lie in promoting community arts and encouraging artists to work outside the comfort zone of their own institutions and to work directly with and for people.

János Zoltán Szabó is a guest lecturer at Eötvös Loránd University, Budapest, and senior adviser at the Ministry of Human Resources, Hungary. Formerly he worked as a research officer at the Budapest Observatory (2003-2012), an independent expert (2000-2003) and theatre manager at Csokonai Theatre, Debrecen (1995-2000). He obtained his PhD in Educational Sciences from Debrecen University (2012).

Rhodri Thomas is Professor of Tourism and Events Policy and Head of the International Centre for Research in Events, Tourism and Hospitality (ICRETH) at Leeds Beckett University, UK. His research interests encompass various issues associated with the influence of public policy on business behaviour in the events and tourism sectors.

Katherine Winkelhorn is responsible for the Masters programme in Culture and Media Production at Malmo University. Her research work includes audience development in collaboration with Roskilde University and with *Malmö Stadsteater, Københavns Musikteater* and *Teater Faar 302*. Other work includes working on a festival in Bangalore, with academics, artists, activists and practitioners, considering how modernity is mediated, in collaboration with the Srishti School of Arts, Design and Technology in Bangalore. For five years she worked for *Copenhagen 96 – European Capital of Culture*, where she was responsible for its large-scale international projects for the performing and visual arts. Following that she has initiated many international collaborations between academia and the arts, in India, South Africa and former Yugoslavia. For some years she has worked at *Hotel Pro Forma* and *Odin Teatret*, both located in Denmark, where she lives.

Preface

Christopher Maughan

The aim of this book, *Focus on Festivals*, is to present a collection of work that adds to the limited literature about one of our most ubiquitous cultural phenomena, festivals, and to stimulate interest in their study and increase understanding about their importance in contemporary society. An important contribution to the development of this book was given by Dragan Klaić. He committed himself to publishing such a book as part of his work for the European Festival Research Project (EFRP), which he set up in 2004. Sadly, he was unable to realise this aspect of his vision but his colleagues in EFRP continued working on the project following his untimely death in 2011.

It was partly in response to Dragan's passionate and critical engagement with festivals that the authors featured in this collection responded to invitations by Franco Bianchini and myself, and agreed to contribute their work as a tribute to Dragan. The editors wish to acknowledge their generosity in agreeing to the inclusion of their essays and in this way enabling many others to benefit from their experience and insights.

EFRP is an international, interdisciplinary consortium, focused on the dynamics of artistic festivals in contemporary life. One of its principal aims is to understand the underlying causes of the current proliferation of festivals, the resource implications and diagnostic perspectives. Dragan's personal interest was predominantly in those festivals that are driven by a firm artistic vision, involving international programming and which benefit from substantial support from public authorities.

The focus on Europe is a reflection of the fact that EFRP was a consortium with a membership drawn largely from researchers, festival managers and policy-makers who are based in Europe. This collection reflects other voices and perspectives on the aims and impacts of festivals in contemporary Europe with the addition of an essay by Robyn Archer, 'A view from Australia'.

In the period 2004 to 2011, EFRP, drawing upon Dragan's inexhaustible address book and personal charisma, encouraged new and established researchers to write research papers, and share their knowledge in intensive research workshops on specific topics where the results of their research were presented and discussed. Such workshops took place in Nitra (2005), Leicester and Le Mans (2006), Barcelona (2007), Helsinki and Moscow (2008) Novi Sad and Leeds (2009), Poznan (2010) and Strasbourg and Maribor (2011).

It was from these myriad sources that Dragan proposed to develop an edited book on festival politics, programming, impacts and governance and which might also serve as a source of conclusions, trends, forecasts and recommendations for festival managers, public authorities (as subsidy givers) and potential sponsors. At the present time all research outcomes are accessible in a public repository at the website of the European Festivals Association (http://www.efa-aef.eu/efahome/efrp.cfm).

The genesis of this book as a final outcome of EFRP has drawn together a collection of research perspectives that reveals the richness of the work and thought that is being applied to the festivals sector in a European context. However, compared to the volume and depth of work available in other cultural sectors, the festivals sector is still relatively under-researched. The scope for future research is wide and many features of this ubiquitous phenomenon are still ripe for investigation.

This collection is a companion to a slimmer publication, *Festivals in Focus*, published by the Budapest Observatory in conjunction with the Central European University in 2014 (Klaić 2014). That book features an important part of Dragan's legacy, four essays with which he intended to introduce a collective volume of work derived from EFRP seminars. Because of his untimely death these chapters have to be seen as work in progress. Nonetheless, these four essays display his sharp critical ability and raise many interesting questions about festivals, not just in Europe but in a global context.

The two themes at the heart of *Festivals in Focus* are echoed in this collection too. The first is the role festivals play in contemporary life. This includes the need to understand the social, cultural, political, economic and physical contexts in which festivals operate. But we should also reflect on how the international dimension of artistic festivals – strongly advocated by Dragan – is precisely what allows them to make a deeper, critical and transformative contribution, by relativising and questioning the fundamentals of our everyday lives, political arrangements and ethical values.

The second insight is to the understanding that Dragan Klaić himself had of the fragile world of festivals. Dragan thought that artistic festivals could make a significant contribution to achieving a more internationalist approach to arts programming, audience development and integration with local policy agendas, ranging from economic regeneration and tourism to education and social inclusion. Dragan's advocacy and promotion of EFRP was an important aspect of his encouragement of a more longitudinal and collegiate approach to research and of his expectation of critical reflection. He profoundly believed that festivals had the potential (denied to many continuously operating organisations) to explore a more risk-oriented arts agenda. Such openness of artistic festivals to innovation and risk would bring them closer to a key feature of his life's work: the idea of 'Europe as a cultural project'.

It is hoped that, as well as being a fitting tribute to him and his passionate evocation of arts festivals, this collection will stimulate greater interest in the sector and a deeper analysis of the benefits that festivals deliver globally as well as within Europe.

Bibliography

Klaić, D. (2014) *Festivals in Focus*, Budapest: Budapest Observatory and CEU

Acknowledgements

We would like to thank staff and students of Arts and Festivals Management at De Montfort University Leicester, for their help and encouragement. Thanks in-particular are due to Maurice Maguire, Tony Graves and Jacqui Norton for their advice and unwavering support of this project.

The editors wish to thank Peter Inkei (Budapest Observatory), Anne-Marie Autissier (Paris VIII University) and Richard Fletcher (De Montfort University) for their editorial support and advice, and Tom Faber for his translation from the French of the chapter by Bernard Faivre d'Arcier.

The editors would like to acknowledge the financial support received from the European Cultural Foundation funding for the establishment of EFRP in 2004, and the support we have received from the European Festivals Association and the British Arts Festivals Association.

Special thanks are due also to Julia Bala, widow of the late Dragan Klaić, for being continuously supportive of this project and its companion *Festivals in Focus*.

Introduction: focusing on festivals

Chris Newbold, Jennie Jordan, Franco Bianchini and Christopher Maughan

In focusing on festivals it is our intention in this introduction to reflect and illustrate the diversity of thought, themes and theories that have emerged from the variety of case studies in this book. Even though festivals have probably been a part of people's experience since human interactions began, their academic study is still in its infancy. Indeed as a relatively new area of critical endeavour, which has yet to find its own language and voice, its researchers are drawing on a wide range of academic approaches from anthropology, sociology and policy analysis (for example, Giorgi et al's, (2011) discussion of festivals as part of the cultural public sphere and Quinn's (2010) work on the policy implications of urban arts festivals), to management theory and economics, in order to shed light on this new field (as discussed in Getz, 2012). This collection is consequently eclectic and broadly based, including contributions from festival organisers, event managers, academics and cultural and community activists. As the case studies in this book illustrate, festivals do not take place in a vacuum, they are the result of a range of social and cultural pressures, organisational and management decisions, and artist and audience expectations. Attending a festival may well be a liminal, 'time out of time' experience for the participants. However for the organisers it is the result of a series of negotiations and actions, within the context of the wider political, economic, social and cultural climate. It is this core understanding that informs the contributions in this book.

Focus on Festivals is divided into four sections, reflecting what we have identified as the major areas of interest for academics, organisers and students of festivals.

♦ In the first section, there are broad issues and perspectives such as festivalisation, sustainability and the role of festivals as part of the 'public sphere'.

♦ In the second section we identify issues concerning leadership and management in the sector, such as entrepreneurship, experiences, volunteering and iterative management practices.

♦ The third section, on festival impacts, looks at potential effects on urban change, culture in a broad sense and the arts more specifically. We focus particularly on community festivals looking at diversity, multiculturalism and issues of identity and place.

♦ The final section examines issues including the future of festivals within the network society, transnational identity and citizenship, and trends which may undermine the important role of festivals as a critical force.

Each of these aspects has their own sets of debates, issues and theories that are illustrated by the case studies and discussed in the introductions to the four sections. This book does not aim to provide an exhaustive explanation and examination of each of these. Readers can amplify for themselves through using the extensive bibliographies. The book rather aims to provide the reader with an indication of the breadth of material that can be applied to contextualising and understanding contemporary festivals in Europe.

Clearly, as this book will demonstrate, there are as many different festivals taking place in Europe as there are definitions of what a festival is. As we are focusing on contemporary festivals in one part of the globe, our definition will inevitably be skewed from the outset. There is always a danger when trying to define festivals of creating a taken-for-granted notion of what a festival is or should be – one which will certainly only ever be partially true. Having said that, it is incumbent upon a text such as this to at least try and establish some shared characteristic features, by which we can say that the events we are describing are worthy of our festivals focus and whether taken-for-granted notions are as sensible as they seem at first glance.

Given their complexity and eclectic nature, it is useful to ask why the study of festivals is important. Understanding and developing a festivals' typology is a prerequisite for achieving a systematic engagement with the festivals sector. Within this book, readers will find examples of festivals that are primarily civic in nature, with values that prioritise community self-celebration; other festivals that place artistic promotion and development at their core; and others that exist principally for profit (Jordan 2014). From a policy perspective, each of these types may be more or less integrated into national or local, urban or cultural policies and may be more or less successful in its own intrinsic or in others' social and political terms (Olsen, 2013).

Embedded within these types are a wide range of potential measures and features that reflect the core aims of each festival. These include the extent to which a festival is: a source of artistic innovation and vitality; transformative (e.g. through educational work); a moment of ambiguity and challenge to the status quo; a source of impacts (which may be cultural/political/social/economic/environmental); a source of local cohesion/pride/identity; a mechanism through which to achieve a change in city/regional identity and to market a locality; an investment in improving the quality of urban life; a project focused on advancing cultural democracy; a way of mobilising new audiences and/or new partners and stakeholders; a source of entertainment/ delight/social networks; a platform for developing intercultural dialogue and intercultural competence; and for achieving change in local and European citizenship/consciousness.

For many people festivals are first and foremost social activities. They serve purposes rooted in collective experience and are part of group living. They are events which punctuate the calendar; they are often short term, a day to a month in length, with a few notable exceptions. They are 'public facing', embedded in social and cultural life, and a 'festive' experience. Activity within festivals tends to have a creative/performance/ritual dimension to its content. They may be formally cultural or commercial (although these are not mutually exclusive) in their outlook and they must attract an audience, who in every sense are equal participants in some or all of the festive activities. The festival experience can be an oppositional one and it should not be banal, trite or trivial. For Pieper, festivity lies in the contrast both to everyday life in which we undertake useful work and to the uselessness of the activity. "To celebrate a festival means to do something which is in no way tied to other goals" (1999: 9). Key to our understanding of a sense of festivity is the disruption of the normal. For many, a festival is a rite of passage in their own personal development and whilst attendance at an arts festival is rarely liminal in its full sense, a deeper understanding of festivals' liminal (Turner, 1987) or life changing/challenging impacts could have significant implications for cultural managers and on policies on programming, management and marketing.

The ancient origins of festivals are often associated with moments of intensive consumption of meat at times of abundance, providing a protein rush leading to mad hedonism, moments of abandonment, the mocking of authority, spectacle, feasts for the senses and aesthetic indulgence. Intensity underlies all these elements. Much of the work on festivals in society historically has been anthropological in its understanding, with rituality at its core (see Bahktin's (1984) seminal work in this area, for example). For anthropologists, festivals are analysed for the functional role they play for societies and groups, providing markers of transition, reaffirmation of status and beliefs, and moments of release. Suffice it to say that the above is only a starting point for thinking about what makes a festival. Readers will inevitably develop a 'thicker' typology as they proceed through the book.

It is obvious that for millennia, festivals have taken place around the globe. However, it may be argued that the 'professionalisation' of the festivals sector began to happen in Europe around the middle of the last century with the emergence of the 'arts and culture' festivals of *Edinburgh* (1947), *Avignon*

(1947) and a heightened awareness of the role of culture in contemporary society in rebuilding Europe after two World Wars. The austerity of the late 1940s and 1950s gave way to a period of great economic growth and social change, and alongside that the development of a cultural infrastructure across Europe. Festivals too became a more familiar part of the landscape, and a career path for cultural professionals began to be made possible through organisations such as the Arts Council of Great Britain, established in 1946, and the development of arts management training courses in the UK and other countries in Western Europe from the 1970s.

Professionally organised expositions and exhibitions, such as *The Great Exhibition* in London in 1851, had been very popular across Britain, Europe and the United States in the nineteenth century. These had been celebrations of industrial achievement, technical and scientific advancement and artistic endeavour. The devastation of two World Wars and the arrival of the mass media and the cultural industries resulted in audiences no longer being drawn to demonstrations of a nations' manufacturing prowess, but rather to its cultural products. The development of cultural festivals such as *Edinburgh*, *Cannes* and the *Berliner Festspiele* can be seen as part of this process.

The development of festivals in Europe from the end of World War Two can be identified as emerging through a number of clear phases. The first period could be defined as 'the age of reconstruction'. This phase, beginning in the late 1940s, was focused on an 'arts for art's sake' notion of cultural policy. The emphasis was not only on the reconstruction of European cities and their cultural facilities after the damage of the Second World War, but also on moral and civic reconstruction. Cultural policies in this period focused on high culture and the main aim was to 'raise' the cultural level of the population through a process of 'democratisation of culture'. The arrival of commercial television, radio and pop culture were all seen as a threat to high cultural standards. This was also the era of the developing Cold War and of the separation of the liberal democratic, capitalist West of Europe from the Communist East. Festivals became important as a counterweight to this process and one of the few ways of brokering East/West dialogue. Artists and other 'cultural ambassadors' were the only people, other than sportsmen and women, to breach the Iron curtain at that time. The re-starting of a cultural dialogue between Eastern and Western Europe was indeed part of the mission of the *Edinburgh* and *Avignon* festivals.

Some festivals in the late 1960s and the 1970s reflected a new phase. They became community-focused and/or explicitly political, and forums for symbolic resistance, an expression of the developing oppositional youth culture and radical movements of that era (including feminism, gay and ethnic minority activism). A new generation of artists working in social contexts (including deprived neighbourhoods, schools, prisons and factories) was instrumental in the development of these events. Socially engaged artists became known by different names in different European countries (e.g, community arts in Britain, *Sozio-Kultur* in Germany, *animation socioculturelle* in France) but they all shared a belief in the revolutionary potential of involving ordinary people in the artistic process. There was in this age a strong emphasis on participation and a shift from 'democratisation of culture' to 'cultural democracy' which, for many socially engaged artists, would encourage people to recognise their condition of subordination and oppression, and would start a process of radical social and political change. Festivals took over whole cities and emblematic spaces (the free festivals held in Windsor Great Park in England in 1972-74, for example). Symbolically occupied city spaces, incorporating street theatre, open air performances, political rallies, all gave access to the city centre to the poorer classes living in the outer areas of the city. Clearly in this era there was a widening of the definition of festival culture, which came to include circus, mime, popular music and films shows, many of which were free and open to all comers.

In the late 1980s and during the 1990s another phase was consolidated. This had a more commercial and economic development orientation, characterised by the greater involvement of the private sector, which recognised the potential for aligning their business with the PR possibilities of festivals with a captive audience or other opportunities for business development as sponsors. Local authorities also became increasingly interested in festivals as vehicles for urban regeneration, to respond to the process of de-industrialisation and economic restructuring in cities including Glasgow, Liverpool, Birmingham, Hamburg, Rotterdam, Lille, Bilbao, Barcelona, Turin and Genoa. Festivals during this phase became increasingly part of tourism promotion and city marketing strategies, aimed at attracting increasingly mobile capital, businesses and skilled personnel.

Alongside such macro developments, festivals have become a focus for differentiating between individuals and communities in terms of physical, intellectual, cultural and emotional access. Bourdieu explains the relationship between social class, educational achievement and cultural taste, as being instilled through socialisation, particularly upbringing and education. Taste is exhibited as well as reinforced by the festival environment, in which audiences can signal their understanding of the rules of a particular cultural field, which Bourdieu (1984) calls *cultural capital*. The link between class and cultural consumption may have weakened amongst younger generations as a result of newer forms of distribution, but familiarity with particular genres reinforces the bonds amongst social groups. Festivals that promote particular art forms are an essential element in reinforcing and developing taste and therefore of reinforcing tribal identities, a factor that sponsors utilise to establish their brands. Understanding more about festival audiences and their decision-making would sharpen marketing and communication.

Alongside this we have already noted the increased professionalisation of the sector. The professionalisation process can strengthen a festival and its future but equaly it can lead to risk aversion and self-censorship by all festivals, especially those which become reliant on sponsorship with the constraints that this can impose. Key questions are: does sponsorship influence programming and decision-making? And will increased reliance on sponsorship lead to more and more similar festival offerings?

Another management issue that is receiving more attention is the sector's reliance on, or exploitation of, volunteers and increasingly internships. Festival organisations are more dependent on casual staff than many other cultural institutions, especially those which are building-based. Part of the explanation may well lie in their history, that of being community or artist-based organisations, but there are also managerial issues, as the festival organisation may have to expand rapidly from a small group of employees (four or five is typical and which may include paid, casual and unpaid staff) to a very large group (several thousand) when the event commences.

The model has become more complex with a mixture of communities of taste and the increasing influence of the urban regeneration, tourism and economic development agendas. This ultimately has led to a post-millennial emphasis on economic impact. Following the economic crash of 2007-8 festivals have had to redefine their relationships with the state, local authorities and the public. In some cases, artists began to take charge themselves, with the emergence of anti-elite, live art, cutting edge art forms, aimed at arts graduates and the informed public. Some festivals have responded to new technologies by becoming immersive, one example being *In Between Time* in Bristol.

This being said, it is clear that the influences of previous historical periods still remain and are reflected across Europe's festivals' calendar. Thus, there are many high culture festivals of the 1950s model, exemplified by *Avignon* and *Edinburgh*, that are now joined by the members of the European Festivals Association, which includes events in *St Petersburg* (Russia), *Valletta* (Malta) and *Reykjavik* (Iceland). The radical movements of the late 1960s and 1970s are represented by a wide range of niche festivals e.g. the *Boom Festival* (Portugal) and *Future Everything* (Manchester, UK). Over the same period the number of community-oriented festivals has grown significantly, in part under the influence of diasporic festivals, such as carnivals and melas, and other civic pride-based events. Some of the community-based festivals that emerged in the 1970s and early 1980s have become subsumed under the 'city' festivals umbrella. Such changes are partly an indication of how mainstream they have become. These festivals are now used as one of the ways to encourage people back into city centres – as strategic agents of urban regeneration.

A feature of commercial practice that has also emerged is the cloned festival, which is commodified, standardised and with no special relationship with place (examples include *Leeds* and *Reading* Festivals; *WOMAD*; *Sónar* in Barcelona and 14 cities worldwide). There is a discernible trend towards larger and larger festivals across Europe, especially with the growth of the big greenfield site music festivals and city festivals. There are questions of economies of scale; larger festivals can be more profitable, but as with shopping malls this can also lead to standardisation of the product on offer.

This homogenisation of the festival product, together with co-productions and the impacts of touring companies (and their schedules and exclusivity contracts), has led to a tendency for festivals' audiences to be attracted by large programmes, which focus on big names and on tried and tested performers. The demand and therefore the scope for programming less established artists may be becoming more difficult. From a commercial point of view, this controlled market has negative consequences for some middle scale festivals that may not have the budgets to secure the bigger names and the audiences that follow them. The festivals in this book have responded to this in a variety of ways; by growing in size themselves in order to compete, as in the case of *Flow* in Helsinki, or by producing their own events (often in collaboration with other festivals), or by creating a niche appeal.

Undoubtedly the economic slump has not been all bad for festivals. Indeed much has been made in the popular press across Europe of festivals being 'recession-proof'. This may be journalistic hyperbole, but there might also be some truth in the idea of the 'staycation', the holiday at home, where people are taking more but shorter breaks within their own vicinity, which is ideal for the festival market.

Much will be made in this book of the debates surrounding *festivalisation* and *hyperfestivity*, the multiplication and mushrooming of festivals. This is partially the result of the growing intervention of local authorities into the festival scene, but is also due to the success of the festivals themselves, making them attractive commercial propositions. Economic impact studies and the success of festival leaders in persuading politicians to support festivals for economic reasons has led to the labelling of multiple events as festivals and the corralling of pseudo-events and pre-existing festivals under the banner of 'festival seasons' or 'city festivals'. There is clearly a debate here about the extent to which artistic visions for cities are being developed and the degree to which they are being integrated into city policies, with festivals in many cases being the lead elements of such policies. Leicester City Council's 2012 Festivals Review and subsequent bid for the UK Capital of Culture title are a recent example of this trend.

Destination tourism is an important aspect of local festivals policy. Festivals provide visibility and this leads to increased media profile and thus potential sponsorship. Festivals are politically popular in particular when they can be demonstrated to contribute positively to the revitalising and regeneration arguments noted above. The possibility of developing synergies between previously unrelated activities, but which may operate as a cluster stimulated by the presence of a festival, is another reason for the adoption of festival strategies. The *Festival international de la bande dessinée d'Angoulême* (FIBD) is a good example of this. There is also an argument that festivals could play a development role in supporting local artists, local productions and in feeding into the generation of local creative industries-style clusters and structures. *Game City Festival* in Nottingham is a good example, where Nottingham Trent University and local games manufacturers are trying to build on a pre-existing industry. Thus festivals can be a stimulus for local policy makers to act on local issues, not only in industrial terms but also socially and culturally; examples of the latter will be found throughout the book. There is an increasing recognition of the strategic role of festivals not only by local government, but by national governments as well.

Another growth area in provision in recent years has been the festival of ideas, not just literary festivals such as those held in Hay-on-Wye in the UK, but also those such as *Cultural eXchanges* held at De Montfort University, Leicester, UK or *The Philosophy Festival (FestivalFilosofia)* in Modena, Carpi and Sassuolo, three cities in the Emilia Romagna region of Northern Italy. In Italy, we find festivals of science (in Genoa), economics (Trento and Rovereto), journalism (Perugia), TV and new media (Dogliani) and creativity (Florence). Such festivals aim to provide arenas in which ideas can be encountered and exchanges of opinions and thoughts are encouraged. In Italy it could be argued that the decline in the quality of national TV has led to festivals providing opportunities to meet others who want to debate serious topics.

This type of festival activity brings to the fore the notion of festivals as providing a kind of 'public sphere', a place where the 'conditions of argument' would be such that a 'reasoning public' could debate issues free from the influence of power, traditional authorities or dogma (Habermas, 1974). The notion of the public sphere is an ideal, but one which allows us to examine the role of festivals outside of the 'entertainment paradigm' and consider their wider role in society. It could be argued that, whilst they are not called festivals of ideas, many of the examples in this book do engage with contemporary political and philosophical debates through the work that they produce and exhibit, the spaces they create for informal public engagement, and the development of their art forms, as well as their more direct involvement in urban public policy. One example is the *Mladi Levi* festival in Ljubljana, discussed by Nevenka Koprivšek (the festival's artistic director) in Chapter 10. Another important example is the *London International Festival of Theatre (LIFT)*, which since its foundation in 1983 has explored the power of theatre as a global force for change (De Wend Fenton and Neal, 2005).

This is clearly understood by organisations such as *Festival Republic*, who use their major festivals (*Latitude* and *Reading/Leeds*) in order to generate an awareness of green issues and actively encourage sustainable living during the festival, through their sustainability co-ordinators and their partnership with Julie's Bicycle. This organisation works to improve understanding of the impact of arts practice (not just festivals) on the environment. Festivals can provide a good way of integrating messages about individual and collective responsibility within the context of an event where the audience is potentially more relaxed and open to such discussions. The popularity of the Greenfields, Healing Fields and Alternative Technology camps at *Glastonbury Festival* (UK), the 20,000 volunteers at *Roskilde*, the environmental values of *Sziget* (Budapest, Hungary) and the Green Operations Europe or GO group (based in Bonn, Germany) are testament to the powerful impacts that festivals can have on audience's engagement and commitment to cleaner and more sustainable ways of living.

This engagement with festivals and the public sphere is taken up further in Chapter 3 by Monica Sassatelli. But this whole debate raises questions about the social impact of festivals and the extent to which a single liminal experience can change the opinions and behaviour of the participants. Is it more realistic to expect that festivals have to present several editions before they can induce change in their audiences and other stakeholders?

The management and leadership of festivals also feature strongly in this book. As has been stated, we are in an era of the professionalisation of festivals. Festival directors may stay in post for a number of years/seasons and festival management may therefore become an iterative process, each festival learning and developing from the last, much as an artist develops a piece of work. Many festival leaders come from art form backgrounds and bring elements of reflexive practice to their organisations.

It could also be said that festivals are outside of some of the laws of business management. Theirs is a very entrepreneurial way of working. They often lack a secure relationship with their audience and may also lack secure access to income streams either from the public sector or from ticket income, so many now rely on commercial sponsorship - a precarious basis for any creative organisation at the best of times. Organic growth is also a feature. Festivals have not been created fully formed. They evolve and change, adapting to changes in economic climate, cultural trends and audience demands. However, they are often driven by the obsessions and passion of the people who start them and managerially reliant, it could be argued, on self-exploitation and enthusiasm. Adizes' (2004a, 2004b) organisational development model is useful here, as it can be applied to the various stages of an organisation's lifecycle. Indeed one of the aspects of festival development we have already alluded to is the movement over the decades from dependence to independence to interdependence, the first state representing the reliance that some festivals have on local authorities.

Festivals exist in reality, but also in a parallel virtual world. Digital networks are vital to festivals, since the virtual world provides more opportunities for global reach and global connections. The overcoming of the local/global dichotomy, what Robertson (1997) calls 'glocalization', 'the simultaneity --- the co-presence --- of both universalizing and particularizing tendencies' is an important theme in this book and features many times in each of the sections. Many festivals may be locally derived but they are also internationally orientated. It is the proud boast of many festivals that they bring international artists to their event. The pressure we have alluded to earlier of providing 'big names', standardised formats, touring artists, illustrates the global influences on festival organisers, but can festivals also be filters for globalisation, by combining global inputs with local cultures and values? Is there a conscious effort by some festivals to achieve this? Festivals create encounters between the global and the local which challenges and changes both. Thus some of the chapters in this book are able to demonstrate how the local can act back on the global, indeed providing a foil for the perceived effects of cultural imperialism.

Multi-cultural festivals and international festivals such as the defunct *Dublin Festival of World Cultures*, or the *London International Festival of Theatre* (LIFT) deliberately set out to bring together international and local performers, as part of their cultural or aspirational remit. These types of festivals also provide a platform for local artists. Festivals such as Asian melas or Caribbean carnivals are found across Europe and provide an interesting mix of multi-cultural community interest events and imported performers, representing 'home' or 'tradition'. Increasingly there is also a generational dimension to these kinds of festivals where the second or third generations have closer links to the host culture and want other types of experiences than the first generations who look to such festivals to recall home and traditions. These later generations, especially South Asian youth, look to global styles such as Bhangra or Bollywood dance to be an integral part of a festival's programme. A key question for these types of festivals is to what extent are multicultural festivals becoming intercultural, incorporating in their remit hybrid and collaborative cultural forms and activities? Would intercultural festivals contribute to counteracting racism and xenophobia, and to producing artistic, social and/or economic innovation more effectively than multicultural festivals? Are the advocates of intercultural festivals in European cities (generally young, often of dual heritage backgrounds) relatively marginalised in urban and cultural policy networks, by comparison with traditional ethnic community leaders (often older men), who tend to favour multicultural festivals?

The development of festivals in postwar Europe also provides an illustration of the growing importance of the cultural economy and of the widespread belief among policy makers that festivals have a major role to play in the tourism industry. Some of the case studies in this book interrogate and challenge these beliefs.

What will become apparent to the reader as they discover the various perspectives and approaches revealed by the case studies in this book, is that the world of festivals is rife with myths and ideals. There are also potent totems and some sacred cows. Each of these will need to be critically reviewed and exhaustively researched. For example, research into audiences is still one of the big gaps. Perhaps because this is a nascent field, a lot of the effects of festivals are presumed, if not distorted in claims made to local authorities or potential sponsors. This book in its aim to turn claims, rhetoric and assertions into research questions and academic debate is only the first step in a grounded discussion of festivals and festival practices.

In short, the focus of this book overall is on the contemporary European experience, and it is designed to provide convenient access to a series of case studies arranged in a 'reader' style in order to allow the book to be accessed in part or whole. As we shall see, the new era of professionalised festivals and mass festival attendance across Europe has brought with it layers of competing interests, from the national to the local, from the commercial to the subsidised, and from the overtly entertaining to the worthily cultural. Europe and the European Union provide an interesting field of study because of the long history of festivals on the continent, the size and scope of the market, the role of EU policy and the power of the European tourism industry, and not only the national but also the transnational nature of the festivals sector.

Bibliography and further reading

Adizes, I. (2004a) *Managing Corporate Lifecycles: How to Get to and Stay at the Top*, Santa Barbara, CA: The Adizes Institute Publishing.

Adizes, I. (2004b) *Leading the Leaders: How to Enrich Your Style of Management and Handle People Whose Style is Different from Yours*, Santa Barbara, CA: The Adizes Institute Publishing.

Bakhtin, M. (1984) *Rabelais and his World*, Bloomington: Indiana University Press

Bourdieu, P. (1984) *Distinction: A Social Critique of the Judgement of Taste*, London: Routledge and Kegan Paul.

De Wend Fenton, R. Neal, L. *et al.* (2005) *The Turning World. Stories from the London International Festival of Theatre*, London: Calouste Gulbenkian Foundation.

Getz, D (2012) *Event Studies: Theory, Research and Policy for Planned Events*, Abingdon: Routledge.

Giorgi, L., Sassatelli, M., & Delanty, G. (eds.) (2011) *Festivals and the Cultural Public Sphere*, London: Routledge.

Habermas, J. (1974) The Public Sphere: An encyclopaedic article, *New German Critique*, 1(3), 49-55.

Jordan, J. 2014, Festival Policy: a typology of local urban festivals and their policy implications, paper from the International Conference on Cultural Policy Research, Hildesheim, Germany, September 2014, http://jenniejordan.co.uk/gallery/festival, accessed 21 October 2014

Olsen, C.S. (2013) Re-thinking Festivals: a Comparative Study of the Integration/Marginalization of Arts Festivals in the Urban Regimes of Manchester, Copenhagen and Vienna. *International Journal of Cultural Policy* 19(4), 481-500.

Pieper, J. (1999) *In Tune with the World: a theory of festivity*, translated by Richard and Clara Winston, South Bend Indiana: St Augustine's Press.

Quinn, B. (2010) Arts festivals, urban tourism and cultural policy, *Journal of Policy Research in Tourism, Leisure and Events*, 2(3), 264-279.

Robertson. R. (1997) *Comments on the global triad and glocalization*, paper presented at the Globalization and Indigenous Culture Conference, Institute for Japanese Culture and Classics, Tokyo: Kokugakuin University.

Turner, V. (1987) Betwixt and between: the liminal period in rites of passage, in L. C. Mahdi, S. Foster and Little, M. (eds.) *Betwixt and Between: Patterns of Masculine and Feminine Initiation*, Peru, Illinois: Open Court Publishing Company.

FOCUS ON
FESTIVALS

SECTION 1
PERSPECTIVES AND DEBATES

Introduction

Christopher Maughan and Jennie Jordan

> European cultural policies foster two goals that produce conflicting effects: through state interventions in the name of 'democratisation' they want to broaden access to cultural goods, but through liberalisation, once again in the name of 'democratisation' they destroy the effects of their own measures and impose limits on the access to culture. (Breznik, 2004)

Whilst not directed at festivals per se, Breznik neatly captures the policy dilemmas that the festivals sector has been negotiating for the past several decades. On the one hand the sector reflects local and national priorities for community cohesion, inter-cultural exchanges, artist and artistic innovation; whilst on the other the sector is a partner in the development of tourism, city and place marketing and other more commercial goals. These and other dilemmas, perspectives and issues will be the focus of the first section of this book. The authors in this section, writing from very different perspectives, challenge us to look afresh at festivals and their value for society.

The value of art is a perennial topic, but a general understanding of the value derived from participation in a festival has received limited attention at an anthropological level. Some of the more quantifiable features of 'value' as measured by economic impact, perception studies and environmental impact are achieving regular attention but methodological challenges and limited time frames limit our understanding of long term benefits and challenges.

Several of the authors writing in this section refer to change they have noticed over time, but longitudinal studies of festivals are limited in number and those that do exist are often not the product of a formal research approach. This means that understanding of how a festival develops over time and the changes that need to be anticipated as part of its life cycle are not known. Possession of these insights would provide a richer matrix of perspectives to consider and reduce, perhaps, the tendency to repeat mistakes and pursue unsustainable festival formulae. A richer palette of perspectives would also inform policy-makers and other stakeholders who, in the absence of festival specific research of a longitudinal nature, may lack targets and other evidence with which to inform their policies on festivals.

One feature of the festivals sector that is routinely referenced is the rapid increase in the size and diversity of the sector, especially since World War Two. In Europe and North America in particular the change in the festivals sector has reflected the changes that have taken place from the late 1700s and the industrial revolution, in the cultural sector as a whole and the change in the relationship between art, culture and society. Section 1 contains chapters that highlight some key features of the festival offer and the change in its relationship to policy, place and people. Hertling (Chapter 1) considers festivals as institutions that are well placed to promote contemporary art forms that the establishment has ignored and as opportunities to support artist development, a point further developed by Comunian in Chapter 5. Négrier (Chapter 2) sees festivals as opportunities to attract new audiences to an art form; whilst Sassatelli (Chapter 3) and Szabó (Chapter 4) discuss festivals as part of debates in public policy and Fletcher (Chapter 6) considers one example of a festival that aims to influence public understanding of the Green agenda.

The European Festival Research Project (EFRP) was set up to focus research precisely on these features in determining how the sector might develop. In the book *Festivals in Focus*, Klaić discriminated between the role that festivals played and can play as "symbolic affirmations of a community's continuity and welfare" (2014: 1) and their manifestation in the 19th century "as festive clusters of concerts" (2014: 7). Klaić noted that from this period "artistic, cultural, social and economic aspects were intertwined and reinforced each other" (2014: 7-8) and that the places where these series took place were "expected to benefit materially and symbolically, to boost the local economy and prestige, while being nominally interested only in the advancement of the arts" (Klaić, 2014: 8). Such tensions remain a common feature of contemporary policy and practice and can be seen in how the festivals sector itself developed after World War Two when as Klaić noted "the festival formulae needed to be reinvented and advanced in order to assert the values of culture against hatred, brutality and persecution" (2013: 11) and stood as "an inspiring and encouraging force that reasserted a promise of future peace" (Klaić, 2014: 11).

Several authors engage with these themes. Hertling provides a personal account of a political and historical process that has energised the cultural sector in Berlin for 40 years and, in particular, how festivals played a major role in the 'unification' of the city from the early 1950s. She discusses how festivals such as the *Berliner Festspiele* can stand as examples of the instrumentalisation of art and culture.

Szabó introduces a comparative historical perspective when, in describing the development of the festivals sector in Central and Eastern Europe, he draws some interesting comparisons between his sample and some festivals in Western Europe and North America. Both he and Hertling explore the political context in which their respective festivals were developing. Hertling also draws attention to the international dimension of many festivals, both as a source of audience understanding about different artistic practices and also about the societies in which they are embedded.

Internationalisation and globalisation are important themes throughout this book, as Klaić argues that "in the new millennium, festivals could be seen as a specific response to globalisation and its ambiguous cultural impact" (2014: 32). Not all festivals seek to have an international profile or to present work from different cultural perspectives, of course, but those that do, and several examples are discussed in this section and the book as a whole, reflect this point (notably Négrier, Hertling, Argano, Autissier, Winkelhorn and Archer). Tomlinson's (1999) discussion about connectivity and global-spatial proximity argues that the experience that many can obtain at a festival is of a 'shrinking world' in which we, as cultural tourists, seek an exotic experience through a religious or secular festival where the art may come to us as part of a multi-disciplinary programme.

Klaić's reference to globalisation's ambiguous cultural impact echoes the statement that "from the instrumental point of view of capitalism, then, connectivity works towards increasing a functional proximity. It doesn't make all places the same, but it creates globalized spaces and connecting corridors which ease the flow of capital (including its commodities and its personnel)" (Tomlinson, 1999). Rock and pop music festivals are a clear example of such development, especially since the late 1990s, when CD sales collapsed in the face of downloading resulting in increasing emphasis on live performance to balance the books, and in festivals becoming an important source of income and profile for aspiring and established artists and a 'rite of passage' for audiences. The anticipation that is attached every year to the headliners at *Glastonbury Festival* in England is a case in point. Négrier identifies an increase in these sorts of festivals and links them to a growing preference for hedonistic cultural consumption practices that allow audiences to simply be 'present' and that do not require much cultural capital.

Klaić also points to the challenges to which festival managers have to respond, "festivals turned out to be a vulnerable part of the cultural infrastructure, quick to collapse in the new circumstances, be defunded, lose credibility" (2014: 28). This is a theme that is explored in more detail in Section 2 but it is an issue that Fletcher discusses in his chapter on the *Greenlight Festival* in Leicester and its first four editions, 2011-2014. As he indicates the relationship of this group to both cultural and environmental policy has been a key factor in shaping the organisation and its festival; this can be a source of both strength and weakness. Such vulnerability can be attributed to the marginal position of festivals in a cultural policy context. Festivals are not homogeneous in terms of their rationales, contexts, or relationship to place and people. Collectively they reflect the state, market and civil/communicative discourses of cultural policy that McGuigan (2004) discusses in *Rethinking Cultural Policy*.

As such, festivals provide an interesting source of reflection on changing trends within society at large and the extent to which cultural experiences inform individual and collective understanding of the world around them. It is interesting to examine how festivals fit into such a typology of discourses, how they are influenced by them and in turn what influence they have upon them[1]. The chapters in this section provide a good starting point for reflection on the topics of festivalisation, the roles of festivals with the (cultural) public sphere, as an expression of community values and social change and as sites for artist and art form development.

Where a festival fits in terms of place or 'situatedness' is an issue that is both under-researched from the perspective of the policy agenda, as Breznik (2004) notes, and that can present cultural managers with a challenge. From the point of view of a festival manager, should the priority for achieving a sustainable future lie in developing a strong artistic proposition, a strong connection with the immediate area, local artists and communities, or a more outward looking programme of national/international work with which they aim to attract audiences from outside of the area, i.e. cultural tourism (and economic impact)? These are not necessarily mutually exclusive but understanding where a festival fits and whether it could or should change its orientation, e.g. local v international, will have major implications for the festival, its mission, aims, staffing, marketing, indeed its whole identity and *raison d' être.*

Négrier provides an overview of the conditions under which festivalisation has developed to shape expectations of festivals as a route to personal and community development, as well as increased economic prosperity. He discusses a range of factors that have changed as the process of festivalisation has gained momentum across Europe; on the one hand, he relates 'festivalisation of culture' to more global trends affecting Western societies and specifically those which social scientists have identified from their research into the cultural field and elsewhere. He then goes on to provide a critical analysis of these changes in the context of research into festivals' audiences and in particular differences in motivation, intensity, style, practices that exist within festivals' audiences.

Négrier argues that we should guard against adopting simple explanations of how festivalisation is occurring and recognise instead that "festivalisation is deeply differentiated" and "potentially a new modality of cultural practices in the 21st century".

Sassatelli tackles similar themes with respect to mixed arts urban festivals in calling for "analytical concepts that can account for the complex, relational and processual nature of festivals, both as organisations and as experiences". Her chapter considers the place of contemporary festivals within the framework of the public sphere, as developed by Habermas, and the Cultural Public Sphere expounded by McGuigan. She prompts us to see festivals not just within the context of these discussions but as phenomena that influence the discourse too. She notes that one of the challenges to researchers is to develop and apply a research methodology that is appropriate to the sector in assessing "the possibility that contemporary festivals, as expressions of the contemporary society in which they flourish, can provide a valuable analytical perspective on its public culture".

Much of the analysis presented in this section and the collection as a whole focuses on Western Europe. The chapter by János Szabó provides a contrast to this with his discussion of how festivals have developed in a Central and Eastern European context. The cultural policy context is influential, but here the narrative includes more discussion of a control culture, especially until the late 1980s. This is reflected in the research agenda too: "In Western Europe, empirical festival research has often focused on a festival's social and economic benefits, by contrast in Hungary and other Eastern European countries festival research is often linked to free time and leisure time research, or cultural consumption and youth research". Szabó uses a social sciences approach to present a festivals typology which embraces cultural and community embeddedness which, as he outlines, "provides conceptual tools with which to define the scope, depth and quality of a festival's support from its community and the strength of its social networks".

Here again we find reference to context, support, integration that was previously noted as 'situatedness'. This has strong echoes of the life cycle theory as described by Adizes (2004), in which of the four key functions that help to locate where an organisation is in its life cycle (Purpose, Administration, Entrepreneur, Integration) that of Integration (with whom and for whom do we do this?) is often the function to mature last. It is one that helps to ensure long term sustainability as it is often associated with an expansion of the aims and rationale (Purpose) of an organisation to incorporate those of other stakeholders (artists, funders, audiences, local business, specialists in festival production) as well as the festival's founders. This does not require compromise but recognition that interdependence, working with others, is the mature state to which most organisations aspire.

Two examples of this are reflected in the final chapters that address issues of networking with artists (Hertling, Szabó and Comunian) and promoting more sustainable ways of living (Fletcher).

Hertling describes how the development of the festivals programme in Berlin also included opportunities for artists to stay and work in Berlin, in order that artists and companies could have a chance to learn from one another. Comunian, writing about the *Fuse Festival* (in Medway, Kent), begins from the point of view that much research on festivals focuses on their external impacts but few studies foreground the artists' experience; and especially understated is how being part of a festival benefits them in terms of their own practice. For many artists, developing and presenting work is, if not solitary, then not something in which feedback from other audiences and producers/promoters may be a regular experience.

Comunian takes theoretical approaches from the regional and organisational studies field to explore the creative practice of artists involved with *Fuse*. She discusses the role of the festival on artists' careers, their creative practice and their ability to learn and connect with other creative producers. Comunian provides an overview of the research paradigm that has been operating for the past two decades in arguing that the neglect of the artists' perspective should be unsustainable as we seek a fuller understanding of the role of festivals as "shared-spaces where learning and knowledge exchange happen".

Klaić in writing about the *LIFT Festival* draws attention to the need for festivals to develop a deep relationship with artists in their immediate vicinity and also to expand their programming ideas to include educational opportunities which together will "enrich the overall artistic identity and social significance of the festival" (2005: 149). A further example of the need to understand how a festival can be most effectively integrated into its location in order to secure its long term future.

These examples of networking are also at the heart of Richard Fletcher's discussion of his personal experience of working with the *Greenlight Festival* in Leicester. Fletcher's paper provides an insight into some of the challenges the team faced in getting started, in terms of financial support, volunteering, partnerships (especially with De Montfort University) and their own identity as an organisation that promotes sustainable living. The policy context to which *Greenlight Festival* relates is multifaceted as the organisation and the festival take account of a rich spectrum of sources/partners. The more influential may be the city council, the university and the Transition network but ultimately the success and future of the festival lie with the communities that it aims to reach.

In this respect, as with most other festivals, *Greenlight Festival* is trying to navigate its way through the opportunities, contradictions and conflicts with which the policy field is populated. How effectively it achieves that will no doubt be reflected in how long it continues. Is its programme one that reflects the City Council's agenda strongly enough to fund it, is its programme lively enough that artists and activists wish to be involved and the general public attend? Questions that are common to all festivals.

Bennett has drawn attention to the centrality of culture in any consideration of underlying tendencies towards pessimism or optimism (Bennett 2001, 2011). It is interesting to reflect on the capacity that festivals have to contribute to either tendency. Festivals are frequently attributed with almost magical qualities, their 'salvific nature' being a potential solution to a wide range of social, cultural and political challenges. Certainly this is a factor in their proliferation and one that is explored in depth by many authors in this collection.

But the key feature of the work in this section of the book is the extent to which the cultural policy context is a positive influence on the sector's growth and development and ultimately its ability to make a positive contribution to the development of society, networks and achieving greater understanding of the human condition. Or is this asking too much of a cultural phenomenon that is often seen as a source of short term pleasure, and largely a social activity to which audiences assign limited significance beyond that it is a break from daily life?

Bibliography and further reading

Adizes, I .(2004) *Managing Corporate Lifecycles: How to Get to and Stay at the Top*, Santa Barbara, CA: Adizes Institute Publishing

Bennett, O. (2001) *Cultural Pessimism: Narratives of Decline in the Postmodern World*, Edinburgh: Edinburgh University Press.

Bennett, O. (2011) Cultures of optimism, *Cultural Sociology*, **5**(2), p 301-320.

Breznik, M. (2004) *Cultural revisionism: culture between neo-liberalism and social responsibility*, Ljubljana: Peace Institute.

European Festivals Association (2008) *Arts Festivals Declaration in the framework of the European Year of Intercultural Dialogue 2008*, Gent: EFA available from: http://www.efa-aef.eu/FestivalsDeclaration

European Festival Research Project (2007) *EFRP recommendations to Public Authorities on support for artistic festivals*, Gent: EFA available from: http://www.efa-aef.eu/newpublic/upload/efrp/ EFRPFestivalPolicyRecommandationsToPublicAuthoriteis2008.pdf

Klaić, D. (2005) LIFT Outgrows its festival clothes, in Fenton, R, De W. and Neal, L. *The Turning World*, London: Calouste Gulbenkian Foundation.

Klaić, D. (2014) *Festivals in Focus*, Budapest: Budapest Observatory.

McGuigan, J. (2004) *Rethinking cultural policy*, Maidenhead: Open University Press.

Tomlinson, J. (1999) *Globalization and culture*, Chichester: Polity Press.

Notes

[1] EFRP worked in conjunction with CIRCLE on a Europe wide research project on public authority policy and support for festivals. An outcome of this was the production of a set of recommendations for public authorities on their support for artistic festivals (EFRP, 2007). The full report and the recommendations are available from the EFRP page on the EFA website (http://www.efa-aef.eu/en/activities/efrp/)

1 Festivals: Why, What, When? A case study of Berlin

Nele Hertling

The focus for this chapter is a reflection on the relevance and role of festivals in contemporary life. It is prompted by reading nearly one hundred applications from young festival managers who were applying to participate in a professional Atelier organised by the European Festivals Association. What became very clear from this exercise was the importance of reflection on why we invest so much energy into festivals. The applicants' submissions also prompted me to consider 'Who are we doing this for?' and more fundamentally to think about how to create, develop or sustain a festival in 2013.

This reflection is not aimed at, nor does it discuss or question the existence of traditional big events, such as Salzburg, Bayreuth, Edinburgh or Avignon. Their continued existence (for the foreseeable future) may be more or less taken for granted. Due to their cultural weight and longevity they have developed as important touristic events and, in this respect therefore, they are atypical and not central to the focus of this debate on festivals today.

But for the vast majority of festivals throughout the world, a spectrum which includes the well-known and active through to those in the early stages of planning, a basic question we should ask is 'Why should this festival continue or be created?' All festivals are (or should be) a unique response to a unique situation, every situation is different and these differences have to be considered carefully.

A key question is therefore: "What would be missing in the city or region without its festival? What does it add to the cultural, artistic or social life, which is not available in other ways/elsewhere?" Further questions would be: "For whom is the festival necessary? How is it a source of support for artists? In what way does it create opportunities for artistic production? Does it give something special or new to the audience? Can it help to develop a new audience and stimulate fresh ways of thinking about the needs of a city or region and its development, and generate new, shared ideas about its image and how culture can enrich people's lives?"

A festival in this sense becomes a process, integrated into the changing situation of its political context and, therefore, with the potential to contribute more than may be achievable by a festival that is an isolated event. This is even truer for festivals in a city that already enjoys a diversity of artistic projects throughout the year.

Berlin in the period 1960-1990 and its international festivals serve as an interesting example of this process for example in the origins, development and conclusion of two particular festivals with which I have worked: *Pantomime, Musik, Tanz, Theater* and *Tanz im August*.

After the end of Fascism and the Second World War, cultural life in the city was quickly re-established; theatres, concerts, exhibitions had already re-started as early as the summer of 1945, albeit sometimes in very provisional spaces. The inhabitants of the city longed to experience again the art and culture that for many years had been unavailable to them.

The political/social situation in the city had changed drastically and, to put it mildly, was difficult. The city was no longer in the centre of Germany but still in the centre of Europe. East Berlin was the centre of the GDR, but West Berlin was a distant region of the Federal Republic, completely dependent on the support of the Federal Government. To become a city with a future and an identity Berlin needed to clarify to itself and others its role in the complex geo-politics of the times; one that would reflect its position between east and west, where it was looking in both directions. For the Federal Republic, where for a long time Europe meant just Western Europe, thinking and acting towards the East was limited to defence and commerce. Berlin's role had to complement these areas and the resource that it chose to concentrate on was culture, strongly supported by the Allied Forces.

But even here East and West were already divided, mostly for ideological reasons. West Berlin newspapers tried to influence their readers not to support any activity controlled by the Soviet Regime – in practice, not to go to any cultural, artistic institutions or events in East Berlin. Against this background, the Americans decided in 1951 to create the *Berliner Festwochen* in West Berlin. Cultural policy-makers now regarded, and used, culture as an 'intellectual defense', and, despite encouragement to have nothing to do with 'the East', the Festival, a child of the Cold War, brought artists and their work from all over the world to West Berlin, including from Eastern Europe.

Another small but typical anecdote underlines the contradictions: the director of the theatre in which the *Festwochen* started invited his colleagues from the East to the opening night, but he was forced by the government to withdraw the invitation, adding that this instruction would apply to all forthcoming premieres in West Berlin (i.e. that no one from East Berlin would be invited).

Six years later the GDR Government founded the *Festtage* in the other part of the city using more or less similar arguments to those of their capitalist enemies.

A discussion of the early days of festivals in Berlin provides a way of examining how these festivals stand as examples of the instrumentalisation of art and culture. The positive aspect then was that the *Berliner Festwochen*, later *Berliner Festspiele*, served the demands of an audience in Berlin eager to enjoy the latest developments in international art and culture. The *Festwochen/Festspiele* offered this possibility and success led to it becoming a project that is still funded by the Federal Government today, albeit in many different formats - for example the renowned *Berliner Filmfestspiele*, the *Musikfest*, the avant garde music festival *Märzmusik*, the *Jazzfest*, the *Theatertreffen*, *Foreign Affairs* - a festival of international performing arts - and others. Most of these formats, especially the music festivals, continued to bring projects, artists, programmes and co-productions to Berlin, which would not otherwise have been available to audiences and artists. But there are also examples where the Berliner *Festwochen*, now a powerful institution, presented artistic concepts and ideas, which also had a presence elsewhere in the city in the programmes being developed by continuously operating organisations and initiatives. This led to unfortunate clashes in programming and created competition with those organisations, many of which often had to work with smaller budgets and under more complicated, restrictive conditions.

Is that wise, necessary? Festivals need to harness their resources wisely and not to dissipate their energies. They should avoid slipping into a routine response to the world, ensure that needs are clearly defined and that their chosen programme clearly and explicitly adds value to the overall artistic life of the city.

Looking at the artistic dimension of projects and productions in the 1970s and 1980s in Berlin and Germany, one can see that most of them were still based in the more traditional German structures of repertory theatre, city theatre, opera, ballet. This left little, if any, space for independent artists and their work, with the result that only a small audience, including professionals, was aware of the new forms, approaches and themes that were developing in the international performing arts world. It was this understanding that led Dirk Scheper and I, working for the music and performing arts sections of the *Akademie der Künste*, to propose to the *Akademie* the creation of a festival that would present the most interesting new independent theatre and dance companies.

The *Akademie der Künste* is one of the oldest cultural institutions in Berlin. It was founded in 1696, a time when Germany was still suffering from the effects of the 30 Years War, with the aim of attracting artists to the city but also to follow the example of other European courts (in particular those in Rome and Paris) to achieve greater visibility, recognition and respect for itself through the quality of its artistic life. This new *Akademie* and its elected members were expected to advise the Court on cultural matters and to help in the support and development of local artists. Over the centuries the *Akademie* developed into an important cultural institution and latterly became part of the financial responsibility of the Federal Government, as with the *Berliner Festspiele*. It is funded still to support the arts and artists and to advise the Government on artistic and cultural matters.

After the Second World War, and the political conflicts that followed, neither party, East or West, could agree on which was the true successor to the Prussian *Akademie* so the institution operated separately in both parts of Berlin, a separation that only ended with the fall of the iron curtain in 1989. In West Berlin, after some years in a temporary space, the *Akademie* moved in 1960 to a newly constructed building near the Tiergarten. It was the first cultural centre to be built in West Berlin following the war and from the beginning it was heralded as a great success. The *Akademie* presented the most important visual art exhibitions, contemporary music concerts, literature readings, debates and performances which attracted large audiences eager to enjoy new productions and to share in new ways of thinking. The contemporary cultural life of Berlin now had a visible presence and a place in which to present this work, where it continued for many years. So it was here that in 1975 a festival for performing arts was created under the simple name *Pantomime, Musik, Tanz, Theater*, in short *PMTT*.

We programmed *PMTT* to run on the same dates as *Theatertreffen*, the Festival that, under the banner of the *Berliner Festwochen*, focused on German spoken theatre performances. We did so to offer an alternative artistic perspective to that presented by *Theatertreffen* and to provoke a dialogue between what we saw as the more traditional German repertory theatre on the one hand and the new international forms and structures on the other. It was in the latter that we were more interested.

In shaping this festival, and choosing the artists and companies, we enjoyed great freedom. *PMTT* was funded well and overall we were allowed to operate without any interference from the *Akademie*. This enabled us to create a programme of great variety and quickly to establish a very successful festival. We brought in theatre, music theatre and dance companies from all over the world, most of which were, up to then, unknown in Berlin and, quite often, in Germany. These included for example Trisha Brown, Laurie Anderson, Tadeus Kantor, Lucinda Childs and many, many others.

This festival offered a growing and enthusiastic audience many surprising discoveries and over the years created an awareness and openness to a new contemporary world of performing arts. The Festival also started and supported an important and necessary debate about the need for change in the institutional infrastructure in the city and encouraged those involved to consider new possibilities of production and presentation. The results are still visible today, but after many very successful and influential years the Festival ended in 1987– other institutions, theatres and other initiatives were established and, influenced by us, began to explore a similar artistic agenda. *PMTT* had brought a whole new world to Berlin, it had opened the eyes and minds of professionals and audiences but at a certain moment it was not necessary any more.

In 1985 the great Greek actress, Melina Mercouri, introduced the idea of the European Capital of Culture (ECoC), she wanted "to highlight the richness and diversity of European cultures, to celebrate the cultural ties that link Europe and foster a feeling of European citizenship". The aim was to define the very specific features, the uniqueness of European cities, to present their diversity as the basis of a united Europe. 'It is in the cultural characteristics of particular places or regions that we recognise Europe's cultural profile'.

Berlin was selected for 1988, after Athens, Florence and Amsterdam. We saw it as both a great challenge and opportunity to devise a festival based on Mercouri's vision and principles. The first challenge we had to address was how to programme a new festival in a city which was already full of artistic/ cultural activities. What could a European Capital of Culture add?

Our response to this was the development of the *Werkstatt Berlin*. This was an innovative development because it sought to engage visiting artists in a different relationship with the city. Artists would not just be part of a programme of performances, exhibitions, concerts and diverse projects from many countries but be encouraged to stay and work in the city, using it as a laboratory in which to devise new work. The *Werkstatt* therefore created a different experience to the 'festival stress' of most international festivals. Artists stayed for longer periods of time and the Festival organised and supported meetings and creative exchanges between colleagues, some of which led to new projects and co-productions.

At that time West Berlin was still physically isolated; travelling across borders was complicated with the result that many local artists, especially young and new ones, were cut off from professional networks, international contacts, or touring circuits . The *Werkstatt* was a catalyst in the development of new artistic exchanges, spontaneous co-operations and co-productions. It also integrated many artists living in Berlin into these discourses and provided them with opportunities to develop their own work. For audiences too it provided a rare opportunity to be a witness to creative processes and their surprising, unfamiliar outcomes. It was a very influential process and when the Festival finished at the end of 1988, the *Werkstatt* was retained for many years as an important element in the cultural life of Berlin.

The second idea for the Cultural Capital Festival was again based on the recognition that Berlin is located in the middle of Europe. It was therefore a great chance to create a platform and a context in which artists, audiences, policymakers could contemplate the future of Europe from more than a Western European perspective. To develop a programme that was based on a shared cultural identity and diversity, which went beyond political and ideological borders and which also aspired to give visibility to the conviction that there was a space for something in between East and West; that the European cultural tradition embraced both Western and Eastern Europe and that they are not separate entities.

This was one of the important guidelines in developing the artistic programme for Berlin as the ECoC in 1988. The intention was to present a project from every European country, including those in Eastern Europe, even though as Berlin was still inside the Iron Curtain there were limited chances to travel through the wall. The result of many years of Cold War was that there was little knowledge about the artistic life in neighbouring countries to the east. The ideological situation had even resulted in the West showing disinterest or worse possibly harbouring feelings of superiority towards the 'poor suppressed artists' in the east.

The ECoC festival therefore had to meet the challenging task of discovering artists, ensembles and companies from our Eastern European neighbours and to find, often subversively, a way to open a door in the Wall to give them the chance to perform to audiences in West Berlin. After some surprises and aesthetic irritations, closer contacts were established, cooperation across borders slowly became 'normal' and after ECoC other structures and venues in (and outside) Berlin continued this exchange. (Although I think it still needs a risk taking festival to look again and again for new and young artists from these countries).

As a festival the 1988 project was convincing, because it did not rely on international events, but it produced contacts, knowledge and sustainability, important for the artists, the audience and the city.

This was possible, based on the rare fact of a very close respectful cooperation between the individuals responsible for programming and the representatives of cultural policy in the city. The questions, why, for whom, how, when, had to be answered for each proposed programme before it could be financed and organised. I think this is a very helpful model.

One more experience from the Festival world in Berlin. A key feature of Berlin's year was the *Werkstatt* and the final example I wish to note is a direct product of this – it is *Tanzwerkstatt* Berlin. In preparing it and choosing the artists and companies, we realised that most of them were creating fascinating new works all over Europe, most of them also touring extensively, but usually they were invited to perform and then leave the Festival the next day because of limited budgets (performers and festivals alike). The result was that of these choreographers/dancers few had ever seen the work of any other. The *Tanzwerkstatt* Berlin 1988 invited some of the most interesting companies to stay together in Berlin for nearly two weeks, to present their work, but also to meet during the days with each other, with local dancers and choreographers for workshops and lectures. These novel interactions produced new ideas for artistic work, initiated co-productions, networks and exchanges; and ultimately were an important catalyst for the development of dance in Berlin and in Europe.

The public success of all the many different dance presentations had a direct impact on the Berlin's cultural department too and as a follow-up to 1988 it was agreed to support, on a smaller scale, the continuation of these dance activities, performances and workshops. Also, as a result of the ECoC year, the city accepted a proposal to use the newly opened *Hebbel Theatre* as a place for production and presentation of international performing arts work. One of the first decisions was to repeat the experience of the year before and to create a dance festival under the name *Tanz im August*. The aim was to keep the format that had been so successful, to again invite companies, dancers and choreographers to stay for a longer period together in Berlin. Those invited were not only to perform, but also to give classes and lectures, to meet and mix in workshops, open new networks for international co-production and to invite local artists to participate. Today this seems to be a 'normal' situation, but at that time it was exceptional. Over the years, in continuing the Festival, these new experiences attracted many professionals to Berlin and created the ground for the development of Berlin as a lively international dance city.

But slowly the situation changed. The founding principle of working, performing and being together in a laboratory and workshop in Berlin became more and more difficult to arrange. First because the producers and presenters experienced major cuts in their budgets (in Germany and across Europe) and second it became more complicated to coordinate the working and touring schedules of the dance companies. As a result the focus of the Festival changed to a programme that consisted mostly of groups and artists that could be seen anywhere and so it lost its innovative edge. At the same time the Foreign Affairs project as part of the *Berliner Festspiele* regularly included dance performances in its programme, often involving the same companies. However, *Tanz im* August, has weathered this difficult period and has implemented a new artistic strategy supported by a new financial and organisational structure and plan. August 2013 was its 25th anniversary, which it celebrated with a very successful programme.

As noted before, this experience gave the questions - why, where, for whom - a particular relevance. As also noted it is necessary to find a balance, to define clearly the content and the context of two festivals which are competing with each other, to make them aware of the need to develop their own identity and through this to keep the possibility for adding new experiences and visions to the city's cultural profile. Not repeating a formula through habit, but ensuring that it continues to be relevant to the situation and time in which it is embedded.

Each festival should be able to give a clear answer to the questions: Why work with these artists in this combination? What outcome is desired from a single invited performance? How can it be related to the overall context, both local and international? How should the Festival respond to and add to the existing cultural offer in the city?

For all festivals, the artistic team needs to refresh its planning and its programme each year with a new set of questions which the Festival will help them to answer. New needs should be defined and new outcomes identified for what the Festival can offer to artists, to the audience, to a city and its citizens – a challenging but essential process and vision.

2 Festivalisation: Patterns and Limits

Emmanuel Négrier

The rapid development of arts festivals in the past quarter century should not make us forget that such festivals are a relatively new phenomenon in Europe and that their current explosion goes hand in hand with a growing differentiation in the events/festivals market (Klaić 2008). Notwithstanding the long history of major events, the social, economic and cultural phenomenon that we associate with the 'festivalisation of culture' is much more recent. It is also linked to a plurality of causes, such as the evolution of democratic regimes (notably in Southern Europe), or the decentralisation of power in France (Négrier and Jourda 2007).

Figure 2.1: Eurockéennes Festival France (photograph Philippe Belossat)

What is meant by 'festivalisation' is the process by which cultural activity, previously presented in a regular, on-going pattern or season, is reconfigured to form a 'new' event, e.g. a regular series of jazz concerts is reconfigured as a jazz festival. Festivalisation also describes the process by which cultural institutions, such as a cinema, theatre, arts centre or gallery orients part of their programme around one or more themes or events, concentrated in space and time. Festivalisation therefore results in part from the explosion of festivals, but also from some 'eventalisation' of regular, cultural offers. The current situation in the European cultural sector shows an interesting tension between the two phenomena.

On the one hand, much research in the cultural field is still focused on building-based, traditional venues, fixed locations and seasons, i.e. the general idea of permanence. On the other hand, the recent focus on cultural development has led to increased attention being paid to cultural activities that are temporary and more ephemeral.

The purpose of this chapter is twofold[1]. On the one hand, it relates festivalisation to more global trends affecting Western societies. The first section will discuss several processes that are at the heart of the transformation of our relationship to culture and particularly to the festivals sector. We make the assumption that festivalisation is something that goes beyond national and European borders and beyond the limits of the performing arts. In the second part of this paper, a critical analysis of these changes will be presented which will draws on research into festivals' audiences. It will focus on the differences in motivation, intensity, style and practices that exist within festivals' audiences. These differences are sometimes traceable to national characteristics (Bonet and Négrier 2011).

Festivalisation as a new cultural repertoire

The first part of the paper considers the development of festivals as expressions of larger developments that affect our relationship to culture. A festival, as an object, and festivalisation, as a phenomenon, can be argued to be the crystallisation of changes that have been identified by a variety of researchers in very different fields of cultural analysis. These developments, because they relate to different research fields, are generally treated separately. Here the object 'festival' enables us to ask questions that relate to both. This will be completed in two stages.

We will first note some categories of change and the associated trends that can be observed today. Figure 2.2 sets out six categories and trends with a classic, older view on the left, and a more contemporary perspective that challenges it, on the right. We could identify further categories with a larger study, but nonetheless, these help us to characterise what the process of festivalisation could mean from a social science perspective.

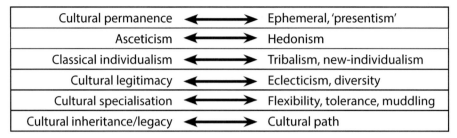

Figure 2.2: Changing trends in society's relationship to culture

The change from cultural permanence towards more ephemeral experiences is one that some might describe as a negative phenomenon. This is because the focus and legitimacy of cultural policies and decisions about which cultural activity merits public support are largely based around places, seasons and the primacy of cultural permanence (Dubois 1999). The spontaneous, unbridled and ephemeral vision of festivals' audiences and their relationship to culture and the arts appear less compatible with this model. The association with cultural permanence also created an association between policy, funding and cultural forms in which the audience brings a commitment to learning and the development of their cultural capital. By comparison, much contemporary cultural development is increasingly being influenced by what Hartog (2003) called 'presentism', i.e. a culture that lives only in the moment or in more or less random patterns, a culture Bauman (2011) has defined as 'liquid'. Permanent zapping, the 'gas' aspect of contemporary cultural practices (Michaud 2003), corresponds to what the philosopher finds in the world of the feast. They also correspond to some more concrete findings too: the decline in the market for subscriptions and increase in late booking by audiences for shows, except for those that the public rates as a truly exceptional event. Amongst others, we could mention here festivals such as *Glastonbury* in the UK, *Bayreuth* in Germany, or the *Paléo Festival de Nyon* in Swizterland, that can sell out several months before they run, on the basis of their reputation, not their programme, which may still be unconfirmed when the tickets are first offered for sale. The nature of our relationship to classical culture is changing and is being rebuilt according to new, distinct rhythms. Festivals are an expression of this development.

The transition from asceticism to hedonism goes hand in hand with this category. It is an old debate of philosophers and sociologists of culture (Veblen 1899, Donnat 2009), some of whom forecast the decline of a culture that society cannot appreciate without experiencing a certain degree of self-discipline, while in its place is substituted a culture more associated with notions of entertainment, leisure, hedonism (Rodriguez Morató 2007). Festivalisation seems to correspond well to the decline of cultural asceticism.

The transition from classical individualism toward tribalism or new individualism is another important perspective. Classical individualism - in the sense of the social construction of the individual - included a personal and institutional relationship to culture (Finkelkraut 2002); a quality embodied in the concept of the honest man, 'mature and calm' (Tocqueville 1892). But what we see more of today is that cultural consumption is inherently a social activity. The number of people who attend a cultural event on their own is small. This collective participation in cultural activity is not limited to what some sociologists have called the ambiguous and vague term 'tribe' (Maffesoli 1991). It also reflects the diverse perspectives of what we might call the 'second individualism' (Corcuff et al. 2010), i.e. a collective practice indeed, but limited, and marked by short-termism and continuous change (Elliot and Lemert 2009). Such a practice is not contradictory but complementary to the end of the great collective narratives and practices, such as activism, for example (Ariño 2010).

Understanding the transition from cultural legitimacy towards eclecticism is partly informed through a sociological analysis of cultural practices. Cultural legitimacy predicts a strong correlation between a person's upbringing in terms of education and family background and their interest in those levels of artistic expression that are colloquially described as high or elitist art (Bourdieu and Darbel 1969). However, other research has not supported that view but instead revealed that people's cultural choices may be more diverse and eclectic (Donnat 1994). This research showed that those who are the most active are not necessarily followers of culture, in an elitist sense. Instead they are essentially eclectic and able to move easily between 'high art' and 'low art', by which we mean art that requires less cultural capital to understand and enjoy it. This shift of legitimacy toward eclecticism led some to think about access to culture in a new way. Inequality was seen as referring less to the quality of cultural consumption by the elite, than to that group's ability to consume more of everything, in all categories, and also in larger quantities than others (Sullivan and Katz-Gerro 2007).

This theme is also closely associated with the sociology of taste (Peterson 1992). While a theory of legitimacy may demonstrate the existence of stratified tastes based on a class hierarchy, empirical studies give us a different perspective. Research on taste has demonstrated that there are a wide variety of taste profiles (Négrier et al 2010) which, whilst relating to the social hierarchy, point to a different conclusion. Consumers of classical music may, on average, be older, female and members of higher academic and social categories than others, but today those who are exclusively lovers of classical music are in the minority. Most of them combine their love of classical music with other genres, some of which can be very different both aesthetically and socially. From our survey at the *Eurockéennes de Belfort Festival* we found spectators who were simultaneously fans of metal and classical music (Négrier et al 2012).

Consequently, some scholars have developed a new vision of the spectator as being less sensitive to the influence of their personal 'cultural legacy' (Bourdieu 1979) in developing their personal 'cultural path'[2] (Djakouane and Pedler 2003). An individual's relationship to culture is no longer thought to be influenced exclusively by genetics but by a very wide range of social factors such as school, family, friends, colleagues or neighbours (Lahire 2004), all of whom can contribute discrete elements to the 'cultural path' that someone may follow through life. Monographs dealing with specific venues or festival experiences (Leveratto 2010) show the importance of local contexts in the acquisition of 'cultural competence', particularly among socially disadvantaged spectators. But the qualitative optimism of such a notion of 'path' has to be related to a greater pessimism about the quantitative magnitude of the phenomena. A person's relationship to culture, beyond the strict notion of inheritance, remains subject to the iron law of unequal access. However, while the quantitative statistical analysis of cultural practices tends to engender a certain fatalism about the reproduction of inequalities, the concept of 'path', more qualitative, offers better opportunities for public action and less pessimism about the 'democratisation of culture'.

Festivalisation is thus a phenomenon that combines a plurality of theoretical and empirical approaches, involving both consumer practices and tastes, on the one hand, and political and economic strategies of many stakeholders on the other. This presentation might suggest that this is an irresistible and widespread process. To test this, the six categories were subjected to further critical analysis because for each dimension, the change is not necessarily inevitable, linear and positive. The next section relates these points to some research into festivals' audiences.

Contrasted changing trends

If the explosion in the number of festivals has been accompanied by a strong differentiation in the nature of the events market, then the social perspectives noted above are definitely affected by these differences. This is the point we will develop in this section through examining how a change of perspective can alter our understanding of the different dimensions. This approach highlights the fact that the categories discussed do not constitute a 'tablet of stone' or a 'road map' but a 'palette' of potential future developments. This reflects previous observations by us that some commentators have misunderstood the theories they were discussing as describing a linear process. If it is not a question of a particular direction, this is because there is not just one, and for several reasons.

What kind of change? From substitution to hybridisation

For most people their relationship to culture is characterised by intermediacy rather than by an affinity to one side or the other. The new practice or behaviour that they adopt does not delete the old one, even if it is now dominant. Thus, when we speak of the rise of eclectic tastes, this does not mean that an individual loses all sense of their own taste or that we become indistinguishable in our selection from the 'taste of others' (Négrier et al. 2012). This can be observed in the tastes for classical music (e.g. fans of baroque) and for more popular aesthetics (e.g. fans of heavy metal). Fans of particular genres have their reasons for retaining their allegiances so, when devising new products, there are good reasons for taking appropriate account of those people who 'resist' eclecticism. Three important reasons are:

♦ One, 'resistors' represent a significant%age of the public. It is therefore logical that they should be taken into account by the organisers of special events.

♦ Two, they form a symbolically important group for the festival. Indeed, fans are at the heart of the programme (e.g. baroque or heavy metal) and often the movers and shakers behind the public success of any event and are likely to be among a festival's most loyal audience.

♦ Three, they are more motivated to express their satisfaction or their dissatisfaction with respect to a festival's programme. They are therefore important social partners and not just targets for a festival.

Finally, these groups of fans represent a singular identity when compared to the average member of the public: fans of baroque are older and more educated than the average audience; heavy metal fans are overwhelmingly male. Therefore while the trend of festivals for popular music is towards feminisation, we must take great care with our interpretation of the thesis of 'triumphant eclecticism'.

Similarly, the new wave of second individualism, which promotes micro-groups and tribes, speed and constant change, has not diminished the importance of the 'solitary aesthete' at a concert or festival. Again, the solitary spectator most often corresponds to specific characteristics in terms of social practices. Our research shows that in addition to it being hard to be 'lonely' at a festival, first time attendees rarely go along alone; when they do, it was found that the solitary spectator is more likely to be male and to have achieved a higher level of education.

One outcome of this research might be that festivalisation is not a source of new practices, but of hybridisation between permanence and transience, between hedonism and asceticism. Thus we observe the growing trend for permanent cultural venues to organise special days. These special days form an important part, in conjunction with the main programme, of many organisations' audience development and long term strategic marketing plans. Such approaches are designed to move people from the outside to the inside in terms of their commitment to a festival and its programme – the future loyal audience. In this way an event can develop a strategic role as part of a long term sustainability plan for a venue.

Consequently, the challenge for a venue becomes one of how to ensure long term benefit from an initiative which can too often be limited to the short term, to the 'coup'. Indeed the first issue of cultural democratisation is certainly the transformation of a non-public into a public cultural offer. Experimental partnership between festivals, cultural venues and social stakeholders generally get a timely success of renewed audiences, with new social profiles, participating in these actions. But the second issue is the transformation of this new public, attracted through an exceptional action, into a sustainable audience. And this goal is difficult to achieve (Oldershaw 2011). This is the problem faced by festivals which cooperate with new communities (e.g. economic migrants) and social centres in outlying municipalities, for example. It is the common challenge of cultural democratisation, how to measure the deeper social impact that festivals may deliver, beyond their economic impact (Maughan and Bianchini 2004).

Thus, for each aspect of the festivalisation process, it would be wrong to talk in terms of substitution, because old cultural behaviours may coexist with the new ones. It is thus better to oppose diversification of regimes (of practices, of goals, of strategies) and their specific combination in the concrete reality of a festival or a family of festivals, of an individual or a social group. In our recent study, we show for instance that practices, goals and strategies developed by a classical music festival differ from those implemented by rock and pop festivals, on important themes such as cooperation, price fixing, or communication. At first glance, we could say that these are two festival worlds, one marked by the old model and the other by the new one. It would be an error, as on each side one can find examples that are different mixes of traditional and innovative tendencies. The mutation is therefore a comparative hypothesis, not the only possible and legitimate trend. This is the reason why this change is structurally uneven (Négrier et al 2013).

Uneven changes

Not all relationships to culture are affected in the same way by these changes. Thus, with respect to audiences, our research shows that participation in a festival is a social activity and rarely something that people do alone. This is the default position but the modality changes according to the types of programming. The dominant form of social modality and participation at classical music festivals is the couple. That at popular music festivals it is the group of friends (Négrier et al 2010).

Against the assumption of widespread hedonism, several cultural offers remain for which an ascetic relationship to culture is dominant, sometimes so demanding with regard to the consumption of cultural goods that it looks like suffering is an intrinsic part of the fun. Dorin's (2011) analysis of the audience of the *Ensemble Intercontemporain de Paris* reflects this high level of requirement with the single statistic: 10% of the audience had a PhD. By contrast other events are more hedonistic, especially the main folk, rock and pop music festivals, which can be seen in the way that the audience 'lives' at the event. But it would be a mistake to confuse hedonism with an uncritical and uneducated relationship of the audience to the cultural offer, or that the audience possessed only limited awareness of the artistic programme they were receiving. On the contrary, in our analysis of *Eurockéennes*, we showed that the audiences' critical knowledge of the artistic offer was at least as high as that of a fan at a great Baroque festival.

Conclusions

The spectacular impact in the phenomenon of festivalisation can be seen in the explosion in the number of events now on offer. But this is a deceptively simple explanation. Behind this apparent simplicity, we are also seeing a strong differentiation in the events market, as has been described by Dragan Klaić (2008). This differentiation not only relates to the strategies and cultural and artistic objectives of festivals but also to the social practices surrounding participation in festivals. At first glance, we consider, that festivalisation does fit with the anthropological and sociological trends that characterise the contemporary Western world. But some festivals still derive their appeal from traditional practices. So instead of being a monolithic and linear movement, festivalisation is deeply differentiated. This is why it could, under certain conditions, appear as a new modality of cultural policies in the 21st century.

Bibliography and further reading

Ariño, A. (2010) *Prácticas culturales en Espa*ña, Desde los años sesenta hasta la actualidad, Barcelona: Ariel.

Baumann, Z. (2011) *Culture in a Liquid Modern World*, London: Polity Press.

Bonet, L. and Négrier, E. (2011) La tensión estandarización-diferenciación en las políticas culturales. El caso de España y Francia, *Gestión y Análisis de Políticas Publicas*, 6, 53-73.

Bonet L. and Schargorodsky, H. (eds.) (2012) *La gestion de festivals por sus protagonistas*, Barcelona: Gescénic.

Bourdieu, P. (1979) *La Distinction*, Paris: Minuit.

Bourdieu, P. and Darbel, A. (1969) *L'Amour de l'art*, Paris: Minuit.

Corcuff, P., Le Bart, C. and De Singly, F. (2010) *L'individu aujourd'hui. Débats sociologiques et contrepoints philosophiques*, Rennes: Presses Universitaires de Rennes.

Djakouane, A. and Pedler, E. (2003) Carrières de spectateurs au théâtre public et à l'opéra, in O. Donnat, P. Tolila, *Le(s) public(s) de la culture*, 203-214. Presses de Sciences Po

Donnat, O. (1994) *Les Français face à la culture : de l'exclusion à l'éclectisme*, Paris: La Découverte.

Donnat, O. (2009) *Les pratiques culturelles des français à l'ère numérique*, Paris: La Découverte..

Dorin, S. (2011) *Le public de l'Ensemble Intercontemporain*, Paris: Séminaire de l'Association Française des Orchestres.

Dubois, V. (1999) *La politique culturelle. Genèse d'une catégorie d'intervention publique*, Paris: Belin.

Elliott, A. and Lemert, C. (2009) The global new individualist debate, in Elliott, A. and du Gay, P. (eds), *Identity in Question*, London: Sage.

Finkelkraut, A. (2002) *L'imparfait du présent*, Paris: Gallimard.

Glevarec, H. and Pinet, M. (2009) La 'tablature' des goûts musicaux : un modèle de structuration des préférences et des jugements, *Revue Française de Sociologie* **50**(3), 599-640.

Hartog, F. (2003) *Régimes d'historicité. Présentisme et expériences du temps*, Paris: Seuil.

Klaić, D. (2008) Festivals: seeking artistic distinction in a crowded field, in H. Anheier, Y. R. Isar and A. Paul *The Cultural Economy*, Los Angeles: Sage.

Lahire, B. (2004) *La Culture des Individus*, Paris: La Découverte.

Leveratto, J. (2010) *Cinéma, Spaghettis, Classe ouvrière, Immigration*, Paris: Éditions La Dispute

Maffesoli, M. (1991) *Le temps des tribus*, Paris: Livre de poche.

Maughan, C. and Bianchini, F. (2004) *The Economic and Social Impact of Cultural Festivals in the East Midlands of England*, London: Arts Council England.

Michaud, Y. (2003) *L'art à l'état gazeux. Essai sur le triomphe de l'esthétique*, Paris: Stock.

Négrier, E. and Jourda, M. (2007) *Les nouveaux territoires des festivals*, Paris: Michel de Maule.

Négrier, E., Djakouane, A. and Jourda, M. (2010) *Les publics des festivals*, Paris: Michel de Maule-France Festivals.

Négrier, E., Djakouane, A., and Jourda, M. (2012) *Un territoire de rock. Le public des Eurockéennes de Belfort*, Paris: L'Harmattan.

Négrier, E., Bonet, L. and Guérin, M. (2013) *Music Festivals : a Changing World*, Paris: Michel de Maule.

Oldershaw, T. (2011) *Circulation des publics entre les offres culturelles : étude de cas à Londres*, communication au séminaire de l'Association Française des Orchestres, 31 Jan, Paris.

Peterson R. A. (1992) Understanding audience segmentation : from elite and mass to omnivore and univore, *Poetics*, **21**(4), 243-258.

Rodriguez Morató, A. (2007) *La sociedad de la cultura*, Barcelona: Ariel.

Sullivan, O. and Katz-Gerro, T. (2007) The omnivore thesis revisited voracious cultural consumers, *European Sociological Review*, **23**(2), 123-137.

Tocqueville, A. de (1892 [2000]) *Democracy in America*, Chicago: University of Chicago Press.

Veblen, T. (1899 [1915]) *The Theory of the Leisure Class*, New York: MacMillan.

Notes

[1] This paper presents analysis already published in Spanish under the title 'La festivalización de la Cultura. Una dialéctica de los cambios de paradigma', in Lluis Bonet et Hector Schargorodsky (dir.), *La gestion de festivales por sus protagonistas*, Barcelona: Gescénic 2012, p.17-32

[2] Djakouane and Pedler use the term of 'carrière' (career) that can be understood, in French, in a broader sense than in English. We use the term 'path' in order to respect this mix of legacy from the past and the plurality of determinations and directions one can take.

3 Festivals, Urbanity and the Public Sphere: reflections on European festivals

Monica Sassatelli

"What is a festival?" is a deceptively simple question – but also a deceptively complex one. This is reflected by much of the literature on festivals, in which discussion of their multiplicity and heterogeneity, their complex etymologies and histories, as well as the expansion in the second half of the 20th century, and exponentially since the 1980s in Europe, has seen festivals transformed into one of the dominant formats in the current cultural realm.

However, beneath the apparent multiplicity, one major feature helps to clarify the issues at stake when considering their cultural significance: festivals tend to be either "'traditional' moments of celebration or… highly orchestrated mega-events" (Waitt, 2008: 513). The first are supposed to be the organic expression of a community; the second, which we may call post-traditional (Giorgi and Sassatelli, 2011: 1-11), are instead mostly associated with the contemporary culture industry and its rationales, their recent exponential growth seen as proof that we are faced by a non-organic, commercially driven phenomenon.

The distinction is relevant because, whilst traditional festivals have been studied, in particular within anthropology and folklore studies, as expressions of a given society and an entry point into its culture, values and identity, post-traditional festivals have been dismissed by some writers as banal, and banalizing 'spectacles' (Debord, 1994). Different approaches and literatures contribute to deepen this gulf, with contemporary festivals on the whole dismissed by mainstream social science and cultural theory and assessed in terms of their (economic) impact only. In this chapter, after a brief review of the dominant approach in urban festivals research, I try to uncouple these associations. That is, to explore the possibility that contemporary festivals, as expressions of the contemporary society in which they flourish, can provide a valuable analytical perspective on its public culture.[1]

As hinted above, this chapter also has a thematic focus on *urban* festivals, or the relationship between festivals and urbanity. It does not come as a surprise that, in a predominantly urban world, contemporary festivals tend to be urban too. The recent festival explosion has meant that today most cities have their own art festival. The majority of recently established festivals are devoted to more than one discipline or art, so that mixed arts festivals outnumber single genre festivals (PAYE, 2008; Allen and Shaw, 2000; Rolfe, 1992). Multidisciplinary festivals draw their specificity precisely from the combination of several artistic genres and types of events, usually reflected in an equally multifaceted mix of venues, audiences and aims (from 'pure' artistic to social activities) that also contributes to this type of contemporary artistic festival being on a continuum, rather than a clear-cut disjuncture, with community based festivals. So, whereas most festivals may stage events from more than one discipline (e.g. literature festivals often have a cinema section, music festivals include visual arts exhibitions, etc.), in mixed arts festivals no single genre dominates and defines the festival. As a result, many of these define themselves by referring to the location that hosts them. The urban dimension becomes a defining feature of most mixed arts festivals, in particular among the more established, international, ones.

Festivals and urbanity

Urban, mixed arts festivals are both intriguing and challenging for scholars. On the one hand, the 'mixed' nature of these festivals, means that their analysis cannot exclusively rely on any specific sectorial body of literature (e.g. music studies, film studies, art history, etc.) or genre development, such as those that kind be found for film festivals (Iordanova, 2009, Iordanova and Torchin, 2012), theatre festivals (Hauptfleisch *et al.*, 2007), or art biennials (Vogel, 2011). On the other, given that some of the major festivals in Europe and beyond are of this kind, empirical research has often concentrated on this type, either focusing on single festivals (see Bruce, 1975; Moffat, 1978 or, more recently, Jamieson (2004) on Edinburgh's festival) or comparing a few of them. Scholarly research on mixed arts urban festivals has drawn mainly from one of two bodies of literature, or, more rarely and mainly in overview articles rather than new empirical investigations, a combination of both (as in Quinn, 2005a, discussed below). In the first approach, contemporary festivals are compared to more 'traditional' community festivals, therefore reflecting on the possible relevance of the extensive anthropological literature on traditional, community festivals, for the study of contemporary, European or more generally 'Western' mixed arts festival, going back to socio-anthropological classics such as Durkheim (1912) and Turner (1982).

In his now classic definition Falassi noted that along with the major distinction between sacred and profane:

> another basic typological distinction that is often made draws upon the setting of the festival, opposing rural to urban festivals. Rural festivals are supposedly older, agrarian, centred on fertility rites and cosmogony myths, while the more recent, urban festivals celebrate prosperity in less archaic forms and may be tied to foundation legends and historical events and feasts (Falassi, 1987: 3).

However, this seems to have given more legitimacy to the study of rural festivals, allegedly more ancient and rooted to community identity and, as noted in the introduction, may be associated with a dismissive account of contemporary, urban festivals. Falassi's own account is mainly geared towards such 'traditional' festivals, which are indeed the focus of most anthropological research. Authors following this approach have thus tended to look for traditional festivals in urban, contemporary contexts, as a result revolving around issues of loss of authenticity and invented traditions. Good examples that question the received clear cut dichotomy between traditional (authentic) and contemporary (inauthentic) are Piette's (1992) study of a Belgian carnival in the city of Binche, Azara and Crouch's (2006) work on the *Cavalcata sarda* in Sassari in Italy and Costa's (2002) study of the *Fallas* festival in Valencia in Spain.

Often, when studying contemporary arts festivals, only slight attention is paid to this literature, before turning to a second, distinct approach, which is also currently a dominant one. This is the so-called culture-led urban regeneration approach. Aimed at defining and assessing the impact of these festivals, the latter feeds a rich and developing literature, especially when considering a wider range of scholarship (including leisure and tourism studies, geography and planning, economy of culture). This field provides the majority of the literature on mixed arts festivals and further confirms the centrality of the urban context. The growing number of festivals in cities across Europe and the growing importance of festivals and more generally of big events (or even 'mega', such as World Expos and the Olympic Games, see Roche, 2000; Gold and Gold, 2004) within urban strategies, suggests that we need to consider relevant urban studies literature and pay appropriate attention to it.

In *Art Festival and the City*, Bernadette Quinn (2005a) focuses on the relationship of festivals to their urban settings, providing both a review of the literature and some insights from her previous empirical research on specific urban festivals (Quinn, 2003, 2005b). Quinn argues that we need more, and more multidimensional, research on festivals to assess whether they meet 'their undoubted potential in animating communities, celebrating diversity and improving quality of life' (Quinn, 2005a: 927). The article notes the remarkable increase in the numbers of art festivals in the past 15 years in cities throughout Europe, but also notes that, as important cultural practices, festivals have a long-established association with cities. The forerunners of contemporary urban arts festivals are traceable as far back as Dionysian festivals in classical Athens, and more recently with the *Bayreuth Festival* founded in 1876 and the *Salzburger Festspiele* in 1920.

The current success of urban festivals and, in particular, their great increase since the late 1970s and 1980s is related to the post-industrial shift of many big European cities, and their search for ways to 'regenerate' themselves. The actual capacity of festivals to meet regeneration objectives remains an open question, with quite a few researchers arguing that using festivals for city marketing and place distinctiveness may be counterproductive, as they run the risk of becoming formulaic and standardised, a form of 'serial reproduction' (Richards and Wilson, 2004; Evans, 2001). Others have noted that this perverse effect is not unavoidable; it is instead linked to:

> urban management approaches that fail to understand how local particularities could be cultivated to counter the globalising influences of cultural production in city arenas […]. Currently, the literature is very uncertain about their [the festivals'] contribution. While there has been a lot of hype about the theoretically catalytic effect that festivals can have in terms of attracting visitors, spearheading the regeneration of derelict city districts and reclaiming public time and space for communal celebrations, hard evidence is in short supply. (Quinn, 2005a, 928, referring also to Bailey et al., 2004, Evans, 2001. See also Maughan and Bianchini 2004.)

Available evidence concentrates on the economic impact, whereas 'the long-term social impact of culture-led urban regeneration remains something of a mystery' (Quinn, 2005a, 931), and this is even more so for cultural impact, in particular in terms of '[w]hat roles has the arts festival played in advancing urban policy, contributing to urban life and facilitating the expression of cultural identities' (Quinn, 2005a, 931). Lacking research to provide evidence, this literature is basically made up of commentaries around a set of common distinctions. In particular it contrasts commodification and globalization with the production of spaces for creativity and difference; tourist orientation with authenticity; reproduction of consolidated social distinctions with countercultural expression within the festivals. Within culture-led regeneration itself, some authors have distinguished two approaches; the 'festival marketplace' (Americanisation) and 'cultural planning' (Europeanisation) (Rowe and Stevenson, 1994, Stevenson 2003).

An example of such commentaries is Kirstie Jamieson's (2004) article on Edinburgh as 'festival city'. Jamieson builds on what can be considered the common stance taken by critical social scientists vis-à-vis the often overenthusiastic and uncritical presentation of festivals as sources of regeneration and 'freedom of expression'. The target of the critique is that contemporary arts festivals do not lead to an actual challenge (a carnivalesque subversion) of the everyday and established differentials of access to cultural production and consumption, because they only provide a tourist, commodified 'encounter with the unexpected', a pseudo-transgression, that celebrates difference but actually aestheticises it and glosses over – thus de facto excluding – actual social differences within the city. This critique also commonly highlights a romantic 'nostalgia for a more sociable and public mode of urban living' (Jamieson, 2004: 73), found in audiences and organisers alike. However, the critique itself seems equally gripped by nostalgia for 'traditional' or 'authentic' festivals, rather than questioning the dichotomy, and by a romantic view of community vs. society. Similarly, Finkel (2004), in an overview of UK combined arts festivals, warns against a rampant 'McFestivalisation'. She contends that a new 'type' of combined arts festival is emerging that is standardised and commercialised: 'the reputation of arts festivals to help the reputation of cities may be at the crux of their upsurge' (Finkel, 2004: 3), however this is why they seem trapped in a vicious circle of imitation, risking failure in what Finkel sees as 'the role of the arts to resist this very kind of conformity' (Finkel, 2004: 6).

This type of critique however has produced a rather dichotomised, or simplified debate, revolving around whether or not festivals can have regeneration effects, whether or not they are sites of more open cultural politics, and whether or not their association with tourism, commodification and globalisation necessarily implies a loss of authenticity, specificity and identity – these latter always remaining the domain of 'traditional' festivals. In this black and white picture there is usually little space for nuanced analysis.

Whilst critical accounts of the salvific nature of festivals can still be found, especially in some policy documents, and whilst most critics seem instead to accept the premise, traceable back to a line of critique from Lefebvre to Debord, that major festivals as 'urban spectacles produced for profit are the outcome of a process of commodification, homogenization and rationalization of time and space' (Gotham, 2005: 234), a more nuanced analysis of the contribution of festivals to public culture or to the 'public sphere' remains to be attempted. It is my contention that in order to overcome this impasse we have to rethink that implicit premise that equates the growing professionalisation, commercialisation and basically popular success of festivals with their becoming both less critical and less significant in terms of their role within wider social life. A useful analytical framework to shift this focus takes the lead from a reformulation of the notion of public sphere.

Festival public sphere

Clearly this is not a totally unexplored avenue. Other authors have pointed out the possibilities of reappropriation that even commodified, invented (traditional) festivals can have for different audiences (de Bres and Davis, 2001; Crespi-Valbona and Richards, 2007). However the opposition between traditional, local, identity-laden on the one side and change, globalisation and extra-cultural instrumentality (tourist and regeneration objectives) is never really challenged, with contemporary festivals framed in terms of what they lack in comparison with their forebears.

A starting point to question this common normative stance is to revisit one of its sources, the theory of the public sphere and its origin within the critical and dismissive position of the Frankfurt school towards 'mass culture' and the culture industry. The original formulation of the public sphere by Jurgen Habermas (1962) was based on the narrative of a progressive degeneration from a 'culture debating' to a 'culture consuming' public sphere. As well as the several critiques that have contextualised, specified and extended this influential theory (Calhoun, 1992) targeting mainly the scope and scale of the 'public' within it, and beyond Habermas's own revisions of his pessimistic conclusions and recognition of 'counter-publics' (Habermas, 1992), some authors have started to question the type of public sphere.

The contention is that a more specific concept is needed, that of aesthetic or cultural public sphere (Jones, 2007; McGuigan, 2005) in order to account for affectivity as well as cognition, particularly with reference to cultural phenomena. In the words of Jim McGuigan:

> The cultural public sphere of late-modernity operates through various channels and circuits of mass-popular culture and entertainment, facilitated routinely by mediated aesthetic and emotional reflections on how we live and imagine the good life. The concept of a cultural public sphere refers to the articulation of politics, public and personal, as a contested terrain through affective – aesthetic and emotional – modes of communication. (2005: 435).

The value of the public sphere theory lies both in its normative character – a critical measure or a guiding principle – and in the rather harsh analysis of how the actual public sphere declined losing its emancipatory potential. Given this, and also Habermas' major revision concerning the potential of popular culture and social movements, festivals are at a curious crossroad. They represent at the same time the apotheosis of the banalisation or 'fun-ification' of everything, and – so their defenders say – places where alternative, resistant or oppositional instances can thrive. It is at this crossroad that the idea of cultural public sphere may be particularly beneficial.

Without explicitly using this notion, Xavier Costa's insights into festivals' peculiar sociability are relevant here. In a study of the *Fallas* festival in Valencia, Costa remarks that: 'festive sociability is shown to have its own public sphere in which reflexivity can be expressed through art and play' (2002: 484). Reflexivity, in other words, is not only that of critical reasoning that characterised Habermas' bourgeois public sphere, but can also take an aesthetic form, as hinted by the notion of cultural public sphere. In the latter both the type of critical distance created and the type of participation are different:

> Habermas' concentration on argumentation divides people's attitudes into two extremes, with a big gap in the middle: either they focus on a rational thematization to solve a problem (critical argumentation as the way to question) or they routinely take for granted stocks of rules, knowledge, etc., which are deposited in the life world. There is no place for a wider questioning, a 'sociable thematization', which is able to retain its content, but in a subordinate form to sociability. The festive sociability of the *Fallas* includes this wider, sociable and festive capacity to convey criticism through the medium of jokes, art or play (Costas, 2002: 486).

The dichotomy between culture debating and culture consuming public spheres – as more generally the reductive vision of 'reception' established by the mass culture school – fails to properly account for the experience of festivals. Rational argument may certainly not figure high in festivals, which may thus appear as yet another instance of a 'culture consuming', corrupted public sphere, but other forms of cultural criticism and sociability are in place.

This approach may also cast new light on previous research. For instance, drawing on Sarah Bonnemaison's account of how Rome successfully used festivals in the 1970s to dispel the climate of fear created by Red Brigade's terrorist attacks (Bonnemaison, 1990), Mark Schuster, concludes his article on *Two Urban Festivals* by offering that:

> to be successful festivals must be part of the shared life of a community, participation must be encouraged if not expected and citizens must be actively involved in creating, conducting and maintaining the festival.

If those who attend are primarily observers or consumers, a golden opportunity will have been missed. For those wishing to redevelop, or indeed establish, the 'civil society' that can be fostered in the best of our cities, they must pay attention to the rise of the new urban festival (Schuster, 1995: 185-186).

There is little more than a hint to 'civil society', but a link has been established. The participatory nature of festivals in general has been long established as one of their defining characteristics, as a distinguishing element from other forms of cultural events, such as concerts, exhibitions, etc. However, once again, it is mostly traditional festivals that have been studied in this respect. A well-argued exception is Willems-Braun's (1994) article on fringe festivals, based both on a solid theoretical background – drawing mainly on Bourdieu for the cultural analysis but also on Laclau and Mouffe for issues of democratic imaginary and Nancy Fraser for the public sphere – and on his own participant observation of two fringe festivals in Canada. Willems-Braun aims at problematising the assumed role of fringe festivals as inherently 'countercultural' sites of a radical cultural politics, without falling into the opposite of dismissing their potential to open up spaces for debate and contestation. Particularly relevant for urban festivals, the focus is on the festivals' 'topography' as key to enquire how cultural practice, social identities and place relate, by considering how they 'reorganize urban spaces into festival spaces, constructing informal discursive arenas within which the interaction of patrons, artists and organizers is encouraged' (Schuster, 1995: 75). As in the case of the classic public sphere, we can use the cultural public sphere found (also) in festivals as a guiding principle, or critical measure (McGuigan, 2011) which allows us to comment on the possibilities opened up within festivals, and within the overall festival culture created by their increasing dominance as a format.

Towards further research

In order to study mixed arts urban festivals and their cultural politics what we need, more than fixed, stable dichotomies, are analytical concepts that can account for the complex, relational and processual nature of festivals, both as organisations and as experiences. A small but growing literature on mixed arts urban festivals is developing, following both the quantitative and qualitative growth in importance of these festivals and of their relevance within the current intellectual climate. This is, on the one hand, still fragmented and lacking a clear theoretical basis. On the other it is providing an increasing set of data that are helping question previously assumed correlations (in terms of festival impacts, audience characteristics and motivations, role within the art worlds). The methodological apparatus is being progressively refined in order to fill the gaps that remain, and that are in particular relative to the proper cultural significance of festivals, as sites where available structures of meanings informing people's dispositions are represented and (re)produced in both discourses and practices.

As for the urban dimension, what seems to hold the key for the interpretation of the specificity of city festivals is an attention to the 'situatedness' of the festivals as cultural artefacts and organisations, linked therefore not only to a specific genre or art world, but to the social and spatial organisation – and therefore the related cultural politics – of the place that hosts them. The peculiar relation of festivals to place and cities makes binary logics particularly reductive. As they are place-specific and performance-based, festivals (even those not devoted to performative arts) create a concentrated space-time frame: they succeed or not as unique, one-off experiences, for which it is important to say '*I was there*', and which therefore bear their own authenticity. It is an authenticity, though, that is less connected to notions of purity than to hybridity, at least this seems to be the case with contemporary festivals, where experience is the result of an array of different, hybrid stimuli. As festivals have something to do with place and as 'place' includes a cultural dimension, 'successful festivals create a powerful but curious sense of place, which is local, as the festival takes place in a locality or region, but which often makes an appeal to a global culture in order to attract both participants and audiences' (Waterman, 1998, 58). This seems to be the case in particular with urban festivals and other major urban events, which often develop a complex, circular relation to the hosting city.

Bibliography and further reading

Allen, K. and Shaw, P. (2000) *Festivals mean Business. The shape of arts festivals in the UK*, London: British Arts Festivals Association.

Azara, I. and Crouch, D. (2006) La cavalcata sarda: performing identities in a contemporary Sardinian festival, in D. Picard and M. Robinson (eds) *Festivals, Tourism and Social Change*, Clevedon: Channel View.

Bailey, C., Miles, S. and Stark, P. (2004) Culture-led urban regeneration and the revitalization of identities in Newcastle, Gateshead and the North East of England, *International Journal of Cultural Policy*, **10** (1): 47-65.

Bonnemaison, S. (1990) City politics and cyclical events, *Design Quarterly - Celebrations: Urban Spaces Transformed*, **147**, 24-32.

Bruce, G. (1975) *Festivals in the North: Story of the Edinburgh Festival*, London: Hale

Calhoun, C. (ed.) (1992) *Habermas and the Public Sphere*, Cambridge, Massachusetts: MIT Press.

Costa, X. (2002) Festive traditions in modernity: the public sphere of the Festival of the 'Fallas' in Valencia, *Sociological Review*, **50** (4): 482-504.

Crespi-Valbona, M.,and Richards, G. (2007) The meaning of cultural festivals. Stakeholder perspectives in Catalunya, *International Journal of Cultural Policy*, **13** (1): 103-122.

De Bres, K. and Davis, J. (2001) Celebrating group and place identity: a case study of a new regional festival, *Tourism Geographies*, **3** (3): 326-337.

Debord, G. (1994) *The Society of the Spectacle*, New York : Nicholson-Smith Zone Books.

Durkheim, E. (1912 [1954]) *The Elementary Forms of the Religious Life*, Glencoe: Free Press.

Evans, G. (2001) *Cultural Planning: an Urban Renaissance*, London: Routledge.

Falassi, A. (1987) Festival: definition and morphology, in A. Falassi (ed.) *Time out of time: essays on the Festival*, Albuquerque: University of New Mexico Press.

Finkel, R. (2004) McFestivalisation? The Role of Combined Arts Festivals in the UK Cultural Economy. in *Journeys of Expression Conference*, published in Conference Proceedings, Sheffield Hallam University, UK, CD-ROM.

Giorgi, L. and Sassatelli, M. (2011) Introduction, in L. Giorgi, M. Sassatelli and G. Delanty (eds) *Festivals and the Cultural Public Sphere*, London: Routledge, pp. 1-11.

Gold, J. R. and Gold, M. M. (2004) *Cities of Culture: Staging International festivals and the Urban Agenda, 1851-2000*, London: Ashgate.

Gotham, K F. (2005) Theorizing urban spectacle: festivals, tourism and the transformation of urban space, *City*, **9** (2): 225-242.

Habermas, J. (1962 [1989]) *The Structural Transformation of the Public Sphere – An inquiry into a Category of Bourgeois Society*, translated by Thomas Burger and Frederick Lawrence, Cambridge: Polity.

Habermas, J. (1992) Further reflections on the public sphere, in C. Calhoun (ed.) (1992) *Habermas and the Public Sphere*, Cambridge, Massachusetts: MIT Press, pp. 421-461.

Jones. P. (2007) Cultural sociology and an aesthetic public sphere, *Cultural Sociology*, **1**(1) 73-95.

Hauptfleisch, T. *et al.* (eds.) (2007) *Festivalising! Theatrical Events, Politics and Culture*, Amsterdam: Rodopi.

Iordanova, D. (ed.) (2009) *Film Festival Yearbook 1: The Festival Circuit*, St. Andrews: St. Andrews Film Studies.

Iordanova, D. and Torchin, L. (eds.) (2012) *Film Festival Yearbook 4: Film Festivals and Activism*, St. Andrews: St. Andrews Film Studies.

Jamieson, K. (2004) Edinburgh: the Festival gaze and its boundaries, *Space and Culture*, **7**(1): 64-75.

McGuigan, J. (2005) The cultural public sphere, *European Journal of Cultural Studies*, **8**(4), 427-443.

McGuigan, J. (2011) The cultural public sphere - A critical measure of public culture?, in L. Giorgi, M. Sassatelli and G. Delanty (eds), *Festivals and the Cultural Public Sphere*, London: Routledge, pp. 79-91

Maughan, C. and Bianchini, F. (2003) *Festivals and the Creative Region*, Leicester: De Montfort University/Arts Council England.

Moffat, A. (1978) *The Edinburgh Fringe,* London: Johnston and Bacon

PAYE (*Performing Arts Yearbook for Europe*). (2008) Manchester: Impromptu Publishing.

Piette, A. (1992) Play, reality and fiction. Toward a theoretical and methodological approach to the festival framework, *Qualitative Sociology,* **15** (1): 37-52.

Quinn, B. (2003) Symbols, practices and myth-making: cultural perspectives on the Wexford Festival Opera, *Tourism Geographies*, **5** (3): 329-349.

Quinn, B. (2005a) Arts festivals and the city, *Urban Studies,* **42** (5/6): 927-43.

Quinn, B. (2005b) Changing festival places: insights from Galway, *Social and Cultural Geography*, **6** (2): 237-252.

Richards, G. and Wilson, J. (2004) The impact of cultural events on city image: Rotterdam, Cultural Capital of Europe 2001, *Urban Studies,* **41** (10): 1931-1951.

Roche, M. (2000) *Mega-Events and Modernity: Olympics and Expos in the Growth of Global Culture*, New York: Routledge.

Rolfe, H. (1992) *Arts Festivals in the UK*, London: Policy Studies Institute.

Rowe, D. and Stevenson, D. (1994) Provincial paradise: urban tourism and city imaging outside the metropolis, *Journal of Sociology,* **30** (2): 178-193.

Schuster, J. M. (1995) Two urban festivals: La Mercè and Fir st Night, *Planning Practice and Research,* **10**(2): 173-87.

Stevenson, D. (2003) *Cities and Urban Cultures*, Buckingham: Open University Press.

Turner, V. (1982) *Celebration: Studies in Festivity and Ritual,* Washington DC: Smithsonian Institution Press.

Vogel, S. (2011) *Biennials, Art on a Global Scale*, Vienna: Springer.

Waitt, G. (2008) Urban festivals; Geographies of hype, helplessness and hope, *Geography Compass*, **2** (2): 513-537.

Waterman, S. (1998) Carnivals for elites? The cultural politics of arts festivals, *Progress in Human Geography,* **22** (1): 55-74.

Willems-Braun, B. (1994) Situating cultural politics: fringe festivals and the production of spaces of intersubjectivity, *Environment and Planning D: Society and Space ,***12** (1): 75-104.

Notes

[1] This chapter elaborates on research conducted within the project 'Art Festivals and the European Public Culture' carried out with a grant of the EU 7th European Framework Programme. More information on the project is available at www.euro-festival.org

4 Festivals, Conformity and Socialisation

János Zoltán Szabó

In the 1970s and 1980s festivals in Eastern Europe were rare but important meeting places for young people and the youth culture movement. However, following the fall of the Iron Curtain in 1989, cultural festivals in 'countries in transition' began to play a more visible role in social and economic affairs. Although the largest summer festivals (e.g. *Exit* in Serbia, *Sziget* in Hungary) are for-profit festivals driven by economic/commercial factors and attract several hundred thousand people, the majority of festivals are not-for-profit events which fulfil important societal functions.

The main aim of this chapter is to present a social science perspective on festivals. The research methodology employed in this research was developed during international meetings of the European Festival Research Project and the monitoring practice (registration and audit – a joint project of five festival unions) of festivals in Hungary[1]. The principal sources were i) a literature review and ii) field research based on a survey of festival organisers[2] and interviews. The interviews were completed with 16 directors of cultural festivals in Hungary, Czech Republic, Slovakia and Slovenia during 2010-2012.

This chapter reports on two aspects of the research project. One part examined the socialisation processes that audiences can experience at cultural festivals, where the features selected for examination were: cultural conformism, community and social networks and learning. The other part focused on the social functions of cultural festivals and their economic efficiency.

Why festivals? – Aspects of festival history

In history, festivals have often been described as part of social play and/or a celebration culture. Every society celebrates, and the way it does so reflects something of that society's world view and group identity. Describing festivals in this way is not a criticism because festivals have been thought of as the highest play-form for many years (Huizinga, 1955:13):

Summing up the formal characteristic of play, we might call it a free activity standing quite consciously outside 'ordinary' life as being 'not serious' but at the same time absorbing the player intensely and utterly. It is an activity connected with no material interest and no profit can be gained by it. It proceeds within its own proper boundaries of time and space according to fixed rules and in an orderly manner. It promotes the formation of social groupings that tend to surround themselves with secrecy and to stress the difference from the common world by disguise or other means.

Play character assumes greatest value when linked to freedom of action for individuals but because of the political context and climate, freedom of action has not always been the norm in different societies, at different times.

Local celebrations became nationwide and well-structured in the ancient Roman and Greek cultures. Festivals in the early Middle Ages were integrated into the Christian liturgical calendar and in many cases subverted the established social order often through mockery, play and laughter.[3] By the end of the Middle Ages, celebration culture had become established as a fundamental feature of society. In the 16th century, the way and the forms of celebration began to change again; festivals began to lose their religious focus and the audience became separated into two social groups: the 'common man' and the 'elite'. This dichotomy was also reflected in the forms of art and play that each experienced and the 'cultural canon' subsequently became different for each group.

Over and above their ceremonial function as part of religious and other observances, festivals, in a general sense, have always been important in Europe and especially for those people who lived and worked on the land. Festivals associated with the seasons provided an important opportunity for the communities to meet, do business and enjoy time away from the rigours of daily life. The arts, especially theatre and music, formed part of that experience but none of these largely social celebrations or festivals were dedicated to the arts. This in part reflected the lowly status of artists but from the Renaissance and especially after the Enlightenment, the social status of artists began to change. That said it was still not until 1876, when Wagner himself set up the *Bayreuther Festspiele* to present his own music and operas, that Europe had its first arts festival. However, this festival was very much a celebration for the elite in society and was not open to the general public (and access is not much easier today as most people have to wait years to obtain tickets). Such was the social prestige now associated with these events that it was a long time before arts festivals were routinely accessible to the general public.

This largely remained the case until the 20th century and the emergence of a mass media – news and entertainment – allied with a 'democratisation of culture' policy to arts funding and promotion. Examples of this can be found in the development of international film festivals. *Festival International du Film* (since 2001 *Festival de Cannes*) opened in 1939, predominantly targeted at professionals and journalists, but this was followed by the *Festival del Film Locarno* (1946) which was targeted at the general public. The celebrity star system and the mass media helped to fuel this and introduced a new concept for the arts world, the arts audience. Sometimes festivals played a specific political role as with Venice and Cannes between the two world wars and later during the reconstruction of Germany (*Berlinale* 1951) or the strengthening of the 'raison d'être' of East-Central European Culture (*Karlovy Vary*, 1946).

By the end of the 1950s increasing ideological and central control meant that the festival calendar of state organised celebrations of Eastern European countries incorporated dates from Soviet history and the international socialist movement (e.g. April 4, November 7). Others replaced events from the Christian calendar (e.g. in Hungary, the *Feast of New Bread and Constitution* replaced the *Feast of St Steven's Day* on August 20). In the early period of the Eastern Block the only international event organised for young people was the *World Youth Festival*. At the national level, public television organised dance song festivals[4] (big bands playing new songs for emerging stars) and provided a platform for new talent but both were strongly controlled by official bodies; for example all lyrics had to be authorised by the Schanson Committee in advance.

Festivals open to the wider public became more common in Western Europe after the Second World War but for political reasons not in Eastern Europe. The hippy or counter culture movement that emerged in the 1960s in the West developed much more slowly in the East, however for both East and West the music festival became the symbol of a younger generation in the manner of *Woodstock* (1969). However, freedom of play, action and assembly of the kind associated with such festivals were unthinkable in the East. Central and Eastern European governments tried to control or postpone all bottom up movements, including festival initiatives.

In the East, rock, hippy and other youth movements only gained momentum in the 1970s with a few autonomous festivals. At that time, a decade or more after the West, alternative culture was emerging as a conscious challenge to politically controlled, official state institutions with their predictable programmes. This alternative culture was characterised by increasing popularity of music groups like the Cure, Pearl Jam, R.E.M. or Nirvana with their national followers including artists and audiences.

On the Western side of the Iron Curtain the political agenda that underpinned investment in arts and culture focused more on instrumental and commercial features of public life such as urban regeneration, tourism and the creative city rather than the more overt political ideology that characterised Central and Eastern Europe until the end of the 1980s (Klaić 2002: 4 - 5).

Role of festivals in socialisation processes

The starting point for a review of the scientific literature in this chapter is celebration culture and public events, and linked to that a history of festivals seen from the perspective of play-forms. Critical to this analysis are two important theories: the exchange concept developed by Marcel Mauss (1990) and the idea of liminality developed by Victor Turner (1969). In this discussion, the examination of socialisation processes is informed by these theoretical frameworks.

As to the concept of a festival, this chapter draws on the definition developed by Alessandro Falassi (1987: 2 and 1997: 296) who defined festivals as recurrent, thematised celebrations 'set up' by ritual events. Such festivals reveal something of the identity, values and world view of the community that celebrates it. In this context I understand 'community' to be the people who participate in the festival, including local residents and visitors. Within this context cultural festivals are events which are endowed with specific meaning and values, both of which sit at the heart of the festival concept.

In Eastern Europe the development of a festivals sector started with traditional arts festivals (*Szeged Open Air* 1931 in Budapest and *Karlovy Vary International Film Festival* 1946 in Bohemia) in which subsidised arts programmes were dominant. It was not until later that the annual calendar of festivals diversified to include more commercially oriented arts or cultural festivals (*Valley of Arts* 1989, *Sziget* 1993, *Exit* 2000), but the majority of the festivals still tend to be local and more general in their focus: for example *Rose Festival* in Kutno (since 1974, Poland), *Flower Festival* in Debrecen (since 1966, Hungary) or days of wine, etc.

Play can be observed in the form of improvisation or feedback, performance, mimicry, games, sports and celebrations created by artists and audience as well. In a general sense this chapter treats festivals as part of a society's celebration culture, but at the highest level of play form. Festivals and events that take place in specific locations (fields, cities, islands and heritage sites) are categorised as part of our material culture, but probably a larger proportion form part of our immaterial culture, because of the role that events play in preserving cultural memory and developing cultural capital. However, undertaking research on the human or social aspects of festivals is harder to investigate than the material aspects.

The label 'arts festival' is widely used in the Western World, while 'cultural festival' may have more resonance in Eastern Europe, but in both East and West there are cultural traditions that make sense of this differentiation. Arts festivals put their artistic programme at the centre of the festival concept, while local festivals usually pay less attention to the artistic dimension of the programme. Cultural festivals share characteristics of both arts and local festivals: they have a distinct artistic programme but they may also offer other activities that provide the audience with specific opportunities for free reaction and play.

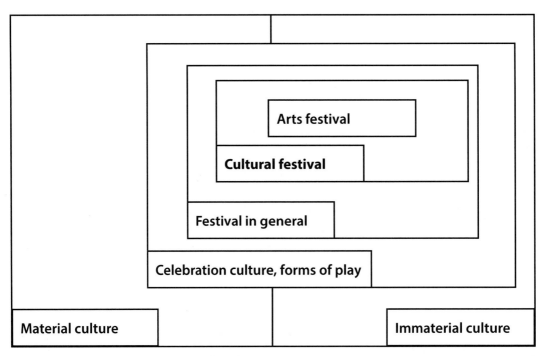

Figure 4.1: Conceptual clarification of the festival phenomenon

With respect to the societal functions, researchers, for example J. Assmann, F. Matarasso, J. Coleman and R. Myerscough, usually focus on *socialisation, cultural memory, community, creative city* and *economic impact*. In Western Europe, empirical festival research has often focused on a festival's social and economic benefits, by contrast in Hungary and other Eastern European countries festival research is often linked to free time and leisure time research, or cultural consumption and youth research, for example the work of I. Vitányi, D. Ilczuk and K. Gábor.

One of the most detailed models of the possible societal function of a festival is that developed by Francois Matarasso (1997) but its application and the indicators that might be defined and measured vary according to the disciplines and practices in use by the festival. One of the aims of the literature review for this research was to develop a structured model of festivals' societal functions, using several disciplines (history, cultural anthropology, economy, political sciences, education, sociology, cultural studies). In this model, different functions were distinguished as three main domains. These are not mutually exclusive but provide a framework for the analysis of specific festival practices as follows:

♦ artistic,

♦ community and

♦ political functions

These societal functions are overarching categories for all the functions identified by the researchers – at least in my opinion. In the field of social sciences, artistic functions can be surveyed as a measure and reflection of cultural embeddedness and their relationship with conformity. The difference between community and political functions can be described as different ways of problem solving and planning, namely community functions based on community needs, while political functions are linked to a positioning process controlled by decision makers. In the sense of marketing, the positioning process focuses on the distinctive features of a city, region or a district, which can then be exploited as part of a branding exercise. Across Europe festivals have now become a significant aspect of a city's identity and brand and can also be employed as part of a strategic response to local problems, e.g. helping to address issues of social exclusion; or the need for urban regeneration.

With regard to their artistic value, the socialisation processes of festivals and their relation to conformity, I analysed the cultural embeddedness of festivals, and the learning processes supported by festival organisers. Cultural embeddedness was understood on the basis of cultural conformity to be delimited by seven variables: name, symbols, artistic genre, autonomy of organisers, festival concept, mediated values and functions. Using these seven variables the following festival typology was set up:

♦ *Old conformist festivals* are generally associated with the canon of Western European art, the classics or classical, the mainstream before the counter culture appeared. Classical music festivals like *Prague Spring International Music Festival* or *Budapest Spring festival* or the *Maribor Theatre Festival* fall into this category. The target group of these festivals are usually people aged 35+, for example the *Szeged Open Air Festival* where research indicates that the typical audience member is a 39 year old woman, educated to secondary school level and who tends to be the decision-maker with respect to her family (at least in terms of choosing which cultural activity to attend)

◆ The category of *new conformist festival* includes music more readily identified with the 70s counter culture, mostly rock and related forms. These events include *Woodstock* style youth music festivals such as *Jarocin Festival* (Poland), *Exit* (Serbia) or *Sziget* (Hungary). The audience at new conformist festivals has a demographic profile which includes a significant number of older people who are aging with the festival (as well as many younger people, of course); the older the festival is, the higher the proportion of older people one can expect to find in the audience. The challenge here relates to something common when we think about audience development, how to retain the existing audience whilst attracting a new generation at the same time.

◆ *Nonconformist events* are those which programme more avant-garde post-modern art. *The Baltic Circle in Suvilahti* (Finland) or *Contemporary Drama Festival* Budapest (Hungary) can be included within this category.

◆ The *heritage reconstruction* category refers to those festivals that mix conformist and new-conformist art forms, and which usually create new understanding of local heritage by recreating it. Sometimes recreated heritage, although it incorporates and uses local symbols, can be quite different to the original local cultural heritage. However, through time the festival itself might become one of the most important elements of local cultural heritage. A good example is the *Valley of Arts*, the week-long festival which is held every July in the village of Kapolcs and adjacent villages, close to the Balaton Lake in Western Hungary. From its modest beginnings in 1989 as a local crafts and arts festival it has developed into one of Hungary's largest and most diverse arts festivals.

Cultural embeddedness combined with community embeddedness provide conceptual tools with which to define the scope, depth and quality of a festival's support from its community and the strength of its social networks. Indicators of community embeddedness can be local or cross sectorial. Local as evidenced by local people working as volunteers or by a festival's relationship with local government, and how closely it is integrated with local policy and planning, or the role it plays in bringing its audience into a different relationship with its physical infrastructure (the material world) and also its local, intangible assets. Cross sector features, i.e. those which cut across specific local loyalties and relations, include the value and range of support received from the private sector support and its other partners in the delivery of the festival's programme.

	Mainstream/ old conformist	Heritage reconstructionist	New conformist	Non-conformist
Label and name	Place, season, historical age, person and arts in the name of the festival	Associations (*Valley of Arts*, *Foothill Festival*), multi/intercultural alternative/contemporary adjectives in the name (e.g. Contemporary Drama Festival)		
Use of symbols	Not characteristic, not innovative	Innovative logos, natural symbols	Innovative typefaces, logos	Avant-garde, unusual visual messages
Typical genres	Theatre, classical music and opera	Folk, classical and popular music, theatre	Popular music	Dance theatre, audio-visual culture
Autonomy of organizers	Low (state or local-government influence)	Middle (nonprofit NGOs)	High (entrepreneurs)	High (NGO or entrepreneurs)
Concept	Culture in general, focusing on quantity of people involved, less articulate	Mature, thoughtful, focus on recreation	Mature, thoughtful, community-focused youth	Radical but thoughtful, focus on contemporary art
Values	Rather instrumental and economic policy	More expressive	More expressive	Rather individualistic
Main functions	Memory: local identity, tradition, entertainment, muster	Renewal: local identity, tradition, diversity, community experience,	Confirmation: community experience, diversity, tolerance and entertainment	Arts reform: presentation of contemporary (avant-garde) art
Typical examples	*Prague Spring International Music Festival (Czech Republic)*	*Valley of Arts (Hungary)*	*Exit* (Serbia), *Jarocin Festival (Poland)*	*Contemporary Drama Festival (Hungary)*

Figure 4.2: Conformity indicators of festivals

Two-thirds of the festivals (N=57) that were surveyed employed volunteers, and the managers of many large festivals indicated that they could not be delivered without them. The private sector can also play an important role with respect to festivals but there is a down side to such cross sector relationships, since support from businesses is often not provided on a regular and long term basis. This research revealed that only half of all sponsorship deals run for more than one year. Similar findings have been reported in other countries (e.g. by Arts and Business in the UK). This means that festival managers not only devote a lot of time and energy to ensuring that sponsors receive the benefits they expect but, as festival managers cannot rely on a sponsor to commit for a second year, they are continuously investing time in attracting new sponsors. This research is an ongoing process for festival organisers and helps to explain the increase in the number of fundraising consultants.

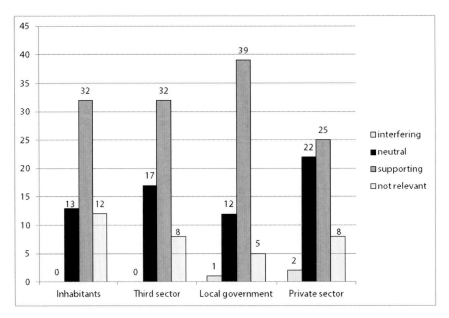

Figure 4.3: The festivals and their relationships with different stakeholders (N=57)

Festival directors were asked to comment on the quality of the relationships that they have with a range of different stakeholders (see Figure 4.3). The data suggests that their relationship with local people, local government and third sector organisations is supportive and positive. The relationship with the private sector is less so. Probably it is the reason why the involvement of local service providers was the most frequently mentioned weakness (e.g. catering, parking, accommodation).

Educational activity as part of a festival (before or during) is not something that has been the subject of much systematic research; however it is an important consideration with respect to an analysis of the socialisation process. Festivals were invited to comment on this aspect of their operation. Whilst this remains an area that needs closer investigation our research revealed the following typology:

♦ Cultural capital of the audience: the more frequently an audience member attends an arts festival the more developed their 'decoding capacity' becomes, i.e. the greater their cultural capital.

♦ Festivals empower artists too: some aspects of an artist's professional development may be achieved through being programmed into a festival; some benefit from competitions, from the impact they can have on their skills and from the positive PR that results; but most of all festivals are meeting places for artists as well.

♦ Arts education: this category was the one that focused most directly on an individual and their learning. It can include audience meeting artists during a festival, but also artists visiting schools, or schools visiting the festival. One example of arts education is from the *Bartók + Opera Festival* held in Miskolc (Hungary) where the festival devised an adult education course on 'what is opera?' This course was targeted at local people who, due to the lack of local provision for opera (no opera house for example), were found to be unengaged with opera as such.

Regarding *political functions,* festival directors were asked to identify what local issues, challenges or problems they could address through their festival programme and other interventions.

Their responses broadly related to one of the following five categories:

♦ political profile (through attracting positive and critical attention)
♦ image (marketing and branding: by helping to project a more dynamic image)
♦ social harmony (bringing energy into an area and people out of their homes)
♦ activist role (making the area a better place in which to live and work)
♦ touristic role (raising the profile amongst potential cultural tourists)

In general, indicators of the political functions of festivals are demonstrated through their impact on the political and economic health of a town, city or region. The research revealed that some places which formerly had a poor or low profile had successfully integrated one or more festivals into their area development strategies and had achieved positive results. A good example is Miskolc, a former industrial centre in North-East Hungary, which since 2001 has been host to the *Bartók + Opera Festival.* Such a programme would not be thought out of place in cities such as Prague or Budapest, but it is in Miskolc where the programme is both extraordinary and has contributed to a major regeneration of the city following de-industrialisation. However, political influence is not just reflected in the impact a festival can have on a city's image but also in the festival's ability to attract development funds and private investment. Therefore festivals may also serve as a catalyst in the planning and implementation of local development programmes.

Local celebration culture and living standards have changed substantially since the 1980s. It is now common for people to eat, drink and rest in public spaces. Festivals through the innovative ways in which they inhabit public space can enable audiences to reconnect with and rediscover the pleasures to be found in their public spaces; it is no surprise therefore that they have become key tools in urban planning. Such interventions are of benefit to local residents who may develop pride in their local area and see their community and its challenges in a more positive light. These interventions are also of benefit to visitors who can experience the area in a more dynamic way, as more than a static environment but one that offers a range of live and spontaneous experiences.

Conclusion

On the basis of a review of the published literature and field research undertaken from 2004-2012 a tentative typology has been developed for the classification of existing and new festivals. A starting point was the societal functions of festivals which are broadly their *cultural, community* and *political* functions. Cultural functions typically correlate with the genre of art programmed and can be assigned to one of the four 'conformity' categories which are: *old conformist, new conformist, heritage reconstructionist* and *non-conformist* festivals. Community functions relate to levels and forms of integration in the local community, common indicators are levels of volunteering, the quality of the relationship with local government, local sponsors and how the festival connects to other factors such as the built and natural environments and engagement with a place's intangible heritage (language, traditions). The political functions of a festival can be understood as being more developmental in nature and to include: contributing to change in a city's profile and its image, making people happier and increasing the economic value of tourism. As a corollary to this, festivals may also be a stimulus to local decision makers to engage with local problems or issues which a festival may help to resolve. But it may also stimulate authorities to identify and tackle local issues that may block the positive benefits that festivals can bring to an area.

With respect to a festival's socialisation process, the main features analysed were cultural and community embeddedness and how these were features of the learning opportunities available to those attending the festival. The research revealed that there is a strong correlation between a festival's cultural embeddedness and its ability to contribute strongly to individual and community learning but also to be recognised in the community as a good thing. Community embeddedness was a prerequisite for achieving the required learning and operational processes. Nearly half of the examined festivals possessed the necessary embeddedness for providing learning opportunities not only to those attending but also to others in the community, e.g. school children.

This chapter has reported on some 'work in progress' which nonetheless has raised some important questions regarding the political and developmental functions of festivals. There is still some way to go, especially with respect to festivals in Central and Eastern Europe for which the historical record is incomplete and the depth of contemporary research is undeveloped. Limitations in understanding are therefore to be expected but I hope that building on this work that future research will continue to examine the artistic, community and political functions of festivals and to sharpen our understanding of these qualities today and how to maximise their contribution to a more vibrant festival sector in the future.

Bibliography and further reading

Bakhtin, M. M. (1984) *Rabelais and His World*, Bloomington: Indiana University Press.

Bourdieu, P. (1998) Gazdasági tőke, kulturális tőke, társadalmi tőke, (Economic capital, cultural capital, social capital), in Z, Lengyel and Z, Szántó, *Tőkefajták: A társadalmi és kulturális erőforrások szociológiája* (Capital Coast: The sociology of social and cultural resources), Budapest: Aula Kiadó

Coleman, J. S. (1998) A társadalmi tőke. (The Social Capital, in Z, Lengyel and Z Szántó (ed.), *A gazdasági élet szociológiája. (Sociology of Economic Life)* Budapest: Aula Kiadó

Falassi, A. (1987) Festival: definition and morphology, in A, Falassi (ed.), *Time out of Time: Essays on the Festival*, Albuquerque: University of New Mexico Press.

Falassi, A. (1997) Festival, in T. A. Green (ed.) *Folklore*, Santa Barbara: ABC-CLIO.

Hahn, I (2006) A római császárkor története (The history of the Roman imperial period), in E. Ferenczy, E. Maróti and S. Hahn (eds.), *Az ókori Róma*, Budapest: Nemzeti Tankönyvkiadó

Hankiss E. and Makkai L. (1965) *Anglia az újkor küszöbén (England on the Verge of a New Age)*, Budapest: Gondolat

Huizinga, J. (1955) *Homo ludens; a study of the play-element in culture*, Boston: Beacon Press

Klaić, D (2002): *The Future of Festival Formulae.* http://www.efa-aef.eu/newpublic/upload/efadoc/11/HFsympbackground%20paper.doc

Matarasso, F. (1997) *Use or Ornament? The Social Impact of Participation in the Arts*, Stroud: Comedia.

Mauss, M. (1990) *The Gift. The Form and Reason for Exchange in Archaic Societies,* London: Routledge.

Turner, V. (1969) *The Ritual Process: Structure and Anti-structure*, Chicago: Aldine Pubications.

Urry, J. (2002) *The Tourist Gaze*, London: Sage.

Notes

[1] http://www.fesztivalregisztracio.hu/index.php?modul=cmsandpage=english

[2] 230 cultural festivals were surveyed in 2004, 56 cultural festivals in 2007.

[3] see Mikhail Bakhtin's work on *Rabelais and His World* (1993)

[4] These events lacked many of the features associated with a real festival, which was largely a label

[5]

5 Festivals as Communities of Practice: Learning by doing and knowledge networks amongst artists

Roberta Comunian

Introduction

Much research and debate on the impact and roles played by arts festivals in regional development concentrates on their external impacts and on two aspects in particular. One is the economic impact of festivals and their potential to attract tourism and therefore benefit the local economy; second is the role they can play in rebranding or regenerating a locality, specifically looking at people's pride in place, social cohesion and the participation of specific social groups. However, instead of looking at the external impacts of festivals on communities and economies, this chapter will examine the impact of festivals on one of their core stakeholders: participating artists (Glow and Caust, 2010).[1] The research takes theoretical approaches from the regional and organisational studies field, such as 'communities of practice' (Wenger, 1998), 'learning by doing' (Arrow, 1962), learning-by-interacting (Lundvall, 1992) and 'temporary clusters' (Bathelt and Schuldt, 2008) to explore the creative practice of artists involved in an emerging UK arts festival (*Fuse Medway Festival*, Kent). It discusses the role of the festival on artists' careers, their creative practice and their ability to learn and connect with other creative producers and asks: 'are festivals also knowledge communities?'

Researching festivals and impact

While the research looking at external impacts is rich and diverse, there is almost no research available which examines the impact of festivals on one of their core stakeholders: the participating artists. Glow and Caust (2010) have explored the benefits artists participating in the *Adelaide Fringe Festival* thought they gained from taking part. They identified a series of activities and services that the festival provided to artists, such as newsletters, making the most of media coverage, free listing in the festival guide, etc. They also considered the importance that the *Fringe* played through inviting producers who might recruit new acts to add to their own programmes for touring and commissions. Their research also examined the significance of local artists in the programme; more than half of the participating artists were originally from Adelaide itself and a high number seem to have returned just to take part in the *Fringe* – which shows that they expect to derive benefit from participation.

The main benefits experienced by artists were summarised as:

♦ **Entrepreneurialism**: 'the festival encouraged an entrepreneurial approach to the task of producing and presenting work.'

♦ **Branding**: allowed artists to increase their visibility and credibility amongst producers and audiences.

♦ **Practising the craft**: helped 'to build the respondents' sense of purpose and identity as artists.'

♦ **A launching pad**: gave an opportunity to artists to test work and develop their craft and career.

♦ **Diverse programming**: linked to the ability of the festival to attract national and international work, commercial and non-commercial work and to create a balanced and varied programme (Glow and Caust, 2010: 419).

Learning, knowledge communities and creative work

The literature on learning and knowledge communities is broad and has been a topic of extensive research across economic geography and organisational studies. Here we are specifically interested in the economic geography perspective as it focuses on place and shared-spaces where learning and knowledge exchange happen. The literature acknowledges the strong relationship between individual and collective learning in the work context. Following Fenwick (2008) we highlight these important dynamics:

♦ **Individual knowledge acquisition**: in particular linked to the idea that alongside codified knowledge (which is easily transferable) there are sets of practice and knowledge that are tacit and hard to teach and transfer.

♦ **Sense-making and reflective dialogue**: this seems particularly relevant for artists. Many consider feedback from peers as pivotal to their development. The 'collective is viewed as prompt for individual critical reflection, a forum for sharing meaning and working through conflicting meanings among individuals to create new knowledge' (Fenwick, 2008: 232).

◆ **Communities of practice (CoP):** As Wenger explains, 'communities of practice are groups of people who share a concern or a passion for something they do and learn how to do it better as they interact regularly'. This broad and fluid definition can be applied to groups that evolve and change both within and outside organisations. The focus is on the members' shared interest, their common ground and reason for engagement and exchange. Although the communities of practice approach has many limits – specifically in relation to the role played by trust, power and structures – it remains a useful framework for understanding motivations and engagement amongst practitioners.

◆ **Co-participation or co-emergence:** embedded in the complexity theory thinking, here the focus is on 'mutual interactions and modification between individual actors, their histories, motivations and perspectives and the collective' (Fenwick, 2008, p.236). The focus here is on micro-interactions and their connections/relationship with macro-level outcomes.

Networks and shared connections are cornerstones of learning and knowledge communities. In particular, it is important to consider the main distinction drawn by Granovetter (1973) that individuals have both strong and weak ties and that these have distinct values and functions in learning processes. While strong ties are based on shared experiences and values developed over time, weak ties are more temporary, requiring less investment and commitment. The role of networks and knowledge exchange has also been a focus in the literature that looks at the nature of creative work where temporary, project-based structures are common across different creative sectors. In these sectors multiple roles and job handling are the norm, with people defining themselves with multiple professional identities.

One important dimension of the way knowledge and expertise is developed is related to 'tacit knowledge'. Tacit knowledge is sticky (often linked to a person or a place/organisation) and learning cannot happen in a codified way (through a manual or an explanation), needing to be transferred through practice, observation, doing or sharing. There is a wealth of literature considering the role of these important dynamics and time and space play a key role as they often imply a co-presence and co-location. The concept of 'learning-by-doing' highlights the need for demonstration and practice to be shared and the concept of 'learning-by-interacting' underlines the role played by exchange and feedback. In particular we see short-term interactions (which are often repeated in time) being part of project-based ecologies when work is commissioned and diverse skills come together. In particular, some have considered how 'clusters' can be understood not only as a permanent geographical co-location but also in temporary forms. While this literature mainly focuses on business fairs and temporary exhibitions, many of the knowledge dynamics described can be considered relevant for the kind of knowledge networks and learning that takes place at festivals. Bathelt and Schuldt (2008) consider two sets of interactions within the context of temporary fairs:

- ◆ **Vertical interactions**: this mainly corresponds to interactions that involve customers or suppliers. In a festival context this can be interaction with audiences (in reference to satisfaction), interaction with artists involved or contributing to the company's work and interaction with other festival directors, funders and promoters attending the festival.

- ◆ **Horizontal interactions**: relates to interactions that involve other companies or competitors. In the festival these could be interactions with other artists/creative companies.

The authors highlight the importance of contacts and exchanges taking place during temporary events such as international fairs. In particular they highlight the importance of learning through comparison and observation. They also consider the value of scouting for complementarity, looking for other companies who might complement or enhance their work as suppliers or partners.

Case study: *Fuse Medway Festival* in Kent

Fuse Medway Festival (Fuse) is a recently established free outdoor arts festival that takes place in Medway (Kent) in June. It started in 2008/2009 with the work of artistic director Kate Hazel and since 2011 has been directed by Lelia Greci, so it can still be considered as an 'emerging festival'. *Fuse* is a weekend of street and performing arts including performances from local, UK-wide and international artists. It is funded and managed by Medway City Council and receives funding from the Arts Council England (through an ACE Grant for the Arts award) in the region of £100,000.

As the festival director explains, artistically the festival aims to give local communities and visitors 'opportunities to engage with arts that are of a really high standard'. For the local council it is about place-making, 'to show that Medway is a very dynamic place and a place where people may want to move to, and students may want to come and study. And a place where they may want to live after they have graduated' (interview with artistic director). Alongside these goals, Fuse aims to support 'local creatives and provide them with opportunities […] by contracting them whenever possible and by offering a programme of commissioning every year' (interview with artistic director).Therefore, this research specifically engaged with the impact of *Fuse* on the artists taking part in the festival.

Overall, *Fuse,* whilst small, has a growing reputation amongst UK performing arts festivals. It is free and this reflects its socio-cultural agenda with respect to engaging the local community and bringing new opportunities for engagement in the arts to a range of demographics (from young children to disadvantaged groups). It is also committed to raising the profile of Medway as a destination and particularly with respect to the creative economy and growing local talent.

Methodology and data collected

Twenty-five artists or cultural organisations were directly involved in the festival via commissions (to present original work) and bookings (to tour previous work) to be showcased during *Fuse 2011*. While further artists and collaboration took part, our data collection specifically focused on these twenty-five. The list of artists/cultural organisations was supplied by *Fuse* organisers, but was also publically available through the *Fuse* programme.

This chapter reports on the use of two different research methodologies. In order to achieve a quantitative overview of the participants and their work and the networks developed or connected with at the festival we used a survey with a social network analysis component that was sent to all twenty-five artists/creative companies.

Social network analysis (SNA) allows researchers to map networks. However, social networks are nested (every network is part of a larger network) and there might be relations which suggest similarities at different scales. Therefore social network analysis can only really offer a snapshot at a given point in time of the social system dynamics of a social system rather than its, evolution. The focus here was mainly to assess the difference in the knowledge networks of participating artists before and after *Fuse 2011*. In particular, we asked the artists participating at the festival to reflect on the social connections established through the festival and the impact of the Festival in creating and supporting an artistic community. Out of the twenty-five artists and cultural organisations contacted, twenty-four responded and completed the questionnaire.

Alongside the survey, we carried out semi-structured qualitative interviews with seven artists/creative practitioners and one with the current festival director. The interviews explored the impact of *Fuse* (and other festivals) on the development of an artist's practice and a career in the creative sector.

Fuse Medway Festival and the artists involved in *Fuse* 2011

The artists and artistic companies who responded to this survey were mainly from the South of England (only one artist/company from the rest of UK). Amongst the Southern companies involved there was a strong presence from the broader South East (eleven), followed by the local Medway (five) and Kent (three) areas and finally the South West (five). Younger companies and organisations (less than six years old) were well represented at the festival, accounting for 50% of the organisations involved.

Respondents were asked to specify how they found out about the opportunity to take part in the festival (they were allowed to select more than one answer if appropriate). The majority of the respondents had already taken part in *Fuse* and therefore had previous contact with the organisers and application process (twelve). However, eight had simply put forward a proposal to be involved and present their work. Seven participants had been contacted directly by the director and invited to submit / propose a piece, while five others had received information through other contacts/colleagues.

Exploring networks of knowledge and learning

The nature of festivals and networks

The interviews underlined the importance of a festival as a source of network activity, indeed it is a fundamental feature and almost hot-wired into their rationales. Some of the networks dynamics are closely linked to the ways in which festivals operate (temporary clustering of performances and activities in a short-time frame). As the director of *Fuse* explains, this also has a strong geographical connotation. For artists to attend a festival requires great commitment as it is time and financially demanding to take part in an event far away from where they are based. This means that naturally – not in a discriminatory way – close-knit geographical networks are quite common. This is also one of the reasons why most of the artists involved in *Fuse* are based in the South of England.

Alongside the geographical and financial constraints, festivals tend to collaborate on joint commissions – this allows them to share the risk, maximise funding opportunities and offer the potential for partnership to artists and companies that may make their work more sustainable and stable (through multiple bookings). Where this happens, careful programming of a mixed programme of shared projects with innovative acts can still make each festival a unique experience.

In particular, festivals – scheduled mainly across the summer – offer the opportunity for artists to showcase work for other festival directors and other sector promoters. This also means that attending any festival expands and stretches the network of each participating act as this artist suggests 'we also then, with this particular piece, went to the *Emerge Festival* […] And that was really pivotal, actually. And the *Emerge Festival* gave us the link through for *Fuse*' (Artist 7).

The festival 'season' and the fact that a limited number of works tour to different festivals means also that amongst artists there is a feeling of a peripatetic community that meets over different weekends in different places. A few of the artists interviewed talked about a sense of community amongst street artists. Festivals fit perfectly (and in part contribute) to the networked and project-based nature of creative work and creative practice. Like other project-based activities, they tend to require the skills and collaboration of different people for a short-time. While usually a company is only formed by one or a hand-full of staff, the number of people involved in collaborative work can expand it considerably. The ever-changing nature of creative companies involved is highlighted here by an artist.

> It is a collaborative company really […] there are about two or three regular members, but the cast and the collaborative teams have got about 30 people [...] I tend to work in a very collaborative way, reaching out to people where my skills are limited (Artist 7).

Within the characteristics of creative work there is also multiple-job handling and identification with multiple professional profiles (i.e. someone defining themselves as actor/producer/musician). This is definitely the case with festivals as at different festivals (and sometimes even at the same festival) artists can take on different roles.

> *Fuse* was different as I had [this piece], but also I worked with […] a dance company who were at *Fuse*. I directed their piece. So there were two pieces happening at the same time. It was the place that the two companies met, that the performers interacted with each other […] always at festivals, there is cross collaboration (Artist 2).

Learning and expanding networks through festivals

There were two key dimensions to the learning process. One was the learning derived from participating in the festival (this was specifically linked to project management, budgets, etc.) and the other was learning derived from performing and working alongside other artists at the festival.

With reference to the first aspect, a few artists – mainly the emerging companies – considered participating in the festival to be a learning opportunity from an administrative and planning perspective. As for the second dimension, artists interviewed highlighted how festivals can also be used as an opportunity to learn from other participating artists.

> So going to festivals is where you get to showcase your work alongside acts from all over the world. And it really highlights the strength and weakness of particular work, technically, creatively so having them there as a marker (Artist 7).

Another important aspect of learning – which interconnected with the analysis of project working within the festival – is the possibility for artists to test their work at a festival.

> We knew we had a show and there were great bits in it and we would get applause but it needed work. […] I mean it's just incredible when you are inside in a rehearsal space, and then you take it outside you think "wow, is it the same show?" it looks totally different and the performers react in a totally different way (Artist 4).

Many artists mentioned that ideas and inspiration taken from a variety of artists and festivals influenced more broadly what they do.

> There is a street arts festival in Mexico and while I was there […] there was a lot of walkabout and absurd costumes and dealing with the crowds, and it made me really want to make something that was along these lines, so there was definitely an influence there […] think that lots of little bits of every show have ended up in this, because of what I see (Artist 6).

Within the SNA questionnaire, artists were asked to consider the impact of *Fuse* on their awareness of others' practice/work. The first network (see Figure 5.1) shows the connections already present before the festival ('I knew/ was already in contact with this artist/creative company before *Fuse Festival 2011*'). This is already a dense network – derived from previous participation in other projects and festivals and previous collaborations amongst these artists. The nodes have been anonymised and instead of the name of the company a general reference to its geographical location is used. In general artists show how festivals can provide an opportunity to expand networks.

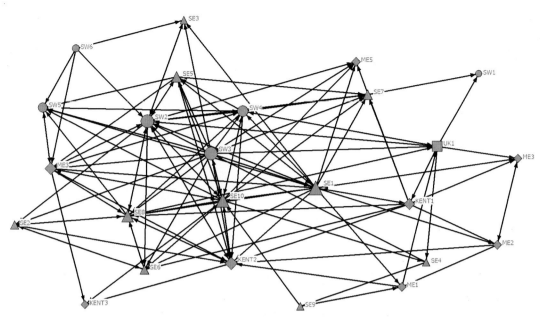

Figure 5.1: Knowledge and awareness connections between participating artists before *Fuse Medway Festival* 2011. The size of the nodes indicates the indegree centrality of the company/artist to the network (the number of lines directed to the company, i.e. the number of times people mentioned they were aware of the company), the different shape of the nodes reflect locations (diamond are Kent and Medway based companies; triangles are the South East based companies; circles are South West based companies and finally a square presents the only UK based participants)

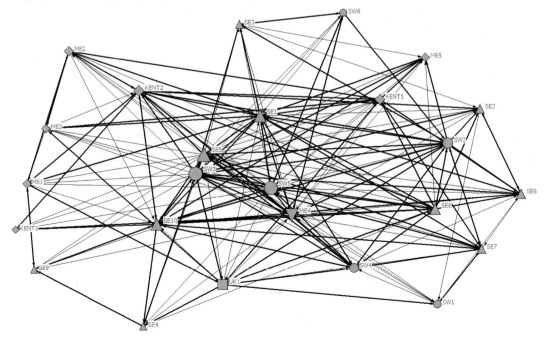

Figure 5.2: Knowledge and awareness connections between participating artists after *Fuse Medway Festival* in 2011. (Thin lines are previous connections; darker lines are the new ones).

A lot of festivals provide opportunities for our work to be seen by other artists so they can come to the director and say we would like you to work with us, on our show. And also to get ideas and see what other people are doing and where the artistic sector is pushing forwards, it helps you to develop your own work. […] Festivals provide something that theatres cannot do which is to pull together a group of different companies and artists and to allow them to all play at the same time and see each other's work (Artist 2).

As can be seen from comparing the network diagrams there is an increase in awareness and knowledge of each others' work. In fact the density is almost doubled (from 135 connections to 227). This knowledge and awareness is considered by the artists themselves to be a key step towards knowledge sharing and possible collaboration.

I mean it was just meeting up with the other artists and having a chat kind or to say "hi, how are you doing? How is the festival?" In terms of marketing and promotion, in terms of where they have been. Artistically it is an opportunity to see other people's work and there were some pieces at *Fuse* I was really looking forward to seeing (Artist 7).

These interactions can be opportunities for future exchanges and mutual support:

for example there is another circus company and they are doing such different things, there are two of them in that company as well, and the guy, one of them had pulled his hamstring, so I was his stand-in last week. (Artist 3).

Competition is not seen as an immediate threat by artists attending the same festival. In part this is because of a shared ethos but also because the artists and acts attending tend to be very different from each other.

The impact of *Fuse* on artists' work and careers

The questionnaire data revealed that twelve of the twenty-five acts involved had previously been involved with *Fuse* before 2011. While in other sectors/ activities this might seem to create a 'cliquey' environment, both the artists and the festival director point out that this is an essential strategy to allow artists to develop their work year on year. It also creates opportunities for artists to maximise their previous project and experiences. As the festival director explains:

> I think it is a very conscious decision. ... if you know that they produce very good work, well, it's a chance of supporting them and saying "okay I will bet on your next work as well". And it is important for them to know they have a regular touring network as it gives them the minimum security that they require to create new work. ... But also in terms of the audience, people don't like what is new, they do not like the unknown. So in a programme we always try to mix new companies, which the audience have never heard of, with companies that were popular in previous years.

In this way *Fuse* has been able to support emerging artists and provide them with valuable opportunity to develop their work.

> The former artistic director was really willing to support us in that and that was really crucial, you just, with this kind of work, you can't see what it is like until you see it outside (Artist 4).

Through its commissioning programme *Fuse* also supports the creative output of local companies. '*Fuse* actually shaped the company in 2009 by commissioning a very large outdoor work and we had to form the company to make that commission' (Artist 3).

Some artists also mentioned the fact that taking part in *Fuse 2011* has helped their confidence.

> She gave us some really positive feedback. They make me feel very confident about any future proposals. Those links, those relationships and conversations ... were real highlights and inspired me to start thinking of the next project (Artist 7).

Conclusions

The data clearly show that *Fuse* plays an important role in supporting artists and creative companies through commissioning new work and showing other works. This is particularly important for emerging companies and *Fuse* is recognised as a supporting partner in the development of new initiatives and new creative companies.

However, the role of *Fuse* is not limited to the activities of a single festival but is part of a broader ecosystem of support that includes opportunities for artistic and professional development. In particular through encouraging companies to return to *Fuse* and giving them long-term professional engagement the festival has created a network of artists and companies. *Fuse* has allowed for experimentation and encouraged young companies to try innovative ideas. Artists particularly value this opportunity as their shows are experienced as 'work in progress' for many months and taking part in the festival – as a process of learning by doing and learning by interacting – plays a key part in allowing them to get where they want to be artistically and professionally.

Furthermore, the results of the social network analysis highlight that *Fuse* provides a good opportunity for artists to interact with each other and learn from each other. While there is room for this kind of opportunity to grow further (and *Fuse* has been keen to develop more professional development opportunities with local artists), generally artists rely on the festival to learn, expand their networks and create more innovative work.

Overall, the results highlight the key role played by the festival in supporting and commissioning artistic work. They also reveal the temporary and explorative nature of many artistic practices and the learning taking place, involving audiences and other creative producers.

Bibliography and further reading

Arcodia, C. and Whitford, M. (2006) Festival attendance and the development of social capital, *Journal of Convention and Event Tourism,* **8**(2), 1-18.

Arrow, K J. (1962) The economic implications of learning by doing, *The Review of Economic Studies,* **29**(3), 155-73.

Bathelt, H. and Schuldt, N. (2008) Between luminaires and meat grinders: international trade fairs as temporary clusters, *Regional Studies,* **42**(6), 853-68.

Crespi-Vallbona, M. and Richards, G. (2007) The meaning of cultural festivals, *International Journal of Cultural Policy,* **13**(1), 103-22.

Crompton, J. L. and McKay, S. L. (1994) Measuring the economic impacts of festivals and events: some myths, misapplications and ethical dilemmas, *Festival Management and Event Tourism,* **2**(1), 33-43.

Fenwick, T. (2008) Understanding relations of individual—collective learning in work: a review of research, *Management Learning,* **39**(3), 227-43.

Gibson, C., Waitt, G., Walmsley, J. and Connell, J. (2010) Cultural festivals and economic development in nonmetropolitan Australia, *Journal of Planning Education and Research,* **29**(3), 280-93.

Glow, H. and Caust, J. (2010) Valuing participation: artists and the Adelaide Fringe Festival, *International Journal of the Humanities,* **8**(2), 413-24.

Grabher, G. (2002) Cool projects, boring institutions: temporary collaboration in social context, *Regional Studies,* **36**(3), 205 - 14.

Granovetter, M. (1973) The strength of weak ties, *American Journal of Sociology,* **78**, 1360-80.

Gursoy, D., Kim, K. and Uysal, M. (2004) Perceived impacts of festivals and special events by organizers: an extension and validation, *Tourism Management*, **25**(2), 171-81.

Lundvall, B. (1992) *National Systems of Innovation. Towards a Theory of Innovation and Interactive Learning*, London: Pinter Publisher.

O'Sullivan, D. and Jackson, M.J. (2002) Festival tourism: a contributor to sustainable local economic development?, *Journal of Sustainable Tourism*, **10**(4), 325-42.

Quinn, B. (2005) Arts festivals and the city, *Urban Studies*, **42**(5-6), 927-43.

Rao, V. (2001) Celebrations as social investments: festival expenditures, unit price variation and social status in rural India, *Journal of Development Studies*, **38**(1), 71-97.

Richards, G. and Wilson, J. (2004) The impact of cultural events on city image: Rotterdam, Cultural Capital of Europe 2001, *Urban Studies*, **41**(10), 1931 - 51.

Robertson, M. and Wardrop, K. (2004) Events and the destination dynamic: Edinburgh Festivals, entrepreneurship and strategic marketing, in I. Yeoman, M. Robertson and J. Ali-Kight (eds.) *Festivals and Events Management: An International Arts and Culture Perspective*, pp 115-29. Oxford: Elsevier Butterworth-Heinemann.

Smith, C. and Jenner, P. (1998) The impact of festivals and special event tourism, *Travel and Tourism Analyst*, **4**, 569-584.

Snowball, J. D. and Willis, K. G. (2006) Building cultural capital: Transforming the South African National Arts Festival, *South African Journal of Economics*, **74**(1), 20-33.

Snowball, J. D. and Willis, K. G. (2006) Estimating the marginal utility of different sections of an arts festival: the case of visitors to the South African National Arts Festival, *Leisure Studies*, **25**(1), 43-56.

Wenger, E. (1998) *Communities of practice: Learning, meaning and identity*, Cambridge: Cambridge University Press.

Notes

[1] The author acknowledges the support of the Arts and Humanities Research Council (AHRC) as part of the Connected Communities Programme (grant number AH/J5001413/1) for the data and materials used in this chapter. Specific acknowledgment and thanks are also due to Lelia Greci, Artistic Director of *Fuse Festival* and all of the artists who gave their time to share experiences and answer questions. All views expressed are solely the responsibility of the author.

6 Festivals of Transition: *Greenlight Festival* Leicester

Richard Fletcher

The Brundtland Commission in its report *Our Common Future* (United Nations, 1987) is widely credited with setting down the first policy definition of sustainable development. In 2017 this report will be thirty years old yet it seems we are still a long way from living sustainably:

> If, as of 2017, there is not a start of a major wave of new and clean investments, the door to 2 degrees [global temperature increase] will be closed. (Birol, 2011)

Green policies have been 'adapted and adopted' by mainstream parties across Europe, despite Green parties being a relatively small political force (Carter, 2013). The European Commission has become a worldwide driver of green policy (Judge, 1992) and market-based innovations such as the Emissions Trading System[1], despite being celebrated and criticised in seemingly equal measure. Media coverage of 'outsider' party growth in the UK has swung towards the libertarian and anti-Europe UKIP recently, despite comparable and longer term growth in support for the Greens (Goodwin & Ford, 2013). Efforts have been made to disassociate Green voices from older clichés of self-deprivation:

> The Green party has changed: partly the personalities within it, partly in response to the changing world outside it….At the same time, ideas that were mainly theoretical 25 years ago – solar and wind technology – have been demonstrably workable…The Greens have become the party of possibilities, not catastrophes. (Williams, 2014).

One attempt to imagine a sustainable future can be found in *The World We Made*, written by Johnathon Porritt from the perspective of a school teacher in the year 2050. The positives of huge renewable investments, progressive economic policies and a panoply of exciting new technologies are matched with equally plausible negatives of stubborn inequality, famines and riots. In the postscript, Porritt states: 'If we can't deliver the necessarily limited vision of a better world mapped out in *The World We Made*, then the hard truth is that no other vision will be available to us anyway, on any terms.' (Porritt, 2013: 276)

This sentiment captures the outlook of many contemporary Green voices. There will be a shift away from a carbon-driven economy, and it is one we can meet with shock and collapse or with prescience and resilience. This chapter aims to discuss how a proactive approach to sustainability is reflected in the UK's festivals sector and in the views of the Transition Network in Leicester and its *Greenlight Festival* of which the author is a founder member. The eponymous 'transition' refers to a world not only without cheap access to fossil fuels and the avoidance of (further) catastrophic climate change; but also to wider socio-economic changes culminating in a more equitable, enjoyable and even enlightened future.

Nationally, the Transition Network was formed in late 2006[2]. At the time of writing, the Transition website lists 475 officially registered Transition Initiatives (Transition Network, 2014a) while the Draft Transition Network Strategy gives a figure of 1,120 across 43 countries. (Transition Network, 2014b) A further estimate of local, community-based groups focusing on climate action in 13 EU countries gave a total of 1999, of which 841 were identified as Transition Initiatives, 367 being based in the UK (O'Hara, 2013). Transition Initiatives are characterised by their community-led approach to organisation. These voluntary initiatives are set up by individuals, with information and advice from the larger network, and commonly span geographic areas such as towns, cities, neighbourhoods and national hubs. The implications of this emergent, small scale yet direct approach embodied by Transition are summarized on their website:

> We're not saying that national governments are irrelevant or that institutions like businesses aren't important...What we are saying is that for most people, their own local community is where they can have the quickest and greatest impact...when governments see what communities can do...it'll be easier for them to make decisions that support this work. (Transition Network, 2014c).

Transition Leicester, the 45th official Transition initiative, was set up in 2008 and to date has acted as an umbrella organisation, or launching pad, for a number of sustainability projects. Practical projects include community supported agriculture (providing around 30 co-op members with a weekly organic veg-box) community owned renewable energy schemes (with £550,000 in shares invested) and a 'swap shop' offering clothes, books and communally owned tools and bicycles. Educational projects include accredited Permaculture design courses, 'Footpaths' group meetings and a number of informal skill sharing sessions. While here we have divided these projects into 'practical' and 'educational', the reality is that the majority of activities retain a strong social learning and community building focus. What role do festivals take in this scenario?

Festivals are commonly defined as periodic events that have as their core function, the embodiment of a defined community's identity and its historical continuity (Falassi, 1987: 1-7); this does not have to be explicitly stated as an aim or desired outcome. A festival can also more directly act as a platform for promotion, experimentation, recruitment, networking, trade and leisure. The community-building dimensions of festivals are clearly appealing to Transition groups. We could even suggest that more formal Transition events such as workshops, annual general meetings commonly exhibit certain festival characteristics; a blend of entertainment, information, participatory activities, frequently free of charge and open in some way to the general public. We are not suggesting that festivals are unique in this respect, but we may consider what particular relevance they have in the wider discourse of culture and sustainability.

Sustainability has been addressed by cultural festivals and the wider events sector principally as an environmental issue and it cannot be denied that these temporary cities, commonly fuelled by diesel generators on the one hand and hedonism on the other, have substantial direct and indirect impacts on the natural environment. Non-profit organisations targeting environmental impacts such as Julie's Bicycle and A Greener Festival have emerged in the UK in the late 2000s, though we may assume longer established festivals and networks will have considered environmental issues prior to this. In Europe, Yourope and GO Events perform a similar role. These groups promote self-regulation and best practice via conferences, online resources and various award schemes; we may identify personal vindications and good PR value as key drivers alongside financial savings. The increasing costs related to energy and/or fuel, waste management (particularly landfill) is a trend likely to continue.

Harder regulations affecting festivals vary across local authority boundaries, although authorities may also see the balance of benefits outweighing the costs; the benefits principally being economic, media coverage and loosely defined social dimensions of cohesion or civic pride and the costs principally being environmental, also social (crime, congestion) and potentially economic whether the authority is invested directly or only via the indirect costs of licensing, policing and other essential services. The development of British Standard BS8901, since replaced by International Standard ISO20121, for Event Sustainability Management, has raised awareness at a corporate level but it is predicted that its impact may increase if it is included as a 'hard' criterion for applications for an event licence or public funding. There are currently no cases to the author's knowledge where this has actually been enforced, however large-scale event organisers agree that certification offers substantial real world and 'prestige' benefits. (International Standards Organisation, 2013). Importantly, and notably unlike the industry-led schemes, ISO20121 treats sustainability as an economic, social and environmental objective, not solely an environmental one.

Additionally, Arts Council England recently became the first arts funding body in the world to make environmental reporting a pre-requisite of its larger funding schemes. In the first year 90% of organisations engaged in the programme and 63% were able to provide data sufficient for reliable analysis (Julie's Bicycle, 2013). Festivals commonly span private, public and voluntary sectors, and with results from only one year to date, it is difficult to estimate how much this specific change has affected them, but it is a further sign to other funders and local authorities on how regulation can be put into effect.

The physical space in which any festival occurs is arguably of less importance than the wider cultural and social factors associated with this geography. In 1986, Leicester was the first city in the UK to launch a city-wide Ecology Strategy. The 'Eco House', an environmental show home was opened in 1989; in 1990 the city was designated as Britain's first Environment City[3]; and in 1996 was one of five awarded a European Sustainable City Award.[4] The city continued to engage with national and international campaigns; it became a Fairtrade city in 2002, joined the 10:10 campaign and was ranked second on the 'Sustainable Cities Index' (Forum for the Future, 2010). The city's parks and open spaces frequently win awards such as the Green Flag. It is worth noting that Leicester City Council has been under Labour control, essentially without interruption, from 1979. The centre-left modern Labour party may be to the right of most European Green parties, at least at a national level. However, its general stance has been broadly pro-environmental regulation, particularly the Climate Change Act (Department for Energy and Climate Change, 2008) and pro-localism; albeit within the context of a free market.

In the author's experience, the environmental side of Leicester's civic heritage does not seem to have played a great part within the city's modern identity.[5] The relationship of environmentalism and the natural environment to civic identity is a subject of debate in its own right. Place attachment and pro-environmental action has been found in some cases to be more associated with natural, rather than civic dimensions, of place (Scannell & Gifford, 2010), whilst at the same time, civic and political engagement has been identified as a key pre-cursor to pro-environmental action (Chawla & Cushing, 2007).

The author's involvement in the Transition festival working group came via discussion with an undergraduate student on the Arts and Festivals Management course at De Montfort University, Leicester. The working group numbered approximately six members for the early meetings and incorporated pre-existing Transition members, the general citizenry of Leicester, individuals from environmental charity Groundwork, De Montfort University staff and under- and post-graduate students. Despite organisational links, little emphasis was placed on individuals acting in their official capacity as representatives of these organisations. Nevertheless, the skills, contacts and resources that individuals were able to access via their respective organisations proved to be valuable.

The first planning cycle took around six months. The viability of the festival's concept was tested and validated by the in-kind support and funds attracted from private and public sources. The Queens Building at De Montfort University was chosen as a venue. This is within Leicester City Centre but not in a high footfall area. Crucially, the building was available at no charge, although this policy did change in future years.

Around 700 individuals attended the first *Greenlight Festival* on Saturday 12th February, 2011 from 11am to 6pm. A key highlight was a talk by Peter Harper, Head of Research and Innovation at the Centre for Alternative Technology, Machynlleth, Wales. The festival coincided with the city's first mayoral elections and a 'Green hustings' debate was organised; with input from all the major political parties and candidates. Alongside these events were film screenings, workshops, food and drink, music and spoken word, activities for children and numerous stalls for traders, charities and community groups. The festival has broadly followed this template for the subsequent three years and is generally 'anchored' by a key lecture or political debate. There were nearly 50 programmed events (workshops, talks, performances) over the course of the day and 40 stalls.

The festival has been delivered with a modest budget of around £2,000 each year with attendance estimated at around 1000 individuals. Accounts from the first year show nearly 70% of the income was from two grant sources with a further 19% provided as seed funding from Transition Leicester. The remainder (11%) was earned via stallholder charges, refreshment sales and donations. Key elements of expenditure at this stage were printing costs for programmes, posters and flyers (31%) and fees for speakers, workshop leaders and performers (28%). The remainder covered consumables and equipment hire. Over time equipment such as a bicycle-powered PA system, a projector and gazebo were purchased for the festival and for use at other events. It is difficult to estimate precisely the in-kind support given to the event, though both volunteer time and the hire cost of the building have been incorporated into subsequent grant applications.[6]

An audience survey was carried out in the first year, achieving a sample of 79, around 10% of the estimated attendance. It found the audience reflected the demographics of Leicester in terms of age (Under 30s: 33% Festival / 47% Leicester) and number of students (In full-time education: 16% Festival / 12% Leicester). In terms of ethnicity, 18% identified as Non White British, which was below the 49% in Leicester.[7] Nevertheless most organisers agreed that the general demography of the audience at *Greenlight Festival* may not conform to the stereotype for such events (and environmentalism as a whole) which is 'muesli-eating, Guardian-reading middle classes' (Birch, 2007). 73% were city residents, 24% from the surrounding county and 3% of the audience were not from Leicester or Leicestershire. The proportion of non-Leicestershire visitors is thought to have increased in subsequent years, perhaps the result of an increasing profile and marketing reach, of both the festival and perhaps also the wider Transition Network.

We can further consider the ongoing challenges and developmental trajectory over the following years in the hopes of identifying risk-of-failure and critical success factors (Getz, 2002). The three themes thought to be of greatest relevance to festivals of this type and stage of development are financial, outward identity and organisational culture.

In common with many voluntary organisations, *Greenlight Festival* is faced by a challenge to move from grants to earned income. The festival has survived through a small but diverse range of income sources, rarely encountering critical problems as a result of the closure of one income stream. The overall level of capital required for the festival is small to begin with, in keeping with its DIY, resilient ethos. On the down side it can be argued that a non-commercial orientation has blunted the entrepreneurial drive of organisers. The approach to soliciting donations has varied over the years, principally through active 'bucket rattling' and the online equivalent. A more structured approach, a 'friends of the festival' scheme has been discussed but never fully materialised. Fees from traders and exhibitors have been structured to allow community groups to participate alongside small companies and sole traders. The traders are not only seen as a source of revenue but as an important part of the overall programme. In some cases this sentiment is also reflected back from the traders, who do not solely participate in the event to maximise their takings.

Maintaining a clear, outward identity for the festival has also been a key challenge. With an uncertain outward identity, stakeholders of all types can be uncertain as to what exactly is on offer and what is expected from them in exchange. The university campus location may act as a double-edged sword, providing an air of academic legitimacy, whilst potentially appearing 'exclusive' for the same reasons. Considerable efforts were made to present a distinct and contemporary brand, through publicity, online channels and on-site signage. Identity is not only shaped by material elements such as publicity materials, but in the experiences of participants and organisers alike. From numerous discussions with audiences and participants, the festival has been described at various times from almost every angle one could think of: too professionalised, too amateur, too radical, too conventional and so on. Individuals will inevitably have different views and experiences of any event, but could this reflect an 'excess of aims'? At what point does holistic, comprehensive ambition collapse into an over-reaching, incomprehensible mess? For example, similar criticisms have been made of other anti-capitalist protests[8] and the Occupy Movement's famous, slogan of 'we are the 99%'. Is aiming to unify such a broad group over equally broad issues achievable? 'The 99% are a lot more numerous than the 1%; they are also a lot more divided, and it's the second fact that counts' (Runciman, 2012).

These financial and identity issues may stem from the organisational culture of the festival working group and perhaps by extension, Transition (or at least Transition Leicester) itself. The standard trade-off for 'flat', non-hierarchical organisations seems to be that while individuals have considerable autonomy and self-determination, a large amount of effort has to be committed, regularly, by all members to forming any meaningful consensus for action. Combined with a voluntary, non-commercial focus, working in a 'flat' organisation can also leave individuals feeling overwhelmed and isolated. The core of most frequent members (i.e. those who have participated for a year or more) has gradually diminished over time, from around 7-8 to around 4-5. Optimistically, we could attribute this to increased efficiency within the group. With a track record and templates to work from members can get more done with less. Perhaps over time the 'excess of aims' has, in truth if not on paper, diminished as the group can more effectively resolve discussions and avoid unrealistic plans. Reducing the work load, potentially also allows individuals more latitude to run their own events, stalls or simply enjoy the hosting and event management role more. Over a longer timescale, the reduction in the size of the core group could be considered a negative trend, as it could reflect a concentration of power in fewer hands and/or a reduction in the skills and energy available.

The future of this festival and, likely of many others, is clearly tied to the festival working group itself, and this is perhaps where we can see the festival's greatest impact. Festivals of this type are a perfect vehicle for small scale, community groups to 'punch above their weight' by participating in a common cause, at least over the short-term. Event-related activities are known to be the most common type of formal participation across all voluntary organisations in the UK, marginally more widespread than actually raising money or taking part in sponsored events[9] (National Council of Voluntary Organisations, 2013). At least at a conceptual level, Transition and festivals also seem to share a close link, both being defined as processes that, in some way should not continue indefinitely.[10]

As festivals are so often tied to their respective geographies, urban/rural and political differences are of ongoing interest. For example, Brighton and Hove, Bristol, Cambridge, Cheltenham and Edinburgh all broadly have 'festivals' of one sort or the other as a significant part of their civic identities; and each have relatively centre-left political histories.[11]

This remains a surface observation for now; we could suggest that festivals, either as a whole concept or a set of their particular characteristics, are more politically valuable to certain parties than others? How are civic and natural dimensions of identity and place attachment expressed through festivals?

The Transition network is of academic interest in its own right and efforts are being made to examine what impact Transition is having, and how community-led organisations can survive, if not thrive, in times of austerity.[12] The Transition Network's Draft Strategy for 2014-2017 shows evidence that the organisation is negotiating some of the dilemmas we have noted, for example, that:

> We also don't want to get too bogged down trying to predict specific outcomes in a fast-changing and very complex world. We're conscious that we probably can't and won't know which bit of what we do will make the most difference. (Transition Network, 2014)

Festivals and sustainability are also a growing focus for policy-makers and activists, though commonly limited to direct environmental impacts such as waste, transport and energy use. The promotion of pro-environmental and pro-social messages at events has been investigated elsewhere, as much for the development of commercial experiential marketing as for 'charitable' purposes.[13] Measuring a festival's economic impact remains one of the most common and versatile research areas for many festivals as partof their strategy for securing their short-term survival. However, the current trend for impact studies, within festivals and the wider cultural sector, is towards a more comprehensive and holistic approach associated with the concept of value (Donovan, 2013; Fletcher, 2013) Such approaches are considerably more resource intensive and technically accomplished than 'single-issue' studies, but methodological and technological improvements are required to meet this demand:

Sustainable data are needed for sustainable development…growing demand for better, faster, more accessible and more disaggregated data for bringing poverty down and achieving sustainable development. (United Nations, 2014: 7)

Finally, both cultural sector and sustainable development actors are increasingly questioning the conceptual role of culture within sustainability. Cultural sector actors seem to have failed to take up a more significant role within development, despite the core and ever widening 'utilitarian' dimensions to which they can contribute. It is a challenging issue of course; should culture be viewed as a 'fourth pillar', an equivalent of economic, social and environmental pillars? Should it be a part of social goals, alongside well-being or education? Is culture a side-effect of development or a fundamental precondition? (Hawkes, 2001).

'Agenda 21 For Culture' now lobbies for the inclusion of culture in the Sustainable Development Goals (post 2015) to be agreed shortly by UN member states. They suggest that 'economic growth, social inclusion and environmental balance no longer reflect all the dimensions of our global societies' and without explicit recognition in policy, 'sustainable development, peace and well-being' are hindered. (United Cities and Local Governments, 2010) Without the cultural dimension, our media-driven, short term society will surely continue towards an increasingly irrational and meaningless future, in which environmental collapse is largely a given; arguably even the least of our worries. Culture is the difference between a full and free life, and mere existence as 'atomized homo economicus' (Hardy, 2013). Advocates of sustainable development, from the grassroots to the mainstream, could benefit from an increased understanding of their own cultural position and how this can shape and be shaped by the wider culture. Cultural sector actors have a critical role to play in shaping the future; if they want it and we should seriously consider whether the sector is structured in such a way as to make this role possible. To this end, festivals like the *Greenlight Festival* aim to provide both 'free theatre tickets for all and open air meetings to decide the future of our communities' (Hardy, 2013: location 1342).

Bibliography and further reading

Birch, S. (2007) A class apart, *Ethical Consumer*, Nov, available online at: www.ethicalconsumer.org/commentanalysis/ethicalsceptic/aclassapart.aspx [Accessed 30/08/2014]

Birol, F. (2011) International Energy Agency website, *Press & Media*, available from: www.worldenergyoutlook.org/pressmedia/quotes/29/index.html [Accessed 30/08/2014]

Carter, N. (2013) Greening the Mainstream: Party politics and the environment, *Environmental Politics*, **22**(1), 73-94.

Chawla, L. & Cushing, D.F. (2007) Education for strategic environmental behaviour, *Environmental Education Research*, **13**(4), 437-452.

Department for Energy and Climate Change (2008) *Climate Change Act 2008*, London: HMSO available from: www.legislation.gov.uk/ukpga/2008/27/contents

Donovan, C. (2013) *A Holistic Approach to Valuing our Culture*, London: Department for Culture Media and Sport.

Falassi, A. (1987) Festival: definition and morphology, in Falassi, A. *Time out of time: essays on the Festival*, Albuquerque: University of New Mexico Press

Fletcher, R. (2013) *Five Capitals for Festivals: integrated reporting of economic, social and environmental impacts*, Discussion papers in Arts & Festivals Management, Leicester: De Montfort University.

Forum for the Future (2010) *The Sustainable Cities Index 2010*, London: Forum for the Future

Getz, D. (2002) Why Festivals Fail, *Event Management*, **7**, 209-219.

Goodwin, M. & Ford, R. (2013) *Just how much coverage does UKIP get?* The New Statesman, available from: http://www.newstatesman.com/politics/2013/11/just-how-much-media-coverage-does-ukip-get [Accessed 30/08/2014]

Hardy, S. (2013) *Destruction of Meaning*, Kindle Edition, ASIN: B00ED2JUFC, [Accessed 30/08/2014]

Hawkes, J. (2001*) The Fourth Pillar of Sustainability: Culture's essential role in public planning*, Victoria, Australia: Common Ground.

International Standards Organisation (2013) *Event Sustainability Management – ISO20121 passes 2012 Olympics Games test*, available from: www.iso.org/iso/home/news_index/news_archive/news.htm?refid=Ref1690, [Accessed 30/08/2014]

Judge, D.A. (1992) A green dimension for the European Community, *Environmental Politics*, **1**(4), 1-9.

Julie's Bicycle (2013) *Sustaining Great Art: Environmental report, Year One results and highlights*, London: Julie's Bicycle.

Leicester City Council, *Environment City*, (n.d.) available from: www.leicester.gov.uk/your-council-services/ep/the-environment/environmental-policies-action/environment-city/ [Accessed 30/08/2014]

National Council of Voluntary Organisations (2013) *What do volunteers do?*, available from: data.ncvo.org.uk/a/almanac12/what-do-volunteers-do/, [Accessed 30/08/2014]

Office for National Statistics (2014) *Neighbourhood Statistics*, London: Crown Copyright, available from: www.neighbourhood.statistics.gov.uk/dissemination/, [Accessed 30/08/2014]

O'Hara, E. (2013) *Europe in Transition: Local communities leading the way to a low-carbon society*, Brussels: European Association for Information on Local Development (AEIDL).

Porritt, J. (2013) *The World We Made*, London: Phaidon.

Runciman, D. (2012) Stiffed, *London Review of Books*, **34**(20), 7-9.

Scannell, L & Gifford, R. (2010) The relations between natural and civic place attachment and pro-environmental behaviour, *Journal of Environmental Psychology*, **30**(3), 287-297.

Transition Network (2014a) *Initiatives list*, available from: www.transitionnetwork.org/ initiatives/by-number, [Accessed 30/08/2014]

Transition Network (2014b) *Draft Transition Network Strategy 2014/2017*, available from: www.transitionnetwork.org/sites/www.transitionnetwork.org/files/Draft%20TN%20 strategy.pdf [Accessed 30/08/2014]

Transition Network (2014c) *What is a Transition initiative?* available from: www. transitionnetwork.org/support/what-transition-initiative, [Accessed 30/08/2014]

United Cities and Local Governments (2010), *Culture: Fourth Pillar of Sustainable Development*, Barcelona: United Cities and Local Governments.

United Nations (1987) *Report of the World Commission on Environment and Development: Our Common Future*, Oxford: Oxford University Press.

United Nations (2014) *The Millennium Development Goals Report*, New York: United Nations.

Williams, Z. (2014) Green party support is surging – but the media prefer to talk about UKIP, *The Guardian*, available from: www.theguardian.com/commentisfree/2014/ may/20/green-party-support-media-ukip [Accessed 30/08/2014]

Notes

[1] In 2011, the trade in permits was worth $150bn per year, compared to the Clean Development Mechanism established by the UN at $1.5bn per year.

[2] Transition Network was established as a company in 2007 and attained charitable status in 2009.

[3] Awarded by the Royal Society for Nature Conservation, now the Royal Society of Wildlife Trusts. Three other Environment Cities were also named during the 1990s - Leeds, Peterborough and Middlesbrough.

[4] This appears to have developed into, or been replaced by the European Green Capital award.

[5] The physical infrastructure, such as the work done to city parks, signage for the 'Environment City' and the Eco House are more commonly recalled; though in later years the Eco House was no longer considered to be the cutting edge

facility it may have been at its launch. Some documents claim the Eco House attracted 15,000 visitors per year, though other individuals involved at stages claim this eventually dropped to around 5,000 per year. The charity running the facility and other projects closed in 2013, with no clear single cause other than the general reduction of public and charitable funding.

[6] The programme for the first festival in 2011 lists eight individuals in the 'core' team, with acknowledgements to many more unnamed casual volunteers and supporters.

[7] All statistics drawn from Office for National Statistics, Neighbourhood Statistics portal.

[8] In particular, Paul Kingsnorth's book *One No, Many Yeses* further reflects on this aspect of anti-capitalist protests in the late 90s and early 2000s. Given the dominance of capitalism and the comparatively booming economy of this time, anti-capitalist protests often struggle to be seen as 'for' anything and only 'against' everything.

[9] Results from the Citizenship Survey 2008/09, 'Formal volunteering activities undertaken at least once a month in the twelve months before interview' – 59% of respondents indicated they had participated by: 'Organising or helping to run an activity or event' compared to 52% who had participated by: 'Raising or handling money/taking part in a sponsored event'

[10] We could argue that a thematically similar, recurring event over multiple years is no longer truly temporary but can be considered instead as a continual organisation. Similar we could also debate whether 'Transition' is or is not something with an end point in mind.

[11] In the case of Brighton & Hove, the first Green local authority.

[12] The Transition Research Network, funded by the Arts and Humanities Research Council, has recently established a knowledge exchange project with the University of Oxford, and has published a *Research Primer* for students and academics looking to investigate and participate in Transition initiatives.

[13] A literature review has not been carried out under this wide topic, but a single blog post on Pixangel advertising agency's website gives: John Lewis, Sephora, Neutrogena, Duracell, Jägermeister and Kellogg's as just some of the many brands carrying out experiential marketing activities at festivals in the UK. http://www.pixangels.co.uk/News/experiential-marketing-at-festivals.html

FOCUS ON
FESTIVALS

SECTION 2
LEADERSHIP AND MANAGEMENT

Introduction

Jennie Jordan

Festivals are strange beasts. They flower once a year or every other year, making a big show for a short period and then they disappear. Yet behind this is an infrastructure that has to be strong enough to survive the months without ticket sales, yet flexible enough to grow from a tiny core team to one of tens, if not hundreds, of staff and volunteers, that can communicate effectively with corporate sponsors, local residents, public funding agencies, artists and audiences, that can enthuse, nurture and select the best art works for their programme from amongst a myriad of ideas, and deliver them on time and on budget. This section considers these management and leadership challenges and uncovers a number of recurring themes within the following chapters.

The leadership of artistic festivals is a complex matter, combining the need for creativity and cultural understanding with the ability to manage cash flow and balance a budget, nurture artists, sponsors and public sector funders, motivate staff and volunteers, understand the needs of audiences and residents and to plan for the future. It is taken for granted by the leaders in this section that artistic quality and the finding and nurturing of new talent are non-negotiable parts of festival leadership. Argano (Chapter 8) calls it 'a normal investment'. It is the belief in the importance of what they are making, what Koprivšek (Chapter 10) describes as passionate devotion, that drives them on – as it does all entrepreneurs and business founders - through the difficult days (Adizes 2004). Whatever the size and longevity of the festival, or the leaders' personal preferences, though, the core managerial skills of planning, co-ordination, direction and control are the foundations upon which the creative and artistic programme is built.

The case studies in this section are all relatively young and are led by their founders; charismatic and entrepreneurial leaders who have imported the skills from their prior lives as artists and arts producers and who have an understanding of the collaborative and iterative processes that artists use in their creative work. Kaiser (1995: 4) describes this planning process as one that allows "the best solutions 'to hatch'". The case studies in the section have, from the outset, had a clear sense of their festival's artistic vision and purpose, and the importance of the programme remains central across the festivals surveyed by myself (Chapter 9). Each has started with an understanding that there is a gap in their community's cultural lives and has turned this in to an opportunity. Koprivšek started the *Mladi Levi Festival* because the venue she ran was too restrictive for her artistic ambition. The *Romaeuropa Festival* launched in 1986 as a challenge to the overwhelmingly traditional and heritage-based cultural offer in Rome. The growth of these events has been organic and opportunistic, testing the ground and responding to the environment rather than trying to control it. In Rotterdam, Dooghe (Chapter 13) discusses the process of festivals starting as local experiments amongst a small team then becoming integrated across the city and into the wider community.

Silvanto (Chapter 7), Koprivšek and Argano all illustrate the juggling act that festival leaders have to manage. They are precariously independent, intermediaries between the established order of municipal regulations and funding body requirements, the desire to do justice to their artists and audience expectations (Smith, Maguire and Matthews 2012). Plus, the next edition is always just round the corner and demands attention, but partnerships and relationships with artists, stakeholders and audiences need to be nurtured over the longer term. Norton (Chapter 11) highlights the importance of thinking several years ahead as she considers the practicalities of organising a procession through the town centre. Balancing the artistic vision and the practical constraints of the budget and the business plan is, in itself, a creative leadership task that demands entrepreneurial skills even when the festival is one that has been long established. Festivals are always looking for new ways to promote their shows, new audiences and new artists to work with. Success for a festival depends on the right mixture of creative vision, management expertise and planning.

Entrepreneurship is usually identified with those individuals who start businesses that grow into hugely financially successful companies. The skills and traits that these individuals demonstrate are vision, creativity, determination, iterative problem solving, a focus on audiences and excellent project-management. These are well understood in the arts world (Daum 2005, Austin and Devin 2003). These are all skills that are clearly demonstrated by the leaders in these case studies who juggle the varied needs of artists, staff, volunteers, funders, partners, suppliers, residents, local authorities, the media and audiences whilst trying to bring the festival in on budget. Norton and Silvanto both discuss the importance of income generation and the need not to let this distract from the festival's core purpose (Moss 2011, Hagoort 2003). What is less well understood in the festival sector are the common barriers and problems that managers face in the different stages of the organisational lifecycle. Whilst founders might struggle to find partners and investors in the early stages when the festival has little profile or credibility, established events might become overly bureaucratic and risk averse, or lose their original vision as they chase funding opportunities (Maughan 2007, Jordan 2013). The *Flow Festival* has been criticised for being overly commercial, for example. Finding a balance between creative risk and management control is the key to sustainable growth, yet my survey in Chapter 9 indicates that the sector is not able to control its environment and is vulnerable to political and economic change and to the whims of donors. Norton's examples of political festivals that are sponsored by trades unions highlight, though, that when the supporters and the festival have the same aims, this relationship can be long-lived and constructive.

As I note, from my research, festival leaders' main priorities are artistic quality and the need to develop new audiences. These chapters show that they also have an awareness of the need to adapt to rapidly changing economic, technological, social and political environments and of the vulnerability of relying too heavily on others. The *Flow Festival* in Helsinki has responded to the need to grow by finding new, bigger venues and using their creativity to turn these in to appropriate festival spaces. The *Diggers' Festival* in Wellingborough in the UK is at an earlier stage, but has introduced a fringe and is now considering adding an annual procession. Managing these processes without alienating audiences and other stakeholders is a tricky task (Hewison and Holden 2011) and it is clear from each of the festival cases in the section that trial and error, keeping the successful parts of one edition and piloting new approaches in the following year have allowed them to grow their programme and structures organically. *Romaeuropa*, for example, started as a partnership with the French Academy in Rome and now works with twenty-six countries' academies within a dedicated association.

Yet growth is not easy. Founders are used to having complete decision-making control, to being the spider at the centre of the organisational web (Handy, 1999). Growth brings the need for more complex systems and leaders have to learn to delegate. They have to trust others to make decisions that might be different from the ones they would make, but still fulfil the organisation's vision. The *Flow Festival* is just at this point – the founders cannot maintain the vigilance that they have to date over every aspect of the festival's design and production, but that attention to detail has been central to the event's success. Koprivšek relies on a regular team of about fifteen trusted collaborators and stresses the importance of letting go of responsibility as soon as possible.

Autissier's research into volunteering (Chapter 12) finds similar dilemmas, with some festivals embracing volunteers, whilst others consider them to be unreliable and a 'necessary evil'. The solution relies on strong teams with a shared vision and culture (Lipman-Blumen and Leavitt 2001, Schein 2004), but these take time to develop and are particularly difficult to create when most of the workforce is temporary. Norton considers the skills that committee members need and concludes that the motivation caused by having a commitment to the festival's vision will encourage volunteers to develop any skills they do not have. I agree, suggesting that the vision of the festival can create a sense of shared purpose, much as a charismatic film or theatre director does when faced with pulling a team together in a short period of time.

One of the leadership questions that this section seeks to answer is why do some festivals start, thrive and grow to become crucial aspects of a city or region's cultural offer, whilst others flourish for a few editions then disappear?

Some of the answers can be found in the literature related to entrepreneurship. Elyas et al (2012), for example, argue that successful entrepreneurs have high levels of social capital that they use to increase their organisational resources. Social capital is the concept that individuals within a community can harness relational resources to achieve desired outcomes (Bourdieu 1985). It can be considered to have three main dimensions: structural (relationships between individuals), relational (trust between individuals) and cognitive (shared values and goals) (Andrews 2010, Nahapiet and Ghoshal 1998). The more social capital an organisation has, the more opportunities it will be aware of. Granovetter (1983) developed the idea of social capital through his research into the strength of the interpersonal ties between individuals. The stronger the ties, the more cohesive and inward looking (closed) the group, the fewer the opportunities. The wider the connections, the weaker the ties and more outward looking (open) the group, the more varied are the possibilities and the more likely it is that a new festival is likely to survive and grow (Elyas et al., 2012).

For festivals, which tend to have small numbers of staff and to operate in complex environments (Hewison and Holden 2011, Hewison 2006), social capital is often developed through networks and partnerships and these relationships are essential components of the festival's risk management. Koprivšek (Chapter 10) discusses her use of networks to access knowledge about emerging artists and production partnerships that give her economies of scale, whilst the *Flow Festival* relied on the founders' personal networks to programme the festival for a number of years. The *Aarhus*, *Holland Dance* and *Nitra Festivals* researched by Autissier consider their volunteers to be essential members of their networks, as well as potential future workers and advocates, whilst *Romaeuropa* has developed interesting artistic projects in the Middle East at the prompting of one of its business partners.

It is clear that producing any festival is a feat that relies on a web of stakeholders, each with their own priorities, requirements and viewpoints. A selection of the stakeholders mentioned in this section includes local and international artists and arts producers; other festivals; local, regional, national or European authorities and funding bodies; audiences; local residents; sponsors; volunteers; workers; and the media. Managing these competing and complementary voices is an essential leadership task and failure is not really an option for such visible organisations that have a public remit. If a festival loses credibility with any of its stakeholders, or the network of stakeholders becomes fractious, its future is at risk (Hewison 2006). Larson categorises stakeholders as primary and secondary, depending on the power they hold within the network that is needed to produce a festival. Audiences, artists, local government, major sponsors staff and volunteers can all be considered a powerful primary stakeholders whose views festival leaders need to consider (2004). When the web is working well it provides a safety net of guidance, contacts, ideas, funds and audiences and ensures that a festival stays in touch with its communities. Their ability to sit within so many different networks gives them a unique position as cultural intermediaries that can be used to bring diverse views together and creatively change perspectives (Sassen 2012, Giorgi et al. 2012). Adizes (2004) and Maughan (2007) both consider the ability to integrate all of its stakeholders to be a sign of an organisation in its prime. Autissier believes that festivals that work with volunteers make an important contribution to their communities, while Koprivšek and Dooghe both reflect on the wider effects of festivals on city policy and local cultural infrastructure. Dooghe argues for festivals to be integrated into urban planning, with spaces being specifically designed to encourage community engagement. Finding practical responses to the constraints imposed by noise and public order regulations are more of a concern for Norton and Silvanto.

These practical matters of regulation and stakeholder management form the backdrop for a festival experience that will transport audiences away from their everyday lives for a period (Pieper 1999). Pine and Gilmore (1998) contend that experiences can be active or passive, immersive (involving many of the senses) or absorbing, and that the best create a balance between them that is memorable. Koprivšek describes trying to design a festival that considers everyone, artists, producers and audiences, as guests, because the experiences she remembered were those where she was able to be fully involved in the life of the festival. Research into festival audiences illustrates the importance of the festive atmosphere and the sensory cues in providing moments of amazement and discovery that motivate people to attend (Morgan n.d., Uysal and Li 2008). This is, of course, a difficult task, particularly as different individual audience members have different tastes and the variables are not all within the organisers' control. Silvanto highlights the role audiences themselves play in creating a festival's image and Dooghe's model of 'thrill zones' and 'chill zones' illustrates the importance of place design to cultural experiences.

One solution is to create a festival event that learns from the collaborative approaches in the games industry and allow audience to co-design their own experience in collaboration with the artists and producers (Walmsley and Franks 2011). Co-creation allows individuals to select their own points of entry and exit, to decide how much they want to interact, or whether, for now, they would prefer to spectate. Festival audiences value novelty more than festival leaders expect (Kim et al., 2001), meaning that a festival that can provide multiple ways of encountering aspects of the programme will usually provide a more enjoyable and memorable experience. It is, however, an approach that is in direct conflict with the traditional auteur beliefs that prioritise a director's artistic vision. I contend that co-creation is increasingly important, though, as a response to technology-induced social expectations.

The importance of social media is touched upon within these case studies. Norton discusses the potential of social media to reach younger audiences, and the *Flow Festival* has kept abreast of the technology as a marketing tool, but the potential of social media to connect festival communities throughout the year, to actively engage audiences as part of the festival production cycle, or to create connections between a festival and communities with similar aims does not yet appear to have been fully developed.

Despite their relatively small numbers of staff, festivals are complex organisations to manage. They sit at the centre of networks that include sometimes global organisations as sponsors and, at the other extreme, individual artists and volunteers, with each being essential to the festival's success. Festival leaders have to understand and engage with the needs of governmental authorities, educational establishments and local communities, motivate and train volunteers whilst programming aesthetically authentic and enticing experiences for increasingly demanding audiences, and keep up to speed with the potential of the new technologies whilst remembering why they are creating this event and trying to balance the books.

The chapters in this section provide case studies of entrepreneurial leaders who have set up and run festivals that reflect and reveal the places in which they are to be found. Their processes have been, by and large, iterative and the growth organic - a process of trial and error similar to that of artists creating new work. And they all know they have more to learn. They are part of national and international networks that provide them with knowledge and economies of scale to produce new work that isn't a 'product' that can be seen anywhere. They are determined to retain their festival's artistic quality and unique appeal without becoming too narrow to attract audiences.

The balancing act between management skills and inspirational cultural leadership is a difficult one to achieve. These chapters give an insight into the hidden effort that is needed to keep a festival afloat and artistically buoyant.

Bibliography and further reading

Adizes, I. (2004) *Managing Corporate Lifecycles: How to Get and Stay at the Top,* Santa Barbara: The Adizes Institute Publishing.

Andrews, R. (2010) Organizational social capital, structure and performance, *Human Relations, 63*(5), 583-608.

Austin, R. and Devin, L. (2003) *Artful Making: What Managers Need to Know About How Artists Work,* New Jersey: Prentice Hall.

Bourdieu, P. (1985) The forms of capital, in J.G. Richardson (ed.), *Handbook of Theory and Research for the Sociology of Education,* New York: Greenwood, pp. 241-258.

Daum, K. (2005) Entrepreneurs: the artists of the business world, *Journal of Business Strategy, 26*(5), 53-57.

Elyas, G.M., Ansari, M. and Mafi, V. (2012) Impact of social capital on the identification and exploitation of entrepreneurial opportunities, *Faculty of Business Economics and Entrepreneurship Belgrade International Review, 3*(4), 5-18.

Giorgi, L., Sassatelli, M. and Delanty, G. (eds.) (2011) *Festivals and the Cultural Public Sphere,* Abingdon: Routledge.

Granovetter, M. (1983) The strength of weak ties: A network theory revisited, *Sociological Theory, 1,* 201-233.

Hagoort, G. (2003) *Art Management: Entrepreneurial Style,* 3rd edn., Delft: Eburon Publishers.

Handy, C. (1999) *Understanding Organisations,* 4th edn, Middlesex: Penguin.

Hewison, R. and Holden, J. 2011, *The Cultural Leadership Handbook: How to Run a Creative Organisation,* Farnham: Gower Publishing.

Hewison, R. (2006) *Not a Sideshow: Leadership and Cultural Value, A matrix for change,* London: Demos.

Jordan, J. (2013) *The Buxton Festival Lifecycle: towards an organisational development model for festivals,* Arts and Festivals Management, Leicester: De Montfort University.

Kaiser, M. (1995) *Strategic Planning in the Arts: A Practical Guide,* Washington DC: DeVos Institute of Arts Management.

Kim, K., Uysal, M. and Chen, J.S. (2001) Festival visitor motivation from the organizer's point of view, *Event Management, 7*(2), 127-34.

Larson, M. (2004) Managing festival stakeholders, *13th Nordic Symposium in Tourism and Hospitality Research*, Aalborg, Denmark, 4-7 November.

Lipman-Blumen, J. and Leavitt, H.J.(2001) *Hot Groups: seeding them, feeding them and using them to ignite your organization*, Oxford: Oxford University Press.

Maughan, C. (2007) The lifecycle of a festival: preliminary thoughts, *International Festivals Association of Europe (IFEA) Conference*, European Festivals Association (EFA), 14-18 September, www.efa-aef.eu/en/activities/efrp/.

Morgan, M. (n.d.) Festival spaces and the visitor experience, available from: http://eprints.bournemouth.ac.uk/4821/1/99__Morgan.pdf.

Moss, S. (2011) Cultural entrepreneurship, in *Key Issues in the Arts and Entertainment Industry*, ed. B. Walmsley, Oxford: Goodfellow Publishers, pp. 161-177.

Nahapiet, J. and Ghoshal, S. (1998) Social capital, intellectual capital and the organizational advantage, *The Academy of Management Review*, **23**(2), 242-266.

Pieper, J. (1999) *In Tune with the World: A Theory of Festivity*, Indiana: St. Augustine's Press.

Pine II, J. and Gilmore, J.H. (1998) Welcome to the experience economy, *Harvard Business Review*, July-August, 97-105.

Sassen, S. (2012) Culture and its many spaces, in *Cities, Cultural Policy and Governance*, H. K. Anheier and Y. R. Isar (eds.), London: Sage, pp. xxiii-xxiv.

Schein, E. (2004) *Organizational Culture and Leadership, 3rd Ed, : Califo*, 3rd edn, San Francisco: Jossey-Bass.

Smith Maguire, J. and Matthews, J. (2012) Are we all cultural intermediaries now? An introduction to cultural intermediaries in context, *European Journal of Cultural Studies*, **15**(5), 551-562.

Uysal, M. and Li, X. (2008) Trends and critical issues in festival and event motivation, in *International Tourism Conference: 05-09 November 2008 AlanyaTurkey: Cultural and Event Tourism: issues & debates, Proceedings Book*, A. Aktas, M. Kesgin, E. Cengiz and E. Yenidip (eds.), Ankara: Detay Yayincilik, pp. 10-20.

Walmsley, B. and Franks, A. (2011) The audience experience: changing roles and relationships, in *Key Issues in the Arts and Entertainment Industry*, B. Walmsley (ed.), Oxford: Goodfellow Publishers, pp. 1-16.

7 How to *Flow*

Satu Silvanto

The *Flow Festival*, which began in 2004, is a rhythm music festival that takes place every August in Helsinki, the Finnish capital. It started out as a small event organised by a group of friends. Ten years later its audience figures have multiplied, the festival organisation has professionalised and the *Flow Festival* is now one of the biggest arts festivals in Finland. In this paper, I describe the development of the festival, how it uses/plays with urban space and why it is especially popular with well-educated young and early-middle-aged local audiences. Furthermore, I discuss key factors that have contributed to the success of the *Flow Festival*: the urban nature of the festival, its strong use of and presence in social media, the role of the festival as an after-holiday meeting point and, last but not least, its artistic quality (Klaić 2007a). *Flow* is certainly an artistic festival. However, commercial aspects have gained importance as the festival has grown. Without commercial knowhow, such a big event would not be viable, no matter how ambitious it is artistically.

The paper is based on several data sources: the festival's user studies conducted by Cantell in 2005 (Cantell 2007) and by the festival organisers in 2007 and 2010–2012; an internet survey on festival participation conducted among the residents of Helsinki Metropolitan area in 2006 (Linko and Silvanto 2011); articles about the festival published in Helsingin Sanomat (the main newspaper in Helsinki and Finland) since 2004; and interviews with the Managing Director of the festival.

Flow at Makasiinit

The *Flow – Nuspirit Helsinki Festival* was first organised at Makasiinit, a cluster of old railway warehouses close to the centre of Helsinki. The previous year, the Nuspirit Helsinki Collective had performed their nu-jazz/nu-soul repertoire at the *Helsinki Festival*. With DJs playing too, the night was more than just a gig and was a great success. Encouraged by this, the current *Helsinki Festival* Director Risto Nieminen asked Tuomas Kallio, the prime mover of the Collective, to organise a series of concerts in 2005 under the auspices of the *Helsinki Festival*.

Kallio and his girlfriend, Suvi Virtanen, who had just finished her degree in Arts Management, took up the task with enthusiasm. Together with their friends from Nuspirit Helsinki they developed a brand for the festival, starting with its name and artistic programme but also thinking about the festival's visual identity and so on. From the very beginning the festival organisers wanted the programme to include extra-musical elements. Other arts were also on show and sushi was served, while the run-down venue was decorated using large-scale design canvases to create the right kind of atmosphere for the festival area.

The redbrick buildings of Makasiinit, the first *Flow Festival* venue, had been a hotspot for urban subculture since 1989 (Hernberg 2012a, Oksanen 2006). When the railway company moved out, artists, alternative shops and a bar moved in. Grass-root activities, such as a popular flea market and cultural happenings, were organised both inside and in the courtyard; the site was also home to commercial events ranging from snowboard competitions to TV galas. In 2000 the Makasiinit buildings formed one of the main stages used during Helsinki's year as European Capital of Culture. The former warehouses were the subject of a fierce political debate at the time: a massive citizens' movement, joined by politicians from the Greens and the Left Alliance, wanted to preserve and renovate them, but lost the battle to those wanting to tear them down. The Helsinki Music Centre was eventually built on the site.

During the first *Flow – Nuspirit Helsinki Festival*s in 2004 and 2005 the former warehouses were working overtime. The Makasiinit stood as a symbol of urban grass root activity and, in the beginning the *Flow Festival* referred to itself as an urban music festival. Besides Nuspirit Helsinki and its members other bands, the festival performers included both Finnish and international friends and acquaintances of the group. Kallio described the artistic policy of the festival somewhat vaguely as 'something old, something new – and the rest in between, without forgetting soulfulness', and hoped that the festival would help to create a new musical movement in the city (Helsingin Sanomat 2006).

In 2004 the *Flow Festival* attracted 4500 visitors, in 2005 5000 – about as many people as one could fit in the Makasiinit area. According to audience research produced for the *Helsinki Festival* in 2005 (Cantell 2007), just over a third of the *Flow* audience were students and approximately the same proportion had a degree. Males accounted for 58% of the audience, with two thirds between 20 and 29 years of age. The audience included more 'heavy users' of culture (those attending more than 20 cultural events a year) than most other *Helsinki Festival* events included in the study. On the other hand, the festival also attracted people who had never visited the *Helsinki Festival* before.

Flow moves to Kallio

In May 2006 the Makasiinit buildings were burned down (there is still some debate about whether this was accidental or not), just before they were due for demolition. The *Flow Festival* had already decided to move to the district of Kallio[1]. The organisers had found, next door to a live-music club, an ideal redbrick courtyard. With the help of volunteers and sponsors, a 'cosy urban oasis', as Suvi Virtanen put it, was created on the site (Helsingin Sanomat 2006). Making this a reality required artificial grass, design furniture, a huge photo collage and enticing restaurants.

A similar attempt at temporary transformation of an old industrial site into an urban oasis had already been seen at *Koneisto* – a festival of electronic music. *Koneisto* was created in 2000 in Turku, a Finnish city of approximately 200,000 inhabitants, and moved to the Cable Factory in Helsinki in 2002. As a deeply urban event, *Koneisto* can be seen as a predecessor to the *Flow Festival*. Previously, music festivals had only been organised in the countryside (Silvanto 2007). Urban festival-goers had nonetheless started to look for something other than 'tent and mud', creating a need for a similar kind of urban happening. *Koneisto* grew rapidly, perhaps too rapidly, losing something of its originality. The links with the local arts scene and audiences were weakened when it moved to Helsinki. The public taste had perhaps changed as well, shifting from electronic to live music. In 2006, *Koneisto* was only a shadow of its glory years of 2002–2005 and no longer attracted large numbers of people.

By contrast, the *Flow Festival* almost doubled its audience in 2006, with the number of visitors rising to 9500. The festival now operated independently, not as part of the *Helsinki Festival*. The programme showcased various musical genres from soul and jazz to electronic music, indie rock and hip hop. Right from the start the organisers wanted to offer the audience the music they liked, but without limiting themselves to any particular genre. Alongside bringing to Helsinki old-school soul divas, such as Candi Staton in 2006, the mission of the organisers was to introduce emerging, cutting edge performers. So, something old, something new, but always with soul…

The Kallio district has undergone 'centrification' and, to some extent, gentrification over recent decades. Traditionally a working-class neighbourhood, Kallio was separated by a sea inlet from the centre and the bourgeoisie, a separation symbolised by the Pitkäsilta (Long Bridge). Since the 1970s the area has been populated by students and artists and has gradually become a part of central Helsinki. Today, Kallio has a reputation as an open-minded neighbourhood, with different nationalities, social classes and personalities living side-by-side – and characterised by a strong 'we' spirit. Various grass-root cultural happenings pop up there. The area is polishing its edgy reputation and turning into a trendy middle-class district that is once again attracting families with young children (Hernberg 2012b). But the grannies and the shabby old men are still there, too!

Despite its popularity, research indicates that *Flow06* could still be described as a local event, albeit a big one. An online survey carried out amongst 1055 15–79 year-old residents of the Helsinki Metropolitan Area in October 2006 found that 81% had never heard of the event. Only 2% of respondents named *Flow* as (one of) the festival(s) they had visited over the last 12 months, while the corresponding figure for the *Helsinki Festival* was 24%[2]. Interestingly, 6% of respondents indicated that they were interested in *Flow* even though they had not yet attended. The interest was biggest (10%) among 15–25 and 26–35 year old residents, amongst whom 3-5% had participated in a *Flow Festival* (Linko and Silvanto 2011).

Despite this narrow audience base the festival was nearly sold out. It seems that demand was greater than the courtyard of an old bakery could accommodate. There were also other problems related to the venue. City ordinance in residential areas meant that the outdoor programme had to be finished by 22:00 and there was only one stage indoors for later shows. Once again, it was time to move on.

Flow conquers Suvilahti

Situated just a few blocks from the old bakery, Suvilahti, the area of an old electrical power plant, was facing a period of transformation. The power plant was built in 1909 and continued to operate until 1976. The area was first used for cultural projects in the 1980s. Since the beginning of the 2000s it had hosted business activities and photography studios. The fourth *Flow Festival* tested the Suvilahti area as a venue in August 2007. Previous audience records were once again beaten as the festival attracted 13,000 visitors. However, criticism was levelled at the practical organisation of the festival, even in the *Helsingin Sanomat* newspaper, which was one of the event sponsors.

Up to this point the *Flow Festival* had been more of a hobby among a group of friends rather than any person's main job. Kallio, Virtanen and local club promoter Toni Rantanen had been responsible for the organisation and, together with other members of Nuspirit Helsinki, had used their personal networks to attract interesting performers to the festival, since there had been no possibility of paying big wages. A survey conducted among visitors to the *Flow* website in the summer of 2007 as part of Virtanen's master's thesis had shown that the festival still had great potential for audience growth. A surprisingly large number of respondents, almost 50% (n=1006), had never been to the *Flow Festival*, whereas almost all (98%) were definitely or possibly going to visit the festival in 2007. Virtanen decided to quit her day job as producer of an international dance group and became the festival's Managing Director with Kallio continuing as Artistic Director.

Between 2008 and 2012 the *Flow Festival* developed together with the Suvilahti area. Each year, as the renovation of the area went on, *Flow* occupied more and more indoor and outdoor spaces. In 2008 the festival attracted 23,000 visitors, 10,000 more than in 2007, and records continued to be broken in subsequent years: 2009 - 41,000; 50,000 in 2010 and 2011 and 63,000 in 2012 when, unlike previous years, it was not sold out. After eight years of tremendous growth, some kind of tipping point had been reached. And with these audience figures, the *Flow Festival* has grown to be one of the biggest in Finland.

The festival's budget has also grown, from €91,000 in 2004 to almost €4 million in 2012. *Flow04* was organised without any public support. In 2005, the City of Helsinki awarded the festival a grant of €8,000, which was increased to €30,000 in 2006. Since then the city's support has remained the same, but the State has supported the festival with a grant of €28,000 since 2010. Public subsidies make up less than 2% of the entire budget, with ticket sales covering approximately 70% and sponsorship and other sales a further 25% of the total expenditure.

Given its success, some might question whether public money is still needed or merited. One response is that the festival pays more money to the city in the form of rents than it receives as grants. The city also utilises *Flow* for its own marketing purposes. And it undertakes artistic projects that others would not touch due to perceived financial risk, for example creating a new kind of stage design in cooperation with the European Architecture Students Assembly that took place in Helsinki in 2012. Visual elements too, such as lighting the entire festival area, have become more impressive year by year. As Suvi Kallio (née Virtanen) puts it: 'We're still thinking carefully about every detail as though we were still a small event. We have thought about the kind of festival we want to offer to our friends, and our vision is to create a total experience. Even though we attract the masses today, we want to combine big and small and include intimate experiences on smaller stages. We do this with a lot of ambition. This might be a much more profitable business if we didn't use so much money on all the extras. On the other hand, this is an essential part of our brand' (September 29, 2012).

Finally, it is the audience that creates the festival. *Flow* has been described in the media as 'Helsinki Fashion Week' or the 'hipster festival' (Helsingin Sanomat, August 16, 2009). Rather than big brands, the participants photographed for newspapers or various websites have been wearing personal combinations of vintage styles and new trends. Achieving such media coverage through these authentic and individual 'fashion shots' has contributed positively to the image of the festival and to raising its local/national profile.

Creative urban audience appreciating artists and good atmosphere

The festival has carried out audience research online since 2010. Respondents have been recruited through its website, mailing list, Facebook site, etc. Flyers explaining the research were also distributed in 2012 in record shops, cafés, etc. in order to reach a more diverse group of respondents. As the *Flow Festival* has almost 40,000 fans on Facebook, and the website is also visited actively when the festival is over, a significant number of participants can be reached through various web and social media channels (such as Twitter, Pinterest, Flickr).

The research carried out in 2011 and 2012 showed that approximately a third of the *Flow* audience worked in the creative sector. Two thirds had a higher education degree, while approximately 30% of respondents were students. Unlike the first *Flow Festival*, there were more women (approximately 60%) than men. More than half the respondents (55%) were aged 25 to 34 and almost 30% were aged between 18 and 24. Around 75% of the respondents came to the festival from the Helsinki Metropolitan Area. A big share of the *Flow* participants probably still came from Kallio and other neighbouring areas, since 29% of the respondents in 2011 walked to the venue and another 23% cycled. Public transport was also popular; only 5% of respondents travelled by car. Approximately three out of four respondents consider it important that the festival organisation takes account of the environment and some are even willing to pay extra for the tickets for this reason. The *Flow* audience is thus well educated, relatively young, urban and ecologically oriented.

For a significant proportion of the audience (43% in 2011 and 36% in 2012) the decision to participate in the festival came immediately after the previous festival. The most important reasons for visiting the *Flow Festival* were the 'festival as a whole' and 'good ambience', followed by the central location and particular artist(s). Social factors such as friends participating were also important. A significant number of respondents (32% in 2011 and 46% in

2012) also obtained information on *Flow* from their friends – word of mouth. By far the most important channels of communication, however, were the festival's website and Facebook site. Approximately 95% of the respondents searched for information on the website, and 71% (in 2011) and 83% (in 2012) on Facebook.

The *Flow Festival* has been very active and successful in developing its use of social media. In 2007, Myspace was the most important social medium and was used by the *Flow Festival* as one of its main communication channels. In 2009 an RSS Feed was added to the festival's website. *Flow* joined Facebook in 2010 and the festival's own playlist was created on Spotify. *Flow* also uses Twitter and photos are uploaded on Flickr. In 2012 links were added to and from Google+ and Pinterest.

In 2011 *Flow* also began publishing its own magazine twice a year. Besides articles on the performers and other artistic and design content of the festival, consideration was given to various phenomena related to music and urban culture. The additional role of publisher, however, is quite a burden for a festival organisation already working to its limits, and the *Flow* magazine now comes out only once a year. Suvi Kallio admits that the *Flow Festival* is facing a dilemma. On the one hand, they cannot continue putting so much energy (and money) into perfecting every single aesthetic and detail. On the other, this careful and insightful output is an essential part of *Flow*'s brand and one reason for its popularity.

If the starting point of the festival has been to create an event that the friends of the organisers would appreciate, this can no longer be the sole guiding principle. The public has not only grown, but diversified. The musical tastes of twenty-somethings are different from those of the main organisers approaching their forties. Because the *Flow Festival* wants to present rising, up-to-the-minute artists, it must rely on its networks and younger staff members to highlight the current interest in the various music genres.

Naturally, the growth of the festival has also attracted criticism. For some, it has become too popular, too commercial, too mainstream. In cooperation with other Nordic festivals, *Øyan* in Oslo and *Way Out West* in Gothenburg, *Flow* has brought to Helsinki such big stars as Kanye West and Björk. On some stages the names of the sponsors appear prominently. Suvi Kallio defends these decisions, saying that sponsors and big names have made it possible to invest in the festival venue and have funded greater diversity in the musical programme.

Some critics have staged their own cultural events. In July 2012, the *Kuudes aisti (Sixth Sense) Festival* occupied the old bakery courtyard with its 'subculture celebration', serving punk in addition to *Flow*'s musical offering. Altogether many smaller-scale art happenings are taking place around Kallio and neighbouring Kalasatama, an old harbour intended for conversion into a residential area and now attracting an alternative art scene and urban activists. The *Flow Festival* has certainly contributed to the image of the area making it more attractive for different cultural actors. The festival also invites these actors to create happenings. As an example, the We Love Helsinki collective, noted for staging urban events, such as cycling days in Kalasatama, have been arranging their urban ball dance events at the *Flow Festival* for some years.

Why *Flow*?

Three aspects need to be considered in concluding why the *Flow Festival* has become so big. First of all, *Flow* is an urban music festival. There was a real need in Helsinki for this kind of stylish urban event with an interesting musical profile and, apart from *Koneisto* in the early years, the *Flow Festival* has had no real competitor. Furthermore, *Flow* has always managed to be where interesting things are happening: first in Makasiinit, then next to a hip club in the old Kallio courtyard and finally in Suvilahti. The *Flow Festival* has participated actively in development of the Suvilahti area as a cultural hub. Suvilahti, in turn, is probably one of the reasons why Kalasatama is now a hotspot for urban grass-root activity. *Flow* is a part of the growing urban resident movement that has been gaining ground in Helsinki since the turn of the 2000s.

Secondly, the main interest of the festival organisers has been in artistic quality. There was a clear vision about the contents and profile of the festival from the outset. Not only the high-profile musical programme, but also the design of the festival venue, its visual elements etc., have all been planned with subtlety. A variety of stages have made it possible to provide different audiences with diverse genres of music, several stages having being designed to create an atmosphere of intimacy, despite this being a big festival. The *Flow Festival* has also systematically asked its audience for feedback on content and organisation, helping to develop the festival in a direction that pleases the public. At the same time, Tuomas Kallio and the people around Nuspirit Helsinki have tried to offer the audience something that inspires them personally. This kind of authentic enthusiasm filters through to the audience.

The third reason for the rapid success of the festival is related to social aspects. This refers largely to the active and successful use of social media in promoting the festival (Klaić 2007b). With the help of media – both new and traditional – *Flow* has managed to profile itself as the place to be for well educated, creative and ecologically oriented young adults. This means that people now come to the *Flow Festival* to meet other people who share the same interests. Even though *Flow* is now a big event, it has managed to retain some of the charm of a 'block party' – as well as its old clientele – while attracting new people every year. *Flow* has also benefited from being part of the *Helsinki Festival* in 2004–2005 and in 2008–2010.

The *Flow Festival* is not aiming to get any bigger. After tremendous growth, its audience figures have remained about the same in 2012–2013. The Festival organisation has matured and may be in its 'prime' phase (Maughan 2007). While the first *Flow Festivals* were organised by amateurs, today the festival office permanently employs six highly professional event organisers. The three key figures, Tuomas and Suvi Kallio together with Toni Rantanen, still take the lead. It seems that they have managed to turn the festival into their permanent employment without getting exhausted on the way, something which happens to many enthusiastic festival organisers; and which can lead to premature aging (and death) of many interesting events.

The *Flow Festival* is now a permanent feature of the Helsinki summer. The Kalasatama area to which Suvilahti belongs has provided a good basis for development of the festival. On the other hand, the festival has also contributed to the revitalisation and rebranding of the area. While the on-going renovations of the Suvilahti area have offered *Flow* a possibility to grow, the continuous development of the area itself has also challenged the festival organisation. As more and more residential buildings rise up in/around Suvilahti, the open spaces *Flow* has been using are taken over by development, little by little. The festival area is therefore reshaped every year. This demands extra work but it also forces the organisers to rethink their festival every year. This is probably one of the reasons why the *Flow Festival*, which celebrated its 10th anniversary in 2013, has succeeded in maintaining its freshness.

Bibliography and further reading

Cantell, T. (2007) Festivaalien tutkimisen tärkeydestä (The value of festival mapping), in *Helsinki – a festival city: the development, actors and audiences of urban festival*, S. Silvanto (ed.), City of Helsinki Urban Facts, Helsinki City of Helsinki Cultural Office pp.166-173.

Helsingin Sanomat (2006) *Interview with Suvi Virtanen.*

Hernberg, H. (2012a) The battle against apathy, in *Helsinki Beyond Dreams. Actions towards a creative and sustainable hometown*, H. Hernberg (ed.), Helsinki:Urban Dream Management, pp.36-41.

Hernberg, H. (2012b) Independent shops make a comeback, in *Helsinki Beyond Dreams. Actions towards a creative and sustainable hometown*, H. Hernberg (ed.), Helsinki: Urban Dream Management, pp.106-113.

Klaić, D. (2007a) 'Festivaalien tutkimisen tärkeydestä (The value of festival mapping)' in *Helsinki – a festival city: the development, actors and audiences of urban festival*, S. Silvanto (ed.), City of Helsinki Urban Facts, Helsinki: City of Helsinki Cultural Office, pp.202-205.

Klaić, D. (2007b) Every weekend a festival! Urban impact of the festivalization of the daily life in Europe, *Time-Space Dynamics in Urban Settings. Third Annual Conference of the Transatlantic Graduate Research Program, Berlin,* Gent:European Festivals Association, May, www.efa-aef.

Linko, M. and Silvanto, S. (2011) Infected by arts festivals: Festival policy and audience experiences in the Helsinki metropolitan area, *The Journal of Arts Management, Law and Society,* **41**(4), 224-239.

Maughan, C. (2007) The lifecycle of a festival: preliminary thoughts, *International Festivals Association of Europe (IFEA) Conference 2007, Gent:* European Festivals Association, 14-18 September, www.efa-aef.eu/en/activities/efrp/.

Oksanen, K. (2006) *Makasiinit 1899–2006*, Helsinki: Helsingin Sanoma.

Silvanto, S. (2007) Tervetuloa kaupunkifestivaaleille! Urbaanin festivaalikulttuurin nousu (Welcome to festivals! The rise of urban festival culture), in *Helsinki – a festival city: the development, actors and audiences of urban festival culture*, S, Silvanto. S., (eds.), Helsinki: City of Helsinki Urban Facts; City of Helsinki Cultural Office, pp.9-15.

Virtanen, S. (2007) *Word-of-mouth: the role of interpersonal communication in arts marketing.*, Masters of Arts edn., City University, London.

Notes

[1] The neighbourhood having the same name as the festival's main organiser is just a coincidence.

[2] In 2006, *Helsinki Festival* was the biggest festival in Finland attracting altogether 247,000 visitors.

8 *Romaeuropa Festival*: A Case Study

Lucio Argano

Different combinations of conditions, circumstances and historical moments trigger festivals. One of the common denominators that characterises their origins and success over the course of time is the role of their founders. The birth of *Romaeuropa Festival*, provides us with a significant case study of visionary leadership.

The story of this festival began in 1986, just ten years after the creation of the *Estate Romana* (*Roman summer*), a programme of cultural events invented by architect Renato Nicolini, the Rome City Council politician in charge of cultural affairs from 1976-1985, which brought life to the city's streets and squares each summer with music, dance, theatre and film. During that period Rome, for the first time since the end of World War Two, was governed by a leftwing administration, led by mayors belonging to the Italian Communist Party (PCI). These were also the dark years of the Red Brigades and Fascist terrorism that bloodied Italy. The *Estate Romana* was conceived as an umbrella event, which was to bring together many independent initiatives from theatre, music, cinema, art and literature and smaller individual festivals, and which soon became a symbol of the rebirth of Rome and of the revitalisation of the deeply scarred city. Nicolini's idea was to enable people to regain possession of public spaces, especially in the historic city centre, by encouraging them to engage with the highly ghettoised suburbs, by fostering democratic access and participation in cultural activities. The initiative also sought to integrate different cultural forms and languages into its programme and to appeal to a variety of audiences.

The *Estate Romana* was an innovation in a city that seemed opposed to modernity and was rather provincial, a prisoner of its great heritage, where the expression of contemporary creativity struggled to find expression. In those years contemporary dance was totally absent from the city and there was only episodic programming of twentieth century music. The theatrical avant-garde may have enjoyed one of its best seasons, but it was confined to alternative indoor spaces, a phenomenon referred to as 'Roman cellars' to indicate its marginal position in the city's cultural offer. One can also say that in those years Rome was not a significant centre for the contemporary arts, accessible to all audiences, unlike other Italian cities such as Milan, which at that time had a livelier, current focus. The *Estate Romana* was the background for the creation of a festival focused on contemporary creativity. It also suggested a model of public intervention in the field of large scale events, which produced a lively debate between, on the one hand, the proponents of this type of ephemeral action and, on the other, the supporters of cultural policies more aimed at establishing permanent cultural infrastructure providing a year-round programme. However the trigger for *Romaeuropa* was actually found in another fertile context: the European academies in Rome and especially the French Academy. One of the lesser known features of Rome is that it plays host to about thirty academies, mostly of different European countries, but also of countries on other continents, such as Japan, the US and Egypt. Based in and around places of great historical and artistic value, these academies host, for a period of a year or more, artists and intellectuals working in different cultural genres and disciplines. In this way they create a sort of continuity with the Grand Tour, the seventeenth century phenomenon that saw rich young European aristocrats, authors, writers and artists travel through Europe, and through Italy in particular, in order to enhance their education and knowledge of European classical culture.

In 1986 the director of the French Academy in Rome, which is housed in the beautiful Villa Medici, was the writer and director Jean-Marie Drot, who, after arriving in Rome in 1984, immediately became a keen supporter of French-Italian cultural dialogue and of the Academy's role as a 'living' place that communicated with the city. Encouraged by the cultural vibrancy generated by the *Estate Romana*, and convinced that Rome needed to internationalise its cultural offer, he decided that it was time to invest in the contemporary arts. In an interview with Eric Jozsef (2010), Drot indicated that the aims of the project included the desire to make Rome less beholden to and reverential towards the Vatican and to increase the city's engagement with and support of contemporary culture. To use an image recalled by Drot, the French Academy and the new festival were 'smugglers of culture', so that in the spaces they controlled they could be daring and able to experiment with the 'bold shapes of new artistic languages'.

Drot's idea soon became central to the festival. To make it feasible Drot persuaded three more people who shared his passion and vision to become accomplices in his project. These people's support was central to the successful development of the event. The first of the three was Giovanni Pieraccini, then President of Assitalia, one of Italy's largest insurance groups. Pieraccini was a patron who had created a large collection of contemporary visual art for Assitalia and was responsible for several cultural sponsorships. The second key person was Monique Veaute, who at the time worked on music programmes for Radio France and was persuaded by Drot to join him at the Academy. The third key figure was Fabrizio Grifasi, a young cultural worker, who had already had seven years' experience in local cultural associations, events and free radio stations.

So it was that with a small staff, two sponsors (Assitalia and Eni, an Italian oil and gas multinational), the embryo of *Romaeuropa* was born as an association under Italian law. For the first four editions it was called *Festival of Villa Medici*. It took place in July (during the *Estate Romana*) and offered a multi-disciplinary programme of concerts, dance, video installations, theatre and poetry readings in the French Academy's gardens. By being an institution that has a public/private form of governance, *Romaeuropa* has developed a balance and been able to maintain its independence in artistic and strategic matters. The decision-making members of the foundation are the Italian Government, the regional and city authorities, representatives of some big companies (such as Telecom Italia) and many well-known figures from civil society and the arts in Italy and abroad.

The festival received criticism, especially from those on the left, who judged it as being too elitist. In France, too, there was dissent amongst some intellectuals, especially the historian André Chastel, towards the use of the French Academy, which he considered was too 'open' to Italian people. This hostility towards the festival is a version of the conflict between the ancient and the modern, a perennial issue. Despite these negative voices, the city and its people reacted positively to this experiment and seized the opportunity the festival offered to learn about the contemporary arts. The festival reported good attendance and the welcome attention of cultural institutions and communities. The response was so positive that the German Academy created its own similar event in Villa Massimo.

After four years the festival had grown in terms of audience numbers, attention by critics and partnerships. The *Festival of Villa Medici* decided to make a leap forward, taking advantage of offers of collaboration from the Hungarian, British and Spanish Academies amongst others and, in 1990, the Foundation *Romaeuropa* was established and the festival renamed. This successful model soon attracted the attention and support of many other countries, including Germany, which closed its own festival to join the foundation. *Romaeuropa* co-operated with national embassies and cultural institutes, in addition to the academies themselves. The festival became the glittering focus of the programming for the *Estate Romana* and a true international showcase. Not only did it enable the city to reveal the existence of, and take advantage of, the academies, it was also able to draw attention to the heritage of places until then completely hidden. The festival also offered Romans and visitors the opportunity to have temporary access to prestigious venues that were normally closed to the public, such as the Farnese Palace, seat of the French Embassy or the Abamelek Villa, the residence of the Ambassador of the Soviet Union.

In addition to the festival's formal programme, between 1989 and 1997 *Romaeuropa* also contributed to the life of the city with events of significant cultural importance such as the celebrations for the Bicentennial of the French Revolution in Piazza Navona in 1989, the *Music Fest* in 1992 and in 1993, *Fiume di Musica* (River of Music), which animated the entire course of the Tiber through the city. In 1997 the festival, now in its prime, decided to move to the autumn and to shift its focus from outdoor spaces to Rome's theatres. This is a festival model closer to the French *Festival d'Automne* and, since 2000, it has run from September to December with a rich contemporary arts programme. This choice, in addition to making the event easier to plan, has ensured better technical standards of production of the events and has been able to use more stages equipped for the needs of its productions and attract more financial support. In 2003 *Romaeuropa*, thanks to a collaboration with the University of Roma Tre, received a commission to manage the historic Palladium Theatre, where the University presented its own annual programme of events in close collaboration with that of the festival, and which included subjects such as science, literature and economics as well as the performing arts.

The artistic line of *Romaeuropa Festival* has been sustained in a consistent way since its foundation. It is primarily focused, like a subtle watermark, on the contemporary arts. These are represented by global players in theatre, dance, music, poetry and literature, as well as by other forms of expression in the performing arts, including those related to new technologies, and to the discovery and promotion of new talent and young artists, thus fostering a new generation of performers and audiences. Since the beginning there have been key components of high merit and value in the actions of the *Romaeuropa* leadership: co-operation; tenaciously researched international cultural dialogue, reflected in the diversity of the programme; the intersection of different languages and national traditions; the rejection of rhetoric and prejudice; the acceptance of breaches of 'private' spaces; a focus on freedom of expression and, finally, attention to voices providing a critical reading of the contemporary world. *Romaeuropa* seeks to pose new questions and find new answers within the worlds of cultural production, management and consumption.

Romaeuropa has always promoted acceptance of the 'other' and valued a sense of wonder and discovery. Monique Veaute's (2010) belief that the fundamentals of culture are always open is at the heart of *Romaeuropa's* vision and its history. The Festival has always strongly felt the responsibility of being a bridge between cultures, a window opened to a free and unlimited view. But *Romaeuropa* is also faithful to the memory and the roots of modern culture, as an additional rudder in the reflection of its own time and its programming, for example in the cinema world by reflecting on the experiments of Méliès and on the work of the Lumière brothers, Griffith, Pastrone and the Indian Ramayana. *Romaeuropa* considers its independence in judgment and programming choices to be a piece of its DNA to be defended strenuously, as it gives rise to aesthetic plurality without the risk of being generic or excessively eclectic. Rather *Romaeuropa* becomes a place of mediation between different audiences and contemporary creation.

The festival has rejected being labelled as traditional or as innovative. For *Romaeuropa* tradition is a successful innovation and innovation is nothing more than a fertile step forward. In the programmes of *Romaeuropa*, tradition and innovation chase and reflect each other, creating multifarious platforms. Moreover, contemporary creativity is free and wandering, mixed and interdisciplinary, unruly if not actually subversive. Because of this, over the long journey of the festival, it is not unusual to find such a wide heterogeneity of artistic offer, which lives in a coherent and unified project. There is a continuous thread between contemporary music, which mingles with other styles and then turns into traditional music of distant lands. *Romaeuropa* also places emphasis on multidisciplinarity, where music, theatre, dance, visual arts, multimedia are compared and harmonised.

Scanning the long list of artists (over 6,000) and shows (more than 1,200) that the festival has showcased in its life, the geographical breadth is impressive. Some examples will have to suffice to illustrate the festival's style and the artistic universe it has succeeded in exploring. In the field of music *Romaeuropa* artists range from Pierre Boulez to Heiner Goebbels, from Philip Glass to Michael Nyman, from the Orchestra of Santa Cecilia to that of the Ile de France, from Giovanna Marini to Ryuichi Sakamoto. Participating artists in the field of dance include Trisha Brown, Martha Graham, Carolyn Carson, Sasha Waltz, Karin Saporta, Jean-Claude Gallotta, Akram Khan, Ohad Naharin, Alan Platel , Sidi Larbi Cherkaoui, Maguy Marin, Anne Theresa De Keersmaeker, the Ballet de l'Opera de Paris, Michail Baryshnikov, La La La Human Steps, DV8, Bill T. Jones and Montalvo-Hervieu. In the field of theatre, we find Carmelo Bene, Societas Raffaello Sanzio, Bartabas with Zingaro, Lev Dodin, Robert Lepage, Peter Sellars, Robert Wilson, Frank Castorf,

Patrice Chereau, Peter Brook, Emma Dante and Motus company. We could also mention the contributions by Marina Abramovic, Alessandro Baricco and sufi musicians and video installations by Giorgio Barberio Corsetti and Studio Azzurro. Dozens of artistic creations are memorable, including: *Oresteia* by Xenakis in 1988, mixing music with science, mathematics and architecture; Maurice Bejart's tribute to Pier Paolo Pasolini called *Episodes* in 1992, made specifically for *Romaeuropa* in the gardens of Villa Medici; the *Magic Flute* by the multi-ethnic Orchestra di Piazza Vittorio; and Sasha Waltz dance company inaugurating the Maxxi Museum in 2009.

The philosophy of *Romaeuropa* moves along different tracks from many of its rivals among contemporary festivals. It has built a relationship with many artists that eludes specific one-off performances and becomes permanent. The festival follows its creative evolution and works with artists over time on the ensuing projects. In many cases *Romaeuropa* has led the way in Italy, presenting many artists who then go on to become fundamental to international artistic movements. For *Romaeuropa* patient and tireless scouting work is a normal investment, born of its natural propensity to be a cultural incubator not only of new artistic poetics but also of new ways of listening, seeing, producing and developing cultural work.

Figure 8.1: Sasha Waltz and guest (Photograph: Piero Tauro)

Over the years the *Romaeuropa* Foundation has made its voice heard internationally through conferences and meetings. It has called for greater cultural Europeanism, the mobility of artists and intellectuals and has contributed to the debate on the economic importance of culture. If the festival has a fully international vocation and identity, does contemporary national artistic production suffer from a lack of recognition by *Romaeuropa*?

To address this potential imbalance, *Romaeuropa* has included in its mission a responsibility to support contemporary Italian dance since the early 1990s and in 1995 the Italian Government recognised the festival as a National Authority for the promotion of dance.

Finally, since 2008, although it was present since the early years in many performances, installations and video art, the relationship with new media and internet has become a line of research and development for the foundation. An agreement with Telecom Italia led to the setting up of Webfactory, an online creative workshop linked to the creation of Opificio Telecom Italia. Webfactory will generate one of the festival's most innovative projects: Digital Life, a show that has offered multimedia installations, sound environments, video art, interactive and photographic works since 2010.

From its very beginning the planning of *Romaeuropa* has favoured a systemic vision of networking. It was the network of European academies (at the present moment 26 countries are involved in *Romaeuropa*) that in the early years allowed the festival to develop and function. Almost immediately, however, *Romaeuropa* invested heavily in building new networks, both formal and informal, with other festivals, in particular internationally, to share information, knowledge, discoveries and project possibilities. It is not a coincidence that many of *Romaeuropa's* shows are the result of worldwide co-productions. *Romaeuropa* has also cultivated its presence in major international cultural networks. It has participated, to date, in IETM (Informal European Theatre Meeting); in the Varèse network for new music; the Theorem network of theatres and festivals; and the Temps d'Image network for the performing and moving image arts. An accurate and patient weaving work helped place the festival among the major players of its field, especially in the international arena, despite having resources which are far lower compared than those available to other similar events in Europe.

The relationship with the private sector has been a key success factor. *Romaeuropa* is one of the few Italian events that has managed to make a virtue out of business sponsorship, understanding it as a form of genuine partnership rather than simply as a source of funds. As an example, Eni, an Italian energy group with a global reach, has stimulated the festival to explore the artistic expressions of countries where the company has strategic interests, as in the case of Middle Eastern countries or along the Silk Road, thus leading to the creation of fascinating projects. Webfactory exists because of close co-operation with partners like Telecom Italia. Sponsors are recognised and regarded as travelling companions, treated with care and listened to, with a view to building specific projects together.

At present, the budget of *Romaeuropa Festival* is approximately €2 million. 60% comes from public and EU funds, 25% from private sources (patronage and partnerships with companies) and 15% from its own revenues, such as the box office. *Romaeuropa* has the great merit of what can be called 'sound management'. The foundation and the festival have been able to maintain a balanced budget, even in the face of the economic crisis that began in 2008 and the subsequent sudden cuts of government grants for the arts. This attitude comes from a managerial approach that transforms each activity into an expertly crafted project. With an agile and lean organisational structure and a small but steady staff, which grows slightly during the event, the foundation has implemented all the necessary activities of programming, planning, management, control, creating, in keeping with its philosophy of continual innovation. It is not a coincidence that *Romaeuropa* has influenced the formation of many other cultural organisations. Many cultural leaders have passed through its doors, before heading off for other institutions and challenges, including the present author who owes much to the experience.

Romaeuropa has a pioneering operational and strategic marketing approach that is fundamental to its success. In the early 1990s, in fact, this discipline was largely unknown in the Italian cultural sector. *Romaeuropa* built one of the first audience databases in 1992 and implemented customer services such as call centres and sales channels. For many years the festival has launched *Romaeuropa* through two different marketing events: the first addressed to the press and public authorities, while the second event was a party aimed at the public. This attention to audiences has led to over 1 million attendances by 2012. Communication is also subject to continuous review and modernisation, from the use of great contemporary visual artists to create the image of each edition, to the formulation of more provocative visual images in order to get the maximise digital communications and networks.

As pointed out by Claudia Cottrer (2010), *Romaeuropa* has given utmost importance to the various stakeholders, be they institutional actors, artists, partners or audiences. It has tried to build optimal organisational and cultural conditions, starting from the quality of the cultural programme, that has given it a valuable brand reputation.

Romaeuropa Festival has had to face many difficulties, battling to affirm its own space and the natural legitimacy it gained over the years, in a country that continues to be rather resistant to and mistrustful of contemporary artistic creation. Progressive reductions in funding, the search each year for free space within Rome's theatre schedules and changes in government are continuing challenges that *Romaeuropa* has to face. Since 1986, however, Rome has changed. Over the years the city's cultural offer overall has been renewed and improved thanks to the restoration of museums and the building of new infrastructure, some of which is devoted to the contemporary arts, such as the Auditorium Parco della Musica, designed by Renzo Piano, the MAXXI (National Museum of the 21st Century Arts), designed by Zaha Hadid, MACRO (Museum of Contemporary Art of Rome) with its two venues and Teatro India. Despite all this, however, it remains difficult to achieve co-operation and joint policies, not only because of financial pressures, but also due to resistance by many of the city's cultural institutions.

The instrument to overcome these barriers is the project of *Romaeuropa* itself and the high quality of its annual programme. Director Fabrizio Grifasi looks to the future by implementing a two-pronged strategy of resilience and continuous renewal that aims to encourage the festival's ability to listen and absorb the complexity and uncertainty characterising our times and, therefore, the process of artistic creation. This also means being part of cultural change and seeing risk as an opportunity. The nourishment and the perseverance of the festival *Romaeuropa* relies on its courage, to continue to be as visionary today as at the beginning, and to be a taste of utopia. That, in the words of Gianni Rodari (1977), an Italian intellectual who has devoted his life to the themes of creativity, says "is the transition from the world of intelligence to the world of will."

Bibliography and further reading

Cottrer, C. (2010) Produrre, organizzare, promuovere cultura: un modello innovativo tra pubblico e privato, in D'Adamo, A. (ed.) (2010) *1986-2010: 25 anni di Romaeuropa Festival*, Milan: Electa.

Grifasi, F. (2010) La passione dell'arte e il senso del futuro, in D'Adamo (2010)

Jozsef, E. (2010) Contrabbandieri della cultura. Conversazione con Jean-Marie Drot, in D'Adamo (2010)

Rodari. G.(1977) *Grammatica della fantasia*, Turin, Einaudi.

Veaute, M. (2010) Romaeuropa: come osare il contemporaneo, in D'Adamo (2010)

9 Festival Leadership in Turbulent Times

Jennie Jordan

Europe is undergoing a period of transformational political change, with the post-war centre-left consensus that dominated the western nations breaking down and being replaced by a neo-liberal belief in the importance of markets in service delivery and a corresponding reduction in state intervention. Combine this with the financial crisis, which has meant cuts to arts and culture budgets in the UK, Netherlands, Italy, Greece and Hungary amongst others. Add in a touch of technologically driven change and then stop to consider the political, economic and social changes arising from the Arab Spring and the growing economic strength of Russia, Turkey and Kazakhstan on Europe's borders. There are opportunities and threats for all arts and cultural organisations, but what does this mean for festivals' leaders in particular? What do they see as the main issues? How are these issues affecting their vision, production and programming polices, their staff, funding, audience development and stakeholder relationships?

In times of great turbulence, leaders are the pathfinders who establish new ways of working. In Europe the auteur tradition has placed artistic leadership at the centre of decision-making, both within festivals themselves and amongst funders. Festivals' artistic directors are often independent cultural intermediaries, standing apart from the establishment but commenting on it; influencing both their own organisations and wider debates about legitimacy and value (Smith Maguire and Matthews, 2012). This is combined with the tendency of festival organisations to be quite small and entrepreneurial, operating what Handy (1999) calls 'power cultures', reliant on a central figure with a strong vision to make decisions. At their best, with visionary leaders, such organisations can create strong, supportive cultures that are flexible and that can react quickly to social, political and economic change. How then are these weather vanes responding to the post 2008 turbulent social and economic times in Europe?

The range of artistic festivals in Europe is considerable, so it might be thought that identifying shared issues and agendas across such a diverse field is a fool's errand. However, conversations with leaders from festivals across

Europe, supplemented by a small online survey [n=38] undertaken using databases from the European Festivals Association and the British Arts Festivals Association during the summer of 2012 indicate that there are three common issues that they consistently place at the top of their agendas: artistic vision and quality, audiences and income generation. The challenges these present are considered alongside technological, economic and demographic change.

A turbulent environment

Europe's economic situation has been dire since 2008; the Euro in crisis, indebted, lacking growth and with high levels of unemployment in many countries. In this climate making the case for public subsidy of festivals can be very difficult, so it is no surprise that festival directors have been thinking creatively about diversifying their income sources. Previous research across Europe indicates that financial and institutional support for festivals varies widely across the continent, with some festivals receiving almost all of their income from public sources and others almost entirely reliant on sponsorship or earned income (Ilczuk and Kulikowska 2007: 35-37). This places festivals in an interesting place in relation to policy makers – they are not entirely reliant on public subsidy, so can be an independent voice, but they might not be valued as highly as other cultural institutions. Diversifying income streams is at the top of festival leaders' concerns across the continent, indicating some uncertainty about the level of support they can expect from the public and commercial sectors.

At the national level, the approach and commitment of Europe's politicians to culture is changing rapidly. Since World War Two, most Western European nations have taken a benign approach to the arts, providing subsidy without overt artistic intervention (McGuigan 2004). Festival policy has largely focused on large-scale celebrations of national pride, or festivals aimed at encouraging tourism, with the latter often being initiated locally, but success being hailed centrally later, such as the *Edinburgh International Festival* in Scotland (Garcia 2004, Getz 2009).

For festival directors this is both an opportunity and a danger; the very point that requires sure-footed leadership. Do you accept the potential windfall that might come your way if you associate your festival with a celebration of national pride? Or do you perceive this as a dangerous short-termism that might leave you isolated if the political wind changes?

As can be seen from some of the other chapters in this book, festival leaders tend to be entrepreneurial. Jonker et al define festival entrepreneurs as being driven, resourceful, explorative, focused on personal benefits and with good organisational and communication skills (2009: 387). The leaders interviewed and surveyed for this research shrugged off concerns about funding in the belief that their festival product was good enough and important enough that they would find supporters to finance it. This may be partly a desire not to wash their dirty linen in public, partly bravado and partly confidence, but it was surprisingly common as a survey response (50%), regardless of the political landscape in the festival's country.

Although it did not feature strongly as a concern, festival leaders reported declining national support in Germany, the Netherlands, the UK and the Czech Republic in the online survey completed in 2012. Festivals are turning to commercial sponsorship (although this source is also fragile and declining in some places) and some to individual giving. One leader commented "the Festival is seeking to diversify its income streams and increase revenue from corporate partners and private donors", whilst another said "most money is now from grants; sponsorship is less than before…", illustrating the complexity of the environments that festivals are having to contend with.

In some ways, festivals may be benefiting from the lack of consistent public subsidy and policy frameworks identified by Ilczuk and Kulikowska – as there are few policies about festivals, there have been few dedicated subsidy streams, so they have never been able to rely on this source of income and have had to think more creatively than some other parts of the public cultural sector about income generation (2007). In the survey of festival leaders undertaken for this study, an average of 45% of their income came from sponsorship and sales. Contrast this with the criteria for Dutch performing arts companies and festivals for funding from 2013-16 (Fonds Podium Kunsten, 2012), which for the first time asked for 30% match funding.

In the UK, the *Buxton Festival*, which produces rarely seen opera, survived its first quarter century with minimal subsidy. As a result, it has developed a culture of philanthropy amongst its supporters similar to those found in American cultural institutions. It has certainly benefited from opera's appeal to the older, relatively affluent audiences, but the main impetus to fundraise has always been a question of survival: without the Friends, there would be no festival. The Friends provide a significant slice of the festival's funding, sometimes as much as 10% of turnover. They paid for the production of an additional opera in the 2011 edition, for example (Jordan 2013).

Funding, however, is not the only reason for festival leaders to be concerned about a lack of relevant cultural policies and most are well aware of the need for good relationships with their municipalities. Festivals can be important symbols of community pride locally, regionally and nationally, and politicians do engage with them, if only as a PR opportunity (Quinn, 2010; Getz, 2009). Engaging with the policy-making process does not, however, appear to be high on leaders' agendas. This may be a capacity issue: with few full-time permanent staff, festivals are not well placed to engage with the slow pace of government bureaucracy. It may also be a preference issue; festival leaders are focused on the quality of the artistic product and regularly network with artists and their local communities, but perhaps do not see the relevance of planning or legislative decisions until the square they use for major productions has been redesigned or new regulations about arts in education mean a project is no longer viable financially. This is a challenge for all cultural sector leaders (Hewison, 2006), but continuously operating organisations such as theatres and orchestras are probably better placed than festivals to maintain the broad range of necessary relationships with their stakeholders.

As well as economic and political change, the European Union is facing unprecedented demographic change. Internally these include an ageing population, low birth rates and higher divorce rates, all of which are contributing to change in family structures; and externally these include migration from North Africa and the Middle East, as well as from the accession countries. One of the important roles for many cultural festivals is to help us to make sense of the society that we find ourselves living in. For some, particularly those with an artistic programme that covers the classical music and theatre canon, for example, the growth in the number of older people is a boon, as many of the baby boomers have plenty of leisure time, good health and reasonable pensions. Immigration, though, means that their traditional programme may not be relevant to a proportion of the population. The line between celebrating a cultural icon and excluding newer communities can be very thin, as the narrow audience base of those attending many European concert halls and theatres attests. For other festivals, that perceive their mission as celebrating contemporary arts and culture, the relative decline in younger people and the increase in migration presents the challenge of developing expertise in art forms that the organisers may know little about at the moment. How does a festival director or a funding agency judge the quality of a genre from another culture? In Amsterdam, the *Liteside Festival*, which ran from 2006-2012, showcased artists and artforms which were previously little seen in Western Europe (New European Cultural Collaborations, 2014). Having started in 2006 with a focus on Turkish and Moroccan culture the festival's leader responded to the opening up of the old Silk Road countries to the east of the Caspian Sea to find new artists for the 2012 edition. Sourcing excellent artists and understanding how to create and present this work for audiences who are new to it, demands time to travel and absorb new experiences, which a festival director may be able to do more easily than someone running a theatre. *Liteside* struggled for funding after 2012, however, an example of the fact that entrepreneurial festival leaders may run ahead of some of their stakeholders. These risks notwithstanding, the desire to engage with new communities as a source of creativity, income and legitimacy illustrates the health of the sector's leadership.

Stakeholders

So far this chapter has considered the importance of policy makers at a local and national level, but festival leaders have numerous other stakeholder groups to consider: local businesses, the communities who live in their locality, the artistic community that creates the work on show and the venues that will host it, not forgetting the audiences.

Leadership across the cultural sector demands an understanding and ability to manipulate complex environments and relationships (Hewison and Holden, 2011). The arts cross political boundaries and departmental borders to impact upon education, place-making, economic development and employment. Add to this the high visibility of a festival and its ability to define perceptions of a place (Wood, 2006), and it is easy to see why politicians, business leaders and residents have a sense that they should have a say in what the festival does. At the same time, the artists, who have an interest in their genre and want to see it develop, also want to be involved. For performing artists, festivals are one of the few times when they can meet with their peers and see other work; a key part of their personal development. Understanding the needs and priorities of each of these groups, which may conflict with each other, is the key to ensuring that a festival garners support.

The local community can be a festival's greatest strength or greatest weakness, depending on the type of festival and the make-up of the community. A 'high art' festival that takes place in a town or city once a year can be seen as an imposition if little work is done to engage residents. Complaints about parking, noise and road closures can be found in some local newspapers and are a reliable indicator that the festival has not considered sufficiently those living in the vicinity. A lack of engagement by the festival leader with the local community will make a festival vulnerable to a lack of political support at the local level.

The bigger challenge may be when the community around the festival changes rapidly. In some parts of Europe, festival directors perceive that there are new communities growing in their towns and cities as a result of the political turmoil in North Africa and the Middle East and the opening up of borders associated with more countries joining the EU. It can be very difficult for directors to respond artistically, when they themselves lack the specific cultural background. Most artists and festival leaders see the arrival of new populations as an opportunity to learn, a 'culture of curiosity', as one chief executive described it. At their best, festivals can be an excellent bridge for achieving greater understanding between incoming and existing communities, as, having smaller teams, they tend to be fleeter of foot than continuously operating organisations.

Vision and quality

Regardless of the art form, size of festival or its longevity, successful festival leaders have a common interest in the quality of their product and a clear vision for why the festival should exist. This may change over time as the festival strives to remain relevant, but effective leaders maintain a vivid ability to express this vision through words and actions, which draws in stakeholders and supporters. Often these articulations are about development of the artform or of a community. Maintaining this clear vision and avoiding 'mission drift' when public authorities are under pressure to change their own priorities and audiences are suffering the effects of austerity policies, is clearly a major issue for festival leaders across Europe, with half of those responding to the online survey undertaken for this chapter indicating that 'maintaining the festival's artistic vision' was a key area of concern, closely followed by 'maintaining artistic quality'.

But how do festival leaders balance the demand to promote the locality, develop footfall around the festival venues and sites, encourage community feeling and bring the best quality art to their audiences? At their best, festivals achieve all of these outcomes, but it takes time and a large travel budget, supported by excellent information networks to ensure that leaders can go and see work, meet artists and discuss the future. In the case of *Buxton Festival*, the vision 'to produce rarely seen operas' has been consistent since 1976 when the project was first conceived, and is still widely quoted by staff, volunteers and audiences (Jordan 2013). Such as strong vision means that future projects, which may take a number of years to come to fruition, can be kept on track despite changing political agendas. Many European countries appear to be struggling to maintain consistent investment in culture as their governments try to balance market pressure to reduce deficits against the demands of voters to find a way out of recession. In the UK, Italy and the Netherlands, arts and cultural organisations (including festivals) had to contend with their funding bodies rewriting and redefining their long-term funding policies during 2010-2012. Making long-term decisions in such a climate needs very steady nerves and a clear sense of direction.

In the commercial sector, music festivals can spread this risk by programming across several sites, sometimes in different countries. Not-for-profit festivals have more constraints, as they may be supported to provide local distinctiveness to encourage tourism, or to work with local artists and communities. Co-production is a possibility for reducing risk without losing quality and may be the best solution for those festivals that produce. For those that only curate, finding high quality work that is not going to appear on everyone else's bill, from the smaller pool of work that reduced cultural subsidies imply, is one of the major problems with which festival leaders have to contend. Across Europe the emergence of 'light night' festivals (also known as Nuit Blanche, Lange Nacht or Notte Biancha) is providing fresh thinking as the organisers have developed networks to share experiences and encourage co-commissions (Jiwa et al., 2009). Balancing the benefits of collaboration and economies of scale against a potential lack of distinctiveness comes down to high-quality, creative curation undertaken by leaders who truly understand their festival's unique purposes and values (Hewison and Holden, 2011).

Audiences

Audiences feature strongly in the concerns of festival leaders. Balancing the organisation's budget is, of course, important, but most festival leaders appear to have a longer-term view and talk more of the need to develop new audiences for the future, particularly of ways of engaging with younger audiences. This concern does appear to be more than simply having a weather eye on the financial future of the festival; leaders are motivated by the desire to ensure that their art forms, develop and sustain their place in the culture of their communities.

Traditionally audience development has had two approaches – deepening the relationship with existing audiences through education and increasing the number and range of opportunities for them to engage; or encouraging people to attend for the first time (McCarthy and Jinnett, 2001). The first of these often takes the form of instituting a subscription or friends scheme to deepen the relationship with current audiences by asking them to help fundraise, volunteer and advocate for the event. Some develop new projects in response to audience suggestions – innovating and responding in an entrepreneurial way to new technologies or social pressures.

Other approaches to developing loyalty include practices developed by the commercial music festival sector, where audiences are encouraged to engage with the festival experience throughout the year online; uploading their own photographs and videos; talking to other festival goers; participating in competitions and providing on-going ideas and feedback for the organisers in a process of co-creation (Walmsley and Franks, 2011). The top two motivations for young adults aged 25-34 attending *Glastonbury* were 'atmosphere' and 'socialising with friends/family' (Gelder and Robinson, 2009: 88-89) – not the music.

The need for collaboration is not limited to other arts organisations or funders. Social media is changing the way audiences behave and there is a demand for greater participation in decision-making that reflects political movements from the left and the right. From the right, politicians believe that there should be rigorous accountability for public investment and, from the left there is a belief that diverse communities should be involved in defining and developing the services that are appropriate for them (Jancovich, 2013). And audiences demand memorable experiences that fulfil or exceed their expectations. Increasingly they want to be actively involved in curation and production and the technological developments are there to facilitate this co-creation. It is clear that there is momentum behind co-creation initiatives and a challenge to traditional notions of the auteur as the artistic leader whose vision audiences are asked to follow unquestioningly.

True co-creation goes beyond participatory projects that have the focus pre-determined by facilitators, community artists or arts education specialists. The best contemporary example is *Burning Man* in the Black Rock Desert in Nevada, USA (Chen 2009). Each year nearly 50,000 people make their way to a desert and make a festival. No one curates the programme - participants who want to make an artwork or to perform are given a theme to respond to each year and groups often build the work collaboratively. This is the antithesis of the European auteur approach and a major challenge to systems of public subsidy based on judgements of an artist's quality. If you do not know who will be making the art or what they will be making, what criteria can you use to decide whom to fund? One answer is to trust the artistic leaders of the arts and festival institutions that co-ordinate the events – but it will take supreme leadership skills from festival directors to convince politicians to do this.

Conclusions

Whilst the economic and political changes that are taking place across Europe are changing the income generation possibilities for cultural organisations there remains enough public subsidy and influence to mean that government and quasi-governmental organisations are an important source of festivals' finances. Increasingly this is coming with a need to provide evidence of economic or social impacts that fulfil political agendas and hit bureaucratic targets; a factor that sits awkwardly with the auteur tradition of festival leadership in Europe.

Festivals are very well aware of the need to diversity their income streams in this turbulent environment. The online survey revealed that obtaining support from public sources is becoming more competitive, whilst at the same time festival leaders relate that corporate sponsorship is increasingly difficult to secure – leaving individual donations and sales as the other major options.

Good festival directors are well networked within their artistic fields, keen to promote and develop excellence. They place artistic vision and quality high on the list of issues they are concerned about and are keen to develop new audiences. Here the motivation is at least partially instrumental; audiences are important for the festival's future financial health. Technology, though, means that ticket buyers are also key partners in creating the experience. Festivals have always broken down the barriers between artists and audiences better than other cultural institutions (Fabiani, 2011), but how can the audience demand for involvement in the creative process be developed and the opportunities it offers be nurtured without sacrificing artistic excellence? Opening up to motivated, enthusiastic and interested communities may be a way for festivals to develop the new income streams and audiences that directors say they want. The commitment that is built through a shared experience might well translate into a donation; at the very least participation will have increased understanding of the creative process and may encourage future attendance. Co-creation could also be a path that helps festivals to engage with migrant communities and to learn about their artistic values. Achieving audience involvement will help to provide festivals with the legitimacy that will convince stakeholders, whether political, commercial or community, to support them into the future.

Bibliography and further reading

Chen, K. (2009) *Enabling Creative Chaos: The Organization Behind the Burning Man Event*, Chicago: The University of Chicago Press.

Fabiani, J. (2011) Festivals, local and global: Critical intervention, in *Festivals and the Cultural Public Sphere*, L. Giorgi, M. Sassatelli and G. Delanty (eds.), London: Routledge, pp. 92-107.

Fonds Podium Kunsten (2012) Beleidsplan 2013-16 [Online]. Available from: www. fondspodiumkunsten.nl/nl/over_het_fonds/publicaties/beleidsplan_2013_2016_naar_ een_nieuw_evenwicht/ [Accessed 2014, July 14].

Garcia, B. (2004) Cultural policy and urban regeneration in Western European cities: lessons from experience, prospects for the future, *Local Economy*, **19**(4), 312-326.

Gelder, G. and Robinson, P. (2009) A critical comparative study of visitor motivations for attending music festivals: a case study of Glastonbury and V Festival', *Event Management*, **13**, 181-196.

Getz, D. (2009) Policy for sustainable and responsible festivals and events: Institutionalization of a new paradigm, *Journal of Policy Research in Tourism, Leisure and Events*, **1**(1), pp. 61-78.

Handy, C. (1999) *Understanding Organisations*, 4th edn, Penguin, Middlesex: UK.

Hewison, R. and Holden, J. 2011, *The Cultural Leadership Handbook: How to Run a Creative Organisation*, Farnham: Gower Publishing.

Hewison, R. (2006) *Not a Sideshow: Leadership and Cultural Value, A matrix for change*, London: Demos.

Ilczuk, D. and Kulikowska, M. (2007) *Festival Jungle, Policy Desert? Festival Policies of Public Authorities in Europe*, Warsaw: Cultural Information and Research Centres Liaison in Europe (CIRCLE).

Jancovich, L. (2013) Cultural policy in the public eye, *Journal of Policy Research in Tourism, Leisure and Events*, **5**(1), 95-98.

Jiwa, S., Coca-Stefaniak, J.A., Blackwell, M. and Rahman, T. (2009) Light Night: an 'enlightening' place marketing experience, *Journal of Place Management and Development*, **2**(2), 154-166.

Jonker, E., Saayman, M. and De Klerk, S. (2009) The role and attributes of entrepreneurs at South Africa's largest arts festival, *Pasos, Revisita de Turismo y Patrimonio Cultural*, **7**(3), 381-392.

Jordan, J. (2013) *The Buxton Festival Lifecycle: towards an organisational development model for festivals*, Discussion Papers in Arts and Festivals Management, Leicester: De Montfort University.

McCarthy, K. and Jinnett, K. (2001) *A New Framework for Building Participation in the Arts,* Santa Monica: RAND.

McGuigan, J. (2004) *Rethinking Cultural Policy,* Maidenhead: Open University Press.

Négrier, E., Bonet, L. and Guérin, M. (2013) Festivals in seven variables, in *Music Festivals in a Changing World: an international comparison,* E. Négrier, L. Bonet and M. Guérin (eds.), Paris: Editions Michel de Maule pp. 47-55.

New European Cultural Collaborations (2014) *Liteside: Festivals,* www.liteside.nl, accessed 2014, July 14.

Pine II, J. and Gilmore, J.H. (1998) Welcome to the experience economy, *Harvard Business Review,* July-August, 97-105.

Quinn, B. (2010) Arts festivals, urban tourism and cultural policy, *Journal of Policy Research in Tourism,* **2**(3), 264-279.

SAM and University of Brighton (2008) *Festivals Mean Business,* British Arts Festivals Association, London: UK.

Smith Maguire, J. and Matthews, J. (2012) Are we all cultural intermediaries now? An introduction to cultural intermediaries in context, *European Journal of Cultural Studies,* 15(5), 551-562.

Walmsley, B. and Franks, A. (2011) The audience experience: changing roles and relationships, in *Key Issues in the Arts and Entertainment Industry,* B. Walmsley (ed.), Oxford: Goodfellow Publishers pp. 1-16.

Wood, E. (2006) Measuring the social impacts of local authority events: a pilot study for a civic pride scale, *International Journal of Nonprofit and Voluntary Sector Marketing,* **11**(3), 165-179.

10 *Mladi levi* Festival – Reflections and Memories

Nevenska Koprivšek

I have always been a little suspicious about people who have never doubted themselves. Perhaps this is because, while I am still in the whirlwind of joy and enthusiasm over a new project, I am already picturing the worst-case scenarios. This state of uncertainty normally lasts until I find something that answers each doubt and at this point I begin to see the idea as realisable.

However, even I was not counting on the large number of doubters I met before the beginning of the first *Mladi levi Festival* in Ljubljana. "Another festival?" I was asked, "But why? Don't we already have enough? Who needs festivals and who actually attends them? After two or three years they all vanish into thin air anyway..." Not very encouraging. "There is too much of everything already... and in the middle of the summer? You're nuts! Nobody's there then, the theatres are all closed..." "Well, that's exactly why", I answered, "because the theatres *are* all closed, wouldn't that be the best opportunity? The venues are available and we can maybe borrow equipment; people get back from holidays and want to have somewhere to go, they want to spend some quality time socialising... Our festival will be different, open and not hermetic at all." They just doubtfully shook their heads.

It was by a lucky coincidence that at that time I met Irena Štaudohar. She had just left her editor's job at Maska magazine, as I had just left the Glej Theatre. We were both disappointed by the cynicism of the Slovenia arts scene and the politics, but at the same time full of ideas about what the theatre, what a festival could be like – a space without any bad feelings, where people meet, share, learn, get to know other cultures, other landscapes, other visions, where there is room for debate, experiment and development. An open space, where making mistakes is a legitimate possibility. After all, errors pave the way to changing ourselves and the world, right? Are we capable of admitting to ourselves that as a society we have gambled and lost? Or of finding new ways of tackling the challenges of the crisis?

Without Irena, I would probably have given up. We filled each other with enthusiasm, inspiration, got angry a lot, saved the theatre and the world every day, had fun and laughed a lot – all the things we still successfully do today and, if necessary, in one single breath. She was the one who persuaded me: "Nena, you, and only you, are capable of changing things around here!" That shook me every time. I thought she might be seeing something that I was not, but eventually I started believing in what she saw in me. I know how pathetic this sounds, but it really was quite like that. And then we sat down in a cold little office at Rimska Street 2, like in some socialist realist film (the one and only storage heater we had broke down, but the rent was more than friendly), puffing in our cold hands, dreaming and selecting the programme.

Winter went and spring came, Irena got a job as a journalist, the organisation started. I came into the office earlier and earlier and went home later and later, and it became clear to me that I could not do it by myself. Mojca Jug heard I needed help and said: "I've never done anything like this, but I'm very interested." "Let's try", I responded, "maybe we'll get along." Well, we've been getting along well for almost 15 years now. I accidentally (literally) ran into Ira Cecić in the subway at Rimska Street soon afterwards and quickly invited her upstairs. I still do not know how only the three of us managed to organise the whole first edition of the festival. I guess it was a mix of things: we were passionately devoted, the Mladinsko Theatre helped with the facilities and equipment a lot, as did the Dance Theatre Ljubljana and the Glej Theatre. We put up a completely new stage at the Ljubljana Castle, opening the festival with experimental theatre legend Ellen Stewart and Mayor Vika Potočnik. For something that hadn't existed before, it was a major accomplishment. The head technician was Dušan Kohek and the technical co-ordinator Tomaž Štrucl, with whom I used to tour (Tomaž as lighting designer and I as touring manager of Betontanc).

We pulled out our top ten touring experiences list. Initially we focused on the quality of the programme and technical conditions, but it soon became clear that the shows that had left the most lasting impression were those where we had been able to stay for more than one day, where we were able to get to know local life, artists and audiences, nature and people. So, in that spirit we chose to do things differently. To create opportunities where we could invite artists to stay with us for as long as possible, even if, in practical terms, that meant offering modest accommodation in student dormitories.

The festival came to include many distinctive features. One example was the idea of holding a picnic in the countryside, at Ulovka, which turned into a kind of trademark, the highlight of the festival, where we would take artists, volunteers, critics and festival guests. And then there was the obligatory late night meeting point in the bar Druga pomoč. It was exactly at these places that a great many friendships and new co-operations came into being, in a relaxed and hospitable atmosphere, which is so characteristic of the *Mladi levi Festival*.

Another distinctive feature the festival revealed was the importance of analysing what cultural space is missing and to make a story out of it, to find the right people for it and to turn the impossible into the possible, the possible into the realisable and the realisable into the pleasant.

There is no space? Let's find it, let's occupy it!

No international summer programme? Let's create it! No idea how to do it? We'll learn!

There is no real cultural policy? Let's face cultural policy as it is!

People don't co-operate? Let's create conditions for co-operation, let's set an example!

Throughout its life, the *Mladi levi Festival* has been an arena and an opportunity, in which to address all of these things.

Articulating change

Everything has beginnings and endings, or more beginnings and more endings. In the first few years, the *Mladi levi Festival* was closely related to the international network *Junge Hunde* (founded in 1995), in which I participated at the time when I was the artistic director of the Glej Theatre. This network focused on developing conditions for young upcoming artists to be presented and to grow, across Europe.

The 1990s, the post-war, post-independence years, were permeated with the desire for change and the faith in everything being possible. The good and the bad. The cultural space had decreased with the disintegration of Yugoslavia and artists were stifled in their local environments, but the young generation was obstinate and during the 1980s opened up international opportunities. Matjaž Pograjc, Iztok Kovač, Marko Peljhan, Emil Hrvatin, Tomaž Štrucl, Dragan Živadinov were amongst those who helped to change perceptions of the performing arts at home and abroad. Above all, this generation wanted to work differently, independent of the established practices of repertory theatres. There was a sparkling hope in the air for better times, a spirit of curiosity, discovery and travel. Contemporary dance was flourishing, the theatre too, and new names such as Matjaž Farič, Branko Potočan, Maja Delak, Mala Kline, Ivan Peternelj, Sanja Nešković Peršin, Barbara Novakovič, Goran Bogdanovski, Valentina Čabro and Diego de Brea emerged. The Junge Hunde network gave this new generation of Slovenian artists access to the international arena, with guest performances and new connections. Both the 1980s' and 1990s' generations were proving that the Slovenian contemporary performing arts wasn't confined by local boundaries and, because of their international profiles, the domestic scene could no longer ignore them.

The international scene was now interested in us. They were surprised that so much was going on in such a small place. Slovenian ministers found out about us through well-informed ministers from other countries and started to wonder what it was that made us so recognisable abroad. At the Glej Theatre it had seemed that my desire to break through was beyond reach, that it was impossible to internationalise to the point where we could host foreign artists and create spaces where the impossible would collide. That is why my departure was logical. I started anew, from nothing, on my own.

In 1997, I set up a new association, Bunker, the Slovenian version of *Junge Hunde*, and alongside it the new *Mladi levi Festival*. My intention was to open up the space, internationalise it and enable the conditions for the confrontation and exchange of ideas, for new forms of production and co-operation, learning and experimenting. Since the very beginning it was about paving the way towards new spaces, mentally and physically, and about occupying new territories, developing better working conditions, about professionalisation and transnationality, about challenging prejudice and repositioning the contemporary arts at the centre of attention.

Context: occupying a concrete and political space

For a better understanding of the context in which the *Mladi levi Festival* was born, it is necessary to discuss two other closely linked features of the Ljubljana cultural scene in the 1990s.

The first concerned the acute lack of venues able to offer a platform for new contemporary arts. At that time there were just two small venues in which to present work, the Glej Theatre and the Dance Theatre Ljubljana and, occasionally, the Culture and Congress Centre Cankarjev Dom. In response to this Bratko Bibič and I completed a study into venues in the independent sector and the possible transformation of industrial and other buildings in Ljubljana into performing and production venues for contemporary theatre, dance, visual arts and music. This survey influenced capital development in the city and became a source of success stories: Stara mestna elektrarna – now a theatre; Kino Šiška – now a centre for urban culture, especially music; Kinodvor – now an art-house cinema; and the Rog Factory, which is in the process of transforming into a space for visual arts.

A second story related to cultural policy. As it increased its critical mass, the independent scene became more important and articulate. Individual, ad hoc, sometimes passive, sometimes fierce, its actions started to coalesce into a systematic challenge to the existing elite and the public authorities. This included occupying concrete and political space. The origins of Asociacija (the Association of Arts and Culture NGOs and Freelancers) began in the early 1990s with Metelkova (Autonomous Cultural Centre) and Prostori drugačnosti (Spaces of Difference). It professionalised in 2009 when it became a legitimate partner in decision-making and in creating better working conditions for non-governmental organisations and freelance artists in the field of contemporary arts, as well as achieving regular financial support.

So, in these two areas the conditions have improved in the past two decades. By comparison with the situation in Western countries these changes are modest, slow and still fragile, but in comparison with other Eastern countries or with the Balkans, they are a source of envy. What *Mladi levi Festival* also revealed is what can be achieved when local activists nurture dialogue with and through local and international networks. In the case of *Mladi levi Festival* this was achieved through the engagement of individuals, artists and producers, including some officials, without whom the Festival could not have developed into what it is today. It can be argued that the Festival became a hallmark for artists and curators at home and abroad for its programme and the consistent raising of awareness and changing of the social, public, cultural and political perspective.

However, the promised changes are not finished. Sometimes it feels that for every step forward, we have taken three backward and at times even marching on the spot has seemed like progress. Little has changed. The reforms of the public sector never occurred; the prosperity of the 1990s has been stifled. The authorities always tolerated us, sometimes encouraged us, but were unable or unwilling to support the daring wave of the flourishing young generation from the end of the 1990s by enabling stable working conditions in which these young lions could develop their potential. Of those who have made it in the international market, their success was short lived as the market was mostly interested in new young blood.

Programme, networking, the Balkans, Europe and the world

As has been noted earlier, in culture, and especially in theatre, it is impossible to work on your own. The production and making of performances, the ways in which they are presented to and enjoyed by the audience is a collective experience. Festivals encourage this, since an atmosphere emerges and in some special way everyone becomes involved: as if the mere air sprinkles neurones of empathy. Somehow we are ready to accept, to push the boundaries of the ordinary, to look from another perspective and share more than we usually do. This is most evident at the *Mladi levi Festival*, since we make everything together. Every edition is a reflection of ideas and projects that are shared at the Bunker kitchen table (since the beginning we have cooked for each other and shared our thoughts with artists and guests, while holding a cooking spoon) and at other festivals, to which all of Bunker's creative staff are invited more and more often.

Mladi levi Festival is an expression of the fifteen or so people regularly involved in devising, promoting and producing the festival. If I have learned anything over all these years, it is that it is necessary to let go of responsibility as soon as possible, to trust and delegate work to younger colleagues, so that each can grasp, lead and execute a project as quickly as possible, considering its content and organisation, as well as being in control of the budget. Then the younger colleagues can delegate work to new colleagues and this is exactly what is happening today. Eventually everyone, working as if in a web, delegates work to others, including the volunteers. In this way, we always not only know what we are doing, but we are also spared all the things we do not need to know, and can remain calm knowing that everything will be done. That is how we can cover other people's roles when necessary, inspire, support, sometimes console each other and help each other out with refreshing new ideas. At any moment, a project can become a lot bigger than ourselves, fulfilling the heart of each of us, overcoming our egos, regardless of our position on the hierarchical ladder. Making something work together is a great source of ideas and satisfaction.

The *Mladi levi Festival* has been bigger than us for a long time now. This is especially true where the sublime and artistic are concerned and in the way it enriches the Slovenian space. But there is also this heart-felt relationship between the team members and between artists, which is contagious; and the audience, the volunteers and even the journalists get infected with it. We all somehow become more open, attentive and sympathetic.

The programming itself evolves like that too, but in the end Mojca, Irena and I have the final word. However, the selection of performances, following of certain artists and discovery of new trends is a consequence of lasting co-operation and networking in the domestic and international field. Artistic vision isn't limited by themes; we are like butterfly catchers – always alert to seize that which is relevant and up-to-date, that which would resonate with our audiences and spaces. Bunker forms part of different networks all over the world and the more the Bunker team attends seminars, festivals, network meetings, the bigger its social network becomes. First there was the mother network, the international network for contemporary performing arts IETM, our window to the world. This network connects more than 500 producers, directors, festivals, theatres and institutes; mostly from Europe, but more recently also from Africa, Canada and Asia, who are all engaged in intense transnational co-operation. Membership of this network has been an immense source of information, exchange, support, engagement and common effort. Inside this network some other, more focused consortia were born that have been particularly important for the development of the *Mladi levi Festival. Junge Hunde*, for developing young artists, for instance, and later on *Danse Bassin Méditerranée* (D.B.M.), which for a long time encouraged the development of dance in the Mediterranean area, where things often develop more slowly than in the wealthier north of Europe. The Balkan Express network is also very important to us; it has been rather informal for years, but Bunker has been strongly involved in it from the very beginning. It serves as a platform for new connections and solidarity within and with the Balkan area. The *Mladi levi Festival* focuses a lot of attention on artists from the Balkan area and for many of them it has become a stepping stone. These and other networks, and networking itself as a mode of operation, are extremely important, both for the programme itself, as well as for common efforts. After all it was through these networks that the *Mladi levi Festival* has received European Commission funding.

The current state of affairs

If the 1990s were full of energy, full of expectations, good spirits and hope for better times in creating a common space, the general atmosphere in Europe and in Slovenia today is much more oppressive. We wanted more rights and freedom, but we got markets and competition. Despair is in the air. Censorship and self-censorship are increasingly occurring at every step, not only in art but also in other social spheres. It is all rooted in our fear of acknowledging that we have failed, that greed and disdain have prevailed over compassion and empathy. Right now, when we need all the knowledge we have, as well as creativity and courage in order to face the multiplying consequences of the crisis - which is not only financial, but also social and environmental, and for which there seems to be no end in sight. We are faced with mounting budget cuts in culture, science, education and social justice, increasing nationalism, growing inequality between the handful of those who have everything and those who have less and less (or nothing at all). The gap widens between consumption and resource availability and even more so at a global level where the world order offers only weak solutions in the face of all these new challenges. Is it still possible to talk about art and culture being that last field of freedom, where change is possible? Can we do it by ourselves? I doubt it.

How to proceed?

From personal experience and perhaps because of my growing interest in the Feldenkrais Method, which promotes lifelong learning and focuses on raising awareness through movement, I believe change is possible. New mental, emotional and perceptual patterns can be achieved through breaking and re-integrating habitual patterns, and through new ways of moving and sensing. If our brain is always exposed to the same patterns, it can only react in the same way. The more we expose it to new circumstances and challenges through learning, the more neural connections it is capable of. The more space is given to developing a dynamic imagination, the more new ideas and connections are possible to make. In this way I think we are able to rearticulate ways of our social behaviour.

As I was fifteen years ago, I'm at a new crossroads, facing new challenges again. How to articulate what this common space is missing and what our new stories are? If I believe in personal change, the unused potential in each and every one of us, I can also believe that as a society we still have enormous potential for development, learning and discovering how to live together.

In the early years, Bunker was mostly associated with similar festivals and organisations, but it has become increasingly clear to us that culture and art can no longer exist only in their self-sufficient bubble and function as they have been functioning so far. Many new forms of co-operation, ideas and debates searching for common answers will be needed. Two examples of such ideas and debates are the international project Sostenuto, which explored the extent to which culture can be a strong factor for economic and social change, whilst at Bunker we investigated the possibility of the revitalisation of our immediate surroundings, the Tabor neighbourhood with its centre in Stara mestna elektrarna. Both of these indicate how it is possible to look for common local answers to global questions. We established the Cultural Quarter Tabor and, with the group prostoRož, helped to revitalise the Park Tabor (as a dynamic space for encounters and exchanges). With the Cultural Association Obrat we also helped to change the abandoned construction site at Resljeva Street into a community garden called Beyond Construction Site. We learned a lot and changed our working methods. Networking and searching for new alliances has become important not only at the international but also at the local, immediate level. Now more than ever the *Mladi levi Festi-*

val has become a meeting point and a place for contemplating different new ideas, the meeting point for artists from across the world, the expert public and local audiences, whereas through new initiatives and micro-politics we resist global phenomena.

Despite the sad predictions that the crisis has only just begun, we do not intend to give in to defeatism and apathy. The Bunker team is ready, with tentacles spread through various branches of art, culture and also education, urban planning, social welfare and ecology. We are ready for new challenges, issuing new debates and creating new tools for transformation. The *Mladi levi Festival* will remain the peak and crown of Bunker's activities and will continue to set the space for much-needed change in the shared responsibility of creating a world in which quality of life and solidarity have purpose and meaning[1].

Bibliography and further reading

Selimović, A. R. and Štaudohar, I. (2012) *LION Tales : anthology to commemorate the 15th anniversary of the Mladi Levi Festival*, Ljubljana: Bunker.

Notes

[1] This chapter is an abridged version of a longer essay published as part of *LION Tales* edited by Selimović and Štaudohar, 2012.

11 The *Diggers' Festival*: Organising a community festival with political connotations

Jacqui Norton

Introduction

This chapter examines the organisation of a community festival from an ethnographic perspective drawn from the festival organiser's viewpoint. It will provide some context on the reasons for founding the *Diggers' Festival* and examine key issues and difficulties surrounding the launch and development of a small festival that relates to historical political activities in the market town of Wellingborough, Northamptonshire, UK. As we shall see, most current political festivals in the UK tend to be events launched to commemorate historical milestones that have a political resonance. The chapter will make specific reference to the festival's funding, audiences and branding, concluding with recommendations on how to move the festival forward.

During 2010 the author was asked by the Independent Socialists of Wellingborough (ISW) to organise an evening event to commemorate the 17th century radicals known as the Diggers. As an individual with socialist leanings, the author agreed to promote the first event, which was held during March 2011, and was launched and branded as the Wellingborough *Diggers' Festival*. Even though it was in its infancy arguably only an evening event with two professional performers, Ian Saville, a magician who promotes himself as 'Magic for Socialism' (Saville, n.d.), and well-established local folk and Americana band The Old Speckled Men, booked, it was felt necessary to launch the festival name and the branding, with the aim being to produce a steady growth into the fourth or fifth years. It was essential to raise awareness of the identity and purpose of the festival amongst like-minded individuals, the local community and people from surrounding areas. The fourth festival grew from being organised solely by the author to having a committee of an additional five volunteers who coordinated an afternoon fringe event based in a town centre public house with three live music artists/bands, including punk/poet Attila the Stockbroker. A writer who had written historical fiction for teenagers, including one that takes its inspiration from Gerrard Winstanley and the Diggers, was invited as a guest speaker to present her work in the local library. The local museum hosted a week long display on the Diggers including a copy of the declaration and a copy of a field map dated 1838 identifying the location of the Bareshanks field (the site of the Wellingborough digger community). The programme for the evening event commenced with a local author Alan Moore (*V for Vendetta, Watchmen*) as a key speaker, followed by performances by two professional live bands with 'left' tendencies. In addition to the general considerations of organising a festival, for instance audience, budget, funding, licensing, entertainment and promotion, coordinating a festival with such strong socialist values was going to be a challenge because of the political connotations.

A brief history of the Diggers

To put the festival into perspective it is necessary to ascertain what and who the commemorations were for. Led by Gerrard Winstanley, the Diggers' movement was part of the radical ideology that swept England at the time of the Civil War (1642-1651); taking over common land and running it as a 'common Treasury to all' (Winstanley, [1649] 2009). Initially known as the True Levellers, they became known as the Diggers because of their involvement in cultivating land. "Among the many social, political and religious eruptions in the time of the Commonwealth was the little known Digger Movement which commenced in Surrey in 1649 and ended at Wellingborough in 1650" (unknown. 1932: 18). A declaration dated 12th March 1649 (1650) identifies nine men from Wellingborough who briefly occupied the field known as Bareshanks, off Hardwick Road, Wellingborough to plough and sow seeds for the community. This declaration emphasised the commonness of poverty in the local area and the non-existence of support for the poor people (Gurney, 2007). The document "included specific demands that reflected local needs and preoccupations" (Gurney, 2007: 188). Like Winstanley, the Diggers of Wellingborough felt that the common land belonged to the poor and this resulted in them being welcomed by the starving inhabitants of the town. "[S]everal freeholders had agreed to give up their claim to the commons, and some farmers had already offered them seed" (Jones, 1986: 7). Unfortunately, Bareshanks was used for only a short period of time before the Justice of the Peace for Northampton, Thomas Pentlow, put into force laws that were opposed to individuals intruding on other men's properties.

This resulted in "four of the Diggers [being] arrested; the remainder were dispersed with force" (unknown 1932: 20).

Arguably, the Diggers were the first socialist movement, hence the small group of like-minded people, the ISW, deciding to launch the *Diggers Festival*, the first we know of in the country, to remember all those concerned.

Political festivals in the UK

The Wellingborough *Diggers' Festival* is not the first politically themed festival to take place within the UK. During the same year as the first Wellingborough event, the northern town of Wigan, the birthplace of Gerrard Winstanley (1609) also launched their first *Wigan Diggers Festival*. The commemorations began "on a wet morning in September 2011, [when] a small group of marchers passed through the town of Wigan to Mesnes Field, a popular open space threatened with development" (Gurney, 2013: 9). The main event was held in a public house and included "speeches and talks on Gerrard Winstanley, to drink and to listen to bands and choirs including Bolton Clarion Choir singing the Digger anthem 'You Noble Diggers All'" (Gurney, 2013: 9).

In a small village in Dorset, South West England, the *Tolpuddle Martyrs' Festival* and Rally is held to celebrate "trade unionism and to remember the sacrifice of the six farm workers from the village" (Tolpuddle Martyrs' Museum, 2014a). During the period of 1834 the six men had "formed a trade union to protest their meagre pay of six shillings a week" (Tolpuddle Martyrs' Museum, 2014b), which equates to thirty pence sterling in today's money. The men were sentenced to seven years transportation to Australia. "After three years, during which the trade union movement sustained the Martyrs' families by collecting voluntary donations, the government relented and the men returned home with free pardons and as heroes" (Tolpuddle Martyrs' Museum, 2014c). Records show that commemorations for the Tolpuddle Martyrs have been in existence in one form or another since 1875 "when the Agricultural Workers Union presented an engraved watch and illuminated address to James Hammett, the only one of the six Martyrs to return to Tolpuddle" (Tolpuddle Martyrs' Museum, 2014c). Various forms of the commemorations have taken place, including the 150-year anniversary in 1984. The festival in its current form has been running since the late 1990s. It is held annually in July for three days and includes camping and a programme of numerous performances of live music, speeches, debates and poetry. Early afternoon on the Sunday there is wreath laying at Hammett's grave followed by a procession through the village with marching bands accompanied by members and supporters of various trade unions with their colourful embroidered banners. Tickets are sold for the Friday and Saturday activities, but the procession and events that follow are free and it is difficult, therefore, to provide an exact number of attendees at the 2013 event. However, during a conversation in April 2014, with Nigel Costley, Trade Union Congress (TUC) and *Tolpuddle Martyrs Festival* and Rally organiser, he stated that the "festival is licensed for 5,000 people on the main site, but it's possible the number rose to 8,000 on the Sunday which would include additional people in the [Tolpuddle] village". Sponsorship by and the support of the South West TUC branch-organised festival is obvious and apt as it is a trade union commemoration. They include, but are not limited to, the Communication Workers Union (CWU), Musicians Union (MU), National Association of Schoolmasters Union of Women Teachers (NASUWT), Unite, Unison and the Fire Brigades Union (FBU).

The *Women Chainmakers' Festival*, which commemorates an historic strike by women, celebrated its tenth anniversary in 2014. This festival is organised by the Midlands Region of the TUC and Labour-controlled Sandwell Council. In email communication on 8th May 2014 with Alan Weaver, TUC Regional Policy and Campaigns Officer for the Midlands, Weaver advised that the TUC was involved from the beginning and up to and including 2010, "the centenary of the original dispute". Since 2011 the festival has been held at Bearmore Park in Cradley Heath, the location of the 1910 dispute, "which has brought the festival back to its roots".

Another political festival organised by the TUC that is similar to the current *Diggers' Festival* is *Levellers Day*, which is held yearly over one day in May in Burford, Oxfordshire to commemorate the Levellers who had "beliefs in civil rights and religious tolerance" (Levellers Day, n.d.). This event includes speeches, debates and a procession similar to the Sunday activities at the Tolpuddle Martyrs' event.

Funding a political festival

Although the ISW assisted in paying for the first event via member subscriptions, the author felt it was imperative to organise an event that either broke even financially or raised enough money from ticket sales to cover the costs incurred and, optimistically, assist with the early financial expenses of the second event. Taking inspiration from the Diggers' ethos it was also essential that the festival was not-for-profit and therefore any monies received from the first year were to be used for the sole purpose of assisting in the funding of the following year(s).

As the festival was going to have political ideologies the suggestion of funding from the obvious partners such as the local authority, Arts Council England (ACE) or community funding organisations such as Northamptonshire Community Foundation (NCF) would not be possible. The local authority offers £500 under a Small Community Grants Scheme but states that "organisations need to demonstrate, as a minimum, a Constitution or Terms of Reference and a system for recording income and expenditure". The website continues "political parties or organisations intending to support or oppose any particular party" (Borough Council of Wellingborough, 2014) will not be considered for funding. The NCF offers grants of £500 to £5,000 which require 25% match funding, but although this funder welcomes projects that allow members of the community to act as volunteers or gain additional skills leading to future employment (all of which the *Diggers' Festival* could provide), "activities of a political nature" (NCF, 2014) will not be funded. The Heritage Lottery Fund (HLF) offers grants from £3000 to £10,000 under the Sharing Heritage Scheme that recognises heritage as including "histories of people and communities" (2013), which the *Diggers' Festival* would match, but it would need a constitution for funding to be taken to the next stage. There are financial records relating to the festival, but they are part of the ISW's bank statements and there is no separate constitution. Although it could be argued that the event was for members of the community, the bank account and any funding applications would have been in the name of or written on behalf of the ISW and although it is not a political party there are, naturally, strong links to socialist and left-wing political principles and beliefs. This being said, it is important to acknowledge that small amounts of funding have been obtained from the Co-operative Membership, Unison, Unite and the Northampton Trade Union Council, organisations that all have a natural affinity with the Digger movement and left-wing thinking.

Audience development

One of the festival's initial aims was to host an annual event and strive for a steady growth of attendees over the years. However, it is also essential to maintain the Digger ideology and, despite the need to increase the audience numbers, the key is not to focus on how many 'beers and burgers' are sold, but the issues past and present, remembrance and commemoration, to maintain the principles and hope to trigger thought and interest in the community whether political or from an historical standpoint. However, one of the key difficulties has been that the terminologies political and politics have been a barrier and a reason for not attending for some people. It was clear very early on that the ISW wanted to endorse a programme with a left-wing theme, but at the same time see the audience capacity grow and to book artists and speakers who are known on a national or international level. This is a clear goal but the objectives would be difficult to meet using the political theme within any publicity due to the limitations this puts on promoting the festival. Neither the local museum or council run library like to be linked to anything political, nor does the local shopping centre or various retailers with community boards.

> Relationships that engage with communities in the spirit of the congenial host who wishes to know and understand the other members of the community, are more likely to succeed. Consultation with community organisations further allows marketers to determine which will be the most effective method of delivering the message about the product in a timely and appropriate manner (O'Reilly and Kerrigan 2010: 63).

This has been attempted with both the Quakers and members of the Wellingborough Civic Society and the Wellingborough Archaeological and Historical Society. At least two people from the Quaker community have attended each year but, although the members of the Wellingborough Civic Society and Wellingborough Archaeological and Historical Society share an interest in the Diggers, the political theme and political publicity surrounding the events might be discouraging individuals from attending. O'Reilly and Kerrigan continue that one way to assist with audience development is to "identify and create the right point of entry for each audience member" (2010: 63). Politics can be an obstacle to people with an interest in local history, although the irony is that politics and history generally go hand-in-hand. Weaver (2014) stated that the *Women Chainmakers' Festival* is promoted as an historical event, but "speakers are encouraged to relate what they say about the present to the struggles of the Chainmakers in 1910, linking the message". Despite the challenges of moving site in 2011, which Weaver acknowledged had "consequences for footfall and attendance", the 2013 festival was estimated at 2,000 attendees. Therefore, publicising the *Diggers' Festival* as a commemoration and local historical event would no doubt encourage other members of the community and surrounding areas to attend.

Hill and Whitehead discuss the value of a membership base that consists of a group of people who have the same or similar interests and goals, such as members of interest/hobby clubs or pressure groups, and suggest that the members can assist in distributing relevant information. "The enthusiasm and commitment of members can be harnessed to 'spread the word' throughout the communities in which they live" (2004: 39). Established during 2005 the ISW has a small but dedicated membership with one particular member who is excellent at communicating with like-minded individuals on a national level via regular email bulletins. He also posts Digger updates via his Facebook page. There is also a conventional Diggers' mailing list allowing updates for to be disseminated, but the challenge still continues to see the mailing list grow in order to increase the number of ticket sales to fund additional professional performing artists and community activities.

A further issue that requires consideration is that the general age of the current audience is between 50 and 70 years of age. Arguably the older generation currently have more disposable income than the younger generation, but the festival in its fourth year has already seen some previous audience members who are now unable to attend, although there was an overall growth. While the marketing of the 2014 festival included Facebook and Twitter other forms of social media and digital platforms such as YouTube are potential promotional tools to encourage a wider demographic and younger generation. Politics is taught at some educational establishments at 'A' Level (17-18 year old students) within the UK, but lack of political understanding could also be a barrier for the younger generation. Some form of audience participation using social media could be a way forward and assist with the younger generation engaging in future Wellingborough *Diggers' Festivals*. A pipeline for developing and broadening new audiences and awareness is essential for the festival's future. The fringe events could be the beginnings of this and, reflecting the Digger philosophy, there is potential to encourage the younger generation to produce activities themselves; whether it is involvement via the use of social media, inviting a youth theatre group to perform a play on the subject, a young local band or singer/songwriter to perform or promoting a competition through the local schools using the historical theme. "Through the use of social networking platforms the arts marketer can enable audience-to-audience interaction in the generation and dissemination of stories; thus extending the experience" (O'Reilly and Kerrigan 2010: 227). The ISW did have a small youth group before the first *Diggers' Festival* was launched, but with those initially involved leaving the area to go to university this couldn't be sustained and so new contacts and relationships with the younger community need to be established.

Branding the festival

It was felt essential early on to design a logo that demonstrated some relevance to the Diggers but was also in keeping with a local theme or feature. Historically, Wellingborough is renowned for its wells and springs and these have been captured in various local logos for organisations and social clubs. However, it was felt that the wells have no direct relevance to the Diggers and therefore the concept of a wheat sheaf evolved. The wheat sheaf, a bundle of cereal crops, has a strong aesthetic reflecting the Diggers' work on the common land and furthermore a local link as it was also an image used on a local school uniform. Branding is essential and according to Rutter "the brand should effectively 'talk' to the consumer instantly, saying as much as it can" (2011: 233). The wheat sheaf is a simple logo that works well on merchandise such as t-shirts and on posters, flyers and the website, all of which will assist with the brand recognition as the festival grows. "A festival's success depends on its ability to make itself known, to maintain its brand image and to share its program with a large potential audience" (Négrier et al 2013: 121).

A number of the political festivals discussed earlier have a procession as part of their events, which acts to raise their profile locally. A procession has been considered as an additional part of the Wellingborough *Diggers' Festival* programme for the near future. It would start from the town centre, assisting in raising awareness amongst the local community, and lead to the Bareshanks field for a brief speech and memorial service (a walk of approximately two miles), meaning that it was in keeping with the festival's historical purpose. The procession would be programmed as a morning event as part of the developing Fringe.

To put the size of the audiences into perspective, the 2011 festival had an audience of 72 people and the fourth festival, which took place during March 2014, had a collective audience from the daytime and evening events reaching approximately 250 people. There is evidence that members of the committee wearing Wellingborough *Diggers' Festival* t-shirts at other events has helped to raise awareness of the brand; we have examples of people reading the Gerrard Winstanley quotations from his original writings or the Diggers' timeline on the reverse of the t-shirts and wanting to know more about the event. This has resulted in approximately a 5% increase in the audience, including one person travelling from Kendal in Cumbria in the North West of England for the third and fourth festivals. A procession might have a similar effect in raising the brand's profile in Wellingborough.

Managing regulations

There are managerial concerns though. According to Liberty (2008), a leading civil liberties and human rights organisation in the UK, the notification of the procession's date, start time, proposed route and organiser's name and address may be required in writing six 'clear' days before a procession takes place. Additional volunteers may also be required to take on the roles of stewards, depending on the number of people participating. The Public Order Act (1986) in the UK "gives the police extensive controls over processions. Organisers of most processions must give advance notice to the police. The police may impose conditions on processions and, in limited circumstances, have them banned" (Liberty 2008). One of the reasons that the local police authority should be provided with an advance notice by the organiser(s) is if the procession is to "mark or commemorate an event" (Liberty 2008). It would, therefore, be necessary to invite a local police community officer to a *Diggers' Festival* committee meeting prior to providing the relevant notice and to build relationships.

Conclusions

Reflecting on the development of the Wellingborough *Diggers' Festival*, the stable growth has allowed the organisation of the festival to be flexible and manageable in all aspects. It was essential to invite a committee of volunteers to assist in the planning and running of the additional activities as it grew. However, it is necessary to highlight that not all volunteers will have previous experience of committees, organising events or financial skills, but they will have the enthusiasm to learn and acquire some of these skills if the event is important to them. By remaining small, it also allows for the festival to continue commemorating an important part of social history within the UK and not divert from the original ethos of the festival. As identified earlier in this chapter, the festival is not-for-profit and any additional funds are used to develop the following year. Since the first festival, the finances, although small, have been in credit and this now potentially allows for the committee to apply for match funding from a number of organisations.

To bring this chapter to a close there are a number of key recommendations to consider in moving forward and developing the Wellingborough *Diggers' Festival*. It is important to emphasise that the overall aim is not to increase the attendees by thousands, but hundreds. If the audience increased by thousands then the overall organisational infrastructure would need to be altered; in addition to the current committee members, an increase in volunteers would be required and there would be additional costs such as licences for the use of local authority land. Keeping the committee small but raising awareness of the annual event could still allow for further town centre activities by inviting the retailers, community centres, public houses and so on, to host their own events as part of the fringe programme. Reflecting on this research and based on the organisation of the *Tolpuddle Martyrs' Festival* and rally and the *Women Chainmakers' Festival* the following recommendations are presented to assist with the key issues of organising a small community festival with political connotations and are presented as follows:

♦ Compose an official constitution now that there is a committee of volunteers who will establish a membership. The constitution should incorporate items such as, but not be limited to, the membership and voting powers such as the powers to raise funds and spend money on activities specific for the *Diggers' Festival* and *Fringe* and any subsidiary events associated with the original Diggers' ethos. Equally, it should include important details relating to dissolution, such as where any remaining assets would be donated i.e. a charity or social enterprise that reflects the original Diggers' ethos, which could be a homeless charity or a local food-bank.

♦ Open a new bank account that does not reflect or contain any political wording, which includes signatories of at least two members of the Consortium.

♦ Build relations with local authorities whatever their political orientations, particularly the individuals and departments that specialise in environmental health and licensing.

♦ Build relations with the local police authority and in particular the community police officers working within the town centre area.

♦ Build relations with schools and in particular the senior schools/academies that include politics in addition to history on their curriculum for 16+ year olds.

♦ Politics as a word can be a barrier for some individuals. Continue to programme the festival with performers with 'left' tendencies but promote the event as a community and historical festival.

Bibliography and further reading

Borough Council of Wellingborough (2014) Who Can and Who Cannot Apply, www.wellingborough.gov.uk/info/200047/grants/887/community_and_voluntary_grants/3 accessed 31 March 2014.

Gurney, J. (2007) *Brave Community the Digger Movement in the English Revolution,* Manchester: Manchester University Press.

Gurney, J. (2013) *Gerrard Winstanley the Digger's Life and Legacy,* London: Pluto Press.

Heritage Lottery Fund (2013) What We Fund, www.hlf.org.uk/HowToApply/programmes/Documents/SH_Application_Guidance.pdf, accessed 31 March 2014.

Hill, L. and Whitehead, B. (2004) *The Complete Membership Handbook, A Guide to Managing Members and Supports Schemes*, London, Directory of Social Change.

Jones, L. (1986) *The Digger Movement 1649*, [Pamphlet] p. 7.

Jones, T. (2014) *A Pictorial History*, www.johnleaschool.com/, accessed 31 March 2014.

Levellers Day (n.d.) About, levellersday.wordpress.com/, accessed 25 April 2014.

Liberty (2008) Marches and Processions, www.yourrights.org.uk/yourrights/the-right-of-peaceful-protest/marches-and-processions.html, accessed 25 April 2014.

Négrier, E., Boner, L. and Guérin, M. (2013) *Music Festivals in a Changing World: an international comparison*, Paris, Editions Michel de Maule. Translated from French by Andrew Dach.

Northamptonshire Community Foundation (n.d.) NCC Small Grants Programme, www.ncf.uk.com/Grants/NCCsmallgrants, accessed 25 April 2014.

O'Reilly, D. and Kerrigan, F. (2010) *Marketing the Arts a Fresh Approach*, London: Routledge p. 63, p. 227.

Rutter, P. (2011) *The Music Industry Handbook*, London: Routledge.

Saville, I, (n.d.) Magic for Socialism,www.redmagic.co.uk/, accessed 25 April 2014.

Tolpuddle Martyrs' Museum (2014a) Tolpuddle Martyrs' Festival, www.tolpuddlemartyrs.org.uk/index.php?page=martyr-s-festival, accessed 23 April 2014.

Tolpuddle Martyrs' Museum (2014b) Martyrs Story, www.tolpuddlemartyrs.org.uk/index.php?page=martyr-s-story, accessed 23 April 2014.

Tolpuddle Martyrs' Museum (2014c) History of the Festival, www.tolpuddlemartyrs.org.uk/index.php?page=history-of-the-festival, accessed 25 April 2014.

unknown (1932) Diggers at Wellingborough *The Northampton County Magazine*, **5** (49) January 18-20.

Weaver, A. (2014) Women Chainmakers' Festival to Return to Bearmore Park in Cradley Heath, womenchainmakersfestival.blogspot.co.uk/, accessed 30 April 2014.

Wellingborough Bid (2014) About Wellingborough, http://www.discoverwellingborough.co.uk/about/-wellingborough, accessed 9 May 2014.

Winstanley, G. (1649 [2009]), A Watch-Word to the City of London and the Armie, in *The Complete Works of Gerrard Winstanley Volume II*, edited by T.N. Corns, A. Hughes and D. Loewenstein, Oxford: Oxford University Press pp. 79-106.

12 Volunteering for Festivals: Why and How?

Anne-Marie Autissier

This chapter reflects on some features of a topic that is both a source of controversy as well as importance in the cultural sector, that of 'volunteering'. In 2001 Cultural Information and Research Centres Liaison in Europe (CIRCLE) published the results of a Pan-European enquiry which remains today as one of the few authoritative sources of reliable European statistical data on the subject (Dodd, 2001). This chapter will discuss the role of volunteering in different festivals and countries and provide some analysis of more recent research.

What is volunteering? A simple definition is that provided by Canadian authors Gagnon and Fortin (2002: 67): volunteers "are people who freely assume to provide a service without being paid through a group or an organisation".

Self-interest in a collective context

What motivates volunteers? According to Bernd Wagner (Ratzenböck, 2001: 33), motivations appear to have changed from one of Christian brotherly love and solidarity to a stronger connection with self-interest. However it can be argued that beyond solidarity, the idea of self-interest was already a factor in the cultural sector, for example in the motivation of volunteers with the National Trust in the UK, which has had volunteers working for it since 1895. Even here, being able to enjoy some privileged access to heritage sites and acquiring valuable knowledge was still linked to a commitment to collective usefulness.

The idea of renewing the feeling of neighbourhood and place could also be one of the key motivations for volunteering. The research completed by CIRCLE showed that people living in small urban centres or villages were generally more eager to volunteer than residents in cities (Dodd, 2001). Volunteering in one's region may be a part of an identification process, both personal and communal. While building their own identity, volunteers may help to create or recreate a sense of common belonging.

As a general observation it appears that personal reasons for supporting volunteering in the cultural sector have been the focus of limited research. Given its value throughout Europe, it would be useful to explore what motivates people to volunteer in support of an artistic or cultural activity. Some anthropologists have suggested that to remedy Western Europe's potential lack of clear political commitment, volunteering may provide an alternative activism. To people already working volunteering could be a way to reveal or develop another identity, one that could transcend daily life and its hierarchical barriers. The manager of a big French harbour, for example, who devotes his free time to a rock music festival, contributing his technical knowledge to a small team motivated by friendship, shared interests and a break from everyday pressures. Volunteering on the board of cultural associations provides some people with the opportunity to realise a passion undeveloped in paid employment. It is also a way for an individual or a community to feel involved in a cultural event and to feel a sense of ownership, as Silvanto described for many festivals in Helsinki (2009).

Volunteering cannot be investigated independently from people's positions in the labour market, nor from individual and collective representations about the legitimacy of unpaid work. As with any other individual commitment, it is also associated with people's cultural capital. In underprivileged countries, where people must manage several jobs in order to earn their living, there is little time nor will to volunteer. In the UK, CIRCLE's respondents underlined that those in paid employment were more likely to volunteer than unemployed people (Fisher and Fox 2001). By comparison, in Belgium people without professional activities give more time to volunteering. However Belgian citizens with a lower degree of education are less engaged with volunteering (Høbye 2001). The topic of employment may lead to a paradox: in the Netherlands, in a period of economic prosperity and low unemployment, women, who used to volunteer more than men, now prefer paid employment. Interestingly some Dutch national authorities responded to this by launching campaigns to promote the value of voluntary work to both volunteers and to the community (Smithuijsen, 2001). Collective history is clearly a critical factor too, not least in some countries where the word is associated with activities and a culture of control. For example the CIRCLE report noted that the word 'volunteer' – 'dobrovolstvo' – had military connotations in Bulgaria (Varbanova et al., 2001). In Poland the term 'social activist' was associated with 'mandatory volunteering' during the Communist regime (Sicinski et al., 2001).

Young people are interested in volunteering to varying degrees across Europe. The CIRCLE report noted that in Denmark and the UK younger people seldom volunteered (Høbye 2001, Fisher and Fox 2001). However volunteering in France seems to be an accepted way for young people to become a member of a group, learn and develop new skills, make connections and develop networks (Mayol 2001).

On the whole though, there seems to be a 'whiff of scepticism' about volunteering. In the analysis of employment in the cultural sector, volunteering is seen as a 'second option', as something that could hinder the professionalisation of staff or is seen as reflecting negatively on the organisation's managers for having failed to raise enough funds to employ people in a paid capacity. While most analysts admit that volunteering is often helpful, the reality is that much volunteering input is undervalued.

Volunteers as seen from festivals' managers: four case studies

As a complement to being 'undervalued', some festivals may consider volunteering as a necessary evil. Having noted that, the use of volunteering by festivals varies greatly from one to the other: the *Alkantara Festival* in Lisbon (Portugal) – a contemporary dance festival – invites volunteers to sign up through its website, as many other events also do. The biennial *Paléo Rock Festival* in Nyon (Switzerland) recruits up to 4000 volunteers to support its audience of 70,000 people, in a town with a population of 17,871 (2008 figures). The *Interceltic Festival* in Lorient (France) employs 400 volunteers for a paying audience of 300,000 (in a town with a population of 61,844). The *Wexford Opera Festival* in Ireland, which was set up in 1951 in a town with a population of about 20,000, can call on 200 local volunteers every year (for an audience of 9,500).

From Northern to Eastern Europe we surveyed four specific situations: the *Aarhus International Festi*val (Denmark), the *Holland Dance Festival* in The Hague (Netherlands), the *International Book Festival* in Edinburgh (Scotland, UK), the International Dance and Theatre *Divadelna Nitra Festival* in Nitra (Slovakia). To each of the festivals' organisers, we posed the same questions, including: "Why do you recruit (or not) volunteers?" and "How do you evaluate the value of volunteering input to the management of your activities?"

Aarhus Festival

The *Aarhus Festival* is a multidisciplinary event that takes place in the second city of Denmark. Beside its permanent team of ten people the festival employs a hundred people as volunteers before and during the event (late August, early September). Volunteers are mainly women (70%), most of whom are between 50 and 60 years old. The second largest group are young people between 25 and 35 years old. All social groups are represented and half of the volunteers return the following year.

According to Marie Overgaad, the festival volunteer manager, recruitment of new volunteers occurs through the website and through personal recommendation by existing volunteers. The festival reviews a potential volunteer's CV, but no interview process is used in making a final selection. Volunteers undertake one or more of the following tasks: greeting the public, answering the telephone, serving food and drink, running the festival's event information and communication services. Some others provide guiding or babysitting services during the event. Volunteers receive free meals and free tickets for selected shows, and a party is organised for them before and after the event. They are considered pivotal to the festival operation, but local residents do not see their participation as a source of greater engagement.

Holland Dance Festival

The Hague-based *Holland Dance Festival* (HDF) is delivered by a regular team of three paid staff, a further nine temporary staff and two trainees recruited every year. HDF also employs 40 to 50 volunteers before and during the event. 90% of these are women, aged between 25 and 35 years old. The group also includes a few retired people. 80% of volunteers come from the cultural sector and have participated in other artistic events. The new volunteers are recruited by the old ones or through dance and music schools, or yet again through interpersonal nomination. The festival also receives unsolicited applications.

In 2007 the management team introduced a recruitment process on the festival's website. As it has developed significantly over the past few years, input by volunteers has become essential. Volunteers are responsible for greeting audiences and artists, information and communication services, security and logistics. A small number of volunteers are involved with costume design, make up and building work. Volunteers receive free show tickets and free meals in return for their work. Their travel expenses are also covered if needed. While managers admit that the input of its volunteers is critical, they identify some pitfalls: relying on volunteers is risky because there is no guarantee that their commitment will last. Moreover, running the recruitment process is time-consuming. Volunteers lack day-to-day knowledge of the festival and its culture and priorities, so volunteers need guidance on how to integrate themselves into the workplace and to make an effective contribution; they need to be managed. "Volunteers are not stakeholders in the festival design and we need to be aware of that", our respondents wrote. They do agree though that working with volunteers is a good opportunity. Nevertheless, they are not sure whether that contribution has any impact on increasing the engagement with the festival by local residents.

Edinburgh International Book Festival

The managers of the *Edinburgh International Book Festival* expressed a different point of view as regards volunteering. They employ a regular team of 12 people and another hundred people on a seasonal basis but no volunteers. They agree that volunteer recruitment would be a good idea especially as some volunteers are particularly productive. However, the process always carries a risk of disappointment, no matter how much time is devoted to recruitment and interviews. For example, young volunteers may think that volunteering is akin to play and become disheartened when challenges with the work occur. Festival managers emphasise that the pressures and workloads mean that volunteers have to be 100% reliable, otherwise the festival and the audience's experience may suffer. Lastly, respondents from *Edinburgh International Book Festival* stressed that the demands made of volunteers cannot be the same as those applied to paid employees and that *Edinburgh International Book Festival* is 'proud' to pay for the work done.

Divadelna Nitra Festival

As a comparison the *Divadelna Nitra Festival* in Slovakia values volunteering highly and gives special attention to volunteers. The festival employs six paid staff members, 10 to 20 seasonal people, a dozen trainees for three to eight weeks, as well as 80 volunteers, of whom 70% return the following year. Men account for one eighth of the people employed and the average age for trainees is 21. Most of the volunteers are students from Nitra universities and the Bratislava Music and Theatre Academy. The festival recruits volunteers through its website as well as through classified ads in specialised papers, the local press and student publications. Word of mouth also works well with the recruitment of students.

After reviewing their academic CVs, young applicants receive an initial interview. They are recruited before and during the festival, and five of them stay a further week at the end of the festival. They are responsible for greeting the audience, information and communication services, security, logistics and ticketing. According to respondents from *Divadelna Nitra Festival*, some are given additional opportunities to become involved creatively through working on aspects of the programme. In return all receive free tickets for shows as well as free room and board if needed. An evening party, including a concert, is organised for them after the festival. They are encouraged to stay in touch with the festival team as well as the other volunteers.

According to the festival's managers, volunteers are the main talent pool from which *Divadelna Nitra Festival* hopes to recruit new employees. It sees volunteers as contributing to the festival and its culture through their informal friendliness, openness and enthusiasm. They are also an important source of new ideas and a pool of potential new employees – translators, interpreters, cultural producers, etc. They are a 'source of inspiration and progress'. Not that this occurs without commitment of time by the festival's managers who have allocated special attention to volunteers as part of their human resource management. *Divadelna Nitra Festival* staff also recognise that the same levels of performance cannot be expected of their volunteers compared to those in paid employment. Sometimes volunteers lack a professional edge, knowledge and experience.

Nevertheless, *Divadelna Nitra Festival*'s managers are convinced of the beneficial impact of volunteers on the local population. Volunteers persuade their own families into attending the festival and they and their families subsequently become part of the future loyal audience. In addition, local associations and organisations view the fact that the festival provides such good opportunities to so many young people favourably. Festival managers also noted that some young volunteers decide to stay in Nitra after their voluntary work at the festival and develop a career in the city.

Volunteers: the dilemma

The need to understand and question the benefits that can be derived from volunteering is a crucial one. Taking account of the reluctance of the *Edinburgh International Book Festival* managers to employ volunteers, it is clear that employment of volunteers requires an appropriate and robust framework within which to integrate volunteers and to channel their energy, knowledge and enthusiasm; this should be a core requirement for all festivals. Furthermore, given the fact that volunteers offer a kind of short-term or unpredictable contribution, perhaps the number of volunteers that can be employed in a professional organisation should be carefully evaluated. In Hungary, Inkéi and his colleagues found that 50% of the staff in the festivals that they documented were volunteers (Hunyadi et al. 2006). This figure is a product of the fact that, rather than support festivals financially, local authorities offer festivals 'free labour' in the form of their own employees, during their daily work.

This kind of agreement, which does not enable festivals to select their own volunteers, is not ideal and looks like an excuse not to subsidise festivals. Even if some public employees are happy to contribute and their activity turns out to be satisfactory, such a large proportion of volunteers seems to be problematic for a festival's sustainability in the long term. However, according to Négrier's (2008) survey of 86 dance and music festivals for France Festivals, no precise correlation could be established between the numbers of permanent staff and volunteers. Their work also showed that between 2000 and 2007 the number of volunteers had increased globally by 20.4%, Négrier noted that three festivals had cancelled any form of volunteering, however, and that eight of them were relying upon it less. Moreover, those who did report a reliance on volunteering also reported difficulty in sustaining their input – they ran out of steam.

As the CIRCLE report (Dodd, 2001) suggests, now could be the time to provide volunteers with official status and support, for example by offering them training opportunities. The skills acquired by volunteers could be recognised, as well as those of cultural associations working with volunteers, in an effort to help those volunteers with the development of their professional career. An efficiently managed welfare and tax system that encouraged volunteers could also be set up, and the skills of the Young European Volunteers[1] could be taken into account in national skill reviews. Germany, the Netherlands, the UK and Italy seem to have developed some regulations that apply to the field, as well as Canada, where recent developments have made it possible for school children and students to undertake voluntary work as part of their studies.

Conclusions

As a conclusion to this modest survey, it is important to analyse the situation of volunteering not only from a professional viewpoint but also from a social and cultural perspective. Volunteering is a social and cultural phenomenon that has seen continuous increase in importance since the beginning of the 20th century, notably through the first national and international associations which fought for peace, women's rights and so on, to the point that volunteering has become one of society's most distinctive qualities.

Today it plays different roles. In individualistic societies, volunteering appears to be a key contribution to social activism across a wide of topics. Beyond its contribution to professional activities, volunteering seems to have great value in itself. "This socialisation relies on individual differences and affirmation of personal characteristics and particularities; each with multiple partial and often transitional identities" (Elbaz et al. 1996: 75). The type of commitment that it requires and delivers stands in contrast to current productivism. From this perspective, volunteering could act as an indicator of cultural citizenship and as a possible way of breaking borders between professionals and amateurs, in the positive definition that Bernard Stiegler gives to this last word (Stiegler 2004). Efficiently integrated in a professional team, volunteers can make an outstanding contribution to new forms of participative cultural activities.

Bibliography and further reading

Dodd, D. (2001) The extent of volunteerism in the cultural sector in Europe (Presentation of the CIRCLE questionnaire results), *Volunteers at the Heart of Culture: Culture, Civil Society and Volunteerism in Europe,* Conference Report, R. Fisher (ed.), Barcelona: Cultural Information and Research Centres Liaison in Europe (CIRCLE), available from: www.circle-network.org/wp-content/uploads/2010/09/Conference-Reader4.pdf.

Elbaz, M., Fortin, A. and Laforest, G. (1996) *The Boundaries of Identity. Modernity and Postmodernity in Quebec,* Sainte-Foy: Presses de l'Université Laval.

Fisher, R. and Fox, R. (2001) Country report: United Kingdom, *Volunteers at the Heart of Culture: Culture, Civil Society and Volunteerism in Europe,* Conference Report, R. Fisher (ed.), Barcelona: CIRCLE, p.64, available from: www.circle-network.org/wp-content/uploads/2010/09/Conference-Reader4.pdf.

Gagnon, E. and Fortin, A. (2002) L'espace et le temps de l'engagement bénévole : essai de définition, *Nouvelles Pratiques Sociales,* **15**(2), 66-76.

Høbye, L. (2001) Country report: Denmark, *Volunteers at the Heart of Culture: Culture, Civil Society and Volunteerism in Europe,* Conference Report, R. Fisher (ed.), Barcelona: CIRCLE, p.40, available from: www.circle-network.org/wp-content/uploads/2010/09/Conference-Reader4.pdf.

Hunyadi, Z., Inkei, P. and Szabó, J.Z. (2006) *Festival-World Summary Report: national survey on festivals in hungary including deliberations on public funding, evaluation and monitoring,* KultúrPont Iroda and Budapest Observatory, Budapest.

Mayol, P. (2001) Country report: France, *Volunteers at the Heart of Culture: Culture, Civil Society and Volunteerism in Europe,* Conference Report, R. Fisher (ed.), Barcelona: CIRCLE, p.42, available from: www.circle-network.org/wp-content/uploads/2010/09/Conference-Reader4.pdf.

Négrier, E. and Jourda, M. (2008) Les nouveaux territoires des festivals, *France Festivals,* Paris: Michel de Maule.

Ratzenböck, V. (2001) Country report: Austria, *Volunteers at the Heart of Culture: Culture, Civil Society and Volunteerism in Europe*, Conference Report, R. Fisher (ed.), Barcelona: CIRCLE, p.30, available from: www.circle-network.org/wp-content/uploads/2010/09/Conference-Reader4.pdf.

Sicinski, A., Gurba, J. and Ilczuk, D. (2001) Country report: Poland, *Volunteers at the Heart of Culture: Culture, Civil Society and Volunteerism in Europe*, Conference Report, R. Fisher (ed.), Barcelona: CIRCLE, p.54, available from: www.circle-network.org/wp-content/uploads/2010/09/Conference-Reader4.pdf.

Silvanto, S. (2009) City residents' participation in arts festivals: case Helsinki, in *The Europe of Festivals: From Zagreb to Edinburgh, intersecting viewpoints*, A. Autissier (ed.), Toulouse: France: editions de l'attribut / Culture Europe International, pp. 113-124.

Smithuijsen, C. (2001) Country report: The Netherlands, *Volunteers at the Heart of Culture: Culture, Civil Society and Volunteerism in Europe*, Conference Report, R. Fisher (ed.), Barcelona: CIRCLE, p.60, available from: www.circle-network.org/wp-content/uploads/2010/09/Conference-Reader4.pdf.

Stiegler, B. (2004) Amateur, *Ars Industrialis association internationale pour une politique industrielle des technologies de l'espri*, [Online]. Available from: arsindustrialis.org/amateur-english-version.

Varbanova, L., Viacheva, N. and Tomova, B. (2001) Country report: Bulgaria, *Volunteers at the Heart of Culture: Culture, Civil Society and Volunteerism in Europe*, Conference Report, R. Fisher (ed.), Barcelona: CIRCLE, p.36, available from: www.circle-network.org/wp-content/uploads/2010/09/Conference-Reader4.pdf.

Notes

[1] Open to young people between 18 and 28 years of age the European Volunteer Service is part of the Youth in Action EU programme. The Grundtvig, another EU programme, also supports a European Senior Voluntary Service.

13 Festival City – Rotterdam

David Dooghe

In an environment that sees cities vying to attract people, businesses and investments in increasingly competitive markets, many municipalities have identified place identity and image as parts of their unique selling point. The high profile and collaborative nature of festivals means that they are seen by city marketing bodies as an important tool in shaping and widening awareness of the unique qualities of their city's particular cultural and built environments. The extent to which an audience identifies with a festival or a city (and are willing to invest time and money) strongly determines how successful both the festival and the city's further development will be. Accordingly, festivals are being placed at the heart of strategic development of some cities' physical and human infrastructures.

Festival City - Rotterdam is an urban design study that researches the symbiotic collaboration between festivals and urban development to see how they can forge stronger identities for each by working collaboratively. The specific communities that organise and support festivals in Rotterdam are central in this study's findings. Community involvement, the visibility of the festival between editions and the specific audience appeal strongly influence how festivals can be used to catalyse the relationship between the social and urban structure of a city. Without the fertile ground provided by a supporting community, a festival will not flower.

This chapter will examine this strategy in more depth, using two festival case studies from Rotterdam: the *Caribbean Summer* in the Afrikaanderwijk and an example of urban theatre on the Coolsingel. It will also consider *Soundpiece*, an ongoing project on the Schouwburgplein. These case studies and their relationship with Rotterdam's urban development plans are described below.

Rotterdam and its festivals

Rotterdam is a festival city: it is a city where the possibilities of the temporary event are optimally used; where experiments are undertaken and new concepts are developed. Due to this laboratorial function, in which temporary events can mature and in their full maturity can be tested in the daily situation, new elements can be added to the city in an 'almost natural' way. In this way, the different manifestations, events and festivals create a surplus value and become important test sites for the social, spatial and cultural structure of Rotterdam (De Winter, 1988: 13).

Following World War Two, in which its city centre was heavily bombed, Rotterdam pursued a policy of organising events and temporary constructions to keep its city centre vibrant (De Winter ,1988: 7) and to test the popularity of specific urban amenities (De Winter, 1988: 12). There is a clear and strong connection between the identity of events and the urban redevelopment plan during this period. In the *Ahoy'* (1950) and *E55* (1955)[1] events, Rotterdam celebrated the rebuilding of the harbour and the city after the destruction caused by the war. *C70*, the last large event in the city's redevelopment, took place in 1970, a time when the Dutch population was protesting against the large scale development of the Netherlands, demanding that their cities should be more liveable. With *C70*, the organisers wanted to bring people together through communication (De Winter, 1988: 109). As the city has continued to expand, less space has been left undeveloped, potentially putting the strong unity and cooperation between the city festivals' organisers, artists and architects at risk.

The Spatial Development Strategy 2030

In the Spatial Development Strategy 2030 (Gemeente Rotterdam, 2007), Rotterdam presents itself as an attractive, living city. By building new residential areas and improving the public space, Rotterdam has tried to attract the middle and upper classes to come and live in the inner city. The post war 'viable society' ideology is still very apparent in this document, but the experience that festivals can offer residents and audience is largely ignored, even though studies have shown that two-thirds of Rotterdam's residents visit its festivals and the average visitor defines him or herself as middle class (Rijpsma et al., 2006: 44).

The experiences that festivals offer contribute to the bond that residents have with their city. Rotterdam has a wide variety of festivals and temporary events, ranging from classical concerts in the old harbours, to car races in the inner city; from the marathon to a 'wine and dine' festival. There are some large festivals that attract hundreds of thousands of people, and there is a broad base of small, niche, award-winning festivals spread all over the city. In 2012, Rotterdam Festivals, the organisation responsible for the city's events policy, supported a total of 59 events relating to specific aspects of the city: maritime, youth, multiculturalism, modern architecture, (international) culture and sports. These were attended by approximately two million visitors in total. One third attracted fewer than 5000 visitors; just over half between 5000 and 50,000 and 9% attracted more than 50,000 visitors (Rotterdam Festivals, 2013). In short, Rotterdam has something to offer the whole year round. For this reason, urban development and festivals should find ways to collaborate symbiotically.

Symbiosis as a strategy

Festivals are the moments of self-celebration of a community (Dayan, 1997).

It is clear that festivals can play a role in urban development; the question is how? "Each ... festival consists of a number of cooperating and conflicting groups of players, forming together a dense latticework of human relations, temporally coexisting in the same time-space capsule" (Dayan, 1997). When thinking about festivals, most people only consider this time-space-capsule, which is the moment where the audience meets the performer. Behind the festival, however, there is an important driving force: the community, for they are the people who prepare the festival and grow with it.

This community is more than merely a group of people with a shared interest; it also has a spatial component. The group of people become a community when they claim a space to meet, prepare and celebrate. The community is essentially the component that creates continuity between festival editions. After all, the festival only exists due to the existence of the community. By supporting their festivals, the city can assist the communities in developing roots. This is the starting point of the symbiotic collaboration between the city and a community/festival. The relationship may create space for the community to further expand, to become breeding grounds, places and institutions that nurture artistic ambition and creative entrepreneurship in the city, attracting new programmes and developing new uses for public space. They can also become the triggers for gentrification processes.

During the festival, the community becomes a part of the public sphere. It is, therefore, important that the city invests in urban meeting spaces where the audience and performers can meet and celebrate the rich diversity of the different communities.

Case study 1: *Caribbean Summer, Afrikaanderwijk*

This case study illustrates how a community-supported festival can be a catalyst for the future development of a district.

Initiated in 1984, the *Rotterdam Summer Carnival* grew to become one of the largest multicultural events in Western Europe, attracting close to a million (inter)national visitors each year before merging with *Rotterdam Unlimited* in 2013. The annual city centre procession involves months of invisible preparation. In order to root the event in the city, it is important that it has a 'breeding ground' where the festive atmosphere can be kept visible throughout the year.

Every year, the *Summer Carnival* selects a new Carnival Queen: but where in Rotterdam is her kingdom to be found? Looking at the social, cultural and demographic data, the district of Afrikaanderwijk could become the perfect breeding ground in which to create a cultural incubator for the communities that are connected by the *Summer Carnival*. The district has a large proportion of Antillean, Surinamees and Cape Verdian inhabitants, a popular weekly multicultural market and it has the ambition to further develop as a 'meet and eat' district.

Presently, the preparation of the festival consists of making the costumes, building the floats, rehearsing the choreography for the procession and the accompanying music. This takes place in separate private locations all over the city throughout the year. The legacy of each carnival is hard to demonstrate to a wider audience because after the event the physical results of this hard labour are dispersed and appear to vanish. This happens because the groups of people preparing the carnival have no shared space in which to prepare and present the costumes or to rehearse the dance and the music for the procession, which in turn hinders any opportunity to learn from each other or to simply meet between editions. Additionally, out of sight often means out of mind and there is a danger that the carnival, its ambience and beneficial impacts, may be forgotten by the wider public who are not part of the core community.

It is therefore important that the festival programme, whether long term or temporary, is concentrated in order to maintain the tradition and ensure that innovation can take place. Adding new programmes that are connected to the *Summer Carnival* (but not necessarily happening at the same time) could support the festive atmosphere in the district throughout the year. These new programmes could improve innovation by learning and sharing knowledge, for example by offering dance and music schools in which to rehearse, stages on which to perform or encouraging greater attention from local media such as local radio stations to raise the carnival's public profile and public engagement throughout the year. Furthermore, the programmes could create more opportunities for the community to gather, making use of public spaces such as function halls to celebrate cultural or religious holidays.

Figure 13.1: Artist's impression of the daily use of a multifunctional urban location in Afrikaanderwijk.

Figure 13.2: Artist's impression of the Summer Carnival taking place in a multifunctional urban location in Afrikaanderwijk.

The case study has revealed that the process works best if there are at least two developmental phases. The first phase is the experimental phase. A cultural incubator is placed in a discrete area of the district where there is no economic pressure to (re)develop. The entire programme (temporary and long term) is then concentrated in this cultural incubator. If a festival develops and the inhabitants of the district adopt it, then the second 'expansion' phase can start. In the second phase, the programme spreads over the entire district in order to connect itself to the people in the district. In both phases, the design will create multifunctional (in space and time) urban locations for different people and activities.

Case study 2: Rotterdam urban theatre

When mapping Rotterdam's festivals, the Coolsingel stands out for the sheer number and variety of festivals that take place there throughout the year. In 2006 this street hosted ten cultural and five large sports events (Rotterdam Festivals 2006). The Coolsingel is the main boulevard of Rotterdam and home to the City Hall, the World Trade Centre and the main shopping area. What is surprising is that pedestrian traffic along the Coolsingel was very low.

For this case study, the urban plan perceives the city centre as a theatre, with the Coolsingel as a multi-purpose stage at its heart; a public place that invites people to see and to be seen and offers multiple use for urban life during and between the events. All festivals have their own specific target groups and a coherent programme of festivals on the Coolsingel could help transform it into Rotterdam's central meeting space. During research into larger urban festivals that take place in a concentrated area for one or more days it was noted that these festivals usually take place in two areas: the area where the main activities take place, the so-called 'thrillzone'; and a second area, the 'chillzone', where the visitor can experience the main activities from a distance whilst enjoying the supporting services including catering, shops, small exhibitions, etc. These supporting services do not necessarily have to be temporary and organised by the festival itself; they can also be part of the daily urban function of the city. With this in mind, the public space of this boulevard needs to become more pedestrian friendly and attractive for people to use. Festivals could give the Coolsingel a new dimension as a 'thrillzone'.

In the proposed design for this case study, the space for vehicle traffic would be decreased, while the space for pedestrians would be increased. In the middle of the street, a water element with two basins would be introduced. During the day, these basins communicate, bringing the idea of the riverside back to the heart of this port city. The changing water levels would create different possibilities of contact with the water. People could play in the water or walk and rest along it. During other events, these basins could be drained, creating an urban atrium or a lowered festival street. Alternatively, they could also be completely filled with water, giving opportunities for water festivals.

Figure 13.3: Artist's impression of the Coolsingel as a site for a parade in Rotterdam.

Figure 13.4: Artist's impression of the Coolsingel as the central meeting space of Rotterdam in winter.

The routes of the street would be changed, so that the high-rise panorama of the Weena, the City Hall, the old harbour, the main flagship stores of the shopping area and the Erasmus Bridge could be viewed better while driving through the city. During the festivals, these buildings could also create an attractive backdrop for specific festivals/events. Like in a theatre, the foyer is the space between the stage, the 'thrillzone' of the festival and the entrance, parking garages and public transport stops. The foyer of the city is the 'chill-zone' of the festivals: in this zone, shops, restaurant and cafés add to and support the audience's experience of the whole festival.

Figure 13.5: Artist's impression of the Coolsingel as the central meeting space of Rotterdam in summer.

Case Study 3: Soundpiece, Schouwburgplein, learning from practice

Whilst not a festival, this case study explores the ways that urban spaces can be designed to support festivals.

Soundpiece, is a sound installation that is located below the Schouwburgplein in Rotterdam and has had an interesting effect on the audience. Although we are not always aware of it, sound constantly surrounds us in cities. The sounds of the city have changed over the past decades however. New technology and machines create constant noise, which makes it more difficult for us to recognise or locate a specific sound and its source. We therefore no longer fully experience all the aspects of the city. The size of the installation (a 30 metre x30 metre square) has created the effect that when people walk over it they are totally immersed in the sound of the installation. When people recognise a sound, they stop and look around, hoping to find the source which they can't immediately identify. As a result of this hidden quality, the audience experiences the Schouwburgplein in a different way. Could the adjacent cultural institutions (the concert hall, theatre and cinema), be strengthened through sound to emphasise it as the cultural hub of Rotterdam?

The bottom-up approach

Soundpiece is an experimental project in several respects. Firstly, it is the only sound-installation in the world that is permanently installed, open for everybody to use and in a public space. Many installations only combine two of these aspects: there are temporary installations in the public space, used during festivals by different sound artists. There are permanent installations in public spaces that have a continuous sound, but do not allow for different users. Lastly there are permanent installations in museums or galleries that are used by different sound artists. *Soundpiece* is also a project that is strongly dependent on other participants for its success. For these reasons, it was decided that only an open, experimental and participative bottom-up approach was appropriate.

Soundpiece was originally installed temporarily on Schouwburgplein in 2006 by the artists Jasper Niens, Kamiel Verschuren and Thijs Ewalts as part of the *Poetry International Festival*. It was rarely used after this, however, so in 2009 *Rotterdam Festivals* bought the work and I was appointed as its curator.

From the outset it was clear that by using varied sounds related to cultural initiatives in Rotterdam, *Soundpiece* could promote the rich and diverse cultural life in the public space and strengthen the Schouwburgplein as the urban cultural hub of Rotterdam. A sound artist was commissioned to initiate the project during the ten days of the 2010 *International Film Festival* (one of the largest annual festivals in Rotterdam). Other larger festivals such as *Motel Mozaïque* followed and the audience became aware of the installation and its potential.

By 2011, *Soundpiece* was connected to the internet and could live stream sounds recorded from any location to be heard at the installation in the Schouwburgplein. In collaboration with *Poetry International Rotterdam*, *Soundpiece* launched *Lunch with Poetry*, the first stream that plays poetry from all over the world, every weekday between 12.00 and 14.00. Between 2011 and 2013 sound artists Pierre Bastien, Zeno van den Broeck, Georgios Papadakis, Dyane Donck, Sjaak Douma, Falk Hubner, Gerben Kokmeijer, Ronald Rote, Jorg Schellekens, Peter Sterk, Jan Wirken and Rutger Zuydervelt created soundscapes specifically for the installation. This added a new layer to the potential of *Soundpiece* and the goal now is to organise an annual sound gallery, which will exhibit soundscapes from different sound artists.

In 2012, a wooden floor, a small stage and benches replaced the slippery metal square floor above *Soundpiece*. The installation, which was initially mostly experienced as a temporary event when passing through the square, could now also be encountered for longer periods of time while sitting on the benches. This enlarged the influence that the installation had on the public and changed the aesthetic experience. The sounds could not be as repetitive as when people were just walking across the square. Together with the positioning of the permanent stage on the square, the technical possibilities of the sound installation were enlarged to make it easier to use the installation's speakers for performances.

The future position of Schouwburgplein as the urban cultural hub is strongly connected to how people use the square and to what extent this public becomes an audience. People cross it diagonally, they enter or exit the underground parking garage, they meet there before going into the cinema or they sit on the benches to enjoy the sun or to let their children play in the fountain. As many of these activities are short term and take place throughout the whole day, short-term events on the square cannot count on passersby to gather an audience. Experience has shown that the average user of Schouwburgplein is more attracted to installations than performances. Due to this, the programme concept of Schouwburgplein is shifting its focus from a stage with public performances, to a stage with objects, where the public are the performers as well as being the audience.

Conclusions

The two festival case studies and the *Soundpiece* project demonstrate that the Festival City Strategy, which supports festivals as celebrations of the community, has the potential to work as a tool for developing different urban areas into 'breeding grounds', 'urban theatres' and 'urban hubs'. By doing so, Rotterdam would become a more festival-friendly city that offers its visitors new opportunities to explore the different breeding grounds, to spectate at the urban theatres and to gather at the urban hubs. These three creative zones, opened up or specifically shaped by urban planners and used by the communities and audiences, should be capable of presenting a variety of events, whilst remaining vibrant public areas in themselves.

With respect to the development process, *Soundpiece* illustrates that due to its clear goals and its open, experimental and participative process, its bottom-up approach has been successful. The flexibility within the process of *Soundpiece* has ensured that the installation could gradually build up a community of different users and be updated to accommodate the needs and wishes of these users. In this way, *Soundpiece* can gradually strengthen the Schouwburgplein as an urban cultural hub for Rotterdam by serving as a source of surprise for the public on the square, or of information about the programmes of adjacent cultural institutions.

Bibliography and further reading

Dayan, D. (1997) In Quest of a Festival, *National Forum*, **77**(4), 41-47.

De Winter, P. (1988) *Evenementen in Rotterdam: Ahoy, E55, C70,* Rotterdam: Uitgeverij 010.

Gemeente Rotterdam (2007) *Stadsvisie Rotterdam, ruimtelijke ontwikkelingsstrategie 2030,* Rotterdam: Gemeente Rotterdam.

Rijpsma, S.G., de Graaf, P.A., de Vries, C. and Bik, M. (2006) *Rotterdammers in hun vrije tijd,* Rotterdam: Centrum voor Onderzoek en Statistiek.

Rotterdam Festivals (2006), *Jaarsverslag 2006,* Rotterdam: Rotterdam Festivals.

Rotterdam Festivals (2013) *Jaarsverslag 2012,* Rotterdam: Rotterdam Festivals.

Notes

[1] *Ahoy* was a manifestation held from June–October 1950 to celebrate the recovery of the port as a world port and Rotterdam as a metropolis. It housed various pavilions in which trade, industry and art shows were exhibited (De Winter 1988: 8). *E55* was a national event held in Rotterdam between the March and May 1955. It showcased Rotterdam as the 'source of energy' in the post-war redevelopment of the Netherlands (De Winter 1988: 43).

FOCUS ON FESTIVALS

SECTION 3
IMPACTS, COMMUNITIES
AND PLACES

Introduction

Chris Newbold

In the most difficult moments of festival organisation and management, the question inevitably arises, why are we doing this? The answer that often emerges is either configured as a desired impact, a required output, or in the form of some altruistic motivation. Often it is a combination of all three that is sufficient a driver to push the endeavour on to its conclusion. In this section of the book we focus on some of these impacts, both desired and unforeseen, we look at the communities who run and benefit from festivals, and examine the wider effects of festivals on the places that are transformed by serving for a period as their hosts.

As the chapters included in this section and elsewhere in the book demonstrate, there is an increasing preoccupation with impacts in the study of festivals. As the 'modern' era of festival activity has got into full swing, commercial interests, tourism tsars, local authority functionaries, now all vie for occupancy of the high ground held by festivals in their locale, and seek to bend them to their own agenda, targets and ends. Dragan Kliać is critical of this development, stating that:

> the popularity of festivals is generated by the dominance of the economic perspective on culture, seen not any longer for its inherent value and as an investment in the quality of citizenship and vibrancy of the community, but for its earning potential. Economic impact studies aim to convince funders and sponsors that festivals create significant economic benefits, boost consumption and expand employment. (Klaić, 2014: 31 – 32)

Richards and Palmer in *Eventful Cities* are particularly strong on examining and measuring the way that cities are increasingly designing events to deliver complex ranges of cultural, social and economic impacts: "Events have important cultural, social, economic and image impacts for the places that host them. These impacts are ultimately the reason why places want to stage events and the stimulus for increasing numbers of events being held around the globe." (2010: 380)

Katherine Winkelhorn, in Chapter 14, considers the *Holstebro Festuge* (*Holstebro Festive Week*) in Denmark. This festival occurs every third year, and started in 1989 as a celebration for its founding organisations' 25th anniversary. Odin

Teatret, founded in Olso in Norway, moved to Holstebro, Denmark in 1966, as the Nordic Theatre Laboratory. Its guiding principles are based on cultural diversity and 'barter'[1]. Thus it brings together over nine days the local inhabitants with performers, both national and international, to participate in a range of activities within a theatre framework. Whilst reflecting on the changing character of the 'week', Winkelhorn is mainly concerned with its longer term impacts in enriching the city, as well as examining how it has influenced its citizens. Many of the leading citizens she interviews are united by their concerns with the festival delivering cultural a 'good' which they see as having a knock-on-effect on the viability of the city, both commercially and socially. An important concept for understanding and thinking about the role of festivals that emerges here is the idea of 'encounter'; international professionals 'encounter' local amateurs, institutions 'encounter' citizens, performers 'encounter' audiences and neighbour 'encounters' neighbour. She utilises Robert Putnam's (2006) concept of social capital to great effect here as well, pointing us to the importance of festivals in enabling us to 'bridge' to people and cultures that are different to ourselves. Both these notions of 'encounter' and 'bridging' will emerge again in other discussions in this section. Similarly, by using Mikhail Bakhtin's (1984) analysis of the transformative nature of carnival, Winkelhorn sees the key to Festive Week being its relationship to the culture and logic of carnival, allowing new human relations to develop, roles to be reversed and new types of experiences to emerge during the activities of everyday life. The result or impact of the 'invitation' that *Holstebro Festival Week* extends is, for Winkelhorn, the strengthening of local democracy, the establishment of partnerships, the creation of networks and the development of new bonds between people.

In Chapter 15, Luisella Carnelli provides a case study of research practice into festival impacts and analyses those impacts in her report on the *Bassano Operaestate Festival*, Veneto. Founded in 1981 the festival takes place in July and August in the Veneto Hills; it features contemporary dance, theatre and opera, focusing on new contemporary artists both nationally and internationally based. Carnelli takes up some of Winkelhorn's analysis of audiences and impacts, specifically examining the cultural impact generated by the festival, from the perception of its main stakeholders, who she identifies as the audience, the residents, the region and its economic operators, the festival itself and the artists. She is able to look at the multiplicity of effects generated by the festival over thirty years, by conducting primary research of the audience for the festival, the residents of the area, the economic flows to Bassano and the region, the artists themselves and the cultural impact on the area. She demonstrates that the economic impact on the region is twice the value invested, but more than this she indicates the benefits accrued by audiences of sustained and long running cultural activity, of the programming mix of traditional and experimental performance and of the support to artists the festival prides itself on. Undoubtedly what she provides is a methodology and analytical framework that stakeholders can use to help understand the positive effects that cultural initiatives can have not only on the local economy, but also the social impacts of the festival on stakeholders as varied as audiences, authorities and artists.

Floriane Gaber in the following chapter looks at how the agendas of some stakeholders have come to dominate the meaning and direction of street festivals in France, 'hijacking' and transforming their original spirit, that of the old Paris May 68 slogan *Il est interdit d'interdire* (It is forbidden to forbid). This she does by examining changes in the style and nature of street performance in France over the past forty years, in particular by looking at the status of the *In*, *Off* and *Off Off* performers, describing some of the big festivals as resembling 'supermarkets' holding a monopoly in the market and exerting excessive influence over the whole industry. For Gaber, street performers are 'champions' of public spaces, but for managerial and logistical, as well as health and safety reasons, some performers and companies have been led to relocate to more private spaces, removing from them their ability to engage with and address a whole city, its identity, its challenges, its citizens and the priorities of its local and regional authorities.

Clearly in street performance the connection between people and place, that is, between artists, audiences and location, is crucial. A festival can re-present the familiar location to its audience and participants, and build new relationships between them, as we saw in the Holstebro discussion by Winkelhorn. Negotiation of place and its meaning is also crucial for Fu, Long and Thomas in their discussion of diaspora community festivals and tourism in the UK in Chapter 17, where place and image becomes an important dimension of festivals that celebrate the identities, cultures and traditions of diverse minority and ethnic diaspora communities. Earlier we mentioned that some impacts of festivals are unforeseen; Fu, Long and Thomas feel that some prominent diaspora festivals have indeed unintentionally and implicitly developed relationships with tourists and tourism. As they indicate, some diasporic festivals become highlighted tourist attractions for the city, such as the West Indian Carnival in Leeds. For them, this is not just the case for cities that are major tourist attractions already, but also in cities that are less well known as tourist destinations, such as Bradford, Birmingham and Leicester. Picard and Robinson (2006), in their edited book *Festivals Tourism and Social Change*, provide a wide-ranging discussion of the relationship between tourists, the tourist industry and festivals. For them the key is to see festivals in the context of the constantly changing socio-economic and political environment in which such events operate, and that tourism is a key dynamic of that, as they say, "the presence of tourists at the periphery of festivity, and also at its centre, interrogates notions of ritual and tradition, shapes new spaces and creates and renews relationships between participants and observers, and between a festival and its conditions of operation" (2006 p 26). Festival tourism then for Fu, Long and Thomas is a reality and many diasporic communities are taking account of this, however, although they may be more focused on tourism, the traditions they are celebrating are still rooted in their traditional cultures.

In focusing on *Chinese New Year* celebrations Fu, Long and Thomas demonstrate that festivals are an important tool for diaspora communities to assert their rights and desire for legitimacy and recognition within their host communities. Kaushal and Newbold go on to address this in Chapter 18 by looking at mela festivals in the UK. By using the term 'Tamasha', which refers to South Asian cultures' exuberant performance and visuality, they describe how through open and loud display South Asian communities are seen to be embedding themselves within the cultural landscapes of host communities, creating identity spaces, lending legitimacy to their presence, as they become an integral part of the cities and towns of the UK. Similarly, Eugenio Barba director of the *Holstebro Festive Week* clearly states in Winkelhorn's chapter that one of the aims of the festival is to make micro cultures visible, connecting the city.

As suggested earlier, Winkelhorn mentions the idea that festivals can act as a form of 'bridging' between communities. This is a key aspect of mela festivals that Kaushal and Newbold explore, particularly through the debates suggesting that one of the impacts of mela is community cohesion. The idea of community cohesion is seen to be the bringing together of the specific community (South Asian) with the wider community (location/city), and in doing so fostering links and understandings. Following the work of Cantle (2008) Kaushal and Newbold see mela as providing an arena which can encourage social interaction and an intercultural exchange rather than cementing community cohesion. This idea that mela and other cultural events can act as an intercultural bridge is also developed by Wood and Landry (2008) in their study of the intercultural city, as they say:

> There are many good examples of how skilled management can foster new relationships and collaborations and open up a mela to other voices without alienating the traditional sectors. The *Edinburgh Mela* has done this and as it has become more intercultural, it has seen a growth of visitors and participants every year. It has been notable for

the intercultural transfers between India, Pakistan and Scotland, and for the development of hybrids, such as the dhol drummer and bagpipes! (Wood and Landry, 2008: 200)

Carnegie and Smith (2006) provide a very well developed case study of *Edinburgh Mela*, examining some of the themes that are introduced here not only by Kaushal and Newbold but also the ideas on diaspora festivals talked about in Fu, Long and Thomas's chapter. As Kaushal and Newbold demonstrate, mela festivals have not just transplanted a festive aspect of South Asian culture into Britain, but have re-inscribed it into new cultural locations and their specificities. Thus the *Southampton Mela* is different in many of its facets and features to the *Leicester Belgrave Mela*, or the *Bradford Mela*. These differences may be down to the ethnic mix of the locale, the religious or political background of the South Asian population, or the management and financial structure of the mela organisation itself. The authors aim to demonstrate that the success of the mela formula in the UK reflects its ability not only to travel, but also to habituate. For Kaushal and Newbold the key to the use of the term habituate is to understand that mela has not only arrived and acclimatised to a new locality, but it has also adapted to it and indeed, changed the local cultural landscape.

In 'A View from Australia' (Chapter 19), Robyn Archer discusses how emerging out of a traditional European 'best of culture' festivals model typical of the nineteen fifties and sixties, Australian festivals have now reached the point at which they can provide "platforms for cultural negotiation". In many ways she almost reverse engineers the debates we are having in this section, where diasporic cultures work to develop their approach to festivity by interacting with indigenous culture. Here it is the indigenous aboriginal culture that has struggled to assert its presence in the model of festival development imposed by the large Australian cities. Indeed, out of the success of integrating Aboriginal cultural products into festivals, Archer is able to assert that a more internationalist approach to festivals has emerged and Australia/Aboriginal artists have been able to take advantage of international links and take their art and performance to festivals across the globe.

Although clearly this book focuses on Europe, the influence of global cultures is represented in many festivals and aspects of festivals across Europe. Thus from Brazilian actors in Holstebro, to the Jaipur Brass Band in Leicester and Chinese New Year Festivals across Europe, we can see the influence of globalisation on the European festivals scene in no small measure. Debates on the impact of globalisation and culture have been raging for two decades now with key interventions from Giddens (1990), Sklair (1991), Tomlinson (1991 and 1999) and Held et al (1999), all engaging with the cultural imperialism thesis that the flow of global culture is essentially one way, from the dominant West. Archer's chapter makes an interesting intervention here, demonstrating how with enlightened festival management indigenous culture can act back on 'dominant' definitions of culture, and indeed can interweave and negotiate a place alongside them.

For Dragan Klaić, festivals in the new millennium can be seen as a response to globalisation, but globalisation with an ambiguous cultural impact. Yes, there are the elements of festivals that appear as readymade, standardised and as stereotypical cultural commodities, but he feels that there are also festivals that:

> function as strongholds of resistance to the standardising pressures of globalisation, as cultural interventions that seek to reinforce the specificity of a local place, and establish their relationship with the world on their own terms... functioning not in a compensating and representational mode, but in a developmental way, seeking to affirm specific artistic strategies and interests and to induce local developments with allies and collaborators brought in from elsewhere. In their best moments, such festivals articulate a productive dialectic of local and global (Klaić, 2014: 32 – 33)

From an anthropological perspective, Inda and Rosaldo (2002) see the entanglement of local and global as being one of the key characteristic elements of globalisation, the others being: worldwide modes of transport and communication, speeding up global interactions and processes; the intensification and regularisation of the links that interconnect the world; and the stretching of social, cultural, political and economic practices across frontiers. In particular, when discussing the cultural dynamics of globalisation, they talk about globalised culture never being simply deterritorialised, but always being reterritorialised: "there is no dislodging of everyday meanings from their moorings in particular localities without their simultaneous reinsertion in fresh environments. You can't have one without the other. It is a matter of both at once" (2002: 12). Inda and Rosaldo argue that the term 'deterritorialisation' "captures at once the lifting of cultural subjects and objects from fixed spatial locations and their relocation in new cultural settings" (2002: 12). Both the chapters by Fu, Long and Thomas and by Kaushal and Newbold ably demonstrate this idea, where the new cultural setting has the ability to impact on and change the festivals original cultural meanings.

Interestingly, if the process of globalisation described here can be seen to have disconnected the fixed nature of culture, communities and place, then festivals can be seen as a visual incarnation of the change in the relationship between culture and place in a globalised world. Here Klaić issues a warning, clearly stating that:

> the worst mistake festivals can make is to neglect the artists in their immediate vicinity while reaching out to those in far-flung places. The best festivals succeed in creating new synergies from the dialectic between the local and the global and from the fusion and mutual inspiration of artistic energies from both realms (2005: 149).

As we have already mentioned, Winkelhorn's chapter is also very powerful in impressing on the reader the importance in Holstebro of the festival bringing together international professionals and local amateur performers. Kaushal and Newbold also find that alongside the international performers, the providing of a stage for local talent is one of the most successful features of the mela formula in the UK. So if the impact of globalisation can be demonstrated through festivals, it may be that all cultural commodities wherever their origin are subject to reterritorialising, reinterpretation and recontextualising.

Impacts, communities and places as we shall see in this section are amongst the most keenly debated aspects of the study of contemporary festivals. Inevitably the understanding of these impacts is based on research carried out by festival organisations themselves, by consultants or by academics in universities. From the perspectives gathered here it is clear to see that there is a tendency from the festival insiders to see these effects and impacts as positive for society, as a cultural good and as supportive of the festival itself. The more analytical academic based approaches will see the role of festivals more critically, will take a longer view of their impact and their analysis will often be informed by theoretical underpinning. These stances are then reflected in the types of research methodologies employed by researchers and the questions that they ask. Those working with commercial organisations, local authorities, or preparing funding bids will tend to be quantitative in their approach, wanting to produce statistical 'evidence' of impacts and effects, something that can be measured and used to make a case. The more critical approaches will tend to be more qualitative in their methods, and their questioning will often be informed by sociological or cultural theory. The temptation is to categorise these in terms of 'administrative' versus 'critical' approaches, where administrative serves the festival, its organisers and its various stakeholders, and critical examines festivals at a more societal and cultural level creating knowledge and understandings. The assumption from all sides tends to be that festivals have impacts and effects, hence the question at the beginning of the introduction; why are we doing this? Nobody wants to believe that their endeavours are without consequence. Our task as researchers, organisers and students of festivals, is to examine these consequences, by combining different methods and traditions to create a more holistic approach to understanding festivals and their impacts on the contemporary world.

Bibliography and further reading

Bakhtin, M. (1984) *Rabelais and his World*, Indiana: Bloomington.

Cantle, T. (2008) *Community Cohesion: A new framework for race and diversity*, 2nd edition, Basingstoke: Palgrave Macmillan.

Carnegie, E. and Smith, M. (2006) Mobility, diaspora and the hybridisation of festivity: The case of the Edinburgh Mela, in D, Picard and M, Robinson (eds.), *Festivals, Tourism and Social Change: Remaking worlds*, Clevedon: Channel View Publications.

Giddens, A. (1990) *The Consequences of Modernity*, Cambridge: Polity.

Held, D., McGrew, A., Goldblatt, D. and Perraton, J. (1999) *Global Transformation: Politics, Economics and Culture*, Cambridge: Polity Press.

Inda, J. X. and Rosaldo, R. (2002) *The Anthropology of Globalisation: A reader*, Oxford: Blackwell.

Klaić, D. (2005) LIFT Outgrows its festival clothes, in R. De W. Fenton and L. Neal (eds.), *The Turning World*, London: Calouste Gulbenkian Foundation.

Klaić, D. (2014) *Festivals in Focus*, Budapest: The Budapest Observatory.

Picard, D. and Robinson, M. (2006) *Festivals, Tourism and Social Change: Remaking worlds*, Clevedon: Channel View Publications.

Putnam, R (2000) *Bowling Alone: the collapse and revival of American community*, New York: Simon and Schuster.

Richards, G. and Palmer, R. (2010) *Eventful Cities: Cultural managment and urban revitalisation*, Oxford: Butterworth-Heinemann.

Sklair, L. (1991) *Sociology and the Global Process*, Hemel Hempstead: Harvester Wheatsheaf.

Tomlinson, J. (1991) *Cultural Imperialism*, London: Pinter.

Tomlinson, J. (1999) *Globalisation and Culture*, Cambridge: Polity Press.

Wood, P. and Landrey, C. (2008) *The Intercultural City: planning for diversity*, London: Earthscan.

Notes

[1] For Odin Teatret 'barter' is "an exchange of cultural manifestations and offers not only an insight into the other's form of expression, but is equally a social interaction which defies prejudices, linguistic difficulties in thinking, judging and behaving". (wwww.odinteatre.dk/about-us/about-odin-teatret.aspx)

14 The Enchanted City: Holstebro Festive Week – an experiential and social cultural space

Kathrine Winkelhorn

Introduction

In 1989 Odin Teatret established the *Holstebro Festive Week* (Denmark), and did so by involving the entire city and its inhabitants. The Festive Week promptly became an on-going event, which takes place every three years in June. What characterises the *Holstebro Festive Week* in particular? And how has this event influenced the city and its citizens in the longer run? In other words, how can an event like the *Festive Week* contribute to enriching a city for more than just a week? When I interviewed the Mayor about the Festival and the theatre's role in the event, he said: "What the theatre brings us is popular and I think it is crucial that we get common experiences in which we can mirror ourselves – in the selfish society we are currently living in. In Holstebro we have become dependent on Odin Teatret, which makes us take part and which has become a common denominator for the entire city. It is a gift that we have Odin Theatret" (interview with the author, June 2011).[1]

It is a rather unusual statement for a mayor to make that a theatre is a gift for a city and that it has become a 'common denominator'[2] for the city – and, what is more that the city has become dependent on the theatre.

In this chapter I will reveal and explore how Odin Teatret involves the entire city. I will try to give a clear answer as to why the Mayor described the theatre as a 'common denominator'. In my investigation of the theatre's approach to the *Festive Week* I use my personal experience and knowledge from my time as assistant manager at the theatre (1987-88). Most of my research has been carried out in the form of field studies conducted during the *Festival Weeks* in 2008 and 2011. During both festivals I spent one week in Holstebro and the surrounding villages watching and observing how the local audience responded to the activities. In addition I carried out a series of semi-structured interviews with representatives from Holstebro: the head of police, the

Deputy Mayor, the director of a travel agency, a librarian, a policeman, the Chairman of the Cultural Affairs Committee of the City Council, the head of city planning, the project leader from the Odin Theatre and a senior lecturer living in Holstebro and working at Aarhus University and finally the Mayor.

Odin Teatret and Holstebro

For the reader to understand the context in which I am writing, I will briefly introduce the theatre and the city. The theatre was founded in 1964 in Oslo, Norway and was invited in 1966 to move to Holstebro, with the offer of premises in a couple of old farm buildings. When Odin moved to Holstebro in 1966 the city wanted to attract academics. When they settled in Holstebro, the actors were all foreigners, with an Italian director, Eugenio Barba and three Norwegian actors. None of them spoke Danish. Later on more actors were included from Brazil, Chile, Colombia, Denmark, England, Italy, the USA and Sweden. During the first decades it was not easy for the theatre to be truly accepted in and by the city. The Odins, as they are often called, were perceived as strangers, who made odd theatre – often on stilts – and their performances, which do not have a linear narrative, were consequently perceived locally as bizarre.

Over the years, public acceptance has increased and for a number of years Odin Teatret has been a world famous theatre laboratory, characterised by a professional and scholarly milieu, including cross-disciplinary endeavours with a number of international collaborations. The core activity of the theatre is performances, solo performances, workshops, seminars and barters and with these various activities the theatre is touring worldwide some 3-5 months a year. A number of books in several languages have been written about Odin and its practices[3].

In 2011 Odin Teatret played 29 different performances in Danish, Spanish, French, English, Portuguese and Italian, in 16 countries.

Turnover: € 2,084,000
Own revenue: € 770,000
Grants: € 1,314,000
Number of performances played: 274 (108 of which abroad)
Number of students: 4,743, of whom 4,469 in 16 countries across the world
Number of guest performances: 28
Number of people on working visits: 216
Staff members: 30, including 9 actors from 8 different countries

Figure 14.1: Key figures, Odin Teatret in 2011 (in €)[4]

With the theatre group including different languages and nationalities, its cultural diversity has played a fundamental role in the theatre's artistic activities. To simply survive, the theatre had to develop and use alternative artistic strategies to those normally associated with a theatre. With an Italian director residing in Denmark, alienation and otherness have served as sources of artistic challenge and resistance to which solutions had to be found. As the ensemble does not speak the same mother tongue, language cannot be the dramatic engine of the performance. Necessity has forced the theatre to invent a theatrical expression independent of just one language, one that includes music, song, dance and voice. These particular circumstances have contributed to the richness of the theatre's activities in Denmark and abroad. Maybe that is why this relatively small theatre group can deliver such a variety of different activities, within many different political, social and cultural contexts.

A theatre group as a bridge builder

Holstebro is situated in the centre of a landscape of moorland, surrounded by ten smaller villages. Some 17,000 people live in the surrounding rural areas and villages, while the city and the surrounding area have 40,065 inhabitants (in January 2012). A large share of today's retail activity takes place online or in shopping malls that are predominantly located on the city's periphery, which in turn means that urban spaces are often abandoned. In that sense the city is no longer the daily meeting place for people, which means the city has lost some of its soul and identity. It is in this context that the theatre, through its different activities, has developed a role as a co-creator of the city's identity. The Chairman of the Holstebro City Council's Cultural Affairs Committee described the role of Odin Theatre as a bridge builder, which breaks down cultural barriers.

> Commerce knows that we need cultural life. We have known that since the 1960s. One knows that the Odin Theatre is a rather strange theatre that we often meet walking on stilts. Now we have realised that these strange people generate something in the local community that is unique. Now we understand what it offers the city. ... Culture breaks down boundaries and this is what Odin Theatre does in its work. ... Without a good cultural life, we cannot survive here, including attracting settlers and academics. The strength is that during the *Festive Week* the theatre also encompasses the small villages like Ulfborg and Borbjerg Lighthouse in its activities. (interview with the author, June 2008)

Most people I have talked to state clearly that they are very proud of living in Holstebro, since "here we are doing something which nobody else is doing". When I talked to the director of Holstebro Travel Agency (in June 2008) he put it like this: "We are proud that we're doing something different and that we don't merely fly in Dolly Parton to the Stadium, even though she is good." By this statement the director stresses that the *Holstebro Festival* is different from what other cities are doing. They do not just import famous artists to market the city, such as a city close by does. But what is special about what Odin Theatre does in Holstebro? Odin takes on an organisational role as a facilitator for co-operation between amateurs and professionals, and by doing so expands the citizens' cultural scope by engaging them in something they do not know. During a conversation, the librarian summarised the importance of the *Festive Week* as follows:

> To me, the festival is the professionals working with the amateurs. They make the amateurs do something that is unique. ... The extraordinary thing is that Odin Theatre reaches out to the citizens and involves them. Odin makes people do something they did not know they could do and involves them in something they did not know they were interested in. ... and then you see that your neighbour can do something and you get surprised. My neighbour steps into character (interview with the author, June 2008).

Not only does the festival contribute to increased social cohesion and participation, it also contributes to strengthening local democracy. In an interview (June 2011) with a senior lecturer and citizen of Holstebro, he argued that, if we wish to reach consensus, we must accept one another as fellow citizens. In this sense, he indicated that the *Festive Week* has contributed to strengthening local democracy. "It is brilliant to have different organisations and institutions seeing themselves as part of a larger community." Odin Theatre does not represent 'Danishness' in the traditional sense, but 'Otherness', and it is interesting that in this way Odin's work can contribute to the creation of a more inclusive citizenship. You play with the concept of encounter, he says, and if you have this perception of democracy, it has an important function. As such, the theatre represents a new, more cosmopolitan Danishness.

Festival as process

"A whole week of music, dance, theatre, laughter, wonder and poetry." This is how Odin presents the *Festive Week*. The basic idea is to create meetings and dialogue between people who normally do *not* meet or cooperate. Visiting artists – along with Odin Teatret and other cultural institutions, associations, businesses and individual citizens – collaborate to create performances, shows, concerts, exhibitions and much more. "When everyone in this way opens their doors into their own world, a larger space is created where we can meet and share our different values" (Odin Theatre, 2010). Admission to most events is free, which further emphasises a social perspective in Odin's efforts.

How is this comprehensive programme, which predominantly consists of continuous activity squeezed into a single week, organised and carried out? In the early spring, in the year before the *Festive Week*, Odin Teatret invites associations, businesses, cultural institutions and artists to a joint meeting where the theatre presents the overall framework and theme for the *Festive Week*. In 2008 the theme was *Light and Darkness* – two forces existing symbiotically in everyday life. In 2011 the theme was *Love Stories*. "Without Eros nothing is right. The God of love is in control of the elements on which life is founded: friendship, tenderness, solidarity and passion" (Odin Teatret 2011). When the theme is clear, everyone is encouraged to contribute his or her ideas to the festival. In 2014 the theme for the festival will be: *Future Faces - Fantasy and Fictions*.

Often actors from Odin will develop their own major projects, involving an array of local people including athletes, dancers, folk musicians, policemen, soldiers, staff from a horseback riding school and others from Holstebro, elsewhere in Denmark and abroad. The project management and the artistic focal point are the responsibility of Odin and of some 90 groups – ranging from a grocery store and Danish Railroads to Vestjysk Gymnastics Association and Vinderup Citizen and Crafts Association, who all take part one way or another. Everybody contributes as festival organisers, with some 700-800 people taking an active part in the *Festive Week* in 2008 and 2011.

Such a comprehensive programme, made available online and through the local daily newspaper[5], can only be achieved because most activity is independent of the theatre. The festival included some 135 events in 2008 and more or less the same in 2011. Odin Teatret is responsible for the main performances and other happenings, which in 2008 and 2011 included parades in the city, barters, a performance in a castle outside the city, a concert in a medieval church in a local village, a concert arranged for 10 electric guitars on the city's rooftops, as well as activities in other villages and other places. The *Festive Week* finishes in the city's park with a huge performance directed by Eugenio Barba, involving all the performers. The programme runs every day from early morning until midnight and includes jazz music, slapstick and street parades and – in 2008 – *Medea's Wedding*, including 35 Balinese dancers and musicians.

Networking and bridging

A precondition for delivering such an event is that an institution has to lead on the initiative. In an interview with Eugenio Barba[6], he said that the idea of the *Festive Week* was to involve the concealed and unseen environments that constitute people's culture like schools and factories, to try to make these micro cultures visible in the city by connecting them with a common theme. "In this way we want to make the citizens experience their own habitat through a kind of magic and a transformation of daily life"[7] (Barba, YouTube 2011).The challenge for this to take place is that the actors and directors must motivate people to enter actively into the festival. "If we want the police to participate with sirens and blue lights we have to persuade the police to participate." In an interview with actress Julia Varley from Odin Teatret (March 2008 at Odin Teatret), she highlighted the privileged position 'to be in-between' in which the performer serves as a catalyst. It means that the theatre can network and interpret the needs of different people and help to build bridges between institutions/citizens, professionals/ amateurs, periphery/centre, local/foreign, old/new, rural/urban – as well as between academic/practical and technical/ artistic.

It may be useful to invoke here Robert Putnam's concept of *social capital* where he refers to reciprocity and trust, which may arise in meetings with individuals and with social networks (Putnam, 2000). Thus, social capital is closely linked with what Putnam calls the civic virtue and which Landry (2006) refers to as 'social glue'. Putnam distinguishes between two kinds of social capital: *bonding capital* and *bridging capital*. He emphasises that you link with people you already know and who look like yourself in relation to gender and age, but tend to bridge to people who are different from yourself. The theatre is aware that it navigates in many spheres and makes use of multiple logics. This is what Julia Varley has in mind when she refers to the theatre's role as a catalyst. "Being in-between", she says, "allows us to focus on the: inter-cultural, inter-regional, inter-national and the dynamics of complex and complementary realities." It is the caring approach and at the same time the strategic considerations that make it possible to have a Festive Week that has so much popular and political legitimacy.

And as the librarian says: "The Festival does more to tie together the new larger municipality than the municipality itself has been able to do." (interview with the author, June 2008)

A cultural and experiential space of change

The *Festive Week* enables the spectator and the citizen to be part of something else and something more. Russian philosopher and literary critic, Mikhail Bakhtin, writes in his article 'Carnival, Laughter and Culture' (1983: 63): "every party is an important primary custom of human culture". For a party to become a vigorous party one must add a spiritual and ideological dimension. This means that a party must always have meaningful and valuable content to be capable of reaching beyond everyday life. Bakhtin's philosophy is based on the medieval carnival culture and there seems to be some parallels to Odin's dramaturgical practices. He sees the carnival as "a real time celebration, a genesis and a celebration of change and renewal" (1983: 63). During the carnival, status and profession are eliminated, so freer communication can take place between people and new human bonds and relationships can be established. For a short while the carnival suspends the usual sense of truth and order. The carnival does not make a virtue of 'limelight' in the sense that it does not construct any boundaries between actors and spectators. Limelight would spoil the carnival, just as the lack of limelight would spoil a theatre performance. The carnival is not a performance but people live the carnival and take part in the carnival because the very idea includes all people. Bakhtin claims that carnival enables people to be reborn, to experience new human relations. These truly human relations are not just fruits of fantasy or abstract thinking; they can be learned. The ideal of utopia and reality is merged in the carnival experience, which is unique as Bakhtin sees and presents it. The carnival is full of the pathos of change and of renewal and, according to Bakhtin, becomes a *unique experiential space*.

Like a carnival, Odin works with notions of change and renewal in its artistic and cultural practices. Barba describes his approach as "the changed states of dramaturgy" and "the water drop that causes the jar to overflow" (Christoffersen, 2009: 23). This is equivalent to a symbolic blow to the head resulting from an experience that challenges habitual ways of responding/thinking. If one considers a performance as a real time action that intervenes into a context, one can call this dramaturgical level the theatre's transformative power in relation to an individual, but also to a larger cultural context (Christoffersen, 2011). In itself the *Festive Week* is 'disorder' with a cornucopia of events and activities, of song, music and voices interacting with and against each other. The collaboration and the process of creation involving various participants generate a superior dramaturgical strategy with its own rules, where disorder becomes a key concept. Using Bakhtin's words one may say: "a real time celebration, a genesis, a celebration for change and renewal" (Bakthin 1983:63). The *Festive Week* breathes with a delicate balance between disorder and order just like the carnival, which also reveals some boundaries in the middle of the madness. One could argue that the strategy of the *Festive Week* is built on the shoulders of the culture and logic of the carnival.

Through its practice Odin creates live actions in the city, which frame everyday life. Through these actions Odin contributes a renewed urbanity, where the city's values are at play and are re-negotiated through barter and performative actions. During the carnival Bakhtin (1983) describes how new human relations develop and how new types of experiences take place through the staging of everyday life. It is the same kind of mechanism that is present during the *Festive Week*. It reveals and plays with the boundaries between people and even authorities like the police and the military are included. As the head of police says: "We have arrested the polar bear (a famous Odin figure veiled like a polar bear), who was shooting with a water pistol in the pedestrian street and we put him in chains" (June 2008 at the Police Station). The normal roles have been reversed and the police play the game, which everybody in the city appreciates.

In an interview with the Head of City Planning, it is striking that – 20 years later – he recalls the ceremonial burial of a Viking ship in a performance called Skibet Bro[8] as if it was yesterday. What we remember is crucial for our actions and memory is a significant element in our lives. The head of city planning emphasises another aspect – the unorthodox use of urban spaces that consequently challenges the mainstream city discourses on planning and habitation.

> You look upon yourself in a completely different context. This helps to create pride. I am from Holstebro. It's not just like the *Aarhus Festival*. The citizens become a part of this event. You are involved. You are not just a spectator. ... I still remember the day when a Viking ship was buried in the park. I remember it like it was yesterday. It was crazy that we dug it down! That I remember the most. One cannot imagine the *Festive Week* without Odin Theatre as the central figure. It means something to our collective consciousness about the city (Head of City Planning, interview with the author, June 2008).

By using the pronoun *we*, the Town Planner perceives the ceremonial burial of the Viking ship as a collective action in the city. During the *Festive Week* in 2008 I witnessed a young female shepherd shearing a sheep in the railway station in Holstebro, while the Polish Theatre Zar played softly on a violin. This was an action of disorder at the railway station but at the same time there was a poetic order of silence, with a professional shepherd shearing a sheep as inquisitive travellers passed by. The entire *Festive Week* can be viewed as a ritual that breaks spatial boundaries and poetises the cityscape.

The staged square

It is vital for Odin's perception of dramaturgy that you meet *the other* live, on site, the one you rarely talk to or meet. One of the key events during the *Festive Week* in 2008 and 2011 was a barter performance on a square in the heart of Holstebro. "A concept of barter is bound up with an ideology, that understands performance as an activity that must connect people, whilst at the same time celebrating their difference", writes Adam J Ledger (Ledger, 2012). In short, barter is a cultural exchange between Odin Teatret and local residents, for instance musicians or perhaps inmates in a prison or whoever wants to take part and to perform/contribute a bit.

Odin actor and musician Kai Bredholdt directed barter during the *Festive Week* including various events involving amateurs and professionals. There were three daily performances of approximately 30-40 minutes. The Polish Theatre Zar contributed with a series of slapstick performances. Children from the Royal School of Ballet did toe dancing with ten taekwondo fighters dressed in white suits. 25 people from the Senior Citizens Centre joined a parade with walkers and drums. A moving moment was when an 84-year-old dance teacher with a wireless microphone taped to her cheek instructed twenty 80 + people in dancing Zorba, all of them dressed in black trousers and white shirts.

Figure 14.1: Housewives dancing at Holstebro (Photograph: Kathrine Winkelhorn)

By using 60 bales of straw that a local farmer had donated, the performance space was established and by changing the configurations of the straw bales every day, the site achieved an animated and vivid atmosphere. The citizens see each others' changing roles and functions in public space: older people are no longer simply members of the category 'old' but are viewed as performers, and the policeman is not only an authority figure but also a playful human being. Through these performative interventions one experiences groups of other citizens in their diversity. The very fact that a number of the citizens themselves are active participants collaborating with professional artists makes the *Festive Week* different from most other cultural events. One could say that the *Festive Week* in Holstebro is 'strictly homemade' and at the same time professional all the way. This is unique and may be why local people take a certain pride in the *Festive Week* and why the Mayor sees the *Festive Week* as an important shared experience.

Encounter and an invitation

Enchantment is essential to Landry's notion and thinking of what a city may be as "enchantment asks us to rediscover and reanimate the social tissues and repair the severances between us" (Landry, 2006: 268) and to re-establish the bonds between human beings. This may be as simple as giving and receiving courtesy and politeness in our daily actions, such as when we go shopping. "These (small actions) seek to resolve any fissure between being 'me' the individual and being 'us', the collective" (ibid: 268). It is this feeling of urbanity and solidarity that according to Landry may enchant a city. Enchantment is a metaphor for the repetitive act of kindness, which forms the texture and glue from which social capital grows. Landry's notion of enchantment sheds light on Odin's theatrical practice, which through the performative enchantment meets the spectator. Ash Amin (Amin, in Landry, 2006: 268) unfolds this further and talks about "the habit of solidarity towards the stranger as the nervous system of the lived city" and he redefines the good city as "an expanding habit of solidarity, as a practical but unsettled achievement, constantly building...experiments through which difference and multiplicity can be mobilised for common gain and against harm and want" (ibid: 268). Amin points out that the common good can be mobilised through differences, conflict and diversity in an ongoing negotiation. Herein is an ethical point that incorporates principles of social justice, equality and reciprocity that are part of the building blocks of Odin's theatrical practice of barter.

Several words may characterise the *Festive Week*, but if I only had a single word to use, it would be 'invitation'. Embedded in this word lies an element of solidarity with the city and a desire to work together with its citizens. Odin issues a generous and open invitation, which indirectly encourages 'us' to engage and to get involved. Through this practice the theatre contributes to other urban qualities and values as a kind of software that constitutes a living city. The *Festive Week* generates a common point of departure and a united deadline for when the city steps into character. Through events throughout the city - barters, concerts and performances - traditions, symbols and worldviews are formed and are turned into sensuous impressions, with the spectator as an active co-creator of the city's narrative. Looking at the entire programme, the *Festive Week* takes place in a relational tension between the elitist, the strange and the popular. This tension nourishes the micro processes for creating new significance in the city.

Conclusions

By highlighting the cultural macro process (Landry; Amin; Putnam) and the micro processes (Barba; Christoffersen) this chapter has tried to shed light on a particular kind of festival, one whose main aims are to include citizens and encourage them to take an active part. This requires an institution that is committed to engaging and involving local people. For a short period of time, the city of Holstebro turns into a collective living city-laboratory that releases a cultural and transformative energy. Odin's approach revolves around transformation as a practice, which requires but also enables those involved to develop the will or skills to collaborate across visible and invisible borders, and to involve what is outside one's own network of family, colleagues, friends and neighbours. The festival is both a presentation and a process, where the process may be just as important as the result. The *Festive Week* contributes to strengthening local democracy, while also supporting and developing the city's values as they come into play. Partnerships are established, networks are created and new bonds made with people you did not know. *Holstebro Festive Week* is a celebration and a vivid, cultural and political initiative devised and delivered by professional artists and amateurs.

Bibliography and further reading

Amin, A. (2006) The good city, *Urban Studies*, May, **43**(5-6), 1009-1023.

Bakhtin, M. (1983) Karneval og Latterkultur, in: Hans Jørgen Nielsen and Alexander Orloff (eds), *Det andet Karneval*, Copenhagen: Tiderne Skifter.

Barba, E. (2010) *On Directing and Dramaturgy: Burning the House*, Oxford and New York: Routledge.

Christoffersen, E. E. (2009) Odin Teatrets Dramaturgier, *Særnummer Peripeti*.

Christoffersen, E. E. (2011) Interview with Eugenio Barba, June. Kunsten ude på Kanten nr. 5. Downloaded May 2012 from www.peripeti.dk

Christoffersen, E. E. and Winkelhorn, K. (2011) Drømmen om Byen, *Kunsten ude på Kanten* – 5, 2011. Downloaded 5 March 2012 from www.peripeti.dk

Landry, C. (2006) *The Art of City Making*, London: Earthscan.

Landry, C. and Wood, P.(2008) *The Intercultural City*, London: Earthscan.

Ledger, A. (2012) *Odin Teatret, Theatre in a new century*, Basingstoke: Palgrave Macmillan.

Lefebvre, H. (2003) *The Urban Revolution*, Minneapolis: University of Minnesota Press.

Odin Teatrets Årsberetning. (2011) Holstebro: Odin Teatret.

Putnam, R. (2000) *Bowling Alone: The Ccollapse and Revival of American Community*, New York: Simon and Schuster.

Skot-Hansen, D. (2007) *Byen som Scene, kultur og byplanlægning i oplevelessamfundet*, Frederiksberg: Bibliotekarforbundet.

Watson, I. (ed) (2002) *Negotiating Cultures, Eugenio Barba and Intercultural Debate*, Manchester University Press.

Winkelhorn, K. (2012) Odin Teatrets kultur, organisation og ledelse. In: Erik Exe Christoffersen (ed). *Odin Teatret – et dansk verdensteater*, Aarhus: Aarhus Universitetsforlag.

Notes

[1] All interviews have been translated from Danish by the author

[2] In the sense of shared experience, not lowest common denominator

[3] For more information on books, please see www.odinteatret.dk

[4] From Odin Teatrets Årsbetning 2011

[5] *Dagbladet Holstebro*

[6] Interview by Erik Exe Christoffersen, Århus University 2011 http://www.youtube.com/watch?v=aN0jJu7n0nA Den utænkelige festuge. Interview with Eugenio Barba by Erik Exe Christoffersen, June 15th 2011

[7] Interview by Erik Exe Christoffersen, Århus University 2011 http://www.youtube.com/watch?v=aN0jJu7n0nA Den utænkelige festuge. Interview with Eugenio Barba by Erik Exe Christoffersen, June 15th 2011

15 Operaestate Festival Veneto: A socio-cultural and economic analysis

Luisella Carnelli

Introduction

Bassano Operaestate Festival Veneto has presented more than four hundred shows in castles, parks, palaces, villas, squares and museums in thirty municipalities of the region of Veneto in the North East of Italy. The festival hosts artists and productions from all over the world, ranging from contemporary theatre to the most innovative international dance, music, opera, classical, jazz and art films. The diversity, breadth and quality of its programmes are its greatest strengths. The primary objective of the festival is to enable large audiences to experience the performing arts in its many different forms, and to do so through a programme of cultural animation across the entire region. This case study of *Bassano Operaestate* aims to provide a picture of the effects produced by the festival with over three decades of activity, in an area that has experienced vibrant and dynamic growth in the industrial, creative, artistic and cultural sectors, especially in recent years. The research study was commissioned by the festival and carried out by Fondazione Fitzcarraldo (FF). FF is an independent centre, based in Turin, for planning, research, training and documentation on cultural, arts and media management, economics and policies, at the service of those who create, practice, take part in, produce, promote and support arts and cultural activities.

Specifically, the study analysed the following aspects of the festival:

♦ its audience;

♦ its economic flows;

♦ the cultural impacts generated in the region and how these impacts were measured and assessed by *Operaestate's* main stakeholders.

The research therefore puts the festival at the centre of a complex system that reflects the multiplicity of the art forms it works with, and seeks to investigate and interpret the multi-layered system of relationships, and the many interconnections between the festival and the region (considered as a complex system of players). This ambitious research project does not pretend to reveal the full multiplicity of effects that a cultural event like *Operaestate* can generate, but it is a first attempt to produce a multi-level representation of the 'benefits' that a long running cultural activity can generate over time.

The Research Project

This evaluation of the impacts of *Operaestate* aims to describe the multiple dimensions and effects resulting from its work over thirty years. *Operaestate* is deeply rooted in the region, and is especially renowned for how it presents the artistic and cultural challenges of contemporary theatre.

The research methodology began with the key features of the festival, which are:

♦ The temporal dimension: in which key aspects are short term planning (June to September) and sustainability and the festival's longevity (31 editions).

♦ The wide range of stakeholders, which includes about 40 municipalities and 67 venues.

♦ The density and variety of the programme: drama, opera, cinema and contemporary dance and theatre.

♦ Its commitment to best practice in production, programming and support for artists and performers.

These project coordinates allowed for the articulation of some key questions. In particular, whether the nature and history of *Operaestate* required a broad definition of regional development, one which took full account of the different values and benefits that the festival can deliver over time, but which are often difficult to measure.

The research incorporated a multi-layered approach in its use of selected analytical tools in evaluating the different outcomes that *Operaestate* produces in the region.

The research analysed the following topics:

Part	Topics	Target	Tools and Data
I - Analysis of the audience	The audience of the festival	Socio-demographic data Loyalty and participation Satisfaction Audience behaviours	PAPI[1] 1826 questionnaires
II - Residents of Bassano and the festival	The residents of Bassano and the festival	Brand positioning Evaluation of participation Evaluation of the impacts on local residents of their participation in cultural activities	CATI[2] 500 interviews with residents of Bassano
III – The economic impact	The regional economic stakeholders	Economic impact generated by the festival Calculation of the financial benefit generated for different economic sectors Impact on the region's tourism and hospitality sectors	CATI 20 telephone interviews 7 in depth interviews with selected stakeholders
	The festival	Economic impact of the festival's activities and budget	Analysis of administrative data and the operating budget for *Operaestate*
IV - Operaestate under the lens	Artists	Artistic role: evaluation of the festival's artistic focus and content Development role: evaluation of the impacts of the advice and support the festival gives to local artists	In depth Interviews: 8 national artists (5 in choral area and 3 on the theatrical side) 5 international artists

Figure 15.1: *Operaestate* research table

Part I - Analysis of the festival audience

Profile and identity of the audience

(based on analysis of 1826 audience questionnaires):

63% of the audience are female.

Their average age is 43. The largest age group is 30-59 years (over half of respondents are between 40 and 59).

Residency: 65% of the audience are from Bassano, 28.7% from other provinces in the Veneto region, 4.3% from other Italian regions and 2.4% from outside of Italy.

The communication channels used to learn/hear about the festival

Research carried out at previous festivals has revealed important insights into the audience's motivations and some of the factors (e.g. marketing, pricing, programme) that might influence buying decisions. In terms of marketing, 50% have prior knowledge of the festival. 25% learnt about it through word of mouth. 50% revealed that 'traditional' communication, i.e. print, had influenced them, either in the form of advertising in magazines or newspapers, or outdoor advertising – posters, banners, displays. Newer communication tools (web and social networks) were referenced by 21%.

Motivations for attendance

71% prioritised the performance and the artists as their main motivation for attending. *Operaestate's* audience also evidences expectation that both will be of high quality. The dominant motivational feature appears to be the 'show' factor, but audience's buying decisions are also influenced by factors such as the aesthetic nature of the content, wanting a night out, the ambiance/atmosphere of the festival, a personal recommendation from a friend or, simply, curiosity. 12% prioritised the festival experience as a whole in their decision-making. The analysis of what motivates people to attend helps marketing staff to understand their audience's different behavioural attitudes, media diets, tastes, needs and desires. Strategic marketing aims to align marketing strategies and targets to the groups themselves.

Those who loves shows / artists–71%

Knowledgeable and critical, with an average age of about 43, they have attended the festival on average for six years and expect to attend six events. They like the festival, the choice and variety of programming, the courtesy of the staff and the publicity and other information published by the festival. They learn about which shows to attend via several channels (internet, especially, but also articles in newspapers and magazines and the advice of friends). They see the festival as an important element of regional development, but they also appreciate the festival for its programme mix of original and unusual shows and spaces.

The most faithful! - 12%

They love the festival and see *Operaestate* as of fundamental importance to the quality of life in the area and its heritage. They have attended on average for eight years and expect to attend six events. They have a high awareness through various means of communication.

They appreciate the variety of programming, the courtesy and professionalism of the staff and the publicity and other information published by the festival; they are less motivated by the site or the social environment. Among the things they favour are films, great authors and performers in theatre, jazz and contemporary dance.

A night away from home, but not only - 5%

They go to the festival to enjoy a night out, encouraged by the advice of friends and partners. It is a segment that is very supportive of the festival (six shows) and which has attended for about six years. It is an audience that especially loves cinema, but also jazz and contemporary theatre.

Operaestate *mon amour!* - 5%

This segment of the public is supportive of the festival, for its programming, for the courtesy and professionalism of the staff, for where shows are presented and for the prices. Prior knowledge and word of mouth are the main way that this group learns about *Operaestate*, with internet and word of mouth the main sources of more detailed information about specific shows or the programme as a whole. Their main interests lie in cinema, great authors and performers in theatre and jazz. Their average age is 44, they have attended six times and attend seven shows per festival.

Young and recommend to friends... - 3%

Younger (average age 38), they are less loyal (attending the festival two times) and attend fewer shows (three). They learn about the shows from friends. This target group sees the festival as an opportunity to share an evening out with friends or those with whom they share emotional affinity and aesthetic interests.

As well as supporting the festival for its importance for Bassano (image), they also like the festival for its atmosphere and where it is held (space/environment). They favour jazz and contemporary dance, but also contemporary theatre and film.

Occasional and curious - 3%

Those who attend just for curiosity are on average younger than the audience as a whole: their average age is 39. They attend about three shows and the festival for two or three years. They learn about the programme and shows primarily from friends. They favour well known authors and performers in theatre, contemporary theatre and contemporary dance.

Loyalty and frequency

Operaestate's audience is characterised by a long and loyal relationship with the event: almost 40% of the audience has followed it for over seven years and around 50% have attended more than four shows per festival.

Perception and judgments

The overall audience is generally satisfied with the festival although critical about the festival's use of online communication - website and socialweb.

Operaestate is seen to be of benefit to Bassano and the other cities involved in the programme, for a wide array of reasons: artistic, social and financial.

Operaestate fulfils a vital function in audience development: 29% of respondents said that the festival had stimulated their interest in the performing arts and 25% that attendance at *Operaestate* had enabled them to develop better understanding of theatre and contemporary dance (and increased their cultural capital). *Operaestate* is therefore a useful tool for stimulating curiosity and triggering positive diffusion processes - cultural education.

The festival's use of non-conventional spaces for performance is also an attractive feature for much of its audience.

Part II - The residents of Bassano and the festival

Operaestate, after 32 editions, has become a point of reference in the cultural landscape of Bassano: 65% of respondents cite the festival as one of the most important cultural events in the region (spontaneous awareness) and almost all respondents (97%), when asked, claim to know it (induced knowledge).

Spontaneous knowledge of local cultural events is an important indicator because it shows that *Operaestate* is core to the cultural identity and life of the city (and the region).

The level of attendance shows good support by local people: nearly 75% of residents have attended least at one festival. In addition 67% of those indicated that they might attend at least one show in the next festival.

Respondents revealed different behavioural attitudes to the festival with the intention to attend at least one show being highest for those who know and have participated in the past. Among the reasons given by those who have never participated are lack of interest in the festival, its programme and/or that they lack time. Access issues related to interest, non-attendance and lifestyle present this and other festivals with big challenges.

Ultimately, the artistic quality of the programme, or an interest in specific performances, were found to be the main motivators for attendance. Its success indicates that *Operaestate* is perceived as a prestigious festival, and one which understands and meets the needs of its audience through its artistic offer.

Part III - The region and the economic impact

Capturing and measuring the economic impacts of the festival and the benefits to the area requires two things, a measure of the total expenditure and how much of that remains in the region.

This research analysed tourists' ancillary expenditure and the expenditure on artists and workers. The scale of economic impact is a direct reflection of the buy-in by local business to the programme, e.g. through meeting the needs of audience and artists for accommodation, food and drink, etc.

The research focused on the direct effects generated by the festival, in particular:

A. The festival's expenditure

The costs of staging and promoting *Operaestate* were analysed to identify those areas of expenditure that were sourced locally and which contribute to the local economy.

Out of a total expenditure of about €973,132, €677,643 is the direct expenditure for the realisation of *Operaestate*.

B. The audience's ancillary expenditure

This included:

◆ Hotels / Bed & Breakfast

◆ Restaurants / bars / coffee shops

◆ Shopping and leisure

◆ Purchases related to the food and wine industry.

The research revealed specific audience clusters – by reference to residence and patterns of expenditure. These are:

◆ residents in local areas

◆ tourists staying with friends / relatives

◆ tourists - high range

◆ tourists - medium/low range

◆ tourists who do not stay in the area

The methodology employed was as follows:

1 Identify and exclude from the sample those living in the area, as their expenditure is not 'new money' to the local economy.

2 Identify and exclude 'random' attenders

3 Calculate the number of participants - reconstructed from the number of presences and from the average number of visits (excluding local residents and random attenders)

4 Calculate the average time spent in Bassano expressed as days / participant

5 Calculate the average expenditure per day / capita for the main items of expenditure

6 Multiply the days / visitor by the average expenditure.

C. Expenditure on artists

The expenditure on artists and others involved/employed in Bassano during the festival: 420 stayed in the area for the equivalent of 1,705 nights.

The total direct expenditure by the audiences was €1.268 million, of which €876,000 (69%) was spent on foods/bars/restaurants, €200.000 (16%) on accommodation and about €193.000 (15%) on shopping and leisure.

Overall, the additional overnight stays generated by the festival were estimated at 4,145 units – 2,440 tourists, 1,705 artists / professionals.

The direct economic impact generated by *Operaestate* is approximately €1.93million, of which €1.267million is attributed to expenditure by the audience and €662,000 by the festival itself.

€1.93 million is a substantial figure, especially when set against the funding received from public sources (regional, provincial, local) of €360,000. Another feature worth noting is that the benefit to the local economy from this expenditure is seven times the income from ticket sales.

Part IV - *Operaestate* under the lens

The perspective of stakeholders and policy makers

Adopting a stakeholders' perspective allows us, first, to contextualise *Operaestate's* work and role in the context of regional, national and international live events, and secondly, to highlight and examine the role, actions and effects in the region.

The main findings were as follows:

- *Bassano Operaestate* has been able to build its credibility, playing on the idea of a sprawling metropolis.
- The festival is recognised for its role as a creative hub for performing arts: especially by the local authority.
- *Bassano* is a festival with two souls:
  - ❖ vocation and attention to the region and its needs in terms of performing arts;
  - ❖ attention and interest in contemporary and new forms of expression for experimental theatre and dance.

The dual nature of the festival has made it possible to present shows, both belonging to a great tradition, or opening up to contemporary performance and performers.

- *Operaestate* is renowned for its record on finding and promoting new/emerging creative talent, especially Venetian, and its ability to merge them into a coherent programme featuring international artists too, resulting in a sort of osmosis between the disciplines of different countries. The festival is thus not only a showcase for innovations in the field of European contemporary theatre and dance, but also an opportunity for discussion and training between actors from different disciplines at different levels.
- *Operaestate* aims to facilitate contacts and artistic hybrids. Some of that occurs through residencies
- It aims to build a distinctive brand for the festival

The point of view of the artists

National

- Five artists out of eight highlight that the training and support they receive from the festival and its staff is of fundamental importance to them, especially at the beginning of their career path, as well as in their professional career.
- For seven out of eight artists, *Operaestate* is both a source of support for their professional artistic work, but also a reference for employment and management (contracts, etc).
- Collaboration is seen as another key benefit as it reflects a commitment to developing the ability or potential of the young artist, or of the young company.

♦ All artists active in the choral sector say they could count on getting a residency space to develop their work and in two cases have benefited from other services, such as the retrieval of technical sponsors or administrative advice.

♦ All artists interviewed highlighted the positive role that the festival plays, especially in facilitating opportunities for dialogue between artists.

♦ No artist has received direct support for the promotion and communication of their performances, except through the inclusion of their work in the festival programme.

♦ Respondents confirm that they have a good relationship with the creative team.

♦ The system of co-operation between B.motion (the section of the festival dedicated to experimentation) and CSC (Centre for Contemporary Art Scene) is identified by young choreographers/dancers as a fundamental benefit of the festival, and inspiring for their own professional growth.

♦ The festival's brand is recognised, valued, strong, credible and prestigious. The opinion of all the artists was unanimous in stressing the positive image that the festival has constructed and in confirming the help given by PTI (Professional Training Incubator).

♦ The artists of both sections feel part of a long-term process that does not limit them to a single project, but allows space for individual development.

♦ Particularly appreciated by all artists was the opportunity to showcase work that was not complete but 'work in progress'.

International

International artists prioritised three elements:

♦ The mixed programming: which presents a wide range of work from new talent to established members of the international contemporary dance scene.

♦ The city of Bassano itself

♦ Networking: B.motion is not only a showcase of entertainment, but a place to participate/join in international networks and to develop future projects.

Conclusions

An important outcome of this study of *Operaestate's* social and economic impacts is that it has enabled stakeholders to share a common framework through which to understand the scope and value of the benefits that cultural activity can deliver to the local economy. The report's findings will be of interest to many in the sector whilst its methodology can be applied in similar festival research.

The work presented here is new in the Italian context; it has been inspired by similar research carried out in Anglo-Saxon countries around the concept of well-being produced by cultural initiatives and activities. The study employed a multi-variate approach, integrating the tools of Economic Impact Assessment with qualitative and quantitative methods to measure the festival's cultural, artistic and social impacts (for more detailed information see Guerzoni (2008) on the concepts and methods of calculation of the direct, indirect and induced impacts related to the 'spending approach').

Bibliography and further reading

Guerzoni G. (2008) *Effetto festival. L'impatto economico dei festival di approfondimento culturale*, La Sapienza, Fondazione Carispe.

Notes

[1] Pen and paper interview

[2] Computer assisted telephone interviews

16 Street Performance: The unintended consequences of festivals

Floriane Gaber

Introduction

Many describe France as 'the Mecca' for street performance and, world-wide, artists and festival organisers can only dream of the 10 million euros granted by the Ministry of Culture to street companies and festivals; and of the 1000 groups and 250 festivals (or events) dedicated to street performance. Unfortunately, all earthly paradise includes its version of hell, and after 40 years of existence, street performers and organisers in the French context are still struggling to win acknowledgement from the wider cultural sector and public authorities. This chapter will address the issues that have contributed to this difficult situation, one in which some festivals, as 'one shot big events', play a perverse role, albeit perhaps, unwillingly and unwittingly.

The first festival in France that was entirely dedicated to street performance was that held in Aix-en-Provence in 1973. It was called *Aix, ville ouverte aux saltimbanques* (Aix, city open to street acrobats). It presented a mixed programme that ranged from traditional buskers through to young artists who aspired to work in venues/places other than theatres, galleries, museums, cultural centres and their middle class audiences. These were artists who wanted to perform for people who never or rarely attended formal cultural activities; to provide them with artistic experiences that were part of the 'rhythm of their daily lives', not as part of a more formal arts experience as may be enjoyed in a theatre or gallery.

Over time, street performers developed, through their work, their particular identification with their audience, whom they described as 'citizens' or 'public-population'. This has led them to proclaim themselves to be the 'champions' of this cultural practice, and, from this perspective to argue that such forms of arts engagement are of fundamental importance, deserving of critical attention and dedicated funding. To some extent this 'special pleading' has resulted in other parts of the cultural sector (theatre, dance, visual arts) relegating street performances into a category of 'play', 'ephemera' or 'animations' ('activities'), to be bracketed with more socio-cultural activities, i.e. as non-professional in their approach to and use of the arts.

Street performers also claim to be the 'champions' in the use of public spaces, where they have to interact with other users such as pedestrians, cyclists, motorists and other drivers; in both urban and rural contexts; city centres as well as suburbs; and involving heritage and more contemporary sites and locations. To a certain extent this is true but the logistical challenges of working in such spaces have led some performers and companies to relocate into more sheltered and protected spaces such as courtyards or even to perform indoors.

In addition to questions about where to perform, the sector soon had to address the fact that busking on the streets provided very few artists with a steady or adequate income especially those who described themselves as professional street performers, i.e. those for whom it was their job. The sector's response was to diversify the market, but others tried to protect themselves from those 'public spaces', hiding in courtyards even in 1986, 13 years after the first festival in Aix, *Eclat, European festival for street theatre* was created in Aurillac, followed the next year by *Chalon dans la rue* in Chalon-sur-Saône and by *Viva Cité* in Sotteville-les-Rouen, and so on. So that today *Le Goliath* lists 250 events dedicated to street performance in France. *Le Goliath* is published by Hors Les Murs which is France's national resource centre for street arts and circus arts, established in 1993 by the Ministry of Culture, it develops and supports artistic practices 'outside the walls' through information, documentation, training, study, research and publications (for further information visit: www.horslesmurs.fr). These 250 events include big festivals, which attract audiences of up to 400,000, as well as smaller local celebrations in villages. But the biggest festivals now also operate as showcases (or supermarkets as some artists describe them) where the organisers of smaller events can see new work and negotiate with performers to bring the performances they like to their cities, villages, etc. But this symbiotic relationship has not, it will be argued, delivered long term success (though many are happy with the system).

This chapter will continue with an analysis of the key features of this process and examine whether the role played by the big street festivals is beneficial to the artform and ultimately to the companies and organisations themselves. It will present a range of research data that suggests that the process is still in development and that aspects of the current policy, infrastructure and funding have actually had a perverse and negative effect on the nature of street art, and led to a way of working that has weakened the link between performers, companies and people, their daily life and the places where they live; the direct opposite therefore of what the pioneers in this field of work set out to achieve.

The audience

Street performers and organisers claim that they achieve a unique connection with people who never (or rarely) attend cultural activities in formal venues (e.g. theatres, concert halls, museums). But research is showing that at big street festivals this is only partly true. In 2004-5, the street arts network, Eunetstar, commissioned a study of street festivals in eight European countries (Gaber 2005) which revealed the following demographic for the audience:

♦ 64% of the audience identified themselves as middle-class, educated people, employed in professional or non-manual work and who were frequent consumers of cultural activities.

♦ 10% of the audience at these festivals identified themselves as working class, having lower educational qualifications and less frequent attendance at cultural activities (but it should be noted that they were present in higher numbers at street festivals than in more formal, building based venues).

However, a lack of precision in how research data should be interpreted, in particular the extrapolation of evidence collected only from the audience at the big festivals to the whole sector including local celebrations, has led some advocates of street art to make claims that are not supported by the research evidence.

In a study published by Hors Les Murs (2011) the disparity between claims and reality is obvious. Many street performers and festival organisers claim that their events and performances are attended by more people than attend conventional theatres, exhibitions or concerts. At first sight the research data appears to confirm this as 62% of the French population say they have attended a street performance in their life and 34% during the last 12 months (compared with 16 % for theatre and 12% for ballet and contemporary dance). However, the figure of 62% includes those who have attended a national celebration such as La Fête Nationale (on 14th of July) or a local celebration or activity (such as a jumble sale or a charity party, or a 'kermesse' - a formal but local celebration) in a public space where they were able to enjoy live music or clowns. In addition many of these people consider human statues and chalk painters to be 'street artists' but neither of these 'forms' are listed in the 'bible', *Le Goliath*, because they are not categorised as professional street performers.

It means that the figures on which the street performance sector bases its impact do not reflect the reality of the audience or events surveyed. With respect to the events surveyed, the national inquiry reveals that the audience data has been obtained not only from sophisticated artistic performances of street art but also from events that include chalk artists, human statues and also live music. These activities are often features of the programmes presented by the bigger festivals, and which are mainly attended (if we trust the research) by educated middle-class professional people, from towns/cities with a population of over 10,000. These people are not the 'public population' prioritised by street art pioneers but an audience which possesses the cultural capital needed to engage with any artistic activity, including street art.

Big festivals require the audience to understand how to obtain information, to interrogate it in order to plan their schedule (including understanding directions and venue plans to know where the event will take place and when), and to apply in advance for tickets for ticketed performances. In *Chalon* (in *Aurillac*), audiences queue to get their pre-booked tickets or purchase whatever is left for performances that are very often overbooked before the start of the festival. This requirement for a planned schedule means that audiences have less opportunity to encounter something by chance, to enjoy a 'surprise in their daily life'. Few people, without prior experience of these cultural practices, can deal easily with these requirements and many can be disappointed when they cannot get in or when they come late and discover that sightlines are poor. Performances can be presented in places where there is no stage so that there are problems with engagement for people of average height or less, who are therefore disadvantaged.

The space

As the festivals became better known, they attracted even more people, which increased the total population in the area and increased pressure on local resources and space. This led organisers and public authorities to examine the implications for health and safety and subsequently to changes in legislation and local protocols for ensuring public safety. It is precisely because of such problems of overbooking and of poor visibility that in the 1990s big festivals started to control numbers who could attend and to schedule performances in courtyards away from 'daily life', noise and traffic.

The second generation of companies built their reputations in the 1980s through their distinctive large scale creations and performances. Generik Vapeur, Oposito, Transe Express, Les Plasticiens Volants and, later on, Royal de Luxe were the 'champions' of big scale 'wandering projects', both in France and abroad where on tour they were marketed under the 'French label'. At the beginning of the 1990s however, two events happened, which changed the face of street events dramatically. One was the Gulf War during which all events in public spaces were banned and the second was in 1992 when a temporary stand collapsed in Furiani's stadium in Corsica, resulting in 18 deaths and over 2000 injured. These, allied with concerns about the quality of the experience for the audience, also contributed to increased public concern about safety and in turn to a tightening of rules and regulations governing the use of public space.

While it is possible in a small village to work with the local police on matters of audience safety, a similar approach is impossible when managing thousands of festival-goers at a big event. *Aurillac* has estimated its annual audience at 400,000, *Chalon* 350,000 (this may not mean 400k or 350k individuals, as at a four day festival a single person will see more than one performance). In the past although many street performances were full to capacity (even if not ticketed) the companies knew how many people should be able to see a particular show given the right conditions (visibility, audibility). It was their experience from years of work in a range of contexts that enabled them to estimate the maximum audience that they could reach. But by the early 1990s the sheer size of the audience was making it difficult to ensure a high quality experience for everyone who wanted to come.

These concerns led some artists to insulate themselves from the crowd and the background noise of the festival and its ambiance. They showed less enthusiasm for large scale, walking performances and hence their gradual disappearance from the French landscape. In their place more intimate, small scale performances began to appear which used smaller casts, more appropriate for performing in small courtyards or marquee tents. The artists and organisers claimed these delivered better quality, more intimate shows, which were less reliant on visual and sound effects (like the big parades), but which incorporated more acting, use of text and more sophisticated effects (of light and sound). In a way, they were recreating the black box experience familiar from theatres, but outdoors, including facilities such as stages for the actors, seating stands for the audience and technical props. Smaller budgets and a change in the market for large scale performances (discussed below) are not the only reasons therefore why today the majority of street performances are small scale creations. It is also connected with the material conditions in which they are presented in the 'supermarkets', which the big festivals now resemble. This in turn blurs distinctions between the work and explains why some audiences are unable to discriminate between the professionals (the *In* and *Off* companies)[1] as opposed to the non-professionals (the *Off Off* companies).

This is evident when analysing the programme from *Chalon* in 2012. That year the festival was programmed in 83 venues throughout the city, including some in its outskirts. 18 companies presented performances in the official *In* programme, while 163 companies 'participated' in the *Off* programme[2]. 19 venues were used by the official companies, but 109 of the 163 non official companies performed in 12 venues run by 'collective organisations'. Three of these venues were courtyards, the others being gardens or open spaces (like an esplanade). The effect of this was to create a 'privileged space' away from 'real life', it felt like a small village, or a festival within a festival disconnected from the rest of the city. This separation resulted in a reduced presence in the city centre where only 54 *Off* companies (a third of the total in the programme) performed that year. This is a major departure from the 'surprise in the rhythm of daily life' that the 'pioneer' street performers aspired to deliver. This left the free spaces in the city, unused by the *In*/official and *Off*/unofficial programmes, to the *Off Off* artists (who were not subject to any formal selection process to ensure their quality).

In *Chalon*, where the official programme (*In*) is selected by the artistic director of the festival; the 'unofficial' programme (*Off*) is selected by one of his assistants. But everyone who wants to perform in the street is free to do so. In 2012, the best places for street performances, like the City Hall Square, were free at least half of the day. The *Off Off* artists came and performed, as they did in the pedestrian streets, three-quarters of which were available because the selected artists (*In* and *Off*) were not programmed to perform in them. It was a great opportunity for the *Off Off* artists and also for the spectators who did not need to buy tickets, or travel to a venue.

However, this change in programming policy, much as it might meet some of the performers' requirements, does not help with the projection of a clear image of 'street performance' from an artistic point of view. Unlike the *In* and *Off* companies, most of the *Off Off* performers are buskers presenting a routine show that lacks a creative edge, or they are human statues or puppeteers or clowns. These companies and performers make the street arts scene unclear and reduce the attention that is paid to the more professional companies which are listed in *Le Goliath*.

In *Aurilac*, the 'Mecca', it is even worse, since there is no selection for the *Off* programme. In 2012, around 500 *Off* companies were playing, listed by the festival, but there were also *Off Off* companies playing in free spaces in the heart of the city, with loud sound systems that ruined things for other performances situated close to them. This awkward situation is 'tolerated' because 'It is forbidden to forbid' is the mantra of the festival, reflecting its political roots and a 1968 slogan written on walls in Paris. A part of *Aurillac*'s *Off* festival is organised in 19 collective venues, away from the heart of the city, so far that shuttle transport is required. As a result, the main features of the 'festival's atmosphere' in the city centre, are drunk people and junkies who clutter up the pavements, etc with their dogs, who do not pretend to have any interest but whose presence ruins things for the genuine audience and, worse still, whose presence is included in the festivals' audience figures[3].

The budget

Since their 'appearance' in 1986, big street festivals have come to play an increasingly important role in the aesthetics of street performance. One significant change highlighted in this paper is the movement towards smaller casts. These are a product of two things in particular, reduced public sector financial support (both for companies and for festivals) and the smaller venues available for some companies at these big supermarket-events. *Chalon* and *Aurillac* are like Avignon: if the company is not in the official programme, it has *'to pay to perform'*. Companies have no alternative to doing so, because otherwise the companies cannot be seen by other professionals and programmers. How does it work financially? In *Chalon*, if a company is included in the *Off* programme it is provided with one meal a day, but the company has to fund all its other costs, e.g. their other subsistence costs, travel, accommodation and their production costs. Then if there is anything left they may be able to pay the actors and technicians (but most often neither get paid). In *Aurillac*, it is even simpler: the company receives no financial support at all from the Festival!

The inequity in the system is a result of the fact that public grants (from the state, the regions, the cities) go predominantly to the official *In* programmes (which feature those companies that have been in residency at the national centres) and which represent only around 10% of the total number of companies that perform (not counting the *Off Off* ones). In *Chalon*, the festival has a funding relationship with the regional councils with the result that 25% of the *Off* companies receive some funding towards their costs of attending. In *Aurillac*, where no fees or support are offered it is a 'free market' and you come 'because you want to be there'. The presence of 300-400 potential bookers providing the main reason for some to be there.

Would *Chalon* or *Aurillac* be so well known and so overcrowded without the numerous *Off* companies? And how do these unpaid companies benefit in return? In addition to their presence contributing to the overall appeal of the festival; these unpaid companies inject a lot of money into the local economy through their expenditure on food, drink and accommodation in the hotels, or more often in the camping sites. At *Aurillac*, research indicates that for every euro of public sector support the local economy benefits to the tune of 4 euros; a return on investment of 1:4.

In addition, what is sad for the general quality of performances in France is that the big festivals are partnered with a specific national centre of creative production. In turn the national centres invite a performance company to be a company in residence (sometimes several can be in residence simultaneously). When a new show is ready the national centre co-produces the show and it is included in the programme of their 'partner' festival. The main companies can work with several national centres. As this is a recognised way of achieving financial support from the national committee of the Ministry of Culture then the national companies invest much effort in being partnered by a couple of national centres, with the result that several of these chosen companies are programmed by several festivals. That is also why most of the *Off* companies are small scale as they have limited opportunity to invest resources (especially time) in creating and presenting new work that goes beyond familiar 'routines'.

40 years after the emergence of street performance as a contemporary art form (especially in France), street performance is still seeking the official and critical recognition that other art forms receive. The funding received by the best funded national street centre is less than the budget of the smallest *Scène Nationale* (national venue for indoor performances) and the total value of the financial support allocated to street arts projects by the Directorate for Artistic Creation of the Ministry of Culture is 1.5% of the total budget of this department … What a Mecca!

The real sadness and therefore challenge is that street performances and performers still lack basic recognition, from both financial and aesthetic perspectives. Research shows that people confuse the professionals listed in *Le Goliath* with the human statues, clowns and chalk painters they encounter on their streets. They lack understanding of the creativity employed by real street performers, as they do not even know their names. But not only are the general public guilty of such limited understanding, what is worse perhaps is that this is true for other cultural managers too, many of whom still categorise street performance and performers as part of activities that are of limited importance and equivalent to very local celebrations or a children's birthday party.

The French pyramidal and over-networked system is partly responsible for this situation. This is the system, in which the big street festivals, organised as 'supermarket windows', present the work of selected companies to potential buyers. Working as a sort of monopoly in the market, the big festivals exert significant influence through their roles as (co)producers, residency hosts and the main programmers of the chosen few, while 90% of the groups are just left to the market (you 'play if you pay' to come and perform, but few earn income, or receive grants to invest in their R and D process). Unfortunately, even the 10% of *In* companies lack much presence in the mainstream, as few are known by the managers of conventional venues or other kinds of festivals (with one or two honourable exceptions, in Avignon for example, where one street company was programmed in 2012 as a 'sound and light performance' or before that another was presented in a suburb as part of its 'social inclusion programme').

At the same time, dozens of artists, in France and abroad, are more and more conscious of the role they should play in society. They address local and global problems and they work participatively, and site-specifically, engaging with people, in the moment and in the rhythm of their daily lives. By contrast other, less politically motivated street artists choose to develop and present their work in courtyards or in marquee tents, sometimes far away from the heart of the cities; anywhere other than where their 'traditional audience' can be found.

Arising from this analysis the concerns are that what has happened with the format of the big street festivals, the movement away from large scale engagement to more private, smaller scale events will drain the energy and value to be enjoyed in the large scale format. Following this trend, smaller festivals also seem to be making more use of 'controlled spaces' in which to squeeze street artists and the audiences. So increasingly one can find artists and audiences packed into a public park or garden, or in schoolyards. This solution is easier to manage and control than working with an artist to address the whole canvas of a city, its identity, its challenges, its citizens and the local or regional authorities. A show in a park is certainly less controversial than creating a performance or installation which is provocative and challenges people to (re)think the meaning and value of living together and the need to focus their creativity and creative energies on their daily life. Artists and activists all over the world are engaged with this process/work, but unfortunately not enough French street performers, who are muzzled by the French pyramid, within which the big street festivals enjoy significant and perhaps excessive influence.

Bibliography and further reading

Donnat, O. (1973, 1981, 1989, 1997, 2008) *Les Pratiques culturelles des Français*, Paris: La Documentation Française, Available at: http://www.pratiquesculturelles.culture. gouv.fr/enquetes.php

Gaber, F. (2005) *Les Publics des arts de la rue en Europe*, Gent: Eunetstar

Gaber, F. (2009) *40 ans d'arts de la rue*, Paris: Ici et là

Hors Les Murs. (2008) *Le Goliath, L'annuaire des professionnels de la creation hors les murs*, Paris: Hors Les Murs

Hors Les Murs. (2008) *Le Goliath, Le guide arts de la rue*, Paris: Hors les Murs

Hors Les Murs. (2011) *Les Publics des spectacles de rue et du cirque*, Paris: Hors les Murs

Ministère de la Culture / DMDTS (2008) *Les Publics du spectacle vivant*, Paris: Ministère de la Culture / DMDTS Earthscan.

Notes

[1] Street arts performers/companies are defined in this article as being *In*, *Off* or *Off Off*. *In* and *Off* are both part of the professional sector and listed in *Le Goliath*. One year a company may be programmed by a festival in which case they are *In*. another year they may not be formally programmed but still choose to attend, in which case they are *Off*. '*Off Off*' are not considered to be professionals and some critics consider them to be a distraction because the distinctions stated here are not always clear to the general public which attends the Festival/event where representatives of all three can be seen.

[2] Companies in the *Off* programme are actually competing with one another for their audience and also for the attention of potential 'bookers'. *Off Off* artists compete for the audience but not for 'bookers'.

[3] Estimating attendance at street arts events is notoriously difficult and often the figures supplied by festival organisers and an independent authority, such as the police, are very different.

17 Diaspora Community Festivals and Tourism

Yi Fu, Philip Long and Rhodri Thomas

Introduction

Festivals that celebrate the identities, cultures and traditions of diverse minority, ethnic, diaspora communities are significant cultural and social phenomena. They may also contribute to the visitor economy, for example through increasing tourism income, government revenue and employment (Maclinchey, 2008; O'Sullivan and Jackson, 2002; Picard and Robinson, 2006). Furthermore, diaspora community festivals may contribute to enriching the development of place-images and destination marketing themes that seek to reflect diversity and promote a 'globalised' image of the population of the area (usually city) where such festivals take place (Paradis, 2002). As a consequence, 'festival tourism' has entered the language of tourism studies, defined as "a phenomenon in which people from outside a festival locale visit during the festival period" (O'Sullivan and Jackson, 2002: 325). This chapter contributes to festival tourism studies by exploring *Chinese New Year* festivals in the UK and their emerging prominence as tourism attractions. Research in this area examines its potential for building bridges between communities and cultures.

Some scholars problematise the term 'festival tourism' and resist defining it as a particular category of the tourism market. For example, Quinn (2009) refuses to employ this term, arguing that the primary purpose of festivals is not usually the generation of tourism. Some contemporary festivals do possess a strong place-marketing or tourism objective as part of their rationale. However, many 'traditional festivals' that celebrate community beliefs, social values and identities do not have tourism as a primary purpose (though this may be a significant secondary outcome). Examples include festivities associated with belief systems and annual cultural events such as those associated with the *Chinese New Year* (Bakhtin, 1984; Humphrey, 2001; Magliocco, 2006). Although these festivals have changed in their form over time and some of them may have associations with tourism, they cannot be equated with events that are planned primarily for tourism.

Along with the mass international migrations that occurred throughout the nineteenth and twentieth centuries, and particularly from the 1960s, diaspora festivals have emerged as a comparatively recent classification of festival, though many have ancient antecedents (Green and Scher, 2007). Diaspora festivals include "festivals and events that have mobilised and recomposed, to varying extents, aspects of the culture of diasporic populations" (Carnegie and Smith, 2006: 255). Most diaspora festival research has emerged from social science and humanities disciplines, such as anthropology, sociology, the visual arts, languages and literature (Crichow and Armstrong, 2010). Some are inspired by the inter-disciplinary field of diaspora studies (Green and Scher, 2007). These studies usually discuss the meanings and implications of diaspora festivals, for example, Labrador's (2002) research into the Filipino *Pag-ibig sa Tinubuang Lupa* festival in Hawaii and Cohen's (1982) studies of the *Notting Hill Carnival* in London.

However, systematic research into diaspora and/or ethnic minority community festivals in relation to tourism is limited. Do diaspora festivals have impacts on tourism that are comparable and/or distinct from other festivals or events? Are quantitative data, such as visitor numbers or tourism income that are more or less convincingly attributed to a festival sufficient to explain the association between diaspora festivals and tourism? If diaspora festivals do attract tourists to a city, does tourism impose constraints on the nature of the diaspora festival itself? How have diaspora festivals developed their programmes, organisation and audiences in the context of tourism?

Diaspora communities: theoretical perspectives

The word 'diaspora' has a rich historical lineage, deriving from the Greek verb *speiro* (to sow) and the preposition *dia* (over). It was first applied to people who had been forced to leave their national territories after suffering persecution and banishment (Cohen, 1997: ix). Scholars such as Cohen (1997), Safran (1991) and Clifford (1994) suggest that the concept of diaspora has most commonly been linked with the Jewish people's exile from their historical homeland and settlement worldwide. Others have developed the concept of the diaspora based on the forced migrations of black African and Irish peoples (Cohen, 1997; Gilroy, 1993).

However gradually, this traditional definition of diaspora has been enriched with greater meaning, as international migration has diversified in cause and location from the mid-1960s. Voluntary migration has become a more common phenomenon, though still of course subject to constraint and legislation (Ma, 2003). Thus, the concept of diaspora now no longer has exclusive intimations of trauma (Cohen, 1997). Furthermore, a contrast to the pattern of migration that typically occurred before the mid-1960s, characterised by permanent, unidirectional and onetime movement from one country to another now implies more fluid and complex spatial mobilities, (Ma, 2003) with flexible locations, multi-directional movement and complex temporalities (Brinkherhoff, 2006; Clifford, 1994).

The word diaspora is also deployed at times as 'a metaphoric designation' (Safran, 1991: 83) to describe different categories of people and community identities: "Political refugees, alien residents, guest workers, immigrants, expellees, ethnic and racial minorities and overseas communities" (Shuval, 2000:41). The common feature of these diverse groups of people is their experiences of living through cultural differences (Hall, 1990). All diasporas live on cultural borderlands and share spatial experiences with 'porous boundaries' (Ma, 2003: 22). Thus, diasporas construct their identities through negotiation with the cultural influences of 'home' and 'host' countries and also the differences within and between diaspora groups (Shi, 2005). Chan (1999) goes further in this respect, suggesting that diaspora "does not need a country, a kingdom, or a state; it is a condition and that condition is sustained by its place in a community anywhere". In this context, Shi (2005) and Zweig et al (2008), use Chinese students and professionals in the United States as an example to insist that they belong to the global Chinese diaspora community. This is because they have engaged in the community's activities, linking the home and host countries, and share the consciousness of 'Chineseness' with Chinese diaspora communities all over the world. According to these studies, the conventional concept of the diaspora is challengeable and definitions of the word may be updated in relation to research on diaspora communities in specific contexts.

A key issue is whether diaspora communities are more or less actively involved in the life of the host societies (which may, of course, involve engagement with other diaspora communities as well as with the indigenous population) as opposed to focusing their social lives within their communities. The extent to which there is a collective sense of nostalgia for 'home' – an 'imaginative geography and history' (Said, 1978: 55) or an 'imagined community' is also pertinent (Anderson, 1983). Esman (2009) suggests that there are levels of interaction between diasporas and their home and host countries concerning mobilities, education, political activity and culture and that these play an important role in international and inter-communal relations. Zweig,

Fung and Han (2008) claim that 'scientific diasporas' help to connect home and host countries in areas of education, science and technology. According to Lew and Wong (2004), Chinese diaspora people regularly travel back to their ancestral hometown and some may make substantial financial remittances to extended families and communities 'back home'.

The characteristics of diaspora communities also impact in important ways on the festivals that they produce. The following section discusses the association between diaspora festivals and tourism.

Diaspora festivals and tourism

Some diaspora festivals have prominent tourism connections based on the 'exotic' cultures that are on display and also strong attendance from 'diaspora tourists' (Carnegie and Smith, 2006; Wilks, 2011). For example, the *Notting Hill Carnival* in London, which presents Caribbean cultures, typically receives over two million visitors during its two-day programme, with spending estimated at around £30 million (O'Sullivan and Jackson, 2002:325). Other diaspora festivals, such as the carnival in Brooklyn, New York, and the *Asian Mela* in Edinburgh are also claimed to be significant tourist attractions (Carnegie and Smith, 2006; Scher, 1999). However, the attribution of tourist arrivals and expenditure directly to any festival is problematic. A deeper analysis is required in order to better understand the relationships that diaspora communities and their festivals have with tourism. Quinn (2009: 290) suggests that "a key principle underpinning the development of festivals for tourism purposes must be to consolidate and enhance the role that festival practices play in sustaining communities". If a festival lacks the involvement of local communities and focuses primarily on external visitors, it will lose the 'celebratory energy' (Klaić, undated: 34) which will threaten the survival and sustainable development of the festival for tourism (Quinn, 2009).

Therefore, it is important to understand the relationship between diaspora festivals and communities before considering a festival's tourism dimensions. The communities involved in a diaspora festival may consist solely of representatives of the diaspora in its organisation or they may more or less involve the wider population that 'belongs' to the host countries, which may of course be multi-cultural and diverse.

Members of diaspora communities whose ancestries were from the same country may share (*or contest*) values associated with that society, and their festivals may be based on and portray elements of, "a creation myth, a foundation or migratory legend, or a military success particularly relevant in the mythical or historical memory of the community staging the festival" (Falassi, 1987: 5). Through these festivals, community members are reminded of their 'golden age', their tribulations or other stories related to their history (Beezley, Martin and French, 1994; Falassi, 1987). Anderson (1983) considers that the function of these kinds of narratives of history is to construct a community consciousness – to make people think about themselves, and to relate themselves to others, profoundly united in an imagined community. This may explain why diaspora narratives commonly have the subtext of connections with the home (Fu, 2012), which constructs the connections between an individual and the collective. This echoes the arguments made by anthropologists who have examined the functions of festivals for society, such as Durkheim (1976) and Turner (1995), that is, festivals are unifying forces promoting community solidarity.

Members of diaspora communities construct, claim and enhance their ethnic identities when they organise and attend diaspora festivals. The Caribbean diaspora communities in London, Toronto, New York attend the *Notting Hill Carnival*, the *Caribana Carnival* and the *Brooklyn Carnival* respectively in large numbers to celebrate Caribbean community identities. Diaspora communities originally from South Asia may attend the *Edinburgh* or *Bradford Melas* in the UK to express shared identities (Bankston and Henry, 2010; Carnegie and Smith, 2006; Johnson, 2007). Apart from the members of the diaspora communities in such cities, diaspora festivals also attract diaspora tourists from other cities or countries. For example, the *Chinese New Year festival* in Newcastle-upon-Tyne in 2009 attracted Chinese visitors from across the UK who not only attended the event but also consumed in the Chinatown District where the Festival was held (Fu, 2012).

Festivals have been an important tool for diaspora communities to assert their rights and desire for legitimacy and recognition as people from minority ethnic groups incorporated within larger nation-states whose dominant national ideologies have impinged on them (Bankston and Henry, 2010; Becker, 2002). The Notting Hill Carnival in the 1970s and 1980s is a good example in this respect (Cohen, 1982; Jackson, 1987). Through festivals, diaspora communities construct and claim their ethnic identities in the context of the interactions, tensions and at times, conflicts that play out between communities at the levels of nation and neighbourhood (Cohen, 1982). Tourism was, therefore, not a priority or even a consideration in the face of more weighty and politicised concerns. However, if more visitors from 'the outside' were attracted to the festivals, this might contribute to the wider legitimacy of the event. In this sense, tourism can potentially represent communities in a positive light as contributors to local and national economies. Thus, some prominent diaspora festivals have intentionally or unintentionally, explicitly or implicitly, developed relationships with tourists and tourism.

In recent years, many diaspora festivals have become more open to wider participation in festival events and programming. The organising committees of diaspora festivals may consist of individuals or organisations from, for example, local government, private companies, artistic institutions and universities in home and host societies. Such changes to festival organisation closely relate to the transformation of diaspora communities, which in some cases are becoming, or are encouraged to be, more integrated through participation in various political, economic and cultural activities connecting home and host societies. Accordingly, diaspora festivals display multi-faceted and dynamic interactions between diaspora communities and the wider society (Cohen, 1982:24). For example, Johnson (1987) suggests that the *Festival of Lights* in New Zealand, as a transformation of tradition in a multi-cultural context, is a result of organisational intervention, negotiation of ethnic relationships and the blurring of cultural differences.

When tourism agencies and other commercial organisations become more closely involved with diaspora festivals, these events will consequently become more connected to tourism and tourists. In some instances, diaspora festivals may become a highlighted tourist attraction for a city. The *West Indian Carnival* in Leeds, UK, in August each year is a good example. Visiting the festival may be the primary motivation for some tourists to travel to the city during that period. In other instances, diaspora festivals may be featured prominently in the tourist brochures of a city. Tourists encounter the festivals intentionally or unintentionally because they are in the city when the events are taking place. This may happen in cities that are major tourism destinations, but also cities that are less well-known, but that do possess substantial diaspora communities. Bradford, Birmingham and Leicester in the UK are good examples. In such cases, promoting tourism has assumed more importance in the planning and presentation of diaspora festivals. These cases may, therefore, be included in O'Sullivan and Jackson's conceptualisation of 'festival tourism' (2002). However, even though some diaspora festivals are now more focused on tourism, they are still celebrating traditions and identities rooted in diaspora communities, albeit dynamic and hybridised as diasporas have become more or less integrated within the 'mainstream' societies of their adopted 'home' countries and cities. *Chinese New Year festivals* in the UK exemplify this process.

Chinese New Year festivals and tourism in Britain

The *Chinese New Year* festival is the most significant annual event for Chinese people both in China and worldwide. Nowadays it has become a popular phenomenon in cities outside of China, particularly those with large Chinese populations, such as Sydney and San Francisco (Lau, 2002). In Britain, the festival has become a public celebration in cities such as London, Liverpool, Manchester, Nottingham, Sheffield, Leeds and Newcastle-upon-Tyne. At these celebrations, visitors can watch cultural performances, such as martial arts, dragon and lion dances and acrobatics, and taste Chinese food.

Chinese people's New Year celebrations in Britain can be traced back to the 1960s. Newell (1989) suggests that celebrations began in London in 1960. The chair of the martial arts group, the Choi Lee Fut Kung Fu Dragon and Lion Association, described the first time that he and his friends celebrated Chinese New Year at Tiffany's nightclub in Newcastle-upon-Tyne, UK in 1977 (Interview with the chair of Choi Lee Fut Kung Fu Dragon and Lion Association on July 29 2009). At that time, the majority of the Chinese diaspora community in the city was from the New Territories in Hong Kong, where migration was driven by British Government policy after the Second World War and the agricultural policy in Hong Kong (Akilli, 2003). During their early years in Britain, these Chinese immigrants were starting catering businesses and trying to move their families left behind in Hong Kong to Britain (Benton and Gomez, 2011). At that time, most of the Chinese New Year celebrations were on a small scale, based on associations, friendship and workplace or educational groups, schools and other forms of social life (interview with the chair of the Sheffield Chinese New Year Joint Committee in Sheffield on February 10, 2008). They were private occasions limited to certain Chinese individuals or communities through which Chinese people celebrated the Chinese New Year tradition, shared the longing for families left in hometowns and expressed their best wishes for the New Year.

Thus, the Chinese New Year celebrations at that time did not attract much attention from British society, and there were few if any associations with tourism. This phenomenon is closely related to the living condition of the Chinese diaspora community then, as the Chair of the Sheffield Chinese New Year Joint Committee explained:

> In the past, historically, (the) Chinese have been isolated.... (not) because everybody... tried to isolate them, more because themselves acted in that way... when I first came to UK suddenly (in 1975), the Chinese would be looked at in a kind of... not in a favourable way. They were seriously quite secretive...the conception was that usually

they didn't want to be a part of the society. They always somehow looked invisible (from an interview with the chair of the Sheffield Chinese New Year Joint Committee on February 20 2009).

Between the 1970s and the 1980s, racial tension between some ethnic minority communities and some white British people was a serious social problem (Benton and Gomez, 2011; Joppke, 1996). The ethnic immigrants were on the margins of British society and isolated from the wider community. This was also related to the race relations policy at that time which emphasised a multi-cultural agenda and 'self-government' of ethnic minority communities (Joppke, 1996). Compared to the Caribbean communities who use carnival as a 'contest' space (Cohen, 1982:24), the Chinese community's invisible *Chinese New Year* celebration was another way to react to the racial relations at that time, in this case, through exclusive community celebrations.

From the 1980s, the Chinese diaspora community in Britain has become more diversified, which has had consequences for *Chinese New Year* festivals. First, the Chinese immigrants of this period belonged to a spread of occupations including students, scholars, professionals, traders and restaurateurs (Benton and Gomez, 2011). Second, their native places were not limited to one country or area (e.g. Hong Kong). From the end of the 1970s, Britain had started to receive Chinese migration from mainland China, Taiwan, Singapore, Malaysia and other Asian areas, among whom those from mainland China were the largest group (Maclinchey, 2008). Since the end of the last century, *Chinese New Year* celebrations have gradually transformed into city-wide festival celebrations open to a wider public. All (or most) Chinese groups within a city gather together to produce a *Chinese New Year* festival, setting up joint committees to organise and produce local festivals annually. For example, the Chinese New Year Celebration Joint Committee (Sheffield Committee) in Sheffield, the Chinese Festivity Group in Newcastle-upon-Tyne and The Federation of Chinese Associations of Manchester (FCAM) (Fu, Long and Thomas, In press).

Chinese groups and the Chinese New Year organising committees usually play the major role in the Chinese New Year festivals. These 'central stakeholders' are complemented by the contribution of 'peripheral stakeholders' from wider society, which includes visitors, performers, sponsors from private companies and representatives of local governments, universities and the Chinese embassy. These peripheral stakeholders may be either from the Chinese diasporas' native countries or host cities. For example, in the case of the Chinese New Year Festival in Sheffield between 2005 and 2009, the local organisers invited artists and performers from mainland China to perform at the events annually. In Newcastle-upon-Tyne, the City Council has been a member of the event organisation - the Chinese Festivity Group - and has provided human and financial support since it was established (From interviews with the representative of Newcastle Northeast Association on March 1 2009 and with the chair of the Choi Lee Fut Kung Fu Dragon and Lion Association on July 29 2009).

The cooperation between the central stakeholders and the peripheral stakeholders in Chinese New Year celebrations demonstrates Chinese diaspora communities' strong desire to be a part of wider society and to interact with people from 'the outside'. As the Chair of the Sheffield Chinese New Year Joint Committee suggests:

> Chinese New Year is a publicity vehicle, a medium, for the Chinese community to communicate with the society… It is a platform for all the Chinese to come together, to work together to deliver the show, not only for the Chinese to see, but for the non-Chinese to see…They (Chinese people) can be a part of the society. They have got so much to offer to the society. And it's good for the Chinese and it's good for the society. (From an interview with the chair of the Sheffield *Chinese New Year* Joint Committee on February 20 2009)

If the Chinese diaspora community had remained as 'a silent society' in Britain, the Chinese New Year celebrations would not have become festivals open to wider public participation. In addition, peripheral stakeholders can potentially achieve diverse cultural, economic, social and educational objectives through their participation in Chinese New Year celebrations, including the development of their association with tourism.

Some UK cities, such as Manchester, Liverpool and Newcastle, have Chinatown districts where Chinese New Year festivals are celebrated. Local governments, tourist organisations and private companies typically incorporate *Chinese New Year* celebrations within Chinatowns as a tourism package to attract tourists to the cities and these neighbourhoods in particular. For example, Birmingham City Council lists the *Chinese New Year* festival as an item in the 'Tourism and Leisure' section on its official website (Birmingham City Council, 2012) and the Official Visitor Guide of London also uses the *Chinese New Year* festival to highlight the city's tourism offer (Visit London, 2012). As for some smaller-sized cities, the local government tends to regard Chinese New Year celebrations as an opportunity to promote community cohesion, enhance cultural diversity and develop the city-image, which may be helpful to attracting tourism (and business relationships) indirectly or in the long term. For example, in Newcastle-upon-Tyne and Liverpool, the 2009 *Chinese New Year* festival not only displayed 'traditional' Chinese culture (e.g. martial arts, dragon and lion dances), but also employed western music performances and funfair facilities to attract local Chinese and non-Chinese residents and day visitors living in the areas close to those cities.

Furthermore, individual artists or teams are now travelling around British cities to perform at *Chinese New Year*. These performers are usually based in Britain. For example, the martial arts organisation - Jin Long Academy in Manchester - was paid by the Sheffield Chinese New Year Joint Committee for its event in 2009; while it also performed in the Manchester Chinese New Year 2009. The artists may also travel from cities in China, often the hometowns of Chinese diasporas or where there is a twin town relationship with particular British cities. They may also be sent by the central or city government(s) in China or invited by the Chinese Embassy in London to perform the role of cultural envoy to enhance the cultural exchange between the two countries. The visit of the artist delegation team from Chengdu to London and Sheffield for the local *Chinese New Year* celebrations in 2010 is a good example of this. This phenomenon to some extent promotes domestic tourism in Britain and also international tourism, although it is difficult to demonstrate exactly how many people are involved and to what extent economic outcomes are generated by such tours.

If Chinese diaspora communities have expressed their identities through quiet private celebration of Chinese New Year in the past, they currently (re) construct, (re)define and (re)present their identities in a public interactive festival space. In this space, the Chinese diasporas may or may not regard themselves as guests in the host societies. When they put their events in the context of (international) tourism, voluntarily or involuntarily, they mobilise their identity in a format that has rich cultural interchanges and where the diaspora becomes host.

Conclusions

Some diaspora community festivals are increasingly taking account of tourism when they are planned, produced and presented. Many contemporary diaspora communities actively participate in social, cultural and economic activities that connect the home and host societies, which encourage stakeholders from the outside to participate in their festivals. This is an important factor that is enhancing the relationships between diaspora festivals and tourism.

Diaspora festivals more or less attract (international) tourists and tourism. However, it cannot simply be argued that diaspora festivals are produced primarily for tourism purposes. As the case of Chinese New Year festivals in the UK demonstrates, the identities, values, traditions and beliefs of diaspora communities are paramount, though these are of course subject to debate and negotiation within the community and in particular across genders and generations. Diaspora communities are complex, dynamic, fluid and open to hybridisation over time. They are likely, therefore, to be of continuing and growing interest to researchers, policy makers and communities for many years to come, including those with a particular interest in tourism.

Bibliography and further reading

Akilli, S. (2003) *Chinese Immigration to Britain in the Post-WWII Period*, retrieved 19/10/2007, from www.usp.nus.edu.sg/post/uk/mo/sakilli10.html

Anderson, B. (1983) *Imagined Communities*, London: Verso.

Bakhtin, M. (1984) *Rabelais and His World*, Bloomington: Indiana University Press.

Bankston, C. L. and Henry, J. (2010) Spectacles of ethnicity: festivals and the commodification of ethnic culture among Louisiana Cajuns. *Sociological Spectrum*, **20**(4), 377-407.

Becker, C. (2002) We are real slaves, real ismkhan: Memories of the Trans-Saharan slave trade in the Tafilalet of South-Eastern Morocco. *The Journal of North African Studies*, **7**(4), 97-121.

Beezley, W. H., Martin, C. E. and French, W. E. (eds.) (1994) *Rituals of Rule, Rituals of Resistance: Public Celebrations and Popular Culture in Mexico*, Wilmington and Delaware: SR Books.

Benton, G. and Gomez, E. T. (2011) *The Chinese in Britain, 1800 - Present: Economy, Transnationalism, Identity*, Basingstoke: Palgrave Macmillan.

Birmingham City Council. (2012) Chinese New Year in Birmingham, www.birmingham. gov.uk/cny. Retrieved December 9, 2012

Brinkherhoff, J. (2006) Diasporas, skills transfer and remittances: evolving perceptions and potential, in C. Wescott and J. Brinkerhoff, (eds.) *Converting Migration Drains into Gains: Harnessing the Resources of Overseas Professionals*, Manila: Asian Development Bank, 1-32

Carnegie, E. and Smith, M. (2006) Mobility, diaspora and the hybridisation of festivity: The case of the Edinburgh Mela, in D. Picard and M. Robinson (eds.), *Festivals, Tourism and Social Change: Remaking Worlds* (pp. 255-268), Clevedon: Channel View Publications.

Chan, S. (1999) What is this thing called Chinese diaspora? *Contemporary Review*, **274**, 81-83.

Clifford, J. (1994) Diasporas. *Cultural Anthropology*, **9**(3), 302-338.

Cohen, A. (1982) A polyethnic London carnival as a contested cultural performance. *Ethnic and Racial Studies*, **5**(1), 23-41.

Cohen, R. (1997) *Global Diasporas: An Introduction*, London: University College London Press.

Crichow, M. A. and Armstrong, P. (2010) Carnival Praxis, Carnivalesque Strategies and Atlantic Interstices. *Social Identities, 16*(4), 399-414.

Durkheim, E. (1976) *The Elementary Forms of the Religious Life*, London: George Allen and Unwin LTD.

Esman, M. J. (2009) Diasporas and international relations, in M. J. Esman (Ed.), *Diasporas in the Contemporary World* (pp. 120-132). Cambridge and Malden: Polity Press.

Falassi, A. (ed.). (1987) *Time Out of Time: Essays on Festival*, Albuquerque: University of New Mexico Press.

Fu, Y. (2012) *Exploring Diaspora Communities' Festivals: Chinese New Year in England,* Leeds Metropolitan University, Unpublished Phd Thesis.

Fu, Y., Long, P. and Thomas, R. (In press) Guanxi and the Organisation of Chinese New Year Festivals in England. *Event Management.*

Gilroy, P. (1993) *The Black Atlantic: Modernity and Double Consciousness*, London: Verso.

Green, G. L. and Scher, P. W. (eds.). (2007) *Trinidad Carnival: The Cultural Politics of A Transnational Festival*, Bloomington and Indianapolis: Indiana University Press.

Hall, S. (1990) Cultural identity and diaspora, in J. Rutherford (ed.), *Identity: Community, Culture, Difference* (pp. 222-237), London: Lawrence and Wishart.

Humphrey, C. (2001) *The Politics of Carnival: Festive Misrule in Medieval England*, Manchester: Manchester University Press.

Jackson, P. (1987) Street life: the politics of carnival, *Environment and Planning D: Society and Space, 6*(2), 213-227.

Johnson, H. (2007) 'Happy Diwali!' Performance, multicultural soundscapes and intervention in Aotearoa/New Zealand, *Ethnomusiology Forum, 16*(1), 71-94.

Joppke, C. (1996) Multiculturalism and immigration: A comparison of the United States, Germany and Great Britain, *Theory and Society, 25* (4), 449-550.

Klaić, D. (undated) Challenges and strategies. In D. Klaić, A. Bollo and U. Bacchella (eds.), *Festivals: Challenges of Growth, Distinction, Support Base and Internationalisation* (pp. p.28-34), Estonia: Department of Culture, Tartu City Government.

Labrador, R. N. (2002) Performing identity: the public presentation of culture and ethnicity among Filipinos in Hawai'i, *Journal of Cultural Research, 6* (3), 287-307.

Lau, S. C. K. (2002) *Chinatown Britain*, London: Chinatown Online.

Lew, A. A. and Wong, A. (2004) Sojourners, Guanxi and Clan Associations: social capital and overseas Chinese tourism to China, in T. Coles and D. J. Timothy (eds.), *Tourism, Diasporas and Space* (pp. 202-214). London and New York: Routledge.

Ma, L. J. C. (2003) Space, place and transnationalism in the Chinese diaspora, in L. J. C. Ma and C. L. Cartier (eds.), *The Chinese Diaspora, Space, Place, Mobility and Identity* (pp. 1-50), Oxford: Lanham, Rowman and Littlefield.

Maclinchey, K. A. (2008) Urban ethnic festivals, neighbourhoods and the multiple realities of marketing place, *Journal of Travel and Tourism Marketing,* **25**(3), 251-264.

Magliocco, S. (2006) *The Two Madonnas: The Politics of Festival in a Sardinian Community (2nd Edition),* Long Grove: Waveland Press.

Newell, V. (1989) A note on the Chinese New Year celebration in London and Its socio-economic background, *Western Folklore,* **48**(1), 61-66.

O'Sullivan, D. and Jackson, M. J. (2002) Festival tourism: a contributor to sustainable local economic development? *Journal of Sustainable Tourism,* **10**(4), 325-342.

Paradis, T. W. (2002) The political economy of theme development in small urban places: the case of Roswell, New Mexico, *Tourism Geographies,* **4**(1), 22-43.

Picard, D. and Robinson, M. (2006) Remaking worlds: festivals, tourism and change, in D. Picard and M. Robinson (eds.), *Festivals, Tourism and Social Change: Remaking Worlds* (pp. 1-31), Clevedon, Buffalo andToronto: Channel View Publications.

Quinn, B. (2009) Problematising 'festival tourism': arts festivals and sustainable development in Ireland, *Journal of Sustainable Tourism,* **14**(3), 288-306.

Safran, W. (1991) Diasporas in modern societies: myths of homeland and return, *Diaspora,* **1**(1), 83-89.

Said, E. W. (1978) *Orientalism,* London: Penguin.

Scher, P. W. (1999) West Indian American Day: becoming a tile in the gorgeous mosaic: Western Indian American Day in Brooklyn, in J. Pulis (ed.), *Religion, Diaspora and Cultural Identity: A Reader in the Anglophone Caribbean* (pp. 45-66), New York: Gordon and Breach.

Shi, Y. (2005) Identity construction of the Chinese diaspora, ethnic media use, community formation, and the possibility of social activism, *Continuum,* **19**(1), 55-72.

Shuval, J. T. (2000) Diaspora migration: definitional ambiguities and a theoretical paradigm, *International Migration,* **38**(5), 41-56.

Turner, V. (1995) *The Ritual Process: Structure and Anti-structure,* New York: Aldine De Gruyter.

Visit London. (2012) Chinese New Year 2013. Retrieved December 9, 2012, from http://www.visitlondon.com/

Wilks, L. (2011) Bridging and bonding: social capital at music festivals, *Journal of Policy Research in Tourism, Leisure and Events,* **3**(3), 281-297.

Zweig, D., Fung, C. S. and Han, D. (2008) Redefining the brain drain: China's 'diaspora option', *Science Technology Society,* **13**(1), 1-33.

18 Mela in the UK: A 'travelled and habituated' festival

Rakesh Kaushal and Chris Newbold

Introduction

Mela in the United Kingdom has become, in its short thirty year history, one of the most popular forms of festival entertainment. The word 'mela' itself, is based on the Sanskrit, meaning a community gathering or meeting, and in its many forms mela in the UK has remained true to this broad sense of people, families and communities congregating together in an atmosphere of festivity. At its roots, mela in the UK has evolved out of South Asian religious rites and rituals, and can also be seen to be built on South Asian folk and rural culture and traditions. However, at the core of the definition of mela is the notion of a gathering. This is most appropriate here in that it does not necessarily refer to any mono-cultural or religious focus, and is important when we observe how mela has 'travelled' and become 'habituated' in the UK. Carnegie and Smith (2006) identify *Edinburgh Mela* as having travelled but in this chapter, whilst recognising the travelled nature of mela that they refer to, we indicate that it is the habituated nature of mela that more clearly identifies its nature and existence in the UK.

Therefore, this chapter will document that, after 25 to 30 years, mela in the UK can be seen to be adopting its own traditions and connotations. Moreover, by the very nature of the modern diverse British population, mela is now largely urbanised and many continue to reflect South Asian religious festivals, be they *Boishakhi Melas* (Brick Lane London), *Holi Hai Melas* (Oxford) or *Eid Melas* (Birmingham), but others have lost touch with these roots as the demands of festival and cultural event management and venue availability have led to other requirements taking priority. The focus of the research presented here is concerned with the manifestation of mela in the UK and, in particular, how it has adapted to the various town and city locations in which it is now a fundamental part of the cultural events calendar. The importance of mela in terms of economic impact and tourism may be one reason why mela is popular with local authorities. However, as this research will document, other explanations revolve around debates and policy decisions on community cohesion, multi-culturalism and diversity.

The overall approach in this research is that melas do not take place in a vacuum, but are in fact woven into the wider cultural, social and artistic fabric. Thus social, economic, political and cultural contexts are vital to an understanding of mela in the UK. This research advances the argument that mela in the UK is a barometer of the extent to which the South Asian population see themselves and are seen by the wider population as a legitimate part of cities and towns in the United Kingdom. Mela festivals can be seen as the overt displays of the rightful existence of communities and cultures rather than their being viewed as separate, alien or 'other'. The research methodology for this chapter consisted of a case study approach combined with sixteen in-depth qualitative interviews, carried out over the telephone with managers, organisers and representative of sixteen different mela organisations, from Bristol and Swindon in the South West of England, to Middlesbrough in the North East and Dunfermline in Scotland. This research examines the overall state of mela in the UK through the three years of research, 2010 to 2013 (see Newbold and Kaushal 2014)[1].

At the heart of the research questions were a number of key areas to be explored within the sample:

♦ First, the history and development of the particular mela, together with its changing role.

♦ Second, the organisation, management and key stakeholders of the mela, in particular looking at the relationship between these stakeholders, funding and local authorities which emphasises the economic impact of this relationship.

♦ Third, the analysis of community involvement and support is central, since they have a duel stakeholder role as object and subject of the mela.

♦ Fourth, the programming policy is at the heart of the delivery of the melas aims and objectives, and there is often a conflict between traditional South Asian art and culture and the influence of global Bollywood and the hybridisation of modern Indian music. This also leads to questions relating to provisions for first, second and third generation community members.

♦ Last, our questioning explored the role mela played in community cohesion, perceptions of multi-culturalism and diversity and the importance of visuality, legitimacy and references drawn from a bawdy style of theatre from the Indian sub-continent, known historically as Tamasha.

Research into melas calls forth a number of debates and discussions both within the South Asian population, and between that community and the wider population. As an example of one of the most successful forms of festival in the UK at present, the study of mela allows for an opportunity to deepen knowledge of the management and impact of festivals and cultural events in the twenty-first century.

Mela in the UK: origins and development

The oldest established melas in the UK, *Bradford Mela* and *Nottingham Mela*, have their roots in a desire to bring the various South Asian communities together, with their common interests and heritage, rather than on religious grounds. Many melas have become wholly secular, hybridised and eclectic in their content and organisation, as they have become successful local and regional events in their own right, and have thus sought through organisational and economic necessity to attract wider audiences. The story of the movement of mela around the globe is the story of the movement of the South Asian population out of the subcontinent, either by forced or voluntary emigration. South Asian immigration into the UK had started to increase noticeably in the 1950s when citizens of British colonies and the Commonwealth had the automatic right to settle in the UK. It grew through the first years of the 1960s for two main reasons. First, a demand for labour which had seen large scale immigration from the Caribbean and, second, a fear that the UK might impose restrictions on immigration in the face of growing popular, political and press opposition to it. This resulted in the *Commonwealth Immigrants Act* of 1962, introducing an employment voucher system. Subsequent amendments to this system in 1965 did not stop the flow of dependents and by the end of the 1960s the balance of immigration into the UK had shifted from the Caribbean to the Indian subcontinent. This was then boosted in the 1970s by Asian immigration from East Africa, following policies of 'Africanisation' in the newly independent states.

Mela beginnings in the UK can be seen to emerge as a combination of personal action by community leaders and activists and by interventions of entrepreneurs and individuals who recognised a gap in the market for South Asian based arts and entertainment. What was key here was the desire of the communities to have something that represented their cultural interests and heritage. Melas in the UK usually have some common threads that motivate their founding and development. First, to bring South Asian arts and culture to the local community. Second, to provide a free family and community orientated festival. Third, to reflect the diversity of South Asian Arts and to bring South Asian artists and stars to UK audiences. Fourth, to provide a showcase for local talent and arts and performance groups, and for new up and coming South Asian talent. Last, and almost without exception, all mela organisations interviewed stated that they were founded upon the principle of promoting community cohesion and social inclusion. In the 'spirit of mela' the meeting and gathering is central. Melas were thus established with the intention of serving the local communities to whom they were addressed, but increasingly this has developed to the wider community with particular reference to its multicultural make-up. It is this constituency that manifests itself in terms of each particular mela's stakeholders, organisations and the operational procedures.

Mela organisation and management

In terms of mela organisational and management structures there are a large number of variations at play, often tied to the availability and sources of funding. Many melas are run by year round arts organisations (Brouhaha in Liverpool runs the *Liverpool Mela*) and community organisations (*Coventry Vaisakhi Mela* is run by the Sikh Union). There are organisations that are wholly voluntary and just come together to run the event (*Swindon Mela*), whilst others see running a mela as an adjunct to their primary focus, recognising the role of the mela in supporting that focus. For instance, *Fife Dunfermline Mela* is run by the Fairness, Race Awareness and Equality Group while *Loughborough Mela* is formulated in partnership with Charnwood Arts and Human Rights and Equalities Charnwood.

Mela organisations in the UK which employ key event management staff such as Leicester, Nottingham and Bradford for instance, and those run from local council events teams such as Middlesbrough, all emphasise their roles and responsibilities for the professional delivery of an event. The importance to the mela of their relationship with local authorities cannot be overstated, not only in terms of financial assistance, but also for the logistical and organisational support that they provide. This has meant that mela organisers are aware of practical and legal requirements that such events demand. These connections are vitally important, illuminating the strong working relationship mela organisers have had to cultivate with their local authorities. It is the case that community festivals need to meet council requirements which often stipulate concrete outcomes in the way of proposed usage of local amenities and involvement of local communities. Council requirements usually ask for mela organisers to demonstrate that their intended events will do something worthwhile for the local community. It is this condition which is often built into the funding criteria from which applications will be judged.

However, the current economic climate has impacted negatively on mela festivals and the amount of funding they can receive from local authorities. Many of the respondents interviewed within this study expressed concern at the dwindling amount of centralised funding currently being made available for community festivals. In this economic climate the use of volunteers is crucial to the management of most melas in that it is a source of much needed unpaid labour. However, it also connects the mela to its locale and keeps it in touch with the needs and interest of the community it serves. Most volunteers come from within the local communities themselves with the tradition of volunteering for the mela now running into three generations and cementing the place of mela at the heart of many local community arts and cultural activities.

What clearly emerged from the research was that in order to function successfully as a festival in the UK context, mela associations now felt they had to achieve three interconnected objectives: first, they had to be grounded in their local community; second, they had to offer a year round programme of activities, related to and leading up to the mela event itself; and third, they had to become professional in their approach to managing the mela, especially in gaining financial control. All our sample of mela associations have reported struggling with financial pressures and the wider economy, especially in the realm of funding and grants from central organisations such as Arts Council England. This has proved to be a difficult blow especially since the early years of the twenty-first century had seen so many melas brought into existence through schemes like the National Lottery's Arts4Everyone initiative or the Regional Arts Lottery Programme (RALP).

Mela programming

The composition of a mela's programme is important because it is here that the objectives of melas are revealed. The programming of mela in the UK has evolved over its thirty years of development, now encompassing in its many guises not only traditional South Asian entertainments like tabla drums, dhol processions, music and traditional kathak dancing, but also the modern derivations of Bhangra music and Bollywood dance styles such as giddha. Alongside this, melas in the period of this research contained entertainments as diverse as African singer and percussion player Lucky Moyo, The London Philharmonic Orchestra, Japanese drumming from Kakatsitsi and a Blues Brothers tribute band. The music and dance are not the only part of the eclectic mela mix. Key to the mela experience is the arts provision and demonstrations and exhibitions of South Asian artists and arts organisations, work such as rangoli (painting with rice and flour), henna art, shadow puppetry, story-telling about key historical and mythical figures and poems known as geet and quieter ghazal love songs. Additionally, qawwali devotional songs are a feature at many Muslim events.

The need to organise a varied and detailed programme is imperative if community events are to generate as much cross-cultural appeal as possible. Year round educational visits and pre-festival arts workshops, Bollywood workshops, visiting artists doing pre-mela workshops not only give the community a feeling that they have a stake in the content of the mela, but it also reminds them that it is happening. Food is a key element of both the sights, sounds and smells of a mela. Predominantly the fare is South Asian with Indian food dominating, but again the international and the multicultural are increasingly evident, with examples of cuisine from Mexico, Poland and China amongst many others being present, often depending upon the construction of the ethnicity of the locale. Typically at Sikh events, free food is offered, to maintain a tradition known as langaar, whereby community involvement is achieved through the provision of food.

The function of mela festivals extends beyond the celebratory in that they have often acted as channels for public information and education, not only to the host communities but also to the South Asian population, particularly from social services, local authorities and health agencies. This is where notions of civic consciousness are articulated in the programme, because it shows how melas can be a crucial avenue for the delivery of public services. It is important to note how key these functions have become to community festivals and the critical role they perform in providing information to excluded groups, such as the elderly or newly arrived. Melas are a platform for agencies such as the police to talk about crime prevention, the fire service to talk about health and safety at home, and charities that provide services for ethnic minority communities can make people aware of their existence. English language provision can be discussed, or simply information about where to join a Bollywood dance class, or a martial arts group, or a weaving circle can be circulated. Health advocacy is a key area here, with a variety of different health organisations using melas to raise awareness. The presence of a diabetes stall at the *Vaisakhi Sports Festival* in Coventry has been deliberately arranged so that health professionals can reach elderly members of the South Asian community who are more prone to the condition and yet may normally face language barriers. The presence of the army and police as sponsors and stall holders is a strategy designed to connect with and recruit ethnic minority groups. Melas thus provide the initial link for the forging of relationships that can be continued after the event has finished.

Tamasha

Regarding the performative and aesthetic aspects of mela, this research has highlighted how a number of activities rooted within South Asian traditions feature prominently at events. Such performances exude a particular ethos through their 'Asian-ness' and are indicative of the celebratory function of melas. The form of the activities that take place within melas can be classified as 'tamasha' and this will go some way into explaining the composition of the schedule, the types of programming which feature and the overall ethos within South Asian community festivals. Media scholar Daya Thussu (2007: 91) describes tamasha as a particularly Indian form that exhibits a demonstrative, bawdy and exuberant style of performance that is rooted within the sub-continent's theatrical history. There is a long established tradition within South Asian performances that uses a very boisterous style in its engagement with audiences to heighten its appeal. This is indicative of the ways in which South Asian performances have historically transmitted an overt loudness to enhance the spectacle of an activity in order to convey greater emotion and to establish a greater level of empathy with audiences. Historically, the loudness of an activity is increased by audiences joining in with the singing and dancing, both of which are indicative of attempts to fuse closer connections between the performative and spectating realms of South Asian performance. This is achieved with active audience engagement so that spectators become part of the event itself. This also resonates with the principles of integration because it enables people from a non-South Asian background to learn more about the cultural activities than from simply watching.

The notion of tamasha is also concerned with raising the visibility of performances and this is often achieved by increasing the colour within them. So, bright, striking clothes, jewellery and sets have a prominent function within South Asian festivals because they offer a means with which to raise the spectacle of the activities and to heighten their visceral impact. This highlights the centrality of visuality within South Asian culture. Often melas are dressed to discharge colour and decorated with Asian design motifs, so that the event can be easily seen and recognised. For instance, the covering of city centre pavements in rangoli arts is a colourful and overt display of culture in its transformation of the normal into something different. Visuality is thus important to the South Asian aesthetic, possibly because it reinforces the celebratory function that underpins performance and has become embedded within melas to generate greater attention.

Figure 18.1: *Leicester Belgrave Mela*, (Photograph Christopher Maughan)

Melas are a modern effusion of tamasha in that they convey such openly Indian characteristics of being seen and heard, which then lend themselves towards a distinctive method in terms of the style and form of the performances. With regard to the aesthetic of South Asian community festivals, tamasha crucially acts as a means of distinguishing events from the host culture too, which does not have the same approach in terms of its display and type of performance. In this way, tamasha may also be thought of as an expression of cultural belonging as South Asian diasporic communities give a modern meaning to an historical notion. Through open and loud display such communities are embedding themselves within the cultural landscapes of the British cities within which these events are taking place, and showing themselves to be a visible, legitimate and integral part of them. Tamasha therefore captures the difference of some aspects of South Asian culture but also refers to the way in which this is delivered to the mainstream by showing its openly celebratory and exuberant style.

Mela and intercultural communication

Another issue to consider is that as the audiences have diversified and westernised, mela's origins have lost some of their meaning, except to the first generation members of the audience. In particular, as melas have become part of the annual events calendar they have also taken on a more multi-cultural remit. For instance, the inclusion of Scottish folk music and bagpipe bands in the *Edinburgh Mela* shows the expanding nature of mela programming to augment South Asian cultural products with those of the host, thus displaying the habituated nature of mela in the UK. This adds an important dimension to melas in that it reveals a fusion between Eastern and Western cultural habits that is illustrative of the overall purpose of melas to stimulate cultural understanding across different communities. There is also an observable difference between the interests of first, second and third generation Asian communities in what could be perceived as a steady shift away from tradition towards westernised cultural preferences. Mela organisers are therefore tasked with addressing a multitude of audiences that are segmented by age as well as ethnicity, religion and culture.

A new generation wishing to see a homogenous South Asian culture is emerging, one not divided along lines of religion, caste, or national origin - Indian, Pakistan, Bangladesh, East African - is developing in new areas such as Britain where the attachment to traditional affiliations is not so strong. This is indicative of a deviation from the traditional conceptions of mela and more in tune with contemporary notions of multiculturalism.

However, the formal driving forces behind melas are often cultural groups that are committed to the safeguarding of the interests of minority communities as well as to fostering an effective dialogue with the mainstream. This culturally specific starting point could, however, be thought to encapsulate a paradox. While melas have been formulated to provide an outlet for a minority group to showcase its cultural identity, the very act of public expression is often thought to cater towards a minority audience. Tariq Yousuf, a community activist with responsibility for organising the *Bristol Mela*, did find this to be a serious problem in his experiences within the city:

> I could see mela as a platform for delivering messages to different communities as well as enabling integration and participation... Bristol is behind a lot of other cities with regard to these sorts of things. The plans here were to develop an event that could speak to the whole community not one particular religion. This way it could reflect the differences within the South Asian community and culture (Yousuf interview 2011).

The intention is then for melas to act as an initial platform for cultural interaction and by showcasing culturally specific activities enables people from different communities to meet with the possibility of enhancing community relations over and beyond that which is provided in day-to-day life. The extent to which this is inclusive or selective is however very much a point of debate owing to the inclusiveness-selectivity dichotomy that is embedded into the configuration of melas.

Bristol presents a pertinent yet problematic example of these processes. The community festivals in Bristol have very much evolved upon religious lines because they have developed to act as an avenue for cultural expression for one group. To date, there have been three major South Asian community festivals, each of which has been designed to address different communities and principles. The *Arts of Punjab Festival* started in 2004 and ran for five years with the specific remit of raising the profile of the organising group, the Sikh Resource Centre, and to help Sikhs integrate with other cultures and participate within the civic life of Bristol. Similarly, the annual *Islamic Cultural Fayre* began in 1998 because the Bristol Muslim Cultural Society felt that there was not enough provision for the city's Muslims and no significant outlet for connections with the wider community. Both of these events typify many of the essential ideas and elements manifest within South Asian community festivals in that they exemplify the objective of a minority culture's attempt to engage with the mainstream whilst retaining a sense of their own distinctive identity. Organisers of both of these events view their respective purposes as celebratory and cohesive with a religiously orientated focus at the core.

It is this centrality of religion however that has proved problematic for one of the city's other community festivals to introduce another set of concerns into the framework for conceptualising melas. The *Bristol Mela* was begun in 2004 by the community group Awaz Utoah and ran for five years. While it had a programme that was similar to other South Asian community festivals, its objectives were somewhat at odds as compared to the others in Bristol. Its organiser Tariq Yousuf emphasised the event's integrative function operated because it *did not* have a religious core. He explains:

> We had the idea to develop a mela that could be for all South Asians and beyond in order to allow a cohesive voice to be heard so that it would celebrate different religions and cultures. This was missing across a lot of the melas around because they are faith based and specific to a particular group. Many of them do not look beyond their own culture and are only celebrating themselves (Yousuf interview 2011).

It is this notion of separation which characterises the evolution of South Asian community festivals in Bristol, where distinct groups have marked out their own ideas through the development of their own festivals. Thus, the fragmentation of ethnic groups within different parts of the city has been matched by the disparate and separate nature of the community events that have been formulated, indicating a limitation of the power of melas to overcome entrenched cultural beliefs. These caveats highlight a key issue that underpins South Asian festivals in Bristol and which could have implications for the topic as a whole. That is, despite the integrative and celebratory function, melas are sometimes mono-cultural in substance in that they largely speak for and to one particular group. In this way, the research has highlighted a fundamental tension within melas because their exclusive cultural nature could in fact render them as an instrument of separation, isolation and ghettoization rather than one of community cohesion.

Conclusions

This research has raised a set of critical issues central to understanding melas in the UK and the contribution they make to Britain's cultural life. It shows how melas can act as a form of bridge building between a minority culture and the wider mainstream to achieve understanding but also to celebrate the presence and contribution of the minority culture. It has become apparent throughout this research that the act of transportation has shifted the defining features and purposes of individual mela festivals into new directions that are set by the locations in which they are now situated. Such distinctiveness has become a source of local pride as different British cities try and out-do each other in terms of their festival offerings. The original motivation behind the founding of mela was an intention to raise the profile of marginalised groups where they can express and explore issues related to self and society, objectification, exclusion and identity. History and heritage of such groups is central to the experiences of mela communities and it has been intricately woven into the programming schedules. Within these conditions melas offer both an arena in which difference can be viewed but also channels from it can be understood. The ultra-local and global are thus meshed together in melas because of the manner in which long-standing cultural practices from around the world are articulated in a physical space that is representative of a city's civic obligations.

Mela can provide a public space in that they have been formulated to act as a forum for dialogue between different communities to stimulate a healthy interchange between them. The example of *Bristol Mela* shows how tensions and divisions between groups can actually raise barriers to exchanges rather than break them down. On the whole though melas do function as a public forum within which civic issues are articulated and pursued as different groups can engage with the wider social structure that they are a part of.

Aside from acting as a platform for delivering messages to communities, they can act as a forum of civic consciousness by connecting individuals with their communities. They also offer potentially vital information about health, employment and other such key issues and have thus significant implications towards contemporary notions of citizenry.

It is also important to consider the significance of the non-Asian practices that have increasingly been used to increase the popularity of melas and to secure greater funding. There is a need to consider the extent to which the process of cultural intermingling has effectively diluted the original cultural substance of melas away from the original remit. Dilution refers to the watering down of cultural practices that have taken place to generate cross-cultural appeal. Through introducing non-Asian practices, melas have increased their appeal by addressing and including other cultures. However, this could be thought of as a dislocation from their traditional base by compromising their original core. Furthermore, it has implications for the audiences to which these events are orientated and the extent to which South Asian audiences are catered for.

The future of melas seems to be tied to separate locations, each of which will organise the constitutive elements in a manner which the organisers feel best suits the general purposes of integration and celebration that underpin melas. It is this sense of individualisation that makes mela such a fruitful ground for investigation because it illuminates how event organisers have sought to formulate individual festivals in a particular way in the pursuit of certain often localised objectives. Moreover, this process of individualisation shows that melas take into account localised histories in their attempts to address broader concerns to the extent that they have become permanent features of a city's cultural landscape.

It is abundantly clear from this research that melas have now become a permanent and critical element within the contemporary cultural life of the United Kingdom. It is also apparent that there is a complex array of issues that need to be acknowledged when comprehending the significance of melas because of the piecemeal history, range of cultural issues in operation and disparate development that has taken place in different locations across a number of timeframes. Each of these events has attempted to formulate elements of celebration, unity and multiculturalism in their own way and it is this individuality at the heart of melas which makes the topic both a multifaceted yet complicated cultural vehicle. This chapter has hopefully gone some way towards demystifying mela as a topic by clarifying its 'habituated and travelled' nature whilst also illustrating its cultural importance.

Bibliography and further reading

Carnegie, E. and Smith, M. (2006) Mobility, diaspora and the hybridisation of festivity: the case of the Edinburgh Mela, in D, Picard and M, Robinson, (eds.) *Festivals, Tourism and Social Change: Remaking Worlds*, Clevedon: Channel View.

Newbold, C. and Kaushal, R. (2014) *Mela in the UK: A 'travelled' and 'habituated' festival,* Discussion Papers in Arts and Festivals Management, Leicester: De Montfort University.

Thussu, D. (2007) *News as Entertainment: The Rise of Global Infotainment*, London: Sage.

Notes

[1] This research was funded by Arts Council England, the authors are grateful for their support and assistance.

19 A View from Australia

Robyn Archer

> Its proud and joyous image of an Edinburgh in Europe, of the Festival as the enactment of a European communion (a more demanding word than 'community') looked to an eclipse of tribalism, of sectarian violence, of brute power-relations. This foresight of hope had, after Europe's near self-slaughter, every rational legitimacy.
>
> George Steiner, *A Festival Overture*, 1996

Dragan Klaić's faith in festivals as a uniting cultural force seems to have had much in common with the altruistic beginnings of the *Edinburgh Festival*. While it is true that post-war Edinburgh desperately needed new economic drivers, there is no reason to doubt the founders' desires for a cultural framework that might help to pull Europe together again. Klaić's desire was to deconstruct the silos of national identity and construct in their place platforms on which the differences in language and practice could be better understood and shared. While Melina Mercuri's desires for better understanding between the different cultures of Europe resulted in many positive collaborations and much-needed sources of mobility for artists through the European Capital of Culture programme, the programme has also bred a kind of necessary civic bragging that I doubt Klaić would have found productive.

This account of international arts festivals in Australia is less one of bragging (though that too has had its place) and more one of early ignorance, gradual evolution and a happy present.

International arts festivals in Australia were first built entirely on the Edinburgh model. When first Perth in Western Australia, and then Adelaide in South Australia, cloned that model to their relatively isolated cities, the core desire was to bring 'culture' to those cities. Not that Perth and Adelaide lacked artists and performances, but those who had been to Edinburgh felt that Australian audiences were rarely exposed to the 'best' of culture. The significantly named Elizabethan Theatre Trust and entrepreneurs such as Ken Brodziak, already toured international shows and artists: I myself was taken by our science teacher, along with a few fellow students, to see Vivien Leigh play Portia in *The Merchant of Venice*, in 1962. But these southern and western capitals, unlike Melbourne and Sydney with their significantly larger populations and markets which could support profitable commercial tours of international artists, felt cut off from the culture of the 'old country'. Festivals seemed to offer a solution to this isolation and also a pathway for early cultural tourism and its cash component.

While the desire to support more art is admirable at any time, the drivers for these festivals were not altruistic in Klaić's way. Uniting Australia through culture was not part of the mission, nor was the notion of collaboration. This was to be a feast of audience enjoyment of largely European, with some American, arts and entertainment. Where Australian orchestras were involved, they would be playing largely European repertoire, and theatre companies would be presenting European or American plays. At that time the White Australia Policy was still in force, though starting to undergo the 25 years of change which would see the end of discrimination towards non-Europeans wishing to emigrate to Australia. Uniting Australia with its Asian neighbours was also not on the festival agenda at that time, even though popular singer Khamal, then a student at Adelaide University under the Colombo plan (one of the first attempts to broker positive relationships with Asia), played a role in the first *Adelaide Festival*. Khamal's repertoire was comprehensively the popular and semi-classical songs of Europe and America.

The inaugural 1960 *Adelaide Festival* was held from Saturday, March 12 to Saturday, March 26. The festival's patron was Queen Elizabeth the Queen Mother. Festival highlights included the first *Adelaide Writers' Week*, Eliot's *Murder in the Cathedral* and Dave Brubeck's jazz quartet. Perhaps the most obvious legacy was that the *Edinburgh Festival* had been cloned to a similar city in Adelaide, where you can still book a city hotel and walk to all events. Perth took longer to reconcile the model to the spread out nature of that city, and to the fact that its ownership by the University of Western Australia meant it would take longer to convince the general public that the festival was for them too, not just better educated audiences.

But these worthy pioneering efforts were undertaken in apparent ignorance at that time of the desperate need in Australia for a programme of unification and reconciliation not unlike that which Europe cried out for post-World War Two, and which Dragan Klaić saw as still necessary decades later. The main difference was that the war in Australia had not been waged just a few years prior to the revival of the festival model, but had been going on for 180 years and was still being waged. At the time of the first *Adelaide Festival*, Australian Aboriginal and Torres Strait Islander people, the continent's first people, were still seven years away from suffrage, and even further from the complete cessation of the forcible removal of Aboriginal and Torres Strait

Islander children from their families, and the ultimate closure, in the 1980s, of the last of the institutions which had held them.

Steiner also wrote:

> we now know of the neutrality of the arts and of their performance in the presence of barbarism, of the enigmatic capacity of human beings to appreciate music, art, poetry, profoundly in the evening, indeed to perform such music or write verse, and then to proceed to bestiality the next morning.

In 1960s Australia, the ongoing battle was not obvious. Growing up in suburban Adelaide, I had no idea that Aboriginal people lived there. We are reluctant to blame the early festival pioneers for their ignorance - just as I am reluctant to blame my parents for smoking in small rooms in humble houses when their only infant daughter had been prone to skin and lung disease since birth. But we should not be wary of noting the ignorance and neglect the past now reveals, especially given the progress since and the present strengths.

While the Dutch and the French had already bumped into the Great South Land, they saw no use for it, and it was the British who saw some advantages in a big empty dumping ground for their unwanted – especially those convicted of acts of political inconvenience. No surprise that the Irish were so present in early Australia. The British declared the continent Terra Nullius[1], and thereby, in one stroke, rendered Australia's first peoples non-human, non-existent, and the injustices they encountered invisible. While there are recorded instances of clearer perceptions, sympathetic academic studies and individual instances of kindness, that inhuman treatment was still invisible to the majority of the general public when the Australian international arts festival model was imported into Australia.

The facts are that not only were there people on the continent when the British mistakenly and brutally labelled it Terra Nullius, but they had been there for 40,000 years and had complex systems of clan relationships, land management, protocols and ceremony. In 1950s Australia, there was nothing new about the idea of special gatherings for special celebrations that involved visual arts, song, dance, costume, food, kids: such 'festivals' had been around for tens of thousands of years, as an integral part of indigenous life. This forgetfulness was highlighted in Prime Minister Kevin Rudd's 2020 summit, in the arts stream, when so many Australian artists called out for the arts to be seen as central to Australian life, especially in education, rather than an optional leisure pursuit. Theatre Director Wesley Enoch pointed out that we need look no further than Indigenous Australia, where art had always been central to life and community. It is a sign of the good things that have happened in Australia that Wesley is now the Artistic Director of the Queensland Theatre Company and the first Aboriginal man to direct one of the state theatre companies. Though, in case we go too far in thinking Australia somehow exceptionally backward, it is worth pointing out that it was only in 2006 that Jacques Martial became the first black man to head up one of France's major cultural institutions (*Parc la Villette*).

European festivals also had their antecedents, best evidenced by a carnival such as Basel's *Fasnacht*, where early pagan behaviours mix with the marking of Christianity's Lent, along with those hallmarks of festivals of all kinds – an excess of indulgence compressed into a tight timeframe. There are many such remnants of festivals in which Europeans for thousands of years marked the seasons or times of religious significance, or both. For me, festivals are at their best when they acknowledge those arcane characteristics of excess and compression. These tend to be more clearly observable in generic festivals which cater for passionate fans of the genre – a food or beer festival where there is way too much of both, a film festival from which buffs emerge wide-eyed from weeks in the dark, or the huge music festivals like Hungary's *Sziget*, England's *Glastonbury* or Adelaide's *Womadelaide* where non-stop stages give fans a surfeit of the music they hunger for.

The international festivals in Australia began much more politely and, even by 1972, the fare had not changed dramatically. The *Adelaide Festival's* archive lists: Leo McKern, Timothy West and Timothy Dalton, popular performances of *Jesus Christ Superstar* and The South Australian Theatre Company's production of *The Alchemist* featuring Australian actors. Other highlights included the Academy of St Martin in the Fields, Charlie Byrd Trio and Cleo Laine. *Adelaide Writers' Week* featured Andrei Voznesensky from the Soviet Union (that was a step forward at least) and the beat and experimental American poets Lawrence Ferlinghetti and Allen Ginsberg. Significantly, Ginsberg's desire to interact with Australian Aboriginal people caused controversy at the time.

But the 1970s would see significant change in the Australian political and cultural landscape. Plays were being written in Australian vernacular language, Australian composers like Peter Sculthorpe were writing contemporary classical music with distinctly Australian undertones and the country was starting to understand its place in the Asia-Pacific region. In the wake of Australia's role in the Vietnam War, the Whitlam Government proposed moves away from an Australian dependency on America. Art centres in Aboriginal communities furnished artists with the materials which would allow Indigenous Australians to start recording their stories, painting their landscapes, in ways more portable than the fragile bark paintings, or the environmental art which they had always practiced. We started seeing stage productions of the work of Jack Davis, the first Aboriginal playwright.

While other festivals had started to spring up - such as the *Sydney Festival*, which began from a commercial impulse to bring more shoppers into the city in summer, and *Melbourne Festival* which began as a remote outpost for Menotti's Spoleto, Adelaide welcomed the significant arrival of Anthony Steel who had come from Britain with an established career in music. The far-sighted Premier of South Australia, Don Dunstan, had given the ultimate go-ahead for a new cultural centre to house the festival and other year-round events. Steel became its first director, with the stipulation that he would also be the artistic director of the festival. As a young formally untrained entertainer, still to take my first recognizable step into 'the arts' (which eventually happened because of Steel's desire to open the new black box theatre with a production of Brecht/Weill's *The Seven Deadly Sins* for which I was invited to sing Annie 1), the 1974 *Adelaide Festival*, under his direction, truly gave me my shock of the new. Contemporary opera, performance artists and foreign language theatre all contributed crucially to the next step that Australian international festivals would take.

Defending the sense of having major international arts festivals in Perth and Adelaide, largely because of their genuine remoteness, Anthony went on to champion the notion of diversity in Australian festivals and would establish the first *Queensland Music Festival*, then the National Festival of Australian Theatre (Canberra) and also to direct the *Sydney Festival*. His book *Painful in Daily Doses* is well worth a read.

While the *Queensland Music Festival* is still alive and well, that state decided it also wanted an international arts festival like Adelaide, Perth, Sydney and Melbourne, and the *Brisbane Festival* was born. These are now the big five in Australia: in 2014, four of them are directed by European men. They are flagship cultural events for their respective states, well-funded, well attended and, in addition to Australian and Aboriginal and Torres Strait Islander arts, they embrace local art, commissions, national and international collaborations, and their raison d'être – international art of all kinds.

It is still true that 'festival as marketing tool' works efficiently. Audiences are more prepared to take a risk on something unknown and challenging in these festival contexts. But losing money is now considered fatal for the major festivals– which means taking bigger risks is challenging. You can push your audiences, but not too far. Greater risk and more spontaneous energy are to be found in the smaller festivals, sometimes genre or audience specific, where there is less to lose.

Festivals do bring to Australian audiences, international work which would otherwise never be seen: the subsidies from government and the corporate and philanthropic support the festivals receive make possible the touring of work which simply would not be affordable on a purely commercial basis. They also commission new Australian works, sometimes in collaboration with each other, and sometimes with international artists and companies. Just from my own Adelaide, Melbourne and Ten Days on the Island (Tasmania) festivals there are many heartening tales of the kinds of international collaborations which those events enabled – Nitin Sawney's work with local Melbourne musicians who went on to play with him throughout Europe, the Australian dance companies and individuals who danced in France as a result of our exchange with French companies, Chiara Banchini's baroque experiment with the Adelaide Symphony Orchestra's string section while Jeffrey Tate rehearsed the horns for the upcoming Ring Cycle, the collaboration between Adelaide's Brink Productions and The Wrestling School on Howard Barker's *The Ecstatic Bible*, Jacques Martial's staged version of Aimee Cesaire's *Journal of a Return to my Native Land* and the first appearances in Australia of Saburu Tehsigawara, Ishin-ha, Ong Keng Sen, Dumb Type and Jan Fabre. There are so many good stories of this kind.

At present, despite all the political and economic focus on the Asian century, there is now less of a focus on Asia in the big five. Ten years ago, works from Japan, India, Singapore and Vietnam made regular appearances in these festivals. Yet this focus has now been taken up in other ways – Adelaide has an *OZASIA Festival* in its own right, the Arts Centre Melbourne has a programmer for Asian work, and latecomers to the festival list, *Darwin Festival* and *Ten Days on the Island* both have geographic/thematic reasons for programming the arts of Asia. When I created *Ten Days for Tasmania*, at the request of another Premier enthusiastic about international festivals, I determined, largely for budgetary reasons, that this festival would claim individuality by inviting only artists from other islands. This has meant a continual stream from Japan, Singapore, Sri Lanka and Taiwan as well as the islands of the Pacific and Indian Oceans including Aetoroa/New Zealand, Hawaii, New Caledonia, Isle de la Reunion and Cape Verde.

Sadly, it was announced in October 2014 that the festival's name had changed to the *Tasmanian International Arts Festival*, and that its content would no longer be predicated on artists from islands. It is a sad reflection that this festival's claim to individuality has been abandoned.

Darwin Festival, however, has boldly confirmed its unique nature. It has gradually acknowledged its proximity to Papua New Guinea, Timor and particularly Indonesia and is now programming work from those northern neighbours as well as rightly focusing on the richness of Indigenous arts in the Top End. Its new artistic director will bring a fresh and exciting bridge to Indonesia and Australia's nearest neighbours.

The *National Festival of Australian Theatre* bit the dust after seven editions because of a lack of political will. Canberra remains the only capital lacking a major festival of this kind. There had been hopes that something might emerge from its biggest cultural year ever in 2013 for the *Centenary of Canberra* celebrations. This constituted a year-long programme not dissimilar to a European Capital of Culture and extending not only to the arts, but also to sport, science, ideas, education, environment and all those things which that city is.

Significantly, 2013 was also the 50th anniversary of the Yirrkala bark petitions. Yirrkala is the community that Ginsberg visited. The petitions are paintings on bark presented to the Australian government at the time to demand change in the status of Aboriginal and Torres Strait Island people. Significantly, in the realm of festivals, the *Centenary of Canberra* devoted a large slice of its resources to the commissioning and presentation of works by and with Aboriginal and Torres Strait Islander artists and communities. Works came from all over Australia to the national capital, and the local Indigenous community was also extensively engaged: the latter especially in support of re-imagining a capital which to date, despite the unique nature of its elected Indigenous body which deals with relevant local government matters, lacked the Australian people's understanding that local Indigenous population, artists and nearby rock art sites even existed in the region. Have a look at www.canberra100.com

This is in step with other festivals which now not only do not ignore or neglect the riches of Australian Indigenous culture, but welcome it with open arms as there are enthusiastic audiences for the theatre, dance, music, writing and visual arts of Australia's first peoples. Since the 1970s the growth in Indigenous content has been enormously, and it is now positively sought and commissioned. This is not just because of the vision of artistic directors who are both quick to recognize work which will please/provoke audiences and are also good at understanding the cultural significance of this work; but because of the decades of action by Australian Aboriginal and Torres Strait Islanders. It is they who bring such weight to the cultural significance that lies at the heart of their traditions, their language, their traditional ceremonies, their contemporary art (film is now very important) and their stories – and they who have worked so hard to share their knowledge and their art and, through that process, to draw attention to how much further Australia has to go to close the gap in so many spheres of their lives. There is also a growing number of excellent festivals dedicated entirely to Australian Indigenous cultures.

Author Bill Gammadge has pointed out in his recent book, *The Biggest Estate on Earth: how Aborigines made Australia,* just how complex traditional Aboriginal land management was, how well they sustained the land and how foolish their colonisers were not to recognise this knowledge: more than two hundred years later some of that practice is only now being re-adopted. The stages and spaces that festivals offer have also now been rightly occupied by the cultures of Australia's first peoples: but many ask when their societal principle of arts at the heart of society will also be re-adopted, and reflect on how much has been lost, and how different Australia might have been had the British colonisers recognised the sovereignty which many Aboriginal and Torres Strait Islanders now claim.

Meanwhile, festivals have played an unanticipated role. The model imported from Edinburgh, initially excluding the cultures of Australian first peoples, has morphed via various models and practice from all over the world, but most significantly from Europe where festivals such as the *Kunsten Festival des Arts* (Frie Leysen take a bow), *Weiner Festwochen, Holland Festival* (with former programmer Lieven Bertels now Artistic Director of *Sydney Festival*), *Roma Europa, Malta Festival* (Poznan) and many more, into an all-embracing model which positively seeks out Indigenous work for commissioning , presentation and touring.

For 2013, *The Secret River* was co-commissioned by the *Sydney Theatre Company*, the *Centenary of Canberra*, the *Sydney Festival* and *Perth Festival*. An adaptation of Kate Grenville's novel of the same name, it is an uncompromising work that looks at the fatal consequences of first contact between freed convict landowners and the local Aboriginal population. The work won multiple awards at Australia's prestigious Helpmann Awards (Sir Robert Helpmann being not only dancer and choreographer but the first Australian artistic director of the *Adelaide Festival*). This production was joined in Canberra this year by many other works and events (theatre, dance, visual arts, sports, summits etc) by, with and about creative Indigenous Australians.

Figure 19.1: *The Secret River.* (Nathaniel Dean, Trevor Jamieson, Anita Hegh, Ursula Yovich, Colin Moody, Miranda Tapsell and Jeremy Sims in *The Secret River*, 2013, produced by Sydney Theatre Company, in association with *Sydney Festival*, the *Centenary of Canberra* and the *Perth International Arts Festival*. Photo: Ellis Parrinder.)

And other good news stories abound. *Barramundi Scales* is a painting by Gija artist Lena Niyadbi; it has been sized up to grace the roof of Paris' Musee du Quai Branly and is now seen by the hundreds of thousands who ascend the Tour Eiffel. The Australian company Big hART presented *Namatjira* in London: this theatre production is about the Aboriginal artist Albert Namatjira, famous for his watercolour landscapes of Central Australia. Some of his works appeared in the Royal Academy survey of Australian Landscape. It feels a long way from the time when all Europe wanted was traditional Australian Aboriginal art, and spurned the efforts of contemporary Indigenous Australia.

Many matters of protocols have also been addressed. It is now common practice in Australian festivals for an elder from the traditional custodians of the land where the festival is held to give what is called the 'welcome to country'. In other instances, anyone giving a speech of note, for instance the launch event of a festival, will acknowledge the traditional custodians of that land. The same can be said for Aotearoa/New Zealand where such protocols have been long observed.

This all means that festivals are much healthier than when the model first arrived in Australia, and that model has proved invaluable in providing platforms for Indigenous culture and encouraging the rise of dedicated Aboriginal and Torres Strait Islander festivals. But it is important to say that we cannot be too complacent or too boastful about the achievement of harmony through festivals. Jack Charles is a 70 year old Aboriginal actor whose show *Jack Charles V the Crown*, directed by Rachel Maza, daughter of Aboriginal artist and activist, the late Bob Maza, has been doing the festival rounds, including *The Centenary of Canberra* in his 27 date tour this year. His irony is ours: in the show he talks about his struggle to tour his show to Britain (despite formal invitations) because of his criminal record – strange, he says cheekily, when Britain's first interest in his country was to send their convicted criminals to his land. Thankfully, the work has now been seen in the UK.

Proving just how long and deep some nationalistic resentments lie, the 1999 *Melbourne Festival* proposed an opening including Japanese taiko drummers at the War Memorial: the outcry was so ugly that the festival believed it was better to change their plans and cancel the event. Yet in 2002 I was able to commission and present in Melbourne Jonathan Mills' *Sandakan Threnody*, a piece of working reconciliation with artists from Australia, Singapore and Japan: this perhaps was more possible, sadly, because it was *inside* a theatre and not a large-scale public event. Still in Australia, the media are only too keen to whip up anger and ugliness over arts events which dare to venture beyond the arts precinct to explore in the public domain anything other than safe positions, styles or subject matter. In the festival context this is less likely to happen, but that is only really in more recent years. And it might have something to do with the current somewhat more risk-averse approach the larger festivals seem obliged to adopt.

Smaller festivals are often better equipped to risk more than the state flagships. In 2007 I created *The Light in Winter*, a month long festival which has combined cutting-edge lighting commissions and artists such as Rafael Lozano Hemmer (Montreal), Srinivas Krishna (Toronto), Luz Interruptus (Madrid) and United Visual Artists (UK), along with grassroots culturally diverse activity. In this context we also encouraged participation of all kinds from both well established communities such as the Indian, Chinese and Greek, to very fragile groups including Afghan, Burmese, Ethiopian and an Asylum Seekers Refuge group. The matter of asylum seekers is tearing at the heart of Australia at present, and it is a complex topic we were able to explore candidly in the context of this arts festival which is entirely free to the public and receives no arts funding.

Some important things have happened via that festival – a meeting to reconcile embattled segments of Melbourne's Afghan community, the public ritual of a Tuvalu/Kiribati woman claiming identity as an elder in exile, a ritual in which members of Melbourne's Indigenous community welcomed a group of asylum seekers to the warmth of their campfire, a collaboration between members of the Japanese and Turkish communities, a poetic/visual exploration of young women's challenges in wearing the hijab at school, and more in the same vein.

In a similar way the new festivals associated with David Walsh's *Museum of Old and new Art* in Hobart, and funded largely through his philanthropic generosity, are able to dare a lot in terms of style, experience and subject matter. And festivals for younger audiences appear to attract less attention in the contested space of public morality and tax-payer dollars.

The question we must put to the future is whether the festival model will continue to provide resilient platforms for harmony and reconciliation through artistic collaboration – or will they drift into respectable hubs of entertainment and event spectacle? My own genre, cabaret, began in Paris in the 1880s, spread to Vienna's fin-de-siecle, branched outwards to Barcelona, St Petersburg, Zurich and then to Munich and Berlin, and was flourishing in Germany when the National Socialist Party came to power in the 1930s. When other stages could no longer support the dissident voice, it was cabaret which provided for a time, the platforms for the necessary voice of comment, criticism and protest. Major festivals in Australia have evolved slowly but admirably into heavy but useful beasts; they have also provided a provocation for the evolution of many lighter, bolder, more flexible animals. Let us hope that all of these will not only continue to open our eyes and ears to the awe of artistic invention which our audiences would otherwise have no opportunity to experience, but also to develop even better capabilities to provide platforms for the cultural negotiation of Australia's continuing challenges – including, but not limited to, the healthy future of its first peoples, the resilience of its beautiful land, and the just treatment of those genuinely seeking asylum here.

Bibliography and further reading

Archer, R. (2010) *Detritus*, Perth, Western Australia: University of Western Australia Press.

EFA (2008) *Cahier de l'Atelier: Arts Festivals for the Sake of Art?* Brussels: EFA Books, European Festivals Association.

EFA (2009) *Dialogue. Festivals Act for an Intercultural Society,* Brussels: EFA Books, European Festivals Association.

EFA (2012) *Inside/Insight Festivals. 9 Festival Directors - 9 Stories,* Brussels: EFA Books, European Festivals Association/Culture Link Singapore.

Gammadge, B. (2011) *The Biggest Estate on Earth: How Aborigines made Australia,* Crows Nest, New South Wales: Allen and Unwin.

Keating, P. (2000) *Engagement: Australia faces the Asia-Pacific,* Sydney: Macmillan Press.

Love, H. (1984) *The Australian Stage: A Documentary History,* Sydney: New South Wales University Press.

Macintyre, S. (2009) *A Concise History of Australia,* Cambridge: Cambridge University Press.

Parsons, P. (ed.) (1995) *Companion To Theatre In Australia,* Sydney: Currency Press.

Pascoe, B. (2007) *Convincing Ground: Learning to fall in love with your country,* Canberra: Aboriginal Studies Press.

Steiner, G. (1996) *The University Festival Lecture: 'a Festival Overture',* Edinburgh: University of Edinburgh.

Steel, A. (2009) *Painful in Daily Doses,* Adelaide: Wakefield Press.

Stephenson, P. (2007) *The Outsiders Within: Telling Australia's Indigenous-Asian Story,* Sydney: University of New South Wales Press.

Notes

[1] Terra nullius is a Latin expression derived from Roman law meaning 'land belonging to no one'

FOCUS ON FESTIVALS

SECTION 4
THE FUTURE OF FESTIVALS

Introduction

Franco Bianchini and Christopher Maughan

The themes of identity and citizenship, in the context of the effects of globalisation and of the economic and political crises which started in the second
half of the 2000s, dominate the contributions in this final section of the book.
In his chapter Greg Richards quotes Dragan Klaić's view that "festivals have
become emblematic of the issues, problems and contradictions of current cultural practices, marked by globalisation, European integration, institutional
fatigue, dominance of cultural industry and shrinking public subsidies".
Aspects of Klaić's formulation are explored by the contributors to this section.

Steve Austen argues that many festivals in Europe will have to redefine their
role and legitimacy as a result of the decline of support for the subsidised
arts, which is one of the consequences of the adoption of austerity policies in
European countries, after the onset of the finance-driven economic downturn
in 2007-2008. Festivals' role in the formation of national identity is changing,
as the bonds between the state, arts institutions and the public are weaken-
ing. Festivals should reflect a new political agenda of European citizenship.
This may involve the need for a debate on the responsibilities, as well as the
rights, of European 'cultural citizens'. Austen maintains that European artists in the 1970s had a key political role in prefiguring the end of the Cold
War. Can artists and festivals have a similarly important part to play today in
helping Europe overcome its current economic and political impasse? Could
contemporary arts festivals help us produce a participatory model of European cultural citizenship? This would be constructed as part of a response to
people's increasing suspicion of arts policy establishments and elites, and to
the crisis of 'democratic elitism' (Peffley and Rohrschneider, 2007) as a form
of governance.

According to Kathrin Deventer, the more diverse the actors involved in a
festival, the better the learning process. Increasing diversity tends to enhance
a festival's creativity, a point that was also raised in Section 2 and relates to
the breadth of information and perspectives that complex networks provide
(Granovetter, 1983). Deventer agrees with Bernard Faivre d'Arcier that festivals have a special role in giving artists opportunities to experiment and
innovate. Faivre d'Arcier argues that this is because festival audiences (more
than attenders at cultural events programmed by venues as part of their regu-

lar programmes) are prepared to take risks. Festivals can enhance people's tolerance by diversifying taste and by challenging traditional cultural institutions. However, it would be interesting for further research to explore how complex partnership models for the governance and funding of festivals – which are becoming increasingly the norm – are affecting risk taking. Does the need for consensus between different stakeholders reduce festivals' ability to be innovative and experimental?

A related issue concerns the concept of 'symbiosis', which is referred to explicitly by Tessa Gordziejko and alluded to by other authors when they describe the relationship between a festival and its stakeholders. Essentially symbiosis means that the life cycles of two or more species are dependent upon one another if either is to survive and prosper. All authors in this section conclude that no festival is an island, cut off from the needs and aspirations of its stakeholders. When the relationship is in balance then a festival can deliver what its organisers, partners and audiences want. But not all symbiotic relationships remain in balance. Arguably some festivals behave in a 'parasitic' manner, and have flourished at a time when financial support for some of their partner cultural institutions has been cut. But likewise some festivals may experience 'exploitation' by their stakeholders because of an underlying vulnerability in the expression of their purpose and commitment. In many cases, problematic relationships between festivals and their stakeholders are due to the fact that festival strategies are not properly integrated into wider cultural policies and urban strategies.

The authors in this section and in the rest of the book agree that festivals are key components of the public sphere. There is a link between educating audiences and developing citizenship in a transnational democratic environment. Deventer, like Austen and Autissier, believes that festivals have an important role to play for the future of democracy in Europe. With the rise of neo-nationalism and xenophobia (which are also by-products of the economic crisis) we can no longer take democracy for granted. It needs nurturing. Festivals can help build a European democratic culture, beyond nation states.

Anne-Marie Autissier discusses two French festivals based on international cultural co-operation - *Les Boréales* and *Reims Scenes d'Europe*. She highlights the special value of transnational festivals for the process of European integration and for building an alternative European narrative. She also notes possible conflicts between global cultural corporations and the need to support festivals and local artistic life. This is shown by the debate in France on the private copying levy, which is used to support local cultural activities but is generally opposed by the multinational cultural industries.

Tessa Gordziejko explores the interplay of 'belonging' and 'unbelonging' in festivals and the importance of these events as 'temporary communities', in which alternative forms of identity can be constructed and experienced, and alternative forms of production and development, in the manner of 'slow art', can be employed. However, again further research would be required to assess whether, due to the commercialisation of many festivals, genuine intercultural, 'liminal' encounters between people with different social, educational and ethnic backgrounds are becoming more difficult to achieve. Similarly, it would be interesting to research in more depth the many obstacles and challenges faced by festival organisers wishing to develop intercultural and liminal programmes, that go beyond the confines of established (usually white, middle class and well educated) audience profiles and consolidated patterns of cultural taste and consumption. Such research might also shed light on the impact of a 'slow' philosophy in the commissioning of new artworks and their life and continuing impacts outside of a festival's programme.

Greg Richards discusses in his contribution the concepts of 'hypereventfulness' and 'hyperfestivity'. 'Pseudo-events' (following the definition given by Boorstin, 1962) are becoming more common. Events of this kind, although they often involve large numbers of people, arguably do not generate genuine social interaction. The trend towards manufactured events is related to the fact that people may be experiencing more and more connections in the digital 'space of flows', at the same time as isolation in the 'space of places' of their daily lives (Castells, 2012). Festivals are thus becoming more significant as opportunities for social encounters.

What is the role of festivals in our increasingly 'disembedded' global society? Richards observes that physical presence is increasingly valuable as a sign of commitment. 'Relational aesthetics' (Bourriaud, 2002) is growing in importance and festivals are key vehicles for it. Richards explains that more and more it is not the cultural content that matters, but the social interaction taking place within a festival, or a museum, or another arts space. Richards adds that "the authenticity of festivals and events therefore arguably depends as much on the audience, and on their ability to co-create festivals as a social happening, as it does (on) the artistic programming".

Co-creation and participatory, bottom up approaches, which value spontaneity and authenticity, are indeed central concerns for many festival organisers today. But the emerging rhetoric of participation is not always matched by reality (Jancovich and Bianchini, 2013) as they are often hindered by resistance from traditional cultural policies and arts institutions. In many cases innovative participatory events are produced as part of special, one off programmes like the 2008-2012 *Cultural Olympiad* (discussed by Tessa Gordziejko in her chapter), which was innovative both in its community-based character and in its production of arts-sports aesthetic, audience and policy crossovers. The interdisciplinary nature of the *Cultural Olympiad* helped reach out to non-arts attenders and experimented, as suggested by Greg Richards in his chapter, with "new skills in the areas of ritual design and experience management". However, arguably the important legacy of experiences like the *Cultural Olympiad* has not been sufficiently absorbed and reflected upon by the arts festivals sector and the arts policy establishment.

Faivre d'Arcier adds that festivals also have an important function to build local identity, foster social cohesion and enhance the visibility of the localities in which they take place. But he sees problems with the tendencies of some festivals to be diluted into longer 'seasons' or, conversely, to concentrate on one day and/or night (as in the case of the 'nuit blanche' phenomenon). Faivre d'Arcier notes the attractiveness for the media of the 'nuit blanche' format, but also its superficiality and the illusion of choice given the fact that audiences, presented with a cornucopia of events, will only be able to attend a small portion of them.

Lastly, several contributions in this section, and in the whole book, make claims about the role and impacts of festivals in contemporary Europe, which would need to be explored and substantiated through rigorous empirical research. For example, some of the authors assume that festivals can have a transformative, transgressive and even revolutionary role. However, both Richards and Faivre d'Arcier discuss some of the potentially negative effects of 'over-festivalisation' in relation to this special attribute of festivals. Is the mushrooming of the number of festivals making these events more formulaic? Have festivals become just another facet of the tourism industry? Some festivals may be in danger of losing their deeper, distinctive qualities through the multiplication of features of the event that are consumption-oriented, controlled and handed to audiences on a plate. This may produce disenchantment and ultimately undermine the quality of festivals as special experiences. Will festivals, in Robyn Archer's words in her chapter earlier in this book, increasingly become "respectable hubs of entertainment and event spectacle", unwilling or unable to perform a more critical function?

Festivals, in this way, may be used by audiences as a break from normal life and as such may not be experienced by them as transgressive or revolutionary. Festival experiences may simply reinforce the status quo and social stability, by offering opportunities for recreation, relaxation and distraction from complex economic and political issues. This is understandable. However, we believe that festivals can and should aspire to be stimulating and challenging. They should not become, as Boorstin predicted, events with "no peaks and valleys, no surprises"[1]. In order to realise the full critical potential of festivals we need cultural managers to be bolder and to recognise their capacity, in Eugenio Barba's words, to be "the water drop that causes the jar to overflow"[2] for audiences, artists and society at large.

Bibliography and further reading

Boorstin, D. (1962) *The Image. A guide to pseudo-events in America,* New York: Vintage.

Bourriaud, N. (2002) *Relational Aesthetics,* Paris: Presses du reel.

Castells, M. (2012) Space of flows, space of places: materials for a theory of urbanism in the information age, in S. Bishwapriya, (ed.) *Comparative Planning Cultures,* London: Routledge.

Granovetter, M. (1983), The strength of weak ties: A network theory revisited, *Sociological Theory,* **1**, 201-233

Jancovich. L. and Bianchini, F. (2013) Problematising participation, *Cultural Trend*s, **22**(2), 63-66.

Peffley, M. & Rohrschneider, R. (2007) Elite beliefs and the theory of democratic elitism, in R.J. Dalton and H-D. Klingemann, *The Oxford Handbook of Political Behavior,* Oxford: Oxford University Press.

Notes

[1] As quoted by Greg Richards in the chapter *'Festivals in the Network Society'.*

[2] As quoted by Kathrin Winkelhorn in the chapter *'A cultural experiential space for change - Holstebro Festive Week, Denmark'*

20 Festivals in the Network Society

Greg Richards

Albert Einstein once remarked that "The only reason for time is so that everything doesn't happen at once". In the contemporary network society, however, this system seems to have ceased working. We are constantly bombarded by events. The regular rhythms of events in traditional societies and the ordered series of events in industrial society seem to have given way to a chaotic cacophony of happenings, which we might characterise as 'hyper-eventfulness' or 'hyperfestivity'. As Richards and Palmer (2010) noted, the slogan 'festival city' or 'city of festivals' has become a popular choice as part of a city's brand image. Edmonton refers to itself as 'Canada's Festivals City', setting itself in competition with Montreal and Quebec City that define themselves in similar terms. Milwaukee and Sacramento are two American cities, along with some 30 others, where being 'cities of festivals' has become a prime element of their destination marketing throughout the year. Guadalajara, Mexico's second largest city, similarly tries to gain national and international standing by communicating itself as a festival centre. The world status of Edinburgh is claimed on the official website of the *Edinburgh Festivals*:"'With the stunning Hogmanay celebrations heralding a brand new year and the start of Homecoming Scotland 2009, the World's Leading Festival City is gearing up for spring, and more of its exciting festivals."

The explosion of eventfulness and festivity evident in contemporary society was also one of the reasons that Dragan Klaić founded the European Festivals Research Project in 2004. The project was launched "believing that festivals have become emblematic for the issues, problems and contradictions of the current cultural practices, marked by globalization, European integration, institutional fatigue, dominance of cultural industry and shrinking public subsidies". As these challenges have only become sharper during the past decade, festivals and events have emerged as an essential part of the contemporary cultural landscape.

This brief review considers why events have become so important in modern society and how events are shaped by and in turn influence the contemporary network society.[1]

A brief history of pseudo-events

In the 1960s the American historian Daniel Boorstin was the first to comment on the gathering avalanche of events that seems to have overtaken modern society. Boorstin illustrated the development of what he called 'pseudo-events' through the rise of the media and tourism. He took the example of a hotel that wishes to increase its business. The hotel hires a public relations consultant, whose advice is that the hotel creates an event – a celebration of the hotel's thirtieth anniversary. "Once the celebration has been held, the celebration itself becomes evidence that the hotel really is a distinguished institution. The occasion actually gives the hotel the prestige to which it is pretending" (Boorstin, 1962: xx). According to Boorstin, such pseudo-events are distinguished from 'real' events by:

◆ A lack of sponteaneity – they are purposefully planned

◆ An orientation towards the media – the purpose of a pseudo event is to be reported

◆ Their ambiguous relation to the underlying reality of the situation. Whether it is 'real' or not is less important than its newsworthiness and ability to gain favourable attention.

◆ Their inclination to become a self-fulfilling prophecy.

The result of the proliferation of pseudo-events, according to Boorstin was "the programming of our experiences", with "no peaks and valleys, no surprises". Somewhat ironically, Boorstin himself became something of an event organiser when he was appointed as Librarian of Congress in 1975, as he "installed picnic tables and benches out front, established a centre to encourage reading and arranged midday concerts and multimedia events for all" (McFadden, 2004).

Today Boorstin's predictions about the rise of the media and events seems to have become reality. Places everywhere are celebrating sport, culture and heritage, to the extent that 'eventfulness' has become an essential part of the cultural DNA of cities and regions worldwide (Richards and Palmer, 2010). Contemporary societies increasingly seem to be flooded with events, designed to meet a range of different needs, varying from economic development to stimulating creativity to supporting social cohesion. The result is a feeling of 'festivalisation' or 'hyperfestivity' in certain cities, to the extent that Einstein's vision of time as a separator of events seems to have collapsed.

Although individual events may have blurred into one another, their growth has defined a recognisable 'events industry', with increasing economic and political power. The OECD (2008) recently took an interest in 'global events' and the European Commission (2007) undertook a study of the economic benefits of cultural and sporting events. Before the 2010 World Cup, it was estimated that a Dutch win in this one event alone would be worth €700 million to the national economy (and such was the confidence in a Dutch victory that nobody bothered to calculate what second place might be worth).

Events in the network society

Is the rise of eventfulness all hype and hyperfestivity, or is there a real need for events, beyond the seemingly ubiquitous appeals to economic benefit? Arguably, in modern society social relations have become increasingly 'disembedded' through the creation of abstract global systems (Giddens, 1984). Castells (1996) paints a picture of global society operating at two levels: the global 'space of flows' and the local 'space of places'. Through the rise of information technology we have increasingly become 'networked individuals', connected to people on the other side of the globe through the space of flows in cyberspace, but increasingly isolated from those around us in the space of places.

Castell's vision of the network society appears bleak. But the idea of increasingly isolated networked lives does not completely match reality. The Internet, rather than replacing face to face contact or 'physical co-presence' (Urry, 2002) has in fact generated more demand for social contact. Part of the evidence for this lies in the growth of events and festivals. People deprived of more traditional means of contact with their fellow human beings, such as the chat over the garden fence, the animated conversation of the local bar or the family discussions over a relaxed meal, seem to seek out new ones. One of the potential explanations for this has been provided by the work of Randall Collins (2004) on 'Interaction Ritual Chains' (IRC), or a "theory of individuals' motivation based on where they are located at any moment in time in the aggregate of (Interaction Ritual) chains that makes up their market of possible social relationships" (xiv).

Collins argues that Interaction Ritual Chains can help to explain individual motivation, since they cause people to seek the 'Emotional Energy' (EE) that is generated by participation in IRCs. Emotional Energy seeking is

> the master motive across all institutional arenas; and thus it is the IRs that generate differing levels of EE in economic life that set the motivation to work at a level of intensity ranging from enthusiastically to slackly; to engage in entrepreneurship or shy away from it; to join a wave of investment or to pull one's money and one's emotional attention away from financial markets (Collins, 2006: xv).

Wittel's (2001) analysis of 'network sociality' provides similar examples of social rituals which generate "leeting and transient, yet iterative social relations" which create ephemeral but intense encounters.

The point of such encounters, according to Collins, is that they require face-to-face contact, physical co-presence. In other words, there have to be events to generate the emotional energy that makes social rituals function. In a dis-embedded network society, one could argue, events become a means of re-embedding networked individuals in the space of places. Events are a framing of time that isolates and draws attention to a gathering of people in a specific place at a specific time (Richards, 2013).

The need for co-presence also means that we literally have to make time for each other. We need to coordinate our presence at events and the performers also need to be there at the appointed time in the appointed place. The growing number of calls on our time in contemporary society means that the time we give to each other through events becomes increasingly valuable, and so events themselves also become more valuable containers of time as a result. The value we place on this time also means that the choices we make between different events become more and more important. Today, the fact of paying attention to somebody on Facebook has a particular value (conferring status measured by our number of Facebook friends, for example), but actually turning up in person at an event organised by one of our friends has a much greater value, because it implies an investment of increasingly valuable physical presence.

Relational goods

The problems of choosing from the increasing stream of events in the network society are highlighted by the difficulties posed for Canadian architectural critic Sanford Kwinter in October 1997. Like many of his colleagues he could have been in the Basque Country, attending the opening of the Guggenheim Bilbao. However, as is often the case nowadays, he had another invitation to consider: the fiftieth anniversary re-enactment of the first supersonic flight by Chuck Yeager in the Mojave Desert. He decided on the desert: 'We came because we believe in shock waves, we believe them to be part of the music of modernity, not something to watch a ribbon be cut from, but something to feel with our diaphragms, eardrums, genitals and the soles of our feet. We wanted to be in the desert badlands that day with nothing but the sun, the baked dirt, the pneumatic tremors and the unbroken horizon' (Kwinter, 2010, 89).

The Bilbao Guggenheim had become an event, even before the ribbon was cut. As Gehry's titanium titanic rose out of the ground it became a place of pilgrimage for architects, art critics and leisure scholars. But for Kwinter, the building was an empty shell. He referred to it as an example of 'pseudo innovation' in architecture, echoing Boorstin's complaint about the (post)modern shallowness of events. The real event was in the Mojave Desert, because: 'Out there somewhere we knew was the zero-degree and the future, and that Bilbao was the past' (Pratt, 2008). There was, however, a certain irony in Kwinter's decision. Arguably, by following Boorstin's prescription to attend a 'real' event dedicated to a real American hero he was actually looking back to events of the past. The Mojave Desert celebrations also had many of the trappings of a Boorstin-style pseudo event, including the issue of a US Postage stamp, the unveiling of a statue of Yeager and the re-naming of the main road to Edwards Airbase as 'Yeager Boulevard'.

Like many architects, Kwinter may have disliked the Guggenheim because he was more concerned with form than function and more with structure than context. But one could also see the new museum in a different light. The opening of the Bilbao Guggenheim was arguably an important turning point in the relationship between art, architecture, culture and local development. Before the Guggenheim, Bilbao was a run-down northern Spanish port-city with a filthy river and declining industry. The new museum put Bilbao on the map, with international tourists suddenly flocking to see Gehry's futuristic colossus and urban leaders across the globe scrambling to emulate the 'Guggenheim effect'.

The debate about the economic and image impacts of the Bilbao Guggenhiem has tended to overshadow the role of the museum as a marker of a significant qualitative change in the way in which art was being consumed. The Guggenheim made clear that art museums did not need to worry about content in the same way as they had in the past. Curators used to focus on assembling artworks to tell a meaningful story to people who appreciated art. But the modern harried leisure consumer no longer has time to contemplate art and think about its meaning. Increasingly museum visitors are skimming the artworks on their way to the café or the museum shop. The legendary marketing campaign launched by the Saatchis for the Victoria and Albert Museum in London had already heralded this change in 1988 by calling itself "an ace caff with quite a nice museum attached". People were no longer using museums as location for the serious development of cultural capital, they were seeing them as an extension of socialised leisure. People no longer went to museums as temples of culture, but because the museums in themselves had also become events, places to be.

The example of the art museum is perhaps one of the most interesting for our purposes, because it concerns the transformation of a practice associated by Bourdieu (1984) with elite culture into a form of cultural sport for the masses. This transformation was heralded by the opening of the Pompidou Centre in 1977, the first ludic art museum with no serious collection. The device was rapidly employed in other cities, as the opening of the Tate Modern, the Bilbao Guggenheim and countless other contemporary art museums underline.

The Tate Modern in London has perhaps become the archetypal example of the genre, if for no other reason than its sheer size. Housed in the largest brick building in Europe (a former power station), it attracts over 5 million visitors a year and is due to add a 21,000 square metres extension onto the existing 31,000 square metres to cope with the demand. The reason for this success is obvious to those who visit. The Tate Modern is not so much an art museum as a relational space. Children run (or roll) down the ramp into the turbine hall, to be greeted by a giant sun, or a theme park-like installation of slides, while their parents drink coffee in the Members' Room or browse the shop. The quiet contemplation of art that Bourdieu and his contemporaries would have valued has been replaced by what the contemporary French art critic and curator Nicolas Bourriaud (2002) has termed 'relational aesthetics'. In his view, it is not the art object itself that matters, but the interaction with it. The Tate Modern, and other cultural institutions have become relational spaces where people develop their own meaning through their relationship with art and each other.

As Vickery (2007, 77) discusses, the way in which people relate to culture-led regeneration projects such as the Tate Modern is key, because this determines if relational capital is actually being developed for the wider community, or if the 'audience' is simply being used to add symbolic capital to the physical space. In the ideal case, collective participation can perform an act of symbolic integration of a diverse social and political constituency, such as social minorities usually absent or excluded from social or cultural institutions.

This is certainly true of grass roots cultural production and creativity, such as the *Festes de Gràcia* in Barcelona, where local residents make their own creative landscapes from recycled materials, attracting around 2 million visits to the neighbourhood every year (Crespi Vallbona and Richards, 2007). One of the important spaces in the *Festes* includes the 'gypsy plaza', where this often marginalised group becomes the focus of collective attention in a transcultural ritual of music and dance.

One of the Turbine Hall installations at the Tate Modern in 2009 was Robert Morris' Bodymotionspacesthings, a series of huge props including beams, weights, platforms, rollers, tunnels and ramps built from materials such as plywood, stone, steel plate and rope. This was actually a recreation of Tate Gallery's first fully interactive exhibition which took place in 1971. The original exhibition was actually too successful in its innovative call for people to physically interact with an art work. It was closed just four days after opening, due to the unexpected and over-enthusiastic response of the audience.

The events industry has imitated art by providing many more 'places to be' in the festive calendar. But in addition to carefully constructed commercial events or expensive art museums, there is a whole raft of 'eventfulness' emerging in different spheres of everyday life. Eventfulness can be found in many different public spaces in cities across the globe, as seen in the trend towards watching live football matches on giant screens in city centres, the growth of mega discos, the increasing popularity of live concerts or the proliferation of 'stag and hen' parties.

Festivals in the network society

Festivals have been argued to represent a special case in terms of events, combining the festive atmosphere that gives them their name with the presentation of the arts. Festivals are therefore perhaps the ultimate vehicle for relational aesthetics – the content cannot exist without the context of place and the audience that devotes their precious time to 'being there'.

In the case of festivals, however, the fact that they revolve around cultural programming in specific places at particular times compounds the temporal challenges they face. As the number of festivals has grown, so the festival season has become choked with events, all seemingly presenting a similar panoply of artists and performers. There is competition to be the first event in the season in a particular artistic genre, or to avoid the performance fatigue that affects performers and audiences alike by the end of the season. There is competition to present the key performers who will anchor the programme and attract the large audiences necessary to pay the inflated fees of the star acts. There is a tendency towards sameness in programming that Mary Miller, Director of *Stavanger 2008* and now directing the Bergen Opera House, once neatly characterised in the formula 'Bono and Tall Ships'.

The growth of the network society has ensured that such competition now extends globally. Not only do performers travel, but audiences do too. Why watch Bono in London when you could do so in Benicassim, or Rio, or Tokyo? So the more traditional festivals in North-western Europe or North America now find themselves dealing with more mobile audiences who can opt for warmer climes, or cheaper beer or better atmosphere elsewhere.

One of the reactions from some festivals has been to clone themselves. *Sónar*, the advanced music festival established in Barcelona in the cultural vacuum following the 1992 Olympics, began organising foreign editions in 2002, and since then it has appeared in various guises in more than 20 cities worldwide. Different strategies have been tried to implant this globalised 'local festival' in the space of places in different cities, including partnership with local promoters and a tour of North American cities organised primarily from Barcelona (Colombo and Richards, forthcoming). The question surrounding these developments is an interesting one, since strategies of cloning, copying and franchising are becoming more and more common for festivals (Richards and Palmer, 2010). If so many festival clones or copies exist, what does this do to the original? Does the existence of many copies detract from the value of the original version, or does it add to its authenticity, as Baudrillard (1985) might have argued? The *Sónar* experience seems to suggest the latter, since the 'original' Barcelona version has gone from strength to strength, in spite of the proliferation of copies. This also underlines the power of festivals as rituals that support physical co-presence and generate emotional energy in the network society.

The authenticity of festivals and events therefore arguably depends as much on the audience, and on their ability to co-create festivals as a social happening, as it does the artistic programming. It is the fact of being there that makes the event real or authentic, rather than just the content presented. The implication for festivals in the future may well be that they need to pay more attention to designing the ritual of participation and ensuring that 'emotional energy' is generated as a result. This means that festivals need to look beyond their traditional programming capabilities to embrace new skills in the areas of ritual design and experience management in order to continue being successful.

Conclusions

The development of the network society has linked people together virtually, but rather than replacing face-to-face contact, it seems to have heightened the need for physical co-presence. We need to be with others to participate in the Interaction Ritual Chains, and these need to have a collective focus of attention which can give meaning to our activities. The result seems to be more, rather than less mass participation in festivals and events of all kinds.

Although Boorstin long ago predicted the rise of pseudo-events, one could argue that the current trend towards hyperfestivity is not just a product of PR campaigns or overblown instrumentalism. It is just as much a result of a real individual and social need to build the social fabric and to generate shared, meaningful experiences. The problem with Boorstin's analysis, as Whitfield (1991) pointed out, is that he was very good at identifying the 'unreal' in modern society, but was at a loss to define what was actually 'real' or 'meaningful'.

Although it is easy to be critical of the contemporary festival landscape, there are still plenty of signs that people are capable of using the spaces and places around them to create meaning and shape fulfilling moments of co-presence. The real problem starts when you want to channel that energy to achieve concrete social, cultural and economic goals. As Boorstin pointed out, pseudo-events are lacking in spontaneity and content, which suggests that 'real' events should be spontaneous and creative. The problem is, how do you plan for spontaneity?

In fact, planned spontaneity is already happening in the network society. Trendwatching.com has identified the tendency to make "spontaneous decisions to go somewhere or do something" as one of the main impacts of networked individualism. If this trend continues, then festival organisers will also have to become more spontaneous, or risk being left behind by the creative audiences of tomorrow.

Bibliography and further reading

Baudrillard, J. (1985) *Simulacres et Simulation*, Galilée (Editions): Paris.

Boorstin, Daniel J. (1962) *The Image. A Guide to the Pseudo-Events in America*, Vintage: New York.

Bourriaud, N. (2002) *Relational Aesthetics*, Paris: Presses du reel.

Bourdieu, P. (1984) *Distinction: A Social Critique of the Judgment of Taste*, London: Routledge.

Castells, M. (1996) *The Rise of the Network Society, The Information Age: Economy, Society and Culture Vol. I*, Oxford: Blackwell.

Collins, R. (2004) *Interaction Ritual Chains*, Princeton: Princeton University Press.

Colombo, A. and Richards, G. (forthcoming) The flow of places: Sónar Barcelona International Festival of Advanced Music and New Media Art.

Crespi Vallbona, M. and Richards, G. (2007) The meaning of cultural festivals: Stakeholder perspectives', *International Journal of Cultural Policy* 27, 103-122.

European Commission (2007) *The Impact of Major Cultural and Sporting Events on Tourism-oriented SMEs,* European Commission: Brussels.

Giddens, A. (1984) *The Constitution of Society: Outline of the Theory of Structuration,* Berkeley: University of California Press.

Kwinter, S. (2010) Mach 1 (and other mystic visitations), in: Sykes, A.K. (ed.) *Constructing a New Agenda: Architectural Theory 1993-2009,* New York: Princeton Architectural Press, 80-89.

McFadden, R.D. (2004) Daniel Boorstin, 89, Former Librarian of Congress, Dies. *New York Times,* March 1. www.nytimes.com/2004/03/01/national/01BOOR.html?pagewanted=2

OECD (2008) *Local Development Benefits from Staging Global Events, Local Economic and Employment Development,* OECD Publishing: Paris.

Pratt, K. (2008) The ends of the parabola: Kevin Pratt on Sanford Kwinter's far from Equilibrium, *Artforum International Magazine,* Inc. Accessed 22 June 2014, http://www.thefreelibrary.com/

Richards, G. (2013) Events and the means of attention. *Journal of Tourism Research and Hospitality,* **2** (February), www.scitechnol.com/2324-8807/2324-8807-2-118.pdf

Richards, G. and Palmer, R. (2010) *Eventful Cities: Cultural Management and Urban Regeneration,* Routledge: London.

Urry, J. (2002) Mobility and proximity. *Sociology* **36,** 255-274.

Vickery, J. (2007) *The Emergence of Culture-led Regeneration: A policy concept and its discontents,* Centre for Cultural Policy Studies, University of Warwick, Research Papers No 9.

Whitfield, S.J. (1991) The image: the lost world of Daniel Boorstin, *American History,* **19**(2), 304.

Wittel, A. (2001) Toward a network sociality. *Theory, Culture and Society ,***18,** 51-76.

Notes

[1] This chapter is partly based on *Leisure in the Network Society: From pseudo-events to hyperfestivity?* an inaugural lecture given at Tilburg University, October 2010.

21 The Public Festival: Inspiration and interconnectivity at the heart of festivals

Kathrin Deventer

Festivals have been around, and will always be around; no matter the political context they are embedded in, supported by, or hindered by. Why? Simply because society develops, it transforms, it is dynamic and it needs space for reflection and inspiration. Festivals are platforms for people to meet, and for artists to present their work, their creations. This gives festivals an enduring, quite independent mission and reason to exist: as long as festivals strive to offer a biotope for artists and audiences alike and point to questions which concern the way we live and want to live, they will be a fertile ground for a meaningful development of society – and an offer for serving the public well-being.

What are the challenges festivals are facing today? There are a series of very complex questions related to festivals' positioning us as human beings in an interconnected, global society, our relation to nature and the immediate surroundings, our stories of life so that as many citizens as possible can be part of the societal discourse, can be enriched, can be touched, can be heard, can be moved. Individuals, interest groups, nationalities, countries, even continents are interconnected.

What does this mean for a festival? Travelling across Europe for work and pleasure and meeting citizens from all walks of life has taught me that citizens, a term that connects individuals to some larger constructed community, are just people, everyday people, going about their lives. People connect with other humans and their human stories, real life encounters. Abstract theory and jargon are meaningless when they lack real life connections. Meaningful festivals of the future will offer possibilities for new connections among people: they invite people to travel in time and in space; they inspire to connect human stories, enriching them with new, unexpected, colourful stories!

It is about this task of festivals – almost a 'public' mandate to be part of a transforming society – that I am going to write about, from my personal point of view, but also referring to some key statements by young festival managers because they will be the ones leading the festival business in the future.

I mentioned the need to connect people and to inspire them. A sense of belonging and willingness to build our future together is only possible if people know their neighbours and care about their concerns – so that an individual concern becomes a shared concern.[1] This requires knowledge about the others' concerns, so it requires interaction and the exchange of views. Knowing and experiencing new views adds value to one's own look at the world – it puts one's own views into perspective.

Festivals are part of these relations in the public area, of this relational network; and the public area becomes part of the festival stage. Festivals need to make new connections, install new rituals of connecting and working together, establishing new bonds, through their artistic offer, their take on history and their visions of the future! They look at what keeps people awake, what drives society, and they give artists, alive or as part of history, a platform for this inspirational practice. This makes festivals public players.

So how do festivals assumeresponsibility for their public role? In his book *Resetting the Stage: Public theatre between market and democracy,* published in September 2012, Dragan Klaić argued that arts institutions don't deserve public financial support without the certainty of continuous investment in education and evidence of intercultural audience development.

I very much share Klaić's belief that art takes part in the development of an inclusive society which is the foundation of every democracy. This is why developing an intercultural audience deserves financial support. I also agree that education plays an important role. But let's take a closer look at what is specifically meant by 'education' in this context, because for me, education is simply the way how we inspire one another.

Working with the audience is an important issue among every serious cultural institution, one that takes many different forms. Festivals are doing it: attracting new audiences and maintaining them year after year, and developing specific programmes for specific audience groups. Radically overt, daring to transform cities and communities, festivals benefit from the interlinked society, they transform the urban environments, they fuse established and upcoming artists, they think global and act local.

But what is the essence of the various kinds of audience development instruments that exist? Why work with the audience?

Audience development is not just a simple goal but it responds to the responsibility of a cultural institution to the broader civil society: the responsibility to create a support basis for citizens. The question each festival should ask itself is: What kind of interaction do I want to create with the audience? What about the interaction between the artist and the audience? How do we succeed in building this type of support basis?

In everyday local life, festivals have always been concerned with the ways in which intercultural dialogue can take a tangible form, because it is anyway part of the artistic practice and cultural reality, both thematically as well as intrinsically: sometimes it is an underlying concern; sometimes it takes a more explicit form. During their creation process artists work very intensely on social relations throughout different sectors. They do so as citizens, not as teachers, and they do so voluntarily, without being asked. Artists choose to link an educational dimension with their creation process, at the final stage but also during the process itself.

It seems to me that 'education' is a true concept dealing with 'mutual learning', and as Klaić calls it: a concept to inspire each other, to 'fertilise' each other. The more diverse the involved actors are, the better the mutual learning process will be! An increasing diversity within an environment also enriches the creative process in a festival. This has an immediate impact on increased access to artistic work. So yes, a cultural institution needs to take care of the development of its audience, keeping the following steps in mind:

1   The moment when audience and artist meet is a moment of continuous development of citizenship. Thanks to a creation you reflect on yourself, on others, on your context.

2   Therefore, it is up to each and every cultural institution to create meeting moments between artists and the audience and to adjust its instruments accordingly - starting with the artist's work.

3   Festivals reach millions of people every day in theatre or opera houses, or in the public space. The artists participating in festivals are also citizens who are part of the 'network'.

4   As a result, the cultural world is part of civil society, of the formal and informal relational network; the arts institution is searching for its place in this system of overlapping informal relational networks.

5   Audience development is no longer a goal in itself. Contact with the audience is part of a festival's identity and how it presents itself in the public environment – know-how linked with a clear artistic-ethnic identity that the audience should take home.

6   This all creates a great deal of responsibility for each festival, in the public sphere, and in the context of the established public order.

7 In that way 'education of the audience' is and will always be abpit the development of citizenship.

I think the biggest challenge of every artistic and cultural activity lies in the stimulation of democracy, and in the promotion of an open, trans-national democratic environment (the bigger, the better!). That is why we speak of audience participation and no longer of audience building.[2] Inclusivity equals nothing less than the promotion of a democratic environment, freedom and the development of an open civil society. Mobilising every single individual to assume responsibility in a citizen-led society is a task that is both in the hands of our political decision-makers and of each citizen. Citizens have the responsibility to engage in the creation of a new culture of politics, economics and social life. Their visions, their everyday actions, their sense of community is what will develop a community.[3]

We need to create new and inventive relationships between citizens, politicians and the economy – a new culture of democracy, far beyond the concept of national interests.

The challenge for the European Festivals Association (EFA)[4] is to trigger this new form of citizenship through festivals and offer festival makers a platform to meet and be inspired; and to make the wider world of policy makers and business aware of the impact of festivals. That is why networks such as EFA exist – to bring together different views, provide for exchange, communicate and act on knowledge, insights, trends and tendencies within festivals – and their role in an ever changing society. This through networking meetings, but also through publications[5] and research[6], advocacy and training.

In this context, the Atelier for Young Festival Managers[7] is a significant example of EFA's efforts to create a fertile biotope of reciprocal inspiration. With a rigorous and intentionally tight timeframe, the Atelier allows hungry participants from a wide range of cultures and contexts to be nourished by a feast of festival experience and expertise from across the world.

This Atelier is not so much about technical skills (how to do things), but about people who do the things, who give meaning to festivals and to places. "It is an island", former Atelier participants said last year during EFA's Jubilee in Bergen, "that is offering the world an immense range of artistic views and backgrounds." It provides exclusive surroundings with optimal concentrated working conditions: very special as the new generation steps out of the shadows cast by their forerunners. It is about energy, honesty and openness of individuals; it is about standing up for one's ideas and reviewing them at leisure: a week that frees oneself from the pressure of measures. The Atelier connects and inspires young managers.

As one of the contributions to EFA's 60th anniversary in 2012[8], some of the Atelier alumni - by now 172 young festival leaders from 52 countries and regions - explored the role of festival directors and festivals in today's societies, and reflected on EFA's 60th anniversary discussions about festivals[9]:

♦ "The true role of a festival is to help artists to dare, to engage in new projects. They might have no other opportunity", Bernard Faivre d'Arcier[10] formulated the core meaning of a festival which then became the motto of the Atelier. The festival vocation should be a stimulation of creative activity and should allow artists to test and dare them to change their habits and places, in a sense of renewal. A festival is able to accommodate any show of any length, any language, located in any place, which finds no equivalent in another context. A festival should be a place of risk. Festivals should make a serious contribution to society through artists working at the edge of new ideas and creativity, experimenting, sometimes revealing, sometimes failing, sometimes succeeding.

♦ Creating space for new works and supporting emerging artists is only the second step which could be taken by a festival. The first one is its role of being a litmus test, being the senses of our society, identifying clearly the status quo as a departing point: a departure for reacting, escaping, opposing, neglecting...

♦ All kinds of professions have infinite expertise and wisdom within their own field, but it is only the arts which create awareness across the whole spectrum of society.

♦ Festivals can wake up people and their creativity and raise their awareness of certain issues. If you like to do that – to have a creative, aware and awake population, which will then work actively for a balanced society – you will see that the most essential function of the arts is to stimulate, and funding will go to artists who continue to do exactly that.

♦ While every taste is valid, the best commentators can increase awareness; a context both historical and geographical can start to diversify taste, and thus tolerance for new and different perspectives (Robyn Archer[11], Atelier Mentor).

♦ We have to act here and now, following the artists' work which in many cases is ahead of our times. Hence, a festival could work as a ceremony for real research. We should follow the work of artists, who are the ones researching the challenges of society and who raise awareness. Art should have a knock-on effect – as the result of the innovative and creative process shared with an audience.

◆ We have to bear political and social responsibility in correspondence with the cultural and artistic significance of a festival in a certain region or community. A festival should play a key role in strengthening local identity (or local communities sharing sets of joint values). It can also give shape to the desire for identity. Festivals with strong local anchoring and conceptual clarity can be temporary platforms of resistance to negative side-effects of globalisation, with a capacity to integrate global issues and local circumstances, needs and aspirations.

◆ A festival is a supporting member of the local cultural life including local artists, bringing them together with international artists and thus stimulating and connecting the local and regional cultural scene. "We are to serve artists, in their right. If we serve them to ensure continuing practice of creativity at the edge, then we serve not only audiences but we serve community, society and the world at large"[12] (Robyn Archer).

◆ Festivals can challenge cultural institutions and give them new horizons by using different approaches to production. They can also provide role models for other (cultural or non-cultural) industries.

◆ As part of the global village and a world of access, festivals should reflect this wide range of possibilities and open up towards other art forms: the future of innovative festivals is interdisciplinarity, inter-generational and full of cross-cultural exchange.

◆ We should try to apply resilience thinking – to build resilience we must maintain education and experiment closer to the ground. Resilient thinking caters specifically to our future audience. To build resilience we need to be more robust in our arguments for the value of research and development in the field of artistic endeavour.

◆ Today, the best festivals have a developmental function: to discover new talents, affirm emerging aesthetics, advance professional discourse, transfer skills and methods to younger artists, and contribute to the development of a more diverse public. Festivals that establish a panoply of local partnerships, also including those beyond their own artistic domain, reach out to the educational and civic infrastructure.

The Atelier alumni concluded that in these times of rapid changes and transformative dynamics, we should still ask ourselves some questions:

◆ Crisis – is it a permanent condition or a discursive image?

◆ What if there will be too many festivals developed? Will the public not be exhausted by the concept 'festival'?

◆ What influence will the altered urban demography have on festivals?

- What about our role in terms of leadership: shall we keep our fantasies of a 'Cultural Superman'?
- How will festivals be changed by the development of technology? Will a festival have its audience still *physically* present?
- Do festivals endanger regular institutions like theatres, museums, etc. of being eliminated?
- Festivals have to reflect critically and to work with the logic of the capitalistic economy, its rapidity, its cynicism, its oblivion, its disinterest in the individual. How can festivals work and at the same time not become a sentimental *Gegenwelt* or a cynical flow heater?
- If we look at Europe in the globalised world, how might intercontinental networking and cooperation look like and work in the future?
- Are festivals heteropies in the sense Foucault introduced this concept? Where 'another' thinking can be encouraged, where the 'normal' given systematic behaviour is left outside? Or are festivals at the centre of society? But then where is the renewal coming from?

These and so many others questions are put on the table in the light of discussing the future of festivals. In the beginning of this article I asked: What do people connect with? And my answer was: with other humans and their human stories, real life encounters. To come full circle: The Atelier is yet another moment of encounter, a very special moment of inspiration, connections, reflections, testing, reviewing, and eventually, these reflections will be passed on from the inner circle of festival makers to the outer circle of audiences and citizens.

In particular at a time where the peace project in Europe in many countries is at stake, where nationalistic tendencies and non-solidary acts feature in the news and rule the streets, when we are facing a rapid increase in nationalism within EU member states, growing anti-immigration sentiments and resentment towards Europe for the age of public sector austerity, we have to speak about values such as democracy, interdependence, participation, imagination, or community. We cannot take for granted the freedom that we have achieved over the course of time. On the contrary, we have to build on these achievements, to think and to act for the greater good, for ourselves and for the future generations. Each festival has a task, however modest it might be, in this context. Let's inspire each other to do that!

Notes

[1] See also the European Union's attempt to find new visions for Europe's future through its initiative 'New Narratives for Europe' launched in April 2013. With the input of representatives of a vast network of partner organisations, the New Narrative project aims to give artists, intellectuals and scientists a space for long-term discussion and expression about Europe. It responds to European Commission President José Manuel Barroso's recent call for 'more and better Europe' which he made during his State of the Union speech in 2012, and is part of expanding the public debate on Europe. On 11 July 2013 in Warsaw, Poland, Barroso underlinded "the need to breathe new life into the European spirit and create a genuine European public space," and asked: "Of course there is what Europe can do for science and culture, but also what can culture and science do for you? What ideas can you bring, what new narratives can you write, what new images can you design so to inspire our young people?" More information at www.ec.europa.eu/debate-future-europe/new-narrative

[2] In this context, EFA leads the Access to Culture Platform's (ACP) Working Group on 'Audience Participation'. In December 2011 in Brussels at the European House for Culture, the ACP held a workshop on 'Access to Culture in the digital era - A Citizen's Right'. It discussed practices and policies which are at the basis of the sector triggering and hindering the audiences' access to culture in the digital era. Participants took a critical view and analysed whether the sector is making the most of the opportunities the digital era brings about. A *Compendium of Best Practices* is available for download. In November 2012, the Access to Culture Platform released the research publication *The Cultural Component of Citizenship: An Inventory of Challenges*. In the publication, 19 renowned authors and researchers from all over Europe and the world share their insights on the opportunities and challenges related to developing citizenship in Europe through culture. The book was launched in the framework of the Brussels Conversations 2012, organised by the European House for Culture and partners, where it served as a way of starting discussion for participants and contributors. It is available in print and digital formats. More information at www.access-to-culture.eu

[3] In this context, the European Festivals Association (EFA) engages in the Cultural Coalition for a Citizens' Europe, which was initiated in 2012 by *A Soul for Europe*'s Strategy Group and its partner organisations: European House for Culture, Felix Meritis Foundation, Setepés, Stiftung Zukunft Berlin, AltArt Foundation, Foundation for Urban Projects and Research, Image Aiguë and n-ost. More information at www.asoulforeurope.eu

[4] The European Festivals Association (EFA) is the umbrella organisation for festivals across Europe and beyond. One of the oldest cultural networks in Europe,

it was founded in Geneva, Switzerland, in 1952 as a joint initiative of the eminent conductor Igor Markevitch and the great philosopher Denis de Rougemont. Since its foundation, the Association has grown from 15 festivals into a dynamic network representing more than 100 music, dance, theatre and multidisciplinary festivals, national festival associations and cultural organisations from 44 countries. More information at www.efa-aef.eu.

[5] EFA shares knowledge, insights, trends and tendencies within festivals via its blog 'Festival Bytes' (www.festivalbytes.eu) and via its books series EFA BOOKS, which was launched in 2006. EFA BOOKS puts in the spotlight the role of the arts, culture and festivals in today's society and highlights contemporary challenges. It contributes to and stimulates further discussion on cultural issues and it involves festivals in the international debate with politicians and cultural operators. All volumes are available on EFA's eShop at www.efa-aef.eu/en/activities/shop.

[6] EFA hosts on its website the European Festival Research Project, an international, interdisciplinary consortium, focused on the dynamics of artistic festivals today and seeking to understand the current growth in the number of festivals and its implications. From 2004-2011, the Chair of EFRP was Dragan Klaić, theatre scholar and cultural analyst. More information at www.efa-aef.eu/en/activities/efrp.

[7] The Atelier for Young Festival Managers is a unique, intense, 7-day training programme initiated by the European Festivals Association (EFA) in 2006. The Atelier is especially designed for those who are working or have ambitions to become involved in programming or in programming-related departments within a festival. The Atelier enlarges young festival managers' personal horizons and their perspective on festivals and programming practices all over the world. It equips them with a new network of international contacts which strengthens the dialogue between these 'leaders of now and the future'. After five editions, the Alumni Network counts 172 young festival managers from 52 countries and regions and 28 presenters from 16 countries. Based on the success of the Atelier, EFA set up The Festival Academy in 2012. The Festival Academy incorporates extended partnerships with networks, cultural institutes, embassies and festivals, greater geographical outreach and new training formats in festival management addressed at more diverse target groups. More information about the history, mission and past editions of the Atelier at www.atelierforyoungfestivalmanagers.eu; and about The Festival Academy at www.TheFestivalAcademy.eu.

[8] EFA celebrated its Diamond Jubilee in 2012. Throughout 2012, EFA joined forces with festivals and partners around the world to celebrate, commemorate and in particular reflect on the present and future of arts festivals in the world. Under the motto '60 Years On: Festivals and the World', EFA looked at the responsibility of festivals today to help shape the world tomorrow. More information at: www.efa-aef.eu/efa60.

[9] On the occasion of its 60th anniversary EFA released a Jubilee publication *European Festivals Association: 60 Years On!* – a book about EFA and its 60 years as a network for solidarity, growth, diversity, artistic endeavour and for people; a book about Europe in times of transitions and enlargement; a Europe in the process of re-invention, integration and the creation of Europe as cultural project; a book about the nature of cultural networks and their mission, their added value, their projects and what they mean to their members. And, of course, a book about festivals as platforms for artistic creation and social actions deeply rooted in society. It is available on EFA's eShop at www.efa-aef.eu/en/activities/shop.

[10] Bernard Faivre d'Arcier is the President of the Biennale de la Danse de Lyon and the former Director of the Festival d'Avignon (France).

[11] Robyn Archer is the Creative Director of The Centenary of Canberra (2013) and the Artistic Director of The Light in Winter, Australia.

[12] Robyn Archer's keynote speech at the closing session of the Atelier for Young Festival Managers in Singapore (14 to 21 May 2011). It also inspired a joint e-publication of EFA and the Asia-Europe Foundation (ASEF) entitled *Serving Artists Serves the Public* which was released in April 2013. It is available for download on EFA's eShop at www.efa-aef.eu/en/activities/shop.

22 Belonging and Unbelonging: The cultural purpose of festivals

Tessa Gordziejko

Introduction

This chapter illustrates the inherent dualism of the European festival traditions and how these have translated into contemporary arts festivals. It is not a history, and focuses primarily on contemporary practice, whilst drawing attention to the continuities of cultural purpose which could be interpreted as fulfilling fundamental human and cultural needs – the need to embrace community and identity whilst at the same time giving license to subversion, challenge and the unfamiliar.

In its central section, this chapter examines the London 2012 *Cultural Olympiad*, which enabled a diversity of national and regional identities to be expressed through its programmes of work. It also enabled important new art works to be presented by a number of partner festivals across the UK. But most significantly, the four year *Olympiad* 'period (2008-2012) enabled projects to be grown from ground level upwards and grand ambitions to be realised, demonstrating on a large scale, a previously hidden trend towards 'slow art': the long-term embedding of partnerships between artists and communities.

Background

In February 2012 the Jerwood Charitable Foundation with *LIFT* and the *South Bank Festival* organised a symposium called the 'Future of Festivals' (Jerwood Charitable Foundation 2012). One of the questions asked on the day by Tim Etchells, Director of Forced Entertainment (Etchells, 2012), was: With what purpose do we convene? Belonging or Unbelonging?

The contributions from that symposium made visible a proposition that the model for the 'new' European festival has been developed drawing on the traditional purpose of 'Belonging' - celebrating locality, identity, community

- with the apparently newer purpose of 'Unbelonging' – risk taking, bringing in the new (international), innovation. But as the following section proposes, both concepts are rooted in both an older established dimension and a new dimension.

The artists at the symposium focused strongly on the purpose of the new, "to change the idea of what is possible" (Etchells), for the festival "to re-imagine and rewrite itself at will, spilling into new shapes and new ideas" (Andy Field, Director Forest Fringe). However, my proposition is that for a festival to achieve the "wild amnesiac vitality" (Field) of Unbelonging, it draws on traditions of Belonging: rootedness, community and the cyclical familiarity provided by the calendar.

Belonging and Unbelonging – echoes of the past

A fuller understanding is based on the concept of misrule that runs through festivals ancient and modern. The Lord of Misrule, a figure featuring in medieval festivals across many European countries, symbolises the world turning upside down, the upending of social hierarchies and norms. Misrule or license for dissent is played out in the traditions of the masked carnival, most notably the Venetian carnival. Indeed, as historian James H. Johnson observes, "Today *carnivalesque* can describe an attitude, a frame of mind, a joyously subversive stance toward authority in general" (Johnson 2011: 42). Another key theme which occurred in a number of European festivals and feast days is connection with the spiritual world, with roots which are clearly present in modern Halloween customs and other occasions when "as happens in the feasts of renewal of many cultures, certain types of social disorder were actively encouraged during the period of the festival because this promoted the renewing influence of the Otherworld" (Kontratiev 1997: 4). Clearly the Belonging/Unbelonging dynamic is enacted through these ritual connections with the spirit world of ancestors and with familiar cycles of the seasons that also celebrate place and community.

Contemporary festivals – belonging as shared passion and the artist tribe

This next section will focus on the application of this axis to contemporary festivals and in particular to an examination of how festivals and their cultural purposes relate to it. It can be observed that an 'artist tribe' often forms among groups of artists in a particular area, region or city where there is a vibrant cultural scene. Nowhere is this more evident than during an arts festival, in the festival venues and bars and early morning symposia discussing the work of the day or days before. Because of the often solitary nature of the way artists work, they huddle together in social groups whenever they can. Artists are particularly susceptible to what Tim Etchells calls "the possibility of community - in the world, in the city, across the city, in the theatre or performance space" (2012), in search of a sense of belonging through shared work, which often finds its fulfilment through festivals.

Similarly, the specialist festival of shared cultural passion and art form – jazz, folk, literature, digital art – brings a particular form of cultural belonging among people from often diverse and far flung communities. This is palpable at *Celtic Connections*, Glasgow's annual folk, roots and world music festival in late January. *Celtic Connections* celebrates Celtic music and its connections to cultures across the globe and each year programmes around 2,000 musicians performing music with Celtic roots and resonances from around the world. The festival attributes its phenomenal success – attracting 100,000 people to a festival in Scotland in January is no mean feat – to the passions of its founders, passions which are shared across the world by musicians and audiences, and which create a deep sense of belonging and community across its 300 events celebrating the Celtic cultural diaspora.

So among the Belonging and global interconnection of the contemporary European festival, where do we look to find the Unbelonging, the misrule, the disguise, the Otherworld?

As Jude Kelly put it at the FOF Symposium, "festivals are for getting dialogue between artists and audiences and creating spaces to say difficult and dangerous things; often the festival is a permission to try something new and big which might frighten people in a venue context." Whilst not all festivals achieve this, the examples in the next section show how some contemporary festivals have diversified their models as their content has evolved and expanded increasingly utilising spaces which are not conventional performance venues, and which source content from communities and audiences. Even traditionally venue-based festivals such as *Edinburgh* now feature site specific, immersive work such as Look Left, Look Right's *You Once Said Yes* in 2013.

Parallel cities and co-creation

Rimini Protokoll is a theatre company which creates such new model festivals. *Parallel Cities* is a project described as "an international festival where the artists don't have to travel". There were four partner cities – Berlin, Warsaw,

Zurich and Buenos Aires – and a series of artists were commissioned to create live art projects which would be realised in all four cities over the same period of time, sourcing material and participants/performers locally from each city. Each intervention was the same, yet different in each location, coloured by the flavour of the city, its artists and the responses of the audiences who encountered the work, often unaware they were experiencing an arts project - a walk through Ibis hotel rooms (identical in every city), hearing on screens and headphones the stories of real chambermaids who cleaned that room (*"ghosts who appear when nobody else is there and clean up after other foreigners"*). In each city, participant groups wander through shopping centres receiving live directions on headphones to carry out specific movements simultaneously, at first not very visible (cross legs, fold arms) but gradually building to a detectable choreography as participants were told to walk backwards, walk in rhythm to music, dance and finally (just as security were becoming suspicious) to "walk away as if nothing has happened". In another part of each city, a choir sings and recites legal rulings from the court of that city, in the entrance halls of the court house. And writers create instant stories and observations about passers-by in a busy station concourse, which are projected overhead on a giant screen. *Parallel Cities* is described on the *Rimini Protokoll* website as making "theatre out of public spaces used every day, and seduce the viewers into staying long enough for their perception to change. They invite you to subjectively experience places built for anonymous crowds… in this way, *Ciudades Paralelas* wanders from country to country as a mobile research laboratory, building up an archive of guerrilla tactics for appropriating cities".

It is striking how the elements of medieval festivals can be detected in these projects; the elevation of the ordinary citizen to the status of artist's muse (stories of chambermaids and passengers), in secular society where to be the subject of cultural production could be likened to the peasant being consecrated as bishop; the masked nature of the work – sometimes described as 'invisible performance' – such as the shopping mall choreography; and the resonance of voices from absent beings, from past legal cases, movement which disappears as soon as it is divined, stories which 'haunt' the hotel rooms, the courthouse halls and the shopping malls, the communal spaces of urban contemporary society. And also the deep connections between Belonging and Unbelonging, the sense of place which is mined by each individual project design and the connections created between cities in different parts of the globe by networking the originating artists with each city.

Slow Art and the London 2012 *Cultural Olympiad*

This co-creation model is evidenced in festivals across Europe and beyond. *Nextwave Festival* Melbourne has as its mission:

♦ Obsessed with the new

♦ Adamant about context

♦ Devoted to the extraordinary

♦ In love with locality

♦ Conscious of time[1]

This consciousness of time translates in the biennial festival's producing models, spending two years commissioning and developing around 28 artists and projects. The model is predicated on the notion of 'slow art' – work which takes time to form: "where unique development programs and a bold festival meet".

The model of slow art was evident in the UK in a number of London 2012 *Cultural Olympiad* projects. Because the *Olympiad* is the period of four years between the handover from one host city (Beijing 2008) and the next (London 2012), the idea of a cultural festival spanning this time is on the face of it, problematical – how to sustain focus and momentum and stretch tight budgets to engage the public over such an extended time. This problem was reflected in much of the media reporting on the London 2012 *Cultural Olympiad* during its first two years, with critics such as the BBC arts critic Will Gompertz running repeated stories on how the public and arts cognoscenti were failing to engage with the *Cultural Olympiad* and had no idea what it was. The perception was not aided by the changing models of cultural programme leadership at the London 2012 Organising Committee (LOCOG), and only started to shift on the appointment of Ruth Mackenzie as Director of the *Cultural Olympiad* in January 2010.

However, there was already in place, unnoticed by the media, a structure for slowly developing work across the nations and regions of the UK through a network of Creative Programmers working with local communities and leading regionally based artists, retrospectively described by Olympic cultural commentator Beatriz Garcia as providing "a rare opportunity for a continuity of a cultural vision throughout the *Olympiad*..." and "a much needed degree of flexibility for locally sensitive cultural programming which previous games editions have always found difficult to manage" (Garcia 2012). The result of this five year devolved network of commissioning and producing activity was a multitude of projects which genuinely belonged to, and sprung from, their locations and communities and which gave rise to events throughout the *Olympiad*, which culminated in presentation during the London 2012 festival period, the summer of 2012.

Whilst the many spectacular London based events highlighted London's position as one of the world's cultural capitals, the work which had been grown across the UK made a more complex and layered statement of identity and community for the regions and nations.

In Northern Ireland, the Land of Giants was a fourteen month programme inspired by Giants which have been significant in the history, ancient and modern, of Northern Ireland - from Finn McCool, the giant who created the Giant's Causeway to Samson and Goliath, the two shipyard cranes which have dominated the Belfast skyline for the past forty years. The project engaged large numbers of schools, local groups and volunteers. In the South East of England, the Tree of Light took place in Oxford, Henley, Reading and Windsor/Slough and explored the relationship between humanity and the environment through the science and art of trees, involving 1650 performers in a large scale spectacle performed in July 2012. In Scotland, Speed of Light was a public interaction with technology, art and sport, using movement sensitive 'wearable' technology which changed colour and animated the hillside around Arthur's Seat with trails of patterned light. In the Yorkshire region, Cycle Song was a community opera about the life and achievements of Lal White, a steelworker who won an Olympic medal for cycling at the 1920 Antwerp Olympics, produced and performed in Scunthorpe by a community cast of 1,500[2]. In the East of England, the *Norfolk and Norwich Festival* produced Robert Wilson's Walking project, a three mile interactive engagement with landscape art near Wells-Next-The Sea, part walk, part theatrical experience punctuated by large scale architectural installations.

What these projects have in common and what, as a body of work may prove to be the most significant aspect of the *London 2012 Cultural Festival*, is that they all took around two years to make. All were funded by Legacy Trust UK (LTUK), which provided significant commissioning and development funds from 2009. This slow art process enabled both engagement and quality to be built, with events and presentations through the *Olympiad* period creating a pathway to the 2012 finale. One powerful legacy of LTUK's investment in arts projects for *London 2012* is an archive of slow art projects and their outcomes. Evaluation of the projects to date indicate that their success is derived from the enabling of a particular dialogue over time between artists, producers, participants and audiences, nurturing innovation – Unbelonging - whilst creating identity and meaning at the heart of communities – Belonging. In many cases, such as Cycle Song and the Giants Causeway project, this was finding new ways to express identity and re-surface forgotten history.

From gallery and theatre to and unusual landscapes and public space ...

Another prominent feature of these and many other London 2012 Festival projects, is that they did not inhabit traditional arts venues, but more public spaces, that they take work out of theatres, galleries and concert halls and into the unusual and iconic locations – beaches and coasts, city squares, parks, national landmarks and heritage landscapes, hillsides, the sea, industrial sites among many others. Whilst the predominance of outdoor events holds particular challenges for northern European countries (amply demonstrated during the inclement summer of 2012) the growing appetite and trend for outdoor art of all forms does not limit itself to areas with warmer climates. The network of Dancing Cities, *Cuidades Que Danzan* (CQD), has grown outwards from its creation in 1997 by Associació Marató de l'Espectacle in Barcelona, following a successful outdoor dance festival *Dies de Dansa* in 1992 as part of the Barcelona *Cultural Olympiad*. The network now comprises forty dance festivals in cities across Europe, Central/ South America, Oceania, Asia and Africa, the northernmost being Sweden, Belgium and the UK. What has emerged from this network are city festivals learning from each other and applying that learning to their own urban environments, and increasingly collaborating on projects between groups of members with common interest. For example, Least Common Multiple is a collaborative exploration between eight European cities of the relationship between dance, public space and community. The project sets out:

> to create awareness of the use of public space as a common place of creativity, co-existence and imagination, through conceiving the city as an artistic laboratory and through exploring the similarities and differences of public spaces in different cities (determining, therefore, their Least Common Multiple)... to bring together curators, art organizations, dance companies, experts and academics working from the performing arts, visual arts, public space and site-specific works. In doing so, we would like to create a political, social and urban map of different areas of different cities to open debates around the socio-urban development of contemporary cities. (Cuidades Que Danzan n.d.)

... and digital space

The outdoor location of the activities in the CQD network is central to its evolving manifesto around the democratisation of culture and public space, creativity and social cohesion and the creation of connections between different languages and cultures. A very different arena which has emerged over the past decade as central to the sharing of cultural dialogue and collaboration is digital space. The *Abandon Normal Devices Festival* (AND) of the North West region of the UK was established as part of the *2012 Cultural Olympiad* and during its three years 2010 to 2012 built a diverse programme of commissions, screenings, online projects and installations. It was characterised from the outset by its international profile in terms of participating artists, a large number of public space projection commissions and, most interestingly from the perspective of this essay, by its crowd-sourced online projects. Projects such as *Ask a Teenager* (AND 2012*) which formed a performance and website film from responses to questions submitted online to a panel of teenagers; and Mechanical Games* (AND 2010), inviting participants to submit a 30 second film of them performing a sporting action or manoeuvre.

Established for 25 years, the *Transmediale Festival* in Berlin has been described by the BBC as "big and professional enough to be globally relevant and genuinely thought-provoking" with hundreds of participating artists from across the globe. Importantly, Transmediale has now extended its activities to support year-round collaboration through "reSource transmediale culture berlin", in projects which have "decisive touchdowns at each festival" (Transmedia n.d.) In this way it is another version of the slow art model, recognising that for arts projects to achieve a sense of Belonging with new constituencies and communities, continuity of connection is needed.

Another example of a digital festival which fosters a sense of Belonging transcending national boundaries was the *Stranger Festival* of 2008 and 2009, an initiative of the European Cultural Foundation as part of the European Year of Intercultural Dialogue, with the aim of encouraging "a sense of belonging among young people from very different cultural backgrounds across greater Europe". In the introduction to the evaluation undertaken by Demos, entitled 'Video Republic', the authors articulate why the digital space is a formative public space for young people and young film-makers in particular: "The falling price of digital technology and the proliferation of broadband access have blown open a whole range of ways for young people to express themselves and communicate with each other in video. The internet is increasingly shaped around moving images. Video mash-ups, citizen journalism, vlogging, viral-video marketing, community film-making projects, happyslapping... we can see the audiovisual explosion everywhere" (Hannon et al 2008).

Significantly, the second chapter of Video Republic, 'The Route-around Kids' opens with an account of the YouTube ban in Turkey and the ease and amusement with which young people 'go around' the ban to continue to access material on YouTube. The chapter references the high levels of disaffection with the political establishment, social inequality and youth disadvantage. Yet, on the question of accessing video content, young people would rather deftly and dismissively defy the government's YouTube ban on their computers than take to the streets about it - in order to continue a dialogue in the shared space that matters to them, the street of collective consciousness for a generation. The concern that this might blunt the desire for more direct action is being shown to be unwarranted, with many taking to the real streets in the summer of 2013 in anger and frustration about the lack of the public voice in many aspects of public policy. The international space of online video which were opened by the Stranger Festival, provided another arena for young people to explore issues of identity, democracy, social and political participation.

Rural and urban festivals – still a valid distinction?

The other aspect of the digital space is that it removes the distinction, or question, of rural and urban festivals. In the past, arts festivals have been identified through their locations and have arguably been stereotypically contrasted (often for budgetary reasons) as: urban festivals = high art, international, cutting edge, large scale, edgy, fashionable, combined art form ; rural festivals = local, popular/ conservative (low risk), small/medium scale, gentle, often single art form (literature, music). The *AND* festival programmed physical work across the Northwest from Manchester to rural Cumbria and sourced online content from communities across the region and beyond. Many programmes of the London 2012 *Cultural Olympiad* took place across whole regions and nations. *Imove*, for example, Yorkshire's three year Legacy Trust programme, presented work in city squares, villages, landscapes, coastal and Pennine communities, swimming pools, markets, churches, parks and cricket pitches[3]. The London 2012 *Cultural Olympiad* represented a very visible and large scale manifestation of trends which have been unfolding for some years, the blurring of boundaries between rural and urban festivals, and the growth of cutting edge, international contemporary work in rural festivals, many of which benefit from access to iconic heritage landmarks as venues.

The festival as movement

The familiarity and Belongingness of the annual or biennial festival in itself creates the continuum of history, tradition and living archive. The social energy a festival generates is undoubtedly derived from those aspects of Unbelonging and strangeness it creates, and it is this relentless innovation which characterises European festivals as a body of work from which we will continue to learn. Festival 'movements' borrow from and influence each other, and generate a collective understanding of how work can best be made and presented in different local and global environments. Those new trends can be summarised as:

♦ New commissions and co-creation forming a significant element of the programme for contemporary festivals.

♦ Slow art and year round/ two year commissioning/ development programmes surrounding the presentational period of the festival itself.

♦ The growth of work in in public spaces, outdoor and street art.

♦ The move to digital space.

All of these could be seen as a heightening of the Unbelonging, whilst finding new ways to draw pathways of Belonging. The redefining of shared space, the creation of work sourced from within communities are creative shafts dug by artists and audiences which mine layers of identity and 'found' archive; the digital space as a new salon of shared cultural value. The 'slow' philosophy in the development of a programme gives artists a temporary community from which they can source new ideas; yet the regular, bounded period of a festival and its intensified programming and presentation of work provides a defined moment when the new can be revealed and orthodoxies overturned.

Bibliography and further reading

Abandon Normal Devices (AND) (2010) *Mechanical Games*, available on http://archive-autumn-2010.andfestival.org.uk/event/mechanical-games

Abandon Normal Devices (AND) (2012) *Ask a teenager*, available on www.andfestival.org.uk/events/ask-a-teenager/

Cuidades Que Danzan (n.d.), *Least Common Multiple*, available on www.cqd.info/index.php/en/projects/item/58-lcm

Delanty, G., Giorgi, I. and Sassatelli, M. (eds.) (2011) *Festivals and the Public Cultural Sphere*, Oxford: Routledge

Etchells, T (2012) *Alphabet of Festivals,* blog commissioned by LIFT and the Jerwood Charitable Foundation for The Future of Festivals Symposium held on February 2012, available on www.timetchells.com/notebook/february-2012/alphabet-of-festivals/

Garcia, B. (2012*)* 'The London 2012 Cultural Olympiad : A Model for a Nationwide Cultural Legacy', online article, *Culture@TheOlympics 2012* ,available from: www.culturalolympics.org.uk

Haedicke, S. C. (2013) *Contemporary Street Arts in Europe: Aesthetics and Politics* (Studies in International Performance Series), Basingstoke: Palgrave MacMillan

Hannon C., Bradwell, P. and Timms, C. (2008) *Video Republic,* London: Demos

Jerwood Charitable Foundation (2012) *The Future of Festivals,* report available on www. liftfestival.com/content/12656/archive/2012/the_future_of_festivals/the_future_of_ festivals

Johnson, J.H. (2011) *Venice Incognito: Masks in the Serene Republic,* California: University of California Press

Kontratiev, A. (1997) Samheim Season of Death and Renewal, *An Tríbhís Mhór: The IMBAS Journal of Celtic Reconstructionism,* **2**(1/2), Samhain 1997/Iombolg 1998

Quinn, B. (2010) Arts festivals, urban tourism and cultural policy, *Journal of Policy Research in Tourism, Leisure and Events,* **2**(3), 264-279

Transmediale website (n.d.) reSource transmediale page available on http://www. transmediale.de/content/resource-transmedial-culture-berlin

Notes

[1] Nextwave website available on http://nextwave.org.au/about-next-wave/

[2] Available on Imove website archive area www.imovearts.co.uk/past-projects/ cultural-olympiad/cycle-song/

[3] For the full range of projects, see www.imovearts.co.uk/past-projects/cultural-olympiad/

23 Transnational Festivals, a European Alternative: *Les Boréales* and *Reims Scènes d'Europe*

Anne-Marie Autissier

At a time when concepts of European identity and integration are receiving increased critical comment, something to which Dragan Klaić devoted much of his attention, it is appropriate that research on festivals should examine and discuss the extent to which they are able to provide special opportunities for promoting knowledge, understanding and experience of Europe across borders and beyond. For those festivals that possess such qualities of 'Europeanness', such focused research should analyse those qualities and what can be learnt from studying the festivals that possess them. This chapter proposes to explore these important questions and themes through an examination of *Les Boréales* and the *Reims Scènes d'Europe* festivals. Analysis of the latter was undertaken in the context of the European Festival Research Project[1], and of the former for a research project piloted by the Observatory for Cultural Policies in Grenoble for the Ministry for Culture and Communication of France[2] (Autissier and Deniau, 2013).

This chapter is also the continuation of an investigation published in *The Europe of Festivals* (Autissier, 2008)[4]. This analysed the role of cross-border festivals and cross-border festival 'twinning' schemes. It highlighted in particular the pioneering role played by events such as *Perspectives*, a live performing arts festival based in Sarrebrück (Germany), which operates in close collaboration with cultural organisations in Forbach and Sarreguemines (France), and of the *Mira!* Festival, which takes place in the south of France and which introduces its audience to contemporary work from Spain and Portugal. Also analysed were the blossoming cross-border initiatives between France and Belgium. From reconciliation to a culture of cross-border sharing, I believe such initiatives aim to promote borders as meeting sites, as well as places for mutual discovery[5] (Autissier, 2008, pp73-87). For the purposes of this chapter, I will examine two festivals that take place in regional French capitals, and which aim to straddle European borders, criss-crossing the continent from north to south and east to west.

The two festivals, *Les Boréales* in Caen (Basse-Normandie) and *Reims Scènes d'Europe* in Reims (Champagne-Ardenne), have several features in common the first of which is that they were developed in regional contexts that were badly affected by World War Two. Normandy paid a heavy cost as the site of the landing by the Allied forces. Similarly, Champagne-Ardenne bore the brunt of the May-June 1940 campaign, in which thousands of people died. This conflict had a devastating impact specifically on the commune of Sedan and the department of Aisne. In addition to this history, both regions have also experienced economic difficulties. Basse-Normandie is one of the most agriculturally and rurally-oriented French regions, but here the fishing industry has suffered badly. Following the closure of its textile factories too, the automotive industry is currently the main source of industrial employment. The nuclear clusters in the Hague and Flamanville give the Cotentin peninsula a special role in the energy sector.

Champagne-Ardenne is one of the French industrial regions that were heavily affected by the economic crisis that has affected most of Europe since 2008. The manufacturing of intermediate goods, which was a strong feature of the region, was hit hard by the downturn in automobile production.

However, both regions benefit from a rich heritage and popular tourist sites, such as the landing beaches and the Caen Memorial. Hikers, champagne lovers and business visitors are all similarly interested in Champagne-Ardenne for the quality of its natural beauty and its location within Europe.

In this interesting, yet complex regional context, what role could festivals like *Les Boréales* and *Reims, Scènes d'Europe* play? In the following section, we will learn more about the origins of both festivals.

In Caen it began in 1951 when the Swedish Government sent kit houses and nurses to the city. This prompted translators and academics at the University of Caen[6] to see an opportunity for cultural co-operation and exchange and to develop the teaching of Nordic languages at the university, by establishing a programme in the spirit and name of modernity and peace. In 1992, *Les Boréales de Basse-Normandie* was established at the behest of the Norden Association, which had been set up by an academic, Eric Eydoux, and involved teachers and translators from Caen University's Nordic Languages Department. Initially centred on literature, with cameos by other artistic disciplines, from 1999 onwards, *Boréales* was organised by the Basse-Normandie Regional Centre of Letters (CRL)[7] and expanded its programme to include a wider selection of cultural and artistic activities. Although, partly because CRL was at the helm, the focus of the festival was still on literature and translation, the idea was to promote awareness and appreciation of the multifaceted, multi-societal Nordic imaginary(ies). "We are not only aiming to present Nordic contemporary art, but also provide insight into the lifestyles, the know-how and the values of these countries (status of the child, parity, environmentalism, the promotion of peace…)", explained Jérôme Rémy, *Les Boréales'* Artistic Director in 2012. The festival contributes to reaffirming the Nordic identity of the Basse-Normandie, whose regional logo actually alludes to the Vikings[7]. Norman fishermen also recall their ancestors sailing away to Icelandic waters and Newfoundland.[8] The festival therefore offers audiences a different experience and perspective of the ocean to reflect on, one that is alternative to that familiar from films about World War Two.

Where *Les Boréales* involves extensive input by academics, *Reims Scènes d'Europe* is driven more by an artistic perspective. Both festivals depend on the involvement of specific individuals. *Reims Scènes d'Europe* was a product of the vision of the director and actor, Emmanuel Demarcy-Mota, Artistic Director of the *Comédie de Reims* in 2007. His idea was to invite three or four European companies each year and the *Comédie* built a new performance space for the purpose. Thus a festival was born: *À Scènes ouvertes.* In 2009, with the arrival of a new Artistic Director, theatre director Ludovic Lagarde, *À Scènes ouvertes* became *Reims Scènes d'Europe.* In other words, the affirmation of the European reference point became a selling point, something that is not common in the French festival landscape. The festival's cross-border dimension subsequently became a central feature. Certain editions of the festival are themed and others feature specific countries, such as Sweden in 2010. The 2012 festival revolved around a 'border and exile' theme. For Ludovic Lagarde, the key challenge has been to develop the festival as an international repository of resources and competences, but also for the festival to serve as a platform for public debate about the meaning and importance of 'cultural Europe'.

Another distinctive feature of *Boréales* and *Reims Scènes d'Europe* is how they unify the cultural institutions of the cities and regions involved. Unlike many organisations that preserve the exclusivity of their programming, the CRL of Basse-Normandie and the *Comédie de Reims* are gradually opening up to other local cultural organisations and collectively developing an annual programme. Twenty-four institutions in Caen and the surrounding region are festival partners, including the Caen Theatre, the *Comédie de Caen*, the Caen Fine Arts Museum, the *Arthothèque*, the Basse-Normandie Contemporary Art Centre and, of course, the Nordic Languages Department of the University of Caen. *Reims Scènes d'Europe* brings together six different, complementary local organisations of varying dimensions and competences: the *Manège*, the Reims Opera, *Césarée*, *Nova Villa*, the *Cartonnerie* and the Champagne-Ardenne Regional Fund for Contemporary Art.

What drives this bold approach to sharing resources, which many others find difficult to achieve? For Jérôme Rémy, it is driven by a desire to 'irrigate' the whole Basse-Normandie territory, by co-operating with a variety of urban and rural institutions (thirty different communes in three departments). An additional challenge for this small French region, which is not particularly conscious of Europe, was to embrace continental contemporary art. According to the director of the *Comédie de Caen*, Jean Lambert-Wild, *Les Boréales* also serves as a meeting point and 'showcase' for increasingly fragile regional theatre companies. For Ludovic Lagarde, the objective is basically to present 'another Europe'. By establishing a shared 'capital' of trust and knowledge, both for cultural organisations and local government, and promoting a diverse and polyphonic Europe, the impulse to look for a 'pre-conceived' Europe is thwarted. But how were Rémy and Lagarde able to harness so many contradictory energies and motivations?

Negotiation is at the heart of the process. According to Jérôme Rémy, 80% of proposals come from the CRL. However each proposal must be agreed upon collectively. The CRL's strength is that it is able to set up artistic residencies and co-productions with its partners, including the *Comédie de Caen*. The CRL can also propose a shared European communication plan, which relies on the support of key French media organisations, such as *Télérama*, *France Culture* and *Le Monde*. Another distinctive feature and strength of the festival is that the partners share their resources and facilities. The festival is presented to the public as an 'adventure' and an opportunity for lifelong learning, including workshops and debates.

In the case of *Reims Scènes d'Europe*, the arguments for unification are the co-production between local partners (with the development of theatre and dance premières) and the possibility of shared residencies for foreign artists. A person from the cultural sector in Reims described the advantages of the system: "We base it on what we would spend each December and the financial endorsements abound." The different partners similarly seek to bring together and intertwine their different audiences. In 2012, the director of the *Manège,* a national stage for dance, circus and theatre, Stéphanie Aubin explained: "we must accept that we are all actors in the festival, but that there also needs to be a leader, so it's essential that we make propositions, as well as adopting those of the Comédie de Reims. It is a question of shared convictions and collective discipline".

Finally, are *Boréales* and *Reims Scènes d'Europe* successful in 'irrigating' the regions where they seek to have an influence and in turn to 'Europeanise' the practices of local government and other public authorities, who are essential as partners for the festivals? This is a question of fundamental importance, because as will be shown the evidence is contradictory.

With respect to *Boréales*, the Regional Council of Basse-Normandie has a particular interest in their activities because of the region's strategic position and international reach and influence. An aspect of this strategy is the agreement between the Basse-Normandie region and the Norwegian region of Hordaland.

How does local government respond to and support such initiatives? For both the City of Caen as well as the Basse-Normandie Region, the festival and its partnerships represent an interesting proposition. We can also see that local government can be involved at a variety of levels – departments, communes – and that this began from the moment that the multidisciplinary nature of the festivals became clearer.

Reims Scènes d'Europe is first and foremost a city event. It contributes to a new urban narrative, introducing festival-goers to both heritage sites and other lesser known, alternative sites. The opening night, which is free and held in a public space, helps in the development of a collective ownership. But the success of the festival is not without its tensions. The regional authorities would like *Reims Scènes d'Europe* to become a regional event, forging links with other non-local entities, such as the International Institute of the Marionette in Charleville-Mézières. However, if the festival chooses to work with and bring together the different echelons of local government, it will have to deal with the reality that they are in competition with one another. Each level of government is protective of its image and its prerogatives. In other words, links that may unite the cultural organisations may result in having to deal with the consequences, i.e. the local authorities do not speak with a single voice.

As such, both festivals need to be involved in continuous negotiation with all partners. Such activity requires someone to manage and drive such negotiations. Jérôme Rémy dedicates himself to this task throughout the year. The *Comédie de Reims* also appointed a co-ordinator to take charge of these relationships.

Which Europe?

Thanks to their contacts, the people in charge of *Boréales* and *Reims Scènes d'Europe* are at the heart of European creative and cultural sector professional networks. From 2010 onwards, they became aware that big cuts were forecast in public funding for cultural organisations throughout Europe. When Ludovic Lagarde evaluated his key responsibilities, he came up with the following: first, to enable artists from countries in difficulty to continue to do their jobs; second, to analyse the social and cultural realities of countries often presented in an overly simplistic fashion by the mainstream press, such as with Greece in 2010 and 2011; and third and last, to enable young people to take on programming tasks and other challenges associated with the *Reims Scènes d'Europe*. This is why the Young Performing Arts Lovers (YPAL) group was created. Supported by the European Union's Youth In Action programme. YPAL provides workshops and debating opportunities during the festival.

Europe is thus perceived as a means of reinforcing the appeal of local areas by creating a sense of proximity with distant countries, thus provoking unexpected dialogues and offering festival-goers an intimate relationship with unfamiliar cultures.

At the same time, the European Union has to address a series of worrying developments; cuts in public authorities' budgets for culture and cultural activity, cultural isolationism and xenophobia. Meanwhile both festivals seek to animate the practice of sharing between European creative individuals and groups and which, some might claim, they achieve despite the European Union itself. It is thus to a continental Europe, larger than the EU and also more flexible in terms of collaboration, that the people in charge of the two festivals choose to look for inspiration and support. Here we see a new trend emerging: rather than being limited by EU institutional procedures, cultural sector professionals are promoting a Europe of circulation and exchange, a 'European learning zone' linked to the motivations of the people. While it is not explicitly articulated as such, here we are seeing real co-operation occurring through subversion of the institutional framework. Thus an alternative European narrative is being created, seen and heard.

A study published in July 2012[9] (KEA report) discussed the gap between, on the one hand, the capacity of regional and local authorities to use the EU's Structural Funds to promote cultural activities and, on the other, the limited attention given to cultural activities by the regulatory framework of the Regional and Cohesion Policy: "cities and regions throughout the Union interpreted their approach to culture using the Cohesion Policy in a very broad fashion. The 2007-2013 regulatory framework (…) links culture primarily (but not exclusively) to tourism, to the renovation and construction of cultural infrastructure, to the provision of cultural services and to the preservation and the development of cultural products and heritage. It does not, however, make reference to the potential culture has to be a source of social innovation in itself, nor to the way in which culture contributes to urban renovation, or how the cultural and creative sectors influence the green economy."

The success of these experiences does not mask the difficulties. Young graduates need to be encouraged to stay, as without available professional opportunities, there exists the temptation to leave the region and make their lives elsewhere. These festivals also attempt to address the problem of 'brain drain'. Whilst the booming French cultural ecosystem is currently in better shape than in Italy, England, Spain or Hungary, the future still looks pretty grim. The presumption of paid employment provided by the unemployment scheme for 'intermittent performers' has once again been called into question. Similarly, the time-consuming EU discussions on copyright and the private copying levy are a product of the current argument between copyright collection societies and electronics manufacturing companies (e.g. cd players, mp3 players etc.), who wish the fee would just disappear.

"By choosing to pay their taxes in Luxembourg or Dublin, the burgeoning companies of the digital world are effectively engaging in tax-optimisation. By planning the death of private copying, they hope to exempt themselves from any form of solidarity", writes musician Jean-Jacques Milteau, President of the ADAMI Administrative Council[10]. One fifth of the revenue generated by festivals in France comes from the 25% private copying levy, which is in turn redistributed by the French organisations who work in favour of artists. "Given that it equals roughly the amount allocated for artist fees by the big theatre, dance and music events in our country, they're going to need to get busy organising festivals without artists", commented Jean-Jacques Milteau (Milteau, 2013).

What *Les Boréales*, *Reims Scènes d'Europe* and other festivals envisage and offer is a Europe of artistic and cultural exchange, a united Europe keen for institutional innovation. However, the dominant paradigms at the level of the EU – both in financial and regulatory terms – are out of 'sync' with such frames of reference. If the European narrative is to be positive, mobilising, a source of creation and hope, then these contradictions must be minimised. In order for this to happen, different political decisions need to be made at the level of the 27 EU Member States – is this possible?

Les Boréales

21st Edition – 15th November -1st December 2012

Guest country: Sweden

Featuring authors and artists from Denmark, Estonia, Finland, Iceland, Latvia and Norway. Literature, cinema, exhibitions, live performances, debates and meetings are all part of the programme.

Reims Scènes d'Europe

4th Edition – 29th November-15th December, 2012

Theme: Exile and the Border

200 artists from a range of different disciplines: theatre, dance, music, circus, visual arts.

Selected highlights: Romeo Castellucci (*The Four Seasons Restaurant*), Claude Régy (*La barque le soir*) and Johan Simons (*Macbeth*). French Première: *Crash Course Chit Chat* from young Dutch-Croatian director, Sanja Mitrovic

Bibliography and further reading

Autissier, A-M (ed.) (2008) *The Europe of festivals: from Zagreb to Edinburgh, intersecting viewpoints*, Toulouse: éditions de l'attribut / Culture Europe International.

Autissier, A-M. and Deniau, M. (with Martin C., Périgois S. and Saez J.P.) (2013) *Prospective study on the creation of European poles of artistic production*, (*Étude prospective sur la mise en place de pôles européens de production artistique*) Grenoble and Paris: Observatory for Cultural Policies, Observatoire des politiques culturelles.

Capellin R. (2000) Urban agglomeration and regional development policies in an enlarged Europe, in J. Bröcker and H. Herrmann (eds.) *Spatial Change and Interregional Flows in the Integrating Europe: Essays in Honour of Karin Peschel*, Physica, Verlag, Heidelberg, pp. 117-129.

Greffe X. (2008) New European cultural enterprises in turmoil, in H. Anheir, H and R. Isar (eds.), *The Cultures and Globarization Series: The Cultural Economy 2008*, California: Booknet, pp. 210-222.

Iglesias M., Kern P. and Montalto V. (2012) *Utilisation des Fonds structurels pour des projets culturels, Brussels*: July. Report commissioned by the European Parliament (Culture and Education Commission)

Milteau, J-J. (2013) La fin des festivals… et 50% de nos droits en danger! Édito, in *La lettre de l'ADAMI* n. 78, March, p.3

Notes

[1] The EFRP research workshop was organised in 2011 in conjunction with the University of Strasbourg's Centre for European Sociology.

[2] Research team: Anne-Marie Autissier and Marie Deniau. Project Steering Committee: Observatory for Cultural Policies: Jean-Pierre Saez, Cécile Martin and Samuel Périgois.

[3] This publication, available in French and English language versions, aimed to present the initial results of the EFRP project, as well as research projects undertaken separately by partner institutions (notably De Montfort University in Leicester, UK and the Budapest Observatory, Hungary)

[4] *Festivals transfrontaliers, enjeux et paradoxes*, in Autissier, 2008.

[5] The University of Caen is today one of the few French tertiary education establishments that offers teaching in a full range of Nordic languages.

[6] This organisation was set up jointly in 1994 by the French Ministry for Culture and by the Regional Government of Basse-Normandie. The festival of Nordic art and literature, *The Lights of Normandy,* was created in 1992 on the initiative of Eric Eydoux and Lena Christensen, with the co-operation of the OFNEC and the Department of Nordic Studies in Caen. The festival was therefore able to call upon the experience of teachers, translators and Nordic specialists' to advise on the programme. The first festivals were largely dedicated to Nordic literature, Shortly thereafter the festival opened up to the other artistic areas, presenting authors, musicians, photographers, choreographers, actors and artists from Denmark, Finland, Iceland, Norway and Sweden or directly linked to them. Since 1999 and henceforth, the festival has been organised by the *Regional Centre of Arts, Lower Normandy.*

[7] Viking migrants who had arrived in Basse-Normandie were granted royal licenses to stay in 911, Treaty of Saint-Clair-sur-Epte

[8] As early as the 15th century, Norman fishermen were eager to conquer new markets. At that time, fishing occupied the majority of the coastal population, a time when fish were considered as the best food for soldiers.

[9] Commissioned by the EU's Directorate-General of Internal Policies.

[10] L'ADAMI is a French civil society organisation established for administering the rights of artists and performers.

24 The Future of European Festivals

Bernard Faivre d'Arcier

Even if we sometimes trace the word 'festival' back to its ancient root (calling to mind the traditional events of *Bayreuth*, *Orange* and *Verona*), the idea of the arts festival as we know it is relatively recent. The modern festival has evolved as part of the 'leisure society', with its extended summer holidays and its all-pervasive media. The theatre festival in *Avignon*, the oldest and best known of all the French festivals, was founded in 1947 by actor and director Jean Vilar. Yet Vilar would never have imagined the success and geographical expansion that the future would bring to the festival phenomenon. For him, the festival was just another one of the many methods he used to bring young people together to share his aesthetic and moral values.

Immediately after World War Two, festivals sprang up simultaneously in several countries. At the same time as *Avignon* and *Aix-en-Provence* were started in France, similar events in *Edinburgh* and *Recklinghausen* were born. This synchronicity implies that the festival is both a social and a historical phenomenon, one both rooted in and responding to the spirit of the times and to our consumer society.

Since then festivals have spread widely, to the extent that there are now innumerable iterations across the globe. Unfortunately it appears that we have now reached saturation point and these events more often than not have become formulaic rather than more individual creative enterprises. Aren't there too many festivals now? Hasn't the public got tired of the very concept of a festival? Has the festival itself dissolved into just another facet of the tourism industry?

It is important to remember that festivals can play a significant role in introducing new works to the public. All over Western Europe more and more plays struggle to reach a wider audience, mainly in the world of public theatre, in countries where theatre comprises a multitude of small companies working on a project by project basis. While countries such as Germany or those in Central Europe perform repertory theatre so that actors are assured work all season, in France there is an imbalance between the number of plays produced and the availability of venues. This overproduction of plays can ultimately lead to media overkill and exhaust the interest of the public. Yet despite these problems, the festival is still capable of breathing fresh life into a city's theatrical scene: indeed, some plays are written with this exact revitalising purpose in mind. The festival can still serve to increase audience numbers and expand what Brecht called 'the circle of connoisseurs'.

While this all may be true of Western Europe, we cannot complain of the same level of saturation in the rest of the continent. Eastern Europe may have adopted the festival format some time ago, but there is still remarkably little opportunity to take shows from one country to another.

Does the festival still retain its original meaning? A festival is characterised by its exceptional nature. The word 'festival' is as synonymous with 'carnival' as it is 'estival' {a French term derived from the Latin word for 'summer', *aestivalis*}. This exceptional nature is what has granted festivals such as *Avignon* or *Edinburgh* their longevity (66 years, that is retirement age!) They offer a summer gathering over three or four weeks in a historic city, where all venues are accessible by foot and where theatre lovers can unite in their shared passion.

Festivals have their fair share of detractors. Certain critics, often permanent institutions (such as the *Centre Dramatique* in France or the *Teatro Stabile* in Italy) frequently object to festivals as mere cultural frivolity. These institutions, because of their very permanence, take it upon themselves to act as cultural advisors and educators. Over time, this kind of objection has fortunately become less frequent for a number of reasons. First there is the clear role which festivals play in initiating and teaching the public about theatre and other art forms, as well as their ability to lend a marked visibility to continuously operating venues and institutions. Second there is the fact that after a festival has taken place, arts groups know that they need only introduce festive moments to their annual programme to rekindle the flame of public interest.

So what is the point of festivals today?

Local politicians tend to justify official support for a festival in their city with reference to at least four reasons

1   The first reason is the ability of the festival to democratise culture. A festival offers a far simpler introduction to the arts than those cultural institutions that we walk past every day and never enter (due for example to a lack of information, ticket prices, cultural barriers, fear of

not being 'of that world'). At a festival, audiences are prepared to take risks. This is particularly the case in open air festivals, where people make the most of the summer and the holiday spirit by making friends, taking a chance on something together, flirting – and doing all this in a space where theatre is accessible, and where one can easily mingle with the performers.

These benefits also account for the success of street theatre and circus performers, without which many festivals would not be nearly so enjoyable. For many local politicians, the accessibility of the arts in the festival space is a useful tool to further the democratisation of culture.

2 Second, holding a festival serves as a means to forge new social connections and reinforce a sense of local identity. The festival can be a balm which heals social wounds; it can give rise to new friendships with neighbours or an intermingling of different groups, even if only for a moment. A festival can also give shape to a shared desire for identity, whether that is of a community, a neighbourhood, or of a professional environment.

3 The third argument, and surely the most recent and successful, is the idea that a festival provides a good economic opportunity. Over the last fifteen years, economic impact studies have convinced not only politicians but also shopkeepers and local businesses that a festival is, on the whole, a positive force in most economic sectors. The service industries are a good example: hotels, car parks, cafes, dry cleaners, souvenir shops and travel agents all can benefit from festivals.

4 Alongside the economic benefits, a festival brings visibility to any community which welcomes it - an image which it could not gain by other means. So the festival is often a key part of a local tourism policy which can extend well beyond the period of the festival itself. A city can also earn long-lasting prestige for only a fraction of what it would have to spend to achieve a similar result through advertising and media promotion. In fact, a good festival can create much more media coverage than any publicity campaign for considerably less expenditure.

5 Obviously, there is a fifth and final reason for the existence of festivals, and in fact it is the most important (although it does not always receive a mention when it should): festivals have unique artistic and cultural value.

- Artistic in the sense that if a festival has the desire and means to truly engender creativity, it will encourage its artists to dare to change their habits and locales, permitting them to reinvent themselves and to break free from conventional modes of performance and artistic production. During a festival, a play can last half an hour or an entire night. It could be played out in Korean or Turkish, or even in an incredible space where a play would never normally be performed. A festival must always create a space for risks to be taken.

The cultural value of festivals lies in the fact that they present an opportunity for audiences to discover new things (for just like the artist, the audience itself takes more risks), a chance to learn and to discuss with like-minded people. Festivals are great occasions for debate, whether formal or informal: at a festival, words, rumours and reputations run wild. Most festivals are places where different aesthetics and disciplines meet and confront each other on an international scale. They also provide a unique opportunity for artists to meet their public and for the critic him/herself to be criticised.

Two distinct types of festival have evolved in recent years:

Some festivals – particularly those in big capitals – have transformed themselves into 'seasons' by lengthening their duration and making space for multiple artistic disciplines. These festivals programme works from a diverse range of foreign countries in order to encourage international artistic exchange, some alternatively choosing a particular theme or contributors from a specific region. This can lead to a festival becoming somewhat diluted. These festivals may lack the Aristotelian unities of place, time and action. If they do not take place in a centralised space, the public may feel that they are not living the festival experience. What is more plays, for example, are generally performed in different spaces; one night in the town centre, another in the suburbs. In these circumstances the festival, which is often not allocated its dedicated space, must come to an agreement with existing theatres and superimpose its own image onto that of its host. We can see examples of this in Paris (*Festival d'Automne*), Tokyo, Berlin and Rome (*Romaeuropa*).

This sense of dilution is accentuated by the lengthening of the festival's run, which makes it lose the unique quality of a concentrated event, and perhaps even surrender the explosive impact of performance. In such cases, the festival plays more on the reputation of its brand. These festivals need to be known as unmissable events to win the loyalty of the public. The unfortunate result of this is that it distances the artists from their audiences, making the exciting communication between the two more difficult and uncertain. In this way festivals which run for too long court the risk of losing their exceptional character. However they may also be said to enrich the theatrical, musical and choreographic life of their cities thanks to their selection of works and their international reputation.

The other possible evolution of the festival format is quite the opposite: they are cut extremely short and can be reduced to only a weekend or even a single night, which can result in large attendance figures and increased media coverage. We can see this evolution in the 'Nuits Blanche'[1] which take place in Paris one night in October, a format which has already been adopted by scores of cities throughout the world. At the moment this format is mainly centred on the visual arts, although theatre, music and other cultural forms are often also incorporated. These festivals rely on huge crowds which, while they may not be able to see everything, may still discover or rediscover monuments and open spaces in an unusual or original way. These kinds of events are a godsend for the fickle media which rarely covers longer artistic events for their whole duration. On the other hand, these one-night festivals make it impossible for people to see everything, and so their experience of the arts may become somewhat impoverished. They operate in the spirit of our age of advertising and hedonism, providing a short-lived pleasure.

The fact remains that arts festivals retain their legitimacy as long as they endeavour to support artistic creativity, particularly at an international level. The true role of a festival is to encourage artists to dare and to undertake projects that they might not risk while working in more permanent institutions

Notes

[1] Launched by the Mayor of Paris in October 2002, and every year since, the 'Nuit Blanche' is an annual all-night or night-time arts festival. Based on an idea first developed in Helsinki and Nantes, a 'Nuit Blanche' will typically have museums, private and public art galleries and other cultural institutions open and free of charge, with the centre of the city itself being turned into a *de facto* art gallery, providing space for art installations, performances (music, film, dance, performance art), themed social gatherings and other activities.

25 Some Reflections on the Future of Festival Practice in Europe

Steve Austen

After many years participating in meetings of festival directors, an interesting thing that can often be observed is that even after days of serious discussion one can be hard pushed to find a common denominator between them. An easy conclusion? Festivals differ from each other; even if they share the same artistic discipline or specialism within a discipline or sometimes even the same artists, the environments in which festivals operate are different so that they defy easy comparisons. From this perspective a primary benefit of meetings of festival organisers is that they may provide participants with a reality check which may validate their claims to uniqueness. This is not to suggest that such meetings are therefore of limited value for festival directors and other professionals. On the contrary, the more festivals have to fight for funding, the more they need objective legitimacy, and that legitimacy is often derived from dialogue between festival directors.

This chapter will therefore focus on the legitimacy issue for those festivals that depend on taxpayers' money and which are now faced with the prospect of diminishing support from public bodies, ministries, regional and local governments, less appreciation from taxpayers and more and more competition from alternative leisure-oriented goods and services. Already, many festivals which began during a period of stronger public support for arts and cultural activity are indicating that the earlier prestige associated with professional cultural products has diminished (the art for art's sake paradigm). And that nowadays financial sustainability can only be achieved through a demonstration of the role that culture and in particular festivals can play in society (the instrumentation paradigm).

Beyond cultural diplomacy

History reveals the important role that festivals have played as part of a country's cultural diplomacy. There is no doubting that *Avignon*, *Salzburg* and

Edinburgh have contributed massively to the national image and profile of France, Austria and Scotland abroad. These festivals simply cannot change that by-product of their existence (and why would they want to?). Although cultural diplomacy is par excellence a mutual activity between states; as a rule it does not include communication with citizens except as recipients, this form of (foreign) cultural policy raises the question of whether policy for culture is still the best instrument to highlight the role of the state as the representative body of the citizens – and not just for the benefit of citizens from other countries, but of its own citizens too. The representative function of art, after all, lies in sublimating the relation between the state and its citizens. Within this perspective, citizenship is a privilege that cannot be enjoyed outside the boundary of the national state. State-subsidised culture is intended to stimulate, reinforce or at least arouse a national feeling in its citizens – their sense of identity. In a situation of this kind, arts institutions, the state and its citizens are caught up in a symbiotic relationship of mutual dependence on one another, an ongoing process of showing, presenting, producing and consuming national values and myths.

Pure enjoyment of art is not excluded, but is rather a by-product of a construct of this kind. The embedding of a festival policy into the process of fabricating a national cultural identity ensures that the relationship between the state and its citizens acquires a (cultural) added value, which in turn may justify the expenditure of taxpayers' money on prestigious arts festivals.

Subsidised artistic expressions are no longer necessary to determine identity

This symbiosis is now in danger of coming to an end. The nation state is no longer the main source of its citizens' personal and cultural identity. Rights, obligations and services are becoming valid and applicable in all the member states of the Union, and that includes citizens of the other 27 member states. This calls into question the role of art as the route for citizens to identify with a nation and its culture. The fact that the latest austerity measures have had particular impact on the national culture budgets of many member states without much opposition from their citizens seems to indicate that the traditional bonds between state, arts institutions and public have been weakened. One response to this is to focus critical attention on the need to re-evaluate the relationship of culture with politics, and its relationship with civil society too. But in so doing this is not a call to return to the relationships of the 20th century.

Reorientation

One outcome of present change and the spending cuts is to make people realise that splendid isolation has its drawbacks. Moreover, that we actually require a review and potentially a reorientation of the role that arts institutions, and festivals in particular, play in society.

What is called for is a deepening of the relationship with the citizen rather than a restoration of the ties to the state. Citizens are looking for coherence, meaning, togetherness and a prospect for the future. These are not available in the supermarket or from the desks of government offices. And we also need to recognise the extent to which globalisation and digitisation have left their mark on the younger generation. Desperate attempts by some political and religious leaders to praise forms of orthodoxy as an automatic guarantee of happiness cannot prevent the fact that transnationalism and the mobility of commodities, services, ideas, customs and insights have become the norms for the local and national orientation of maturing individuals. Understanding their own situation is a prerequisite we need to encourage in these individuals. Some festivals have already realised that historical and cultural context is important as well as the provision of content; important with respect to the festival's capacity to add value to society through reflecting on its past as well as its current context.

So a reorientation by a festival to its political and social context can no longer be postponed, first of all to that of European citizenship. Some of those in the arts sector see the festival as an excellent instrument for cultivating citizenship[1]. An official step towards a broad promotion of active citizenship and the involvement of the arts world in it is a 2007 publication of the Netherlands Council for Culture[2] (hereafter: Council), the official advisory body to the government in the field of culture. This document was the first in the institutionalised and subsided arts world to speak of role and responsibilities in civil society. In the recommendation to the government the Dutch arts world was called upon to take a broader and longer term view of the future than the continued existence of specific institutions. This was when the Council introduced the notion of 'cultural citizenship'.

The Council called for more attention to be paid to the role of the individual, the relationship between past, present and future, meaning and depth, and called upon the arts world to operate in an interdisciplinary and international way that transcended sectoral boundaries. This anticipated the possible development of alliances with other partners in the fields of education, science, the world of industry and commerce and social organisations.

The interesting aspect of this position is that the Council apparently assumed that the arts world was part of civil society and was therefore not only responsible for the generation of arts productions, but could also be held accountable for the links that (subsidised) arts institutions developed with their surroundings.

The arts as intermediary

Arts institutions throughout Europe are confronted with a process in which the classical role that was a shared assumption in Europe from the Restoration on, namely to be connected in one way or another with the nation state's need for representation, is rapidly declining in significance. As providers of meanings, value orientations and historical and social contexts, their role lies precisely in the performing of an intermediary role between different citizens and between civil society and the political class. Festivals are by their very nature natural meeting places for gaining depth and orientation with respect to the principles of the 'value community'[3] that forms the basis of a democratic Europe. Having said that, new alliances are necessary if that potential is to be exploited to the full in the 21st Century.

Whether the term 'cultural citizenship' helps us any further is highly questionable. Through the introduction of this concept, different notions of citizenship have come into collision with one another. The traditionalists point out that citizenship is an individual matter. After all, it is a question of a personal relationship between the citizen and the state, a relationship that is usually anchored in the constitution, which guarantees everyone equality before the law. According to this view, the state ensures that civil rights in relationships between citizens and between citizens and the state are guaranteed through independent institutions that monitor compliance with the constitution.

The protagonists of cultural citizenship consider that collective rights must be recognised, such as for ethnic groups, but also for women, transsexuals, etc. The influence of this collective perspective on government policy in Europe has been and still is substantial. The notion of the multicultural society is grounded in sociological studies that take the group rights mentioned above, based on group identity, as their starting point. However, although a vigorous debate has been conducted about multicultural society, a fundamental, broad discussion of the concept of citizenship is not yet in sight.

It seems to me that introducing special cases of the notion of citizenship such as 'cultural citizenship' does not further the debate on citizenship or that of the role of festivals. After all, we cannot rule out the possibility that those who devise these terms are arguing for special rights for certain groups of citizens, rights that 'normal' citizens will be denied.

Moreover, it might mean that groups that fall under such definitions ought to accept different responsibilities for the public space, the general interest, the functioning of civil society and the democratic constitutional state. This is separate from the implicit suggestion that group identities, in so far as they exist, must lead to legislation by category, which erodes the principle that all citizens are equal before the law. A notion that implicitly is included in most festival programmes and the role of festivals.

Towards new relations

By now the question is no longer whether citizens are prepared to assume a share of the responsibility for how the public domain is organised, but rather: how can it be organised in such a way that political decision-making processes can be stimulated by it? Is there still a role for festivals and artists here, and if so, how is it to be understood?

In an ever increasing mesh of national, regional and urban interdependencies in Europe, the early medieval citizen seems to be a good starting point for thinking about the meaning of European citizenship. The concept of citizen harks back to the Latin *civis*, a member of the *civitas*, a political community that is not necessarily tied to a particular territory.

Citizenship and Europe

Citizenship as it will gradually have to be expressed in the EU, will lead to a complex discussion that makes it difficult to make hasty decisions. That immediately explains the attraction of the European concept: how the future will look is partly up to us. This process makes the greatest demands on the cultural competencies of Europeans. For many the idea of European citizenship is new and one of the reasons why it is vigorously rejected by large groups of voters in almost every member state. Nevertheless, these defensive phenomena are part of an inevitable cultural process that marks the transition from exclusively national to more European solutions.

The letters to the editors in many major European dailies are eloquent: there is no longer any way for either the nation state or the European Union to impose on their citizens a generally accepted definition of belonging together, or patriotism if you like. Whether we like it or not we live in the century of the citizen, of citizens on the road to a new equilibrium with their surroundings and the state. This creates a need for gatherings and celebrations which reflect this new political agenda and festivals could play a significant role in meeting such needs. In the process the cultural dimension of citizenship has come increasingly to the fore. There is therefore little point in rejecting the debate on identity, as some intellectuals do, although they are right in pointing out that the urge to define (cultural) identity irrevocably leads to new forms of demarcation and thus in its most extreme form to new conflicts.

However true this may be, and however much it can be backed up with terrifying examples from the recent history of Europe – especially in former Yugoslavia – without a debate on this all too human tendency to position oneself vis-à-vis others it will never be possible to take a step towards genuine citizenship, a citizenship that both recognises the different levels of mutual dependence, involvement and local patriotism and exploits them for the benefit of a flourishing civil society.

The link with the arts

Arts institutions can play an important role in this. The arts ask something of us that is not common in everyday life. They urge us to abandon familiar and well-trodden paths, to make ourselves receptive to unconventional panoramas and to accept complexity and ambiguity as a condition of progress. In the process, festivals can and do find themselves associated with the need to abandon the fiction of political neutrality, to abandon representation that is too closely linked to the state, and to unambiguously form relations with their community of citizens. After all, the debate on our future in Europe is conducted with them and by them. It is this debate that deserves more attention in the everyday practice of the politicians at the municipal, regional, national and European level. Politics is itself a principal subject of that debate and cannot stand aloof.

Not so long ago, from the 1970s to the aftermath of the Cold War, art and artists were an important catalyst of social progress. The 'decalogue' of the Helsinki Accords from 1975, which with hindsight can be seen to have heralded the beginning of the end of the Cold War, encouraged artists and intellectuals to take initiatives that would bridge the political boundaries that existed at the time between Eastern and Western Europe.

Nowadays it is young intellectuals and highly-trained professionals who not only analyse the present impasse, but who also provide the necessary depth that enables active citizens to arrive at important insights regarding the role of the citizen, the position of the state and the place of religion in a mature democracy that recognises civil rights and provides active protection.

What they have in common is that they transcend the formation of networks as we have known them so far because they are not primarily aimed at exclusively defending the interests of a group, but are orientated towards the general interest, which for that and other reasons is ripe for a thorough redefinition. An initiative that first attracted attention in Brussels and later in the Netherlands, Germany and elsewhere is that of the Flemish writer David van Rijbroeck. His G 1000[4] has been influential in many countries.

For some member states the prospect of a flourishing and thus uncontrollable civil society is an unwelcome idea. The notion that a democracy can be organised, run and further developed without consulting citizens is still prevalent, especially in the new member states of the Union. In some cases a parliamentary majority is used to curb civil rights 'democratically', for example by introducing legislation that limits freedom of expression, freedom of meeting or association, or the pluriformity of the press. However, they increasingly find the European Commission on their trail. By signing the Treaty of Lisbon, member states have accepted the transfer of national sovereignty to the prerogatives of Brussels, such as the authority to maintain the democratic, European 'value community' which is protected by the European Court and other European institutions, as outlined by the Treaty of Lisbon.

A relatively new phenomenon is that recent regulations, such as the joint measures taken in Brussels, directly affect the lives of all individual citizens in Europe. This is why some people appeal to their national governments with regard to effects that they feel to be detrimental. In reaction to this, in some cases we see governments bending over backwards to curry favour with their citizens – it may be for electoral reasons, for example – by suggesting that they regret the measures emanating from Brussels as well. There is an interesting tension in cases of this kind between citizens who call upon their government to correct measures dictated by Brussels, on the one hand, and citizens who appeal to Brussels to try to prevent their government from adopting measures that would curb civil rights, on the other. In such cases, in spite of the alleged scepticism about Europe, it is increasingly common for citizens to not take everything that their national governments consider to be in the national interest lying down. They know, after all, that they have the backing of the citizenship of the EU that has been laid down in the treaty regulations and accepted by their own government.

It is thus logical for the public space in Europe to be increasingly full of initiatives from young European citizens who point to the 'value community' that must form the core of every society at local, regional, national or international level.

Towards a citizens' Europe

Whenever there is a question of giving form to entirely new concepts, and especially when governments and citizens of 28 democratic member states must participate, this necessitates a continuous process of trial and error and harmonisation. Perhaps the best comparison is with the procession to Echternach[5] in which the pilgrims progressed by taking three steps forwards and two steps backwards – a good exercise in European progress.

Conclusion: A new toolkit

The fact that festivals are organic meeting places of interested and motivated citizens offers great opportunities for a more intensive interaction between them as consumers of art and culture and as voters, citizens and taxpayers. If festival managers are tuned in to, and therefore derive some of their artistic focus and direction from, these changes in the global, political context then they can contribute to citizens achieving a deeper understanding of the principles of the 'value community' that now form the foundation of a democratic Europe. Achieving this is not a function of festivals alone but will require new alliances and instruments if we are to exploit this potential to the full.

In terms of festival management this will require more attention to be given to the relationship of festivals to citizenship and civil society; their relationship with stakeholders; the consequences of the family life cycle; the interactive models for communication and programme development and in particular the role of the festival organisation itself as a citizenship educator: by which is meant that a festival should include space in its programme where audiences can learn and engage with the basic notions of what it means to be a citizen and the rights and responsibilities that this carries in terms of being able to vote, carry a passport and enjoy the benefits of citizenship.

If all these topics are part of innovative festival management, we can look forward to seeing festivals[6] more able to adapt to the exciting and challenging times of our contemporary, staccato society by offering a systematic response and approach which draws upon models and practices from business, sociology, psychology, political science as well as European history and citizenship education.

Bibliography and further reading

Access to Culture (2012) *The Cultural Component of Citizenship: an Inventory of Challenges,* Brussels: European House for Culture.

Dahrendorf, R. (1988) *Citizenship. The New Problem,* 6th Van der Leeuw lecture, Groningen, the Netherlands.

Duncan, C. (1991) *Art Museums and the Ritual of Citizenship, Exhibiting Culture,* Washington: Smithsonian Institution Press.

Hoeksma,J. (2011) *The EU as a democratic polity in international law,* The Hague: T.M.C. Asser Institute.

Raad voor Cultuur (2007) *Advies Agenda Cultuurbeleid and Culturele basisinfrastructuur,* available from: http://www.cultuur.nl/

Notes

[1] See Access to Culture, *The Cultural Component of Citizenship: an Inventory of Challenges*

[2] Raad voor Cultuur, *Advies Agenda Cultuurbeleid and Culturele basisinfrastructuur,* http://www.cultuur.nl/

[3] Here the concept of 'value community' is a metonym for the shared values/principles that now reflect discussion about European citizenship since the Treaty of Lisbon was signed by member states in December 2007 and came into power in December 2009.

[4] http://www.g1000.org/en/introduction.php

[5] http://www.iechternach.lu/echternach%20procession.html

[6] One example of an attempt to create new festival practice is the *AAA Festival Muziek en Kunst* see: http://www.aaaserie.nl/

A Author index

Adizes, I xxiv, 6
Anderson, B 203, 205
Ariño, A 21
Autissier, A-M 276
Autissier, A-M and Deniau, M 276

Bakhtin, M xvii, 161, 174
Bathelt, H and Schuldt, N 56
Bauman, Z 20
Benton and Gomez 208
Bonnemaison, S 34–35
Boorstin, D 242, 246
Bourdieu, P xix, 22
Bourdieu, P and Darbel, A 21
Bourriaud, N 242, 250
Breznik, M 2, 5
Brundtland Commission 66

Carnegie, E and Smith, M 164, 204, 214
Castells, M 242, 247
Chawla, L and Cushing, D F 69
Chen, K 114
Cohen, A 202, 205
Collins, R 247
Corcuff, P, Le Bart, C and De Singly, F 21
Costa, X 34
Cottrer, C 105
Crichow, M A and Armstrong, P 202

Dayan, D 149
Debord, G 28
de Tocqueville, A 21
De Winter, P 148
Djakouane, A and Pedler, E 22
Dodd, D 138, 144
Donnat, O 20, 21
Dorin, S 25

Dubois, V 20

Elbaz, M, Fortin, A and Laforest, G 145
Elliot and Lemert 21

Falassi, A 30, 43
Fenwick, T 54, 55
Finkelkraut, A 21
Finkel, R 32
Fisher, R and Fox, R 139
Fu, Y 205

Gaber, F 193
Gagnon, E and Fortin, A 138
Gammadge, B 234
Garcia, B 108, 269
Gelder, G and Robinson, P 114
Getz, D xv, 71, 108, 110
Giddens, A 247
Giorgi, L and Sassatelli, M 28
Glow, H and Caust, J 53
Gotham, K F 32
Granovetter, M 55, 240
Green, G L and Scher, P W 202
Guerzoni, G 190
Gurney, J 128

Habermas, J xxii, 33
Handy, C 107
Hardy, S 74
Hartog, F 20
Hawkes, J 74
Hill, L and Whitehead, B 132
Høbye, L 139
Huizinga 40
Hunyadi, Z, Inkei, P and Szabó, J Z 143

Ilczuk, D and Kulikowska, M 108
Inda, J X and Rosaldo, R 165

Jamieson, K 32
Jancovich and Bianchini 242
Jiwa, S, Coca-Stefaniak, J A, Blackwell, M and
  Rahman, T 113
Johnson, J H 266
Jones, L 128
Jordan, J 109, 112

Kaiser, M 80
Klaić, D xiii, 3, 18, 25, 88, 95, 160, 165, 166
Kontratiev, A 266

Labrador, R N 202
Landry, C 177
Leveratto 22

Maffesoli, M 21
Ma, L J C 203
Matarasso, F 45
Maughan, C and Bianchini, F 24
Mauss, M 43
Mayol, P 140
McCarthy, K and Jinnett, K 113
McFadden, R D 246
McGuigan, J 5, 33
Michaud, Y 20

Négrier, E and Jourda, M 18, 144
Négrier, E, Djakouane, A and Jourda, M 21,
  23, 25
Newbold, C and Kaushal, R 215
Newell, V 207

Oldershaw 24
O'Reilly,D and Kerrigan, F 132
O'Sullivan, D and Jackson, M 201, 204, 206

Paradis, T W 201
Peffley, M and Rohrschneider, R 240
Peterson, R A 21
Picard, D and Robinson, M 162
Pieper, J xvii
Pine, J and Gilmore, J H 84

Porritt, J 66
Pratt, K 249
Putnam, R 161

Quinn, B xv, 29, 30–31, 110, 204

Richards, G 248
Richards, G and Palmer, R 160, 245
Rijpsma, S G, de Graaf, P A, de Vries, C and
  Bik, M 148
Robertson, R xxiv
Rodriguez Morató, A 21
Runciman, D 72

Safran, W 203
Said, E W 203
Scannell, L and Gifford, R 69
Scher, P W 204
Smith Maguire, J and Matthews, J 107
Smithuijsen, C 139
Steel, A 231
Steiner, G 227, 229
Stiegler, B 145
Sullivan, O and Katz-Gerro, T 21

Thussu, D 220
Tomlinson, J 4
Turner, V 43

Urry 247

Varbanova, L, Viacheva, N and Tomova, B
  139
Veblen 20
Vickery, J 250

Waitt, G 28
Walmsley, B and Franks, A 114
Waterman, S 36
Wenger, E 55
Willems-Braun, B 35
Winstanley, G 128
Wood, E 111

S Subject Index

Aarhus Festival 140–141
Abandon Normal Devices Festival 272
Adelaide Festival 228
Adelaide Fringe Festival 53
Agenda 21 For Culture 74
Aix, ville ouverte aux saltimbanques 191
Akademie der Künste 13
artistic directors 107
artist tribes 266–267
Arts Council England 69
Arts Council of Great Britain xviii
arts festivals 44
  as intermediary 293–294
  Australia 227–238
  impact on artists 53–65
  Romaeuropa 99–106
asceticism and hedonism 20
Atelier for Young Festival Managers 258
audiences
  Bassano Operaestate Festival Veneto 182
  composition, Flow 93
  demographic challenges 133
  developing for future 113
  motivations for attendance 183
  street performance 193
Australia 227–238
  Aboriginal people 229–232
  development of distinct voice in arts 230
  Indigenous work 234
  Terra Nullius 229
Avignon Festival xviii, 285

Bartók + Opera Festival 49
Bassano Operaestate Festival Veneto 180–190
  and residents 185
  economic impact 186
  stakeholders 187–189

Basse-Normandie 277–278
  Nordic identity 278
Bayreuther Festspiele 41
Belonging or Unbelonging 265–275
Berlin 11–17
  and Cold War 11
  Cultural Capital Festival 15
Berliner Festspiele 12
Berliner Festwochen 11
Bilbao Guggenheim 249
Bonnemaison, S 34–35
Boom Festival xx
Bradford Mela 205
branding 133–135
Bristol Mela 222
Bunker team, 124-5
  networking 124
Buxton Festival 109

Caribbean Summer, Afrikaanderwijk 150–152
carnival 174
Celtic Connections 267
chillzone 152
Chinese diaspora 207
Chinese New Year festivals 205, 207–210
  as comunication with host society 209
citizenship 255–264, 292
  and Europe 294
cloning xxi
co-creation 114, 170
Cold War xviii
communities of practice 53, 55
community
  building 68
  festivals 127–137
  impact on local 111
  spatial component 149

conformity indicators 47
co-production
  in festival development 279
counter culture movement 42
cross-border 276
cultural capital xix, 48, 265–275
  volunteering 139
Cultural Capital Festival,Berlin 15
cultural citizenship 293
cultural democratisation 24
cultural diplomacy 290–291
cultural embeddedness 45
Cultural eXchanges festival xxii
cultural festival 44
cultural legitimacy 21
cultural permanence 20
cultural policy 122
culture-led regeneration 31
current challenges 108

Darwin Festival 232
destination tourism xxii
development of festivals, late 20th C xviii
diaspora communities 202
  and ethnic identities 205
  and host societies 203
diaspora festivals 201–213
Diggers, brief history 128
Diggers' Festival 127–137
Divadelna Nitra Festival, volunteers 142–143
Dublin Festival of World Cultures xxiv

Eastern Europe 42, 43
Eclat, European festival for street theatre 192
eclecticism 21
  resistance to 23
Edinburgh Festival xviii
Edinburgh International Book Festival
  volunteers 142
Edinburgh Mela 205, 214
education 257
Emerge Festival 59
entrepreneurship 81
Estate Romana (Roman summer) 98
European Capital of Culture 14
European Festivals Association 258
European Festivals Research Project 3, 245
European Sustainable City Award 69

European Union, support for arts 281
Event Sustainability Management, standards
  68

Facebook, for marketing 93
Festival City - Rotterdam 147–158
Festival del Film Locarno 42
Festival international de la bande dessinée
  *d'Angoulêm*e xxii
festivalisation xxi, 18–27
  as a cultural repertoire 19
  definition 19
festival leaders, importance of vision 112
Festival International du Film 42
Festival Republic xxiii
festivals
  as moments of celebration 28
  as orchestrated mega-events 28
  as platforms for reconciliation 237
  as public players 256
  as social activity 25
  nature of xvii
  of ideas xxii
  participatory nature 35
  possible societal function 45
  purpose 10
festival tourism 201–213
festivity, sense of xvii
Festwochen 12
film festivals, development of 42
Flow Festival 88–97
  management 82
funding 113
Fuse Medway Festival 56–63
  artists involved 58
  connections mapped 61
Future Everything Festival xx

Glastonbury Festival xxiii
globalisation 165
government support 280
Great Exhibition xviii
Greenlight Festival 66–78
Green policies 66–78

Helsinki 88–97
hippy culture 42
Holland Dance Festival, volunteers 141–142

Holstebro Festive Week 168–179
hyperfestivity xxi

impacts 160–167
   cultural, social and economic 160
   on artists' work 62
In Between Time festival xx
income sources 108
individualism 21
interconnectivity 255–264

Julie's Bicycle 68
Junge Hunde network 120
justifications for festivals 286

Karlovy Vary International Film Festival 43

Lange Nacht 113
leadership 80–83, 107–117
   Romaeuropa 98–106
learning and knowledge communities 54–56
learning by doing 53
learning experiences for artists 60
Leicester 66–78
Les Boréales de Basse-Normandie 276–284
Levellers Day 130
Leveratto 22
'light night' festivals 113
Liteside Festival 110
London 2012 Cultural Olympiad 265, 269
London International Festival of Theatre xxiii,
   xxiv
Lord of Misrule 266

mela 214–226
   food 219
   intercultural communication 221–223
   meaning of term 214
   organisation and management 217–218
   origins and development, in UK
    216–217
   programming 218–219
   religious divisions 222
   social contexts 215
   traditional and modern entertainments 218
Melbourne Festival 231
misrule 266

Mladi levi Festival 118–126
mutual learning 257

National Festival of Australian Theatre 233
networking 104, 173
   and festival development 122–124
   Junge Hunde 120
network society 245–254
   events 247–248
   festivals 251
   need for co-presence 248
networks of knowledge 58–61
Notte Biancha 113
Notting Hill Carnival 204
Nuit Blanche 113

Odin Teatret 168–179
Operaestate Festival Veneto 180–190
origins of festivals xvii
OZASIA Festival 232

Parallel Cities 267
play, characteristics 41
policy dilemmas 2
political festivals 129
   funding issues 130
   UK, Public Order Act 134
political functions 49
presentism 20
professionalisation of festivals sector xx
pseudo-events 246
public spaces 271
public sphere xxii, 33–35
   culture debating and culture consuming 34

Queensland Music Festival 231

reconstruction, post-War xviii
reflexivity 34
Reims Scènes d'Europe 276–284
   origins 278
relational aesthetics 250
relational space 250
religious origins 41
role
   in contemporary life 10–17
   in introducing new works 285
   in socialisation processes 43

Romaeuropa Festival 98–106
Rotterdam
  festival city 147–158
  Soundpiece 154–156
  Spatial Development Strategy 148
  urban theatre 152–154

seasonal celebrations 41
second individualism 24
Slow Art 269–270
social capital 173
social impact xxiii
social media 95
social network analysis 57
social networks 124
sociology of taste 21
Soundpiece 154–156
sponsorship 104, 109
stakeholders 48, 83–84 , 105, 111–112,
    187–189
Stranger Festival 272
street festivals 197–200
street performance 191–200
  as a contemporary art form 198
  audience 193
  In, Off and Off Off 196
  sharing public space 194
subsidies 108
sustainability xxiii, 66–78
Sydney Festival 231
symbiosis 149–150
  states and festivals 291

tacit knowledge 55
tamasha, performance style 220
Tanzwerkstatt Berlin 16

taste and class hierarchy 21
Tate Modern 250
Ten Days on the Island 232
The Philosophy Festival (FestivalFilosofia) xxii
thrillzone 152
Tolpuddle Martyrs' Festival 129
'traditional' festivals 30
Transition Network 67–78
Transmediale Festival 272
transnational festivals 276–284
tribalism 21
typology of festivals xvi, 45–47, 48–49

urban development 50, 149
urban festivals 28–39
  music 89, 95
urbanity 28–39
urban regeneration xix, 30

value of art 2
volunteering 47, 138–146
  and employment 139
  management of 143
  motivation 138
  roles 141
  varying use of 140

Wellingborough 127
Werkstatt Berlin 14
West Indian Carnival (Leeds, UK) 206
Women Chainmakers' Festival 130
Woodstock 42
World Youth Festival 42

Young Performing Arts Lovers 281